THE UNDARK SKY

A Story of
Four Poor Brothers

GEOFFREY RAISMAN

HAREHILLS PRESS LTD
Newport Pagnell, UK

Published by Harehills Press Ltd
23 Union Street
Newport Pagnell
MK16 8ET
Great Britain 2002

Design
Joe Brock / Ruth Partington

Printed by Antony Rowe Ltd
Chippenham, Wilts
Great Britain

To the long-suffering Vi and Ruth, to my cousin John Michael, and to Barbara Wright and Professor William J ('Bill') Fishman, without whom this book could not have been written. Over the 20 years of its gestation, I have, like the Ancient Mariner, pressed most of my many friends, colleagues and acquaintances into hearing all or part of this story. They have helped me to be midwife to the real authors, the Four Poor Brothers.

Kramer's *Day of Atonement*, 1919 was commissioned by the Leeds Jewish Representative Council and presented to the Leeds City Art Gallery in 1920. Copyright permission kindly granted by the William Roberts Society.

Contents

Contents

'You know,' Harry said, straining his eyes to peer into the gloom, 'even on the darkest nights there's always some light in the sky. However little it is, the sky never gets completely dark.'

'You are stupid,' said the old man. 'It's true that I will soon be gone. But I have children and they have grandchildren. With us people, the more that come, the more there are. But with the stones on the mountain side, the more you move, the less are left.'
Wisdom of Yu Gong

Geoffrey Raisman was born and brought up in Leeds and graduated in medicine at Oxford, where he taught for 11 years. He is a Professor at University College, London, and FRS. His research is stimulated by a fascination with the intricate structure of the brain and the way the brain can change as a result of experience, and after injury. Taking advantage of the million-fold magnification offered by the electron microscope, he was the first to show that the nerve cells in damaged brain automatically form new connections. These observations are a starting point for research into methods for repairing brain injury. He also provided the first evidence that the structure of the brain of males is different from that of females, and showed that this difference arises from the exposure of the prenatal baby to sex hormones. The goal of his team at the National Institute for Medical Research in London is to find a cure for the paralysis caused by spinal cord injury.

Preface

Just over a hundred years ago, my grandparents left their home in Lithuania. With thousands of other refugees, they came to live in Leeds in a slum area called the Leylands. The newcomers soon learned English, and struggled to make a living. My grandfather had two ways of doing this. He gambled on cards, dogs and horses, and he produced eleven children to earn the money to keep him. This book is the story of four of his sons, and of the plan, partly successful and partly disastrous, by which the family attempted to improve their harsh lot.

The history of my family contains no spectacular events. There are no villains, murders, rapes or brutality. The family did not suffer in war or holocausts, nor did strange coincidence bring them good fortune. Yet their story so lured me that in the end I had to write it down.

High up in the Pennines the wind still blows over moorlands as rugged and majestic as they must have been before men ever saw them, but below the moors the City of Leeds changes continually. It is not easy for one community to accept another. When the Leylanders first arrived from Lithuania the people of Leeds thought them very strange. Newcomers and natives were wary of each other. Each wondered at the other's odd customs. But in the narrow bustling streets of the smoky Yorkshire city, the two communities drifted together into the twentieth century. Without their noticing it, what they shared in common gradually became more than their differences. Time had woven them together, like the strands of a rope, each fibre an individual, always separate, always with its own colour, never joining its neighbours, but all blended inseparably into the whole.

The Raisman Family

Louis	*1887 - 1955*
Myer	*1889 - 1971*
Sir Jeremy	*1892 - 1978*
Fanny	*1895 - 1976*
John	*1896 - 1982*
Harry	*1898 - 1992*
Mad Jack	*1899 - 1990*
Sarah	*1903 - 2001*
Ralph	*1905 - 1996*
Sam	*1907 - 1973*
Sidney	*1908 - 2002*

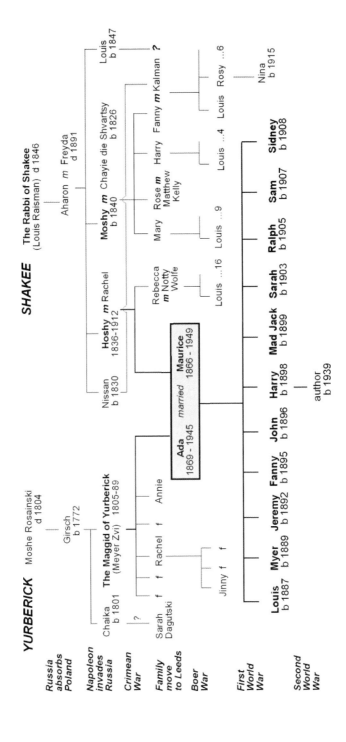

PART I

The Lady Beck

The Leylands

It was six men of Hindostan
To learning much inclined
Who went to see the elephant,
(Though all of them were blind)

Saxe

Truth, like the Hindustani elephant, varies with the position of the observer. It was early one quiet Sunday morning in autumn when I at last persuaded my father to go to the remains of the Leylands. Regent Street was only just coming to life with its first sleepy cars taking this back way to avoid the city centre. We turned off into a little side street. No people lived here now, the houses were long since demolished and replaced by warehouses and gravelled over parking lots. We stopped opposite Gower Street School and I looked across at the ornate brick building, its entrances surmounted by stone slabs with the words:

BOYS   GIRLS   INFANTS

'That's my old school,' my father said.

It was the only time he had shown even the slightest enthusiasm.

Cold white light from a featureless sky revealed only the blank and shabby walls of silent warehouses. Even the noise of the occasional cars swishing by on Regent Street behind us seemed remote, kneading to pulp the autumn leaves, lost in the silence of this deserted side street.

'It wasn't like this,' my father said, looking down the lifeless street. 'At that time there were four narrow little back-alleys here, crammed with slum houses and teeming with unwashed kids.'

I looked down and, to my surprise, at our feet there still remained the curving rows of flagstones that showed where once ran Plum Street, Star Street, Sun Street and Noble Street. For the first time raised the hairs on the back of my neck, that uncanny feeling which was to possess me for most of the next two years - the past was coming to life.

'Let's go to the library and see if they've got any old maps of the

1

Leylands streets,' I said brightly to my father, as if the thought had only just come to me. 'What do I want to see the Leylands for?' he replied sharply. 'I lived there. That's enough for me. It was just a horrible slum. Let's go for a ride in the country,' and he turned away from the scene in front of him, the empty street with its telltale rows of kerbstones. 'It was just Paradise Alley,' he added with a shudder. 'Paradise Alley began here.'

How could I refuse him the rare treat of a ride out to the Dales he so loved, so remote and inaccessible to him now? So I drove off, west through the city, past the silent station, and up towards where the first ridge rises at Gildersome, and the empty Pennine moorsides appear on the horizon, and stopped the car. Reluctant, but accepting this delay to his outing, my father scrambled with me up the ragged track that led to the now disused Hilltop Burial Ground. Around us stood a whole community. My father noticed a fallen headstone. 'Oh dear,' he said, only half curbing an impulse to go over and set it straight. 'He had the cloth shop at the top of Byron Street. I went in there often.'

We wandered on slowly, my father pausing from time to time, to turn desultorily now to the right, now to the left, reading the odd inscription here and there. 'He worked next to me at Burton's for years.' We crossed the road to the *Englisher* cemetery. 'He won five hundred pounds on the Calcutta Sweepstakes.' A little further stood a shiny black marble stone with gold letters and, scattered over the plot in front of it, green marble chips, like a kind of permanent stone grass. 'He was a very wealthy man

- the sort of man who could put in an order for a thousand rolls of cloth - just like that - and so mean that when the bridge section of the club decided to charge an annual fee of half-a-crown, he refused to pay. He left instead.'

My father obviously did not find the *Englisher* dead congenial.

I remained silent. My eyes ranged over the sea of stones all around us. There was a pause in the conversation. Then, gently at my elbow, in a moment all his impatience was gone.

'Well, Geoff, is that enough?' my father asked, in a soft voice. I turned away reluctantly. He didn't want to talk about it any more. I raised my eyes and looked around. Here on the westernmost hill of the city lay the ancestors of our community. Before me on the left, now covered by a threatening cloud, rose the northern hills where their descendants now lived. And eastwards, straight in front, illuminated by faltering shafts of sunlight, was the hollow where all those narrow Leylands streets of back-to-back houses once stood.

It seemed a hopeless task to try to reconstruct the life of those demolished streets. Then one of the perpetual breezes of Gildersome struck my face, with the thought: this is unchanged, this is the same Yorkshire they knew.

Der Hame

Der Hame

Between the east and west parts of Europe, a gloomy tract of land stretches from the Baltic Sea in the north, a thousand miles southwards to the Black Sea. The Russians called this the Pale of Settlement of the Jews. The Jews call this place, so inhospitable to them, *Der Hame*, by which they mean to say Our Home.

On the north bank of the River Niemen, just before it leaves Lithuania, stands a little town. It had been founded nearly a thousand years ago by the Teutonic Knights, who built a castle there and called it Georgenburg. Jews had lived beneath the castle walls for hundreds of years. But, with time and the ebbing and flowing fortunes of many wars, and invaders and counter-invaders, the castle and its Knights had long since disappeared and the Jews now made up most of the population. They called the town Yurberick.

In Yurberick was a school. Its teacher was Reb Meyer the Rum Maker, known as the Maggid of Yurberick. Meyer was born in 1805, the year when Nelson destroyed the combined French and Spanish fleets at Trafalgar. He was seven years old on the buzzing midsummer night when Napoleon's army camped in the forest beyond Shakee, before next day crossing the Niemen on its way to Moscow and annihilation. As a young man, he saw Russia swallow up Poland, and by the time of our story, Reb Meyer was the most famous scholar in the province of Kovno.

Reb Meyer had the distinction of writing one of the Torah Scrolls, which became the treasured possessions of the congregation, and were kept in the elaborately-carved Holy Ark of the Gothic style wooden synagogue. This synagogue was the pride of the Yurberick Jews. It had been built in 1790, and was regarded as the most beautiful synagogue in Lithuania. Reb Meyer had no sons. His wife had died, giving birth to his sixth daughter, Ada. Now she was a little girl, who looked after him, a goat, a few chickens that scratched around behind their wooden house in the muddy Yatever Street, and a cow grazing in the lush green meadows that stretched from the muddy slope of the river bank all the way to the encircling woods.

Maggid is Hebrew for one who tells, a messenger. A Maggid was a local wise man, who wandered from place to place preaching. In Yurberick the

5

Maggid acted as a town clerk, recording legal contracts. In summer his door always stood open, and even when the great frosts of winter came, there was always a chink to show a warm glow from inside. People from all around would travel to visit the Maggid, and ask his advice on all kinds of religious and family problems.

And late one summer's day in 1875, while the westering sun was setting over the River Niemen, and the birch leaves were turning silver and gold, the Tsar Alexander II Romanov, Emperor of all the Russias, sat on his throne in St Petersburg, and Queen Victoria sat on hers in London, and two heavily bearded men with bundles on their backs trudged down the narrow Yatever Street.

Seen from the end of the street, their full black beards made the two men look old. But square little Hoshy Raisman was only just in his forties, and his lantern-jawed brother Moshy was four years younger. They had just got off the raft that ferried back and forth across the River Niemen as it widened on its leisurely way to the sea.

Like so many of the Russian Jews, the Raisman brothers eked out a living by travelling through the little towns and villages selling 'dry goods.' That meant matches, needles and pins, and any other small household things and, when they could, horse-trading with the Lithuanian peasant farmers. Such people were called reisermen, which meant travelling men, and from which they got the family name of Raisman.

The two brothers picked their way carefully between the potholes of Yatever Street, and passed the slaughterers' sheds. Avoiding the blowing heaps of chicken feathers that glinted in the rays of dying sunlight from the River Niemen, they came to the Maggid's open door.

The Maggid stood up from his writing desk, an imposing, patriarchal figure. He had a high domed bald head with thin white hair straggling down the sides and a long black beard straggling down to his waist, and cut off straight. But what was immediately striking to anyone who saw the Maggid was his good-natured expression, his teasing, quizzically-tilted eyebrows, and above all, his mischievous, gently smiling eyes.

'So what's the news?' asked the Maggid.

Hoshy paused in the doorway, and eased the load on his back. 'It can always be worse,' he replied. '… and of course it can always be better.'

'Well, come in!' said the Maggid, and while Hoshy and Moshy took off their packs, the Maggid turned to his little daughter Ada and whispered, 'Put the kettle on. Do you know who these men are? Their grandfather was Louis, the famous Rabbi of Shakee.'

Hoshy and Moshy were always welcome at the Maggid's house. 'And the family?' the Maggid asked.

'In Spring, my son Maurice caught the cholera,' Hoshy said. The Maggid held up a hand in horror. 'He was burning hot with fever. So we put him in a tub of ice-cold water. It took both of us to hold him down,' Hoshy said. 'He's OK now, God be thanked.'

'And the rest of the family?' the Maggid asked.

'Well, may no Evil Eye fall upon them.'

The rest of Hoshy's information was less dramatic, and referred more to the offspring of horses than those of humans, but still the sun had long gone down before they had finished exchanging all the news, and were ready to go on their way.

Tsar Alexander's grandfather, the Tsar Alexander the First, conqueror of Napoleon, had worn the laurel wreath of a victorious Roman Emperor, and the new provinces, named after the style of the Roman Empire, were called Gubernia – Governments. The River Niemen formed one of the internal frontiers of the broad Tsarist empire. North of the river, Yurberick was on the Lithuanian side, in the Russian Government of Kovno. On the south side, Shakee was in the Government of Suwalki, part of Russian Poland. The Lithuanian peasants round Shakee used to breed horses. The big ones were sold across the nearby frontier to East Prussia, for use as the prized chargers of the fierce Uhlan cavalry. Ponies too small to go to war were sold to the local Jews, who in turn traded them into the barges that were towed slowly down the Niemen to the Baltic ports, where they were shipped to the coal mines in England.

The Raismans' house in Shakee was known as the horse dealers' house. It stood at the edge of the town, immediately opposite the cemetery entrance. Behind the house was a large back yard of packed earth, dry in summer, but becoming treacherously muddy the rest of the year, and here the occasional disconsolate pony ambled around, deprived of the chance of military glory, munching the odd apple given it by the kids, and awaiting deportation to the pits. At one side were the remains of a broken-down wooden fence and a shallow pool, with hens pecking around in the dirt. A cat sat under an apple tree laden with worm-eaten fruit. By a wall was a fragrant pile of newly chopped wood, ready for a Baltic winter.

The house was built around a central stove. On the kitchen side, the stove was stoked and used for cooking. The rest of the stove was shared between two rooms, so that each had a part of the stove in the corner. In the bedroom the stove was unadorned. In the living room was a low table, a carpet and a tired sofa that sagged invitingly. The stove was partly tiled, almost to the ceiling, in brown glazed tiles. A small, low stool, covered with worn, soft fabric, allowed their old mother, Frada to sit by the warmth in winter.

Far to the east, the armies of the Russian Empire, now at the height of its power, were advancing across Central Asia, conquering Turkic chiefdoms, and threatening the British in India. It would be a generation before they reached Japan, and their ultimate doom at the hands of another emperor. In 1827, Alexander's son, the Tsar Nicholas I had issued an edict that Jewish children should be drafted for military service. In every Jewish town, the Russians appointed a local Jewish official called the Grabber. He had to countersign the birth record of every new baby boy, and unless he countersigned the death record first, he was personally responsible for delivering the boy to the army.

Officially the boys were taken when they reached the age of twelve, and conscription was for thirty-one years. In practice many of the Nikolaevski soldati were only eight years old. Half the conscripts didn't survive their first journey. Young married men usually divorced their wives so they wouldn't have to wait for them.

Hoshy was born in Shakee in 1836. He had lost nearly all his children through conscription or disease. His two youngest, Rebecca, a girl of twelve, and Maurice, a boy of ten, were all he had left, and he was anxious not to lose this last chance of a son to survive him and pray for his soul.

In 1874, the Tsarist government, always looking for ways to hold down the citizens of their unwilling western provinces, and hungry for soldiers to carry forward the advance of their expanding central Asian empire, had passed an even more severe conscription law.

In the autumn of each year, Moses the Grabber was summoned to the recruiting office, and the names of Jewish boys of age were called out. If a person failed to appear a fine of three hundred roubles was imposed on his family. If they couldn't pay, their property was seized and sold at auction. If the sum raised was still not enough, the Grabber had to pay the rest, and the family were sent to prison. If the parents, brothers and sisters could not be found, the grandparents were arrested.

The Russian Minister of the Interior had decreed:

> *For some time the Russian Government has given its attention to the Jews, and to their relationships with the other inhabitants of the Empire, with a view of ascertaining the sad condition of the Christian inhabitants brought about by the conduct of the Jews. The Government have thought it a matter of urgency and justice to adopt stringent measures in order to put an end to the oppression practised by the Jews. With this in view it has appointed Commissions in all the towns inhabited by the Jews to inquire into what makes it impracticable to put into force the laws limiting the rights of the Jews, and how shall those laws be altered so that they shall no longer be able to evade them.*

In London there was a meeting in the Guildhall, where the following was read:

> *Russia is still, as is well known, in the mediaeval stage of development, where Church and State are identical. Jews are*

thus both heretics and aliens.

A petition was transmitted to St Petersburg addressed to his Imperial Majesty, Emperor of All the Russias. The Memorial of the Citizens of London, in Guildhall assembled, on behalf of the Russian Jews:

> *Pent up in narrow bounds within your Majesty's wide Empire, and even within those bounds forced to reside chiefly in towns that reek and overflow from every form of poverty and wretchedness; forbidden all free movement; hedged in every enterprise by restrictive law; forbidden tenure of land. Education is denied them; they may not freely exercise profession, nor may they gain promotion in the Army.*

The Tsar did not reply, and the Russian Foreign Ministry confined itself to a dignified statement to the effect that it did not interfere in the internal affairs of other states and would appreciate the same courtesy in return.

The Raisman family could see there was no future for them in Lithuania. And to make things worse, Maurice was approaching an age when he would be called up to the army. Hoshy and Moshy went to consult the Maggid. Apart from his other activities, the Maggid of Yurberick had a very important unofficial function. Yurberick was a frontier town. Just across the frontier, on the same bank of the River Niemen, was the East Prussian village of Smalininkai. The Maggid's house was known as a haven for the fleeing conscripts whom he helped to smuggle across the frontier on the first stage of their flight to freedom, a flight that led over the sea to England and then on to the Golden Land of America, whose streets were paved with gold.

To help the refugees, the Maggid had invented a special system of learning English by the sound. Thus to remember the English 'I want' he said you should think of the idea of a wall, the word for which in Yiddish is *vant*.

'We need to get out,' Hoshy told the Maggid. 'There's my wife and our little son Maurice, and his sister Rebecca. a long life to them, there's my mother, Frada, bless her, and there's Moshy. Our kid brothers Nissan and Louis have decided to take their chances and stay to look after the pony business.'

'It'll be more than ten years ago now,' the Maggid said, 'a young man

10

called Maishy Katz came through here on his way from Kovno. And he got across the frontier to Königsberg and got on a boat to Hull. Actually he had wanted to go to America, but he couldn't afford the fare. Now I hear he's living in Leeds in the English county of Yorkshire. He's changed his name to Maishy Goodman, and he's learned to read and write English. They tell me he is doing well there as a tailor. He must be about thirty now. He got married in Leeds, but it didn't last.'

'What was he like, this Maishy Katz?' Hoshy asked.

'Well...' the Maggid paused, 'strong, determined... a hard man...'

'If we get to Leeds, do you think he will help us?'

The Maggid shrugged, thought for a while, and stroked his beard. 'But there will certainly have to be a smear for the guards at the customs house.'

'A smear?' Hoshy asked. In reply, the Maggid only smiled.

The Maggid was well known to the Lithuanians and to the Russian garrison. Rum lubricated the machinery of the Tsarist empire.

'But you will have to go through the marshes,' the Maggid warned.

In 1876, the Raisman family bundled up their umbrellas, and their mattress rolls and their old mother, and left Shakee for the last time. When they got to the River Niemen they took the ferry across to the north bank, and in the afternoon they arrived in the Maggid's house in Yatever Street.

'Go and play with the little girl, long life to her,' Hoshy said to his children, and Maurice and Rebecca followed Ada as she led them out of the house.

'Be careful,' a voice said from inside.

Ada smiled. 'Your mother?' Maurice asked.

'I have no mother. She died when I was born. That's my older sister, Rachel. She's my good mother now.' The children crossed the main street of Yurberick and into the cow pastures, where the valley broadened out, and two little rivers, the Mituva and its tributary the Imsré, flowed into the Niemen. Emerald-green meadows were spangled with brilliant flower gems. Pond weed, like Ophelia's hair, trailed, floating tresses down towards the Niemen, and people in white shirt sleeves rowing.

Meanwhile, the Maggid carefully went over all the details of the route the family must take, and this done, all waited anxiously in the Maggid's house until after dark. Then, following his instructions, the little party huddled close together, with their mattress rolls on their backs and their packs under their arms, and crossed the wooden bridge over the Mituva. They passed the last two wooden houses on the road to Smalininkai, and then, before reaching the customs house, they took the path down to the Niemen. Here was an ancient grove, sacred to the Lithuanians, of birch and sycamore, and oak whose lumpy branches suggested all kinds of strange forms of giants, men and long-ago creatures half-man half-beast.

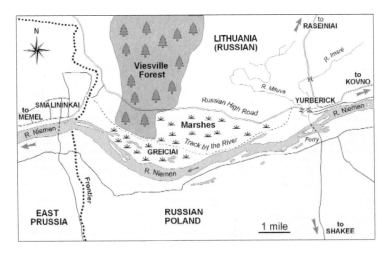

The children clung close to Hoshy, Rebecca holding one hand and Maurice the other.

On their left, the ground fell away into marshy reeds by the river. Fearfully, in the dark, they stepped down. Moshy went first, and the family followed, holding on to each other, fearing, on the right, discovery by the guards on the road, on the left, that they would step out too far and be swept away by the current into the depths of the great river, silent, strong, and luminous as a black mirror against the night sky.

But how would the track get them past the frontier post? The family wondered at this advice from the Maggid. Surely the Russians would be able to cover the few paces of ground to the river?

A little way further down the road, and there was the answer. In a wide sweep, the river turned away from the road. A huge area of marshland with reed forests and bulrushes opened out, further than they could see. In fact, the road was now over a mile from the little cluster of houses at Greiciai, on the bank of the Niemen. The Russians could not possibly have covered this area at night. The Maggid's directions were right! The frontier here was open. They followed a track down towards the river. It intersected another track. They chose a turning, then another, and within a few minutes realised that they had completely lost all sense of direction. They had no choice but to return to the main road. Even in full daylight, they would not have been able to find the way through the marshes.

But no sooner had they started to scramble up on to the road, than the soldiers heard them and shouted: 'Who's that talking? Stop! Show me your papers!'

The soldiers were on the watch. The Maggid's smear had alerted them to the possibility of money. A hurried exchange took place. The Raismans gave what valuables they had, and the Russians gave freedom, a good bargain at any price. And so they reached the end of the marsh. But it was not Smalininkai. There was no sign of Smalininkai. The forest was completely dark, but even though it was totally clouded over, some light still came from the sky. Even on the darkest nights there is always some light from the sky. The sky never gets completely dark. And with the light they made out in front there was a clearing in the forest. Swaying graceful branches and soft leaves of the Russian birch trees bent and sighed and rustled in the wind. But beyond that the great forest of Viesville rose like a black wall. Black and silent, for the stiff leaves of the

13

pine trees and the larch made no sound at all, however fierce the wind.

So, fearfully, like Adam and Eve leaving the Garden of Eden, my great-grandfather, my grandfather, and their family entered between the giant pencils, vertical as guardsmen on parade, the silent woods of bear and hairy boar, of wolf and fallow deer that speckled flit invisible between the trunks. The scent of crushed pine needles was underfoot, and the forest covered them. A red fox with a white tip to its tail ran across the road, fast but unhurried, seeing but not looking, nonchalant and stealthy at the same time, in the way of foxes when they cross a road. Ahead lay the frontier, and they would cross into Germany, and the great Baltic shipping ports of Tilsit, Königsberg, and Memel with their forests of masts at anchor, and the tackle of great overhanging brick warehouses, and the ship that would bring them across the Baltic Sea, following the ancient Hanseatic trade routes, via Hamburg, to the Yorkshire port of Hull.

But in the new country Hoshy's little son, Maurice never forgot the sparkling green meadows, and the bobbing black curls of Ada, the Maggid's youngest daughter, who looked after her father's cow and goat in Yurberick.

El Dorado

During the last twenty years there has been a steady influx to Leeds of Polish-Russian Jews. The greater part come from the province of Kovno, and on starting are often acquainted with but one word of English, and that word is 'Leeds.' They generally land at Hull, proceed direct to Leeds, and know nothing of England or English institutions, save what they have been able to learn in the latter town.

Some of the older immigrants boast that they are Yorkshiremen, but they rarely qualify themselves as Englishmen. It seems evident that, on the whole, they readily earned their living at Leeds, and to the Russian Jew, in dread of obligatory military service or suffering from religious persecution, the name of Leeds was but a modern term for an El Dorado.   The Lancet, June 9th, 1888

My grandfather, Maurice, was the family treasure. His older sister, Rebecca, looked after him like a hen looks after her chick. 'I wouldn't change him for ten sacks of onions,' Rebecca said.

Maurice could remember the boat crossing to Hull, and the baggage-laden trek from Hull to Goole. The house they rented was in one of the long parallel brick terraces which ran down at an angle to the wharves that brought inlets of the River Humber to interlock like fingers with the railway sidings. As yet still without a word of English, Maurice wandered about the little port where the ships berthed and the black church spire towered over the water. He scrambled over the rough fields to see how the River Don came down between high warped banks of mud to enter the Humber. And as he stood on the bank of that vast estuary, watching the muddy tidal water trickling among the roots of the salt marsh grasses at his feet, he looked down to the smoky city of Hull on the distant horizon.

When they first arrived in Goole, Hoshy and Moshy were able to survive on the business of shipping pit-ponies from Lithuania. These little creatures were sold to the mines of the south Yorkshire coalfield to drag the loaded bogeys from the coalface to the waiting railway carts. They lived out their working lives entirely underground, and usually became blind. When a Yorkshire miner retired it was the custom for a small sum to buy from the mine owners one of the worn out ponies to keep him company.

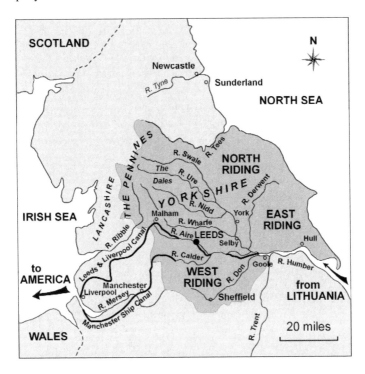

But soon the pit-pony business failed. According to the family legend, it was due to shipwreck. But looking back over the family history, it seems more likely that their downfall would have been caused by quite another sort of horse, one that was ridden round an oval track by a little man in silk colours on the nearby racecourses at Selby or at York. But whatever the cause, with or more likely without paying the rent, Hoshy and Moshy now moved further inland, to Leeds, the centre of the Yorkshire clothing trade, and the glistening El Dorado of the Russian Jews.

Here, in the centre of the city, beneath an imposing statue of the Black

Prince on horseback, the arriving immigrants from all the little towns across the wide provinces of Kovno and Suwalki, and from deeper in the Russian Pale, were met off the train by a crowd of curious kids whose entertainment it was to go down to the station and watch the strange new people coming, and two Yorkshiremen, who spoke only three words of Yiddish: 'Here we are.'

Maurice had completed his journey. Twenty five years later, Britain would fight wars in China and South Africa. Two World Wars would decimate humanity, the Russian Empire would disappear. The last Tsar, Nicholas II, grandson of Alexander II, and all his family would be lined up against a Siberian cellar wall and shot. And the Jews of Yurberick and Shakee too would come to an end. But though this little boy's long life would span all these events, Maurice Raisman was never to move again.

For a penny, the two Yorkshiremen took the bags and bundles, put them on their handcarts, and pulled them from the station along Boar Lane, and down Kirkgate to the Leylands. There was one room in a house on Imperial Street. The four corners were curtained off for married couples. Everyone else slept in the middle of the room, and there the Raismans stayed, with the other people who had come on the same train, until something could be found for them. As soon as the new batch of immigrants arrived, people came rushing in looking for relatives, people from the same village. There were marvellous scenes of crying, laughing, hugging, asking about the people they'd left behind, from Bialystok, from Shakee, from Yurberick, from Marienpol. 'How is it there? How are the children?' and so on.

Next day one of the couples in a corner took in a lodger. There was blue murder - dreadful! And as soon as the week had gone by the family had to be out of Imperial Street because another lot was coming in. So a collection was made among the few people already there to keep the Raismans for another week in Imperial Street. Desperate, Moshy went to find Maishy Katz, who was now called Maishy Goodman, and was known to the immigrants as the poor man's lawyer. 'I'll give the boy a chance,' Maishy Goodman said. 'You're lucky. I've got one machine left. Only one. But that's all I can do. Don't think it's easy here.'

So next morning, Hoshy took his son Maurice by the hand, and they walked up Bridge Street to a little yard. Maishy Goodman led them through an open doorway, past a kitchen with a large family and they climbed two flights of stairs, getting all the dustier as they went up.

An enormous racket came out of the room, and at first the air was so filled with cigarette smoke they could hardly open their eyes. Gradually Maurice made out, all around, at angles, filling every available space, there were sewing machines with men and boys wearing caps and coats, bent over them, hard at work. No one looked up. Maurice was not the only one in short trousers. Maishy Goodman took Maurice to an empty machine, and tapped the next man on the shoulder. 'David, this boy is Maurice. You teach him.' Maishy Goodman stepped back and was going to leave, but Hoshy waited, not knowing what to do.

'So?' Maishy said. Hoshy was silent. 'Let someone bring him something for his dinner,' Maishy said. 'We don't stop. There's a rush on. You should be glad of it. And don't forget it's my time. I'm paying for it.' And with that, Maishy Goodman went off down the stairs, followed by the meek father.

David was only just out of short trousers himself. 'Watch,' he said to Maurice, getting up and sitting at the empty machine. David spread out a piece of cloth on the empty sewing machine, scrabbled a piece of thread from out of the shuttle, threaded the needle with a second thread, flicked round the driving wheel, and started to treadle away furiously. The two edges of the cloth zipped through the machine, and out of the other side, a trouser leg with a straight seam appeared.

Maurice looked bewildered. 'Don't worry,' David laughed. 'We all felt that way when we first saw it.' Then, painstakingly, step by step, he showed Maurice how to slide open the shiny lid of the shuttle box, thread the metal spool, and thread the steel needle. 'Now,' he said, 'You sit.'

Maurice sat, but his legs were too short for his feet to reach the treadle. 'Wait,' David said, and went off to get a wooden box. 'Sit on that.' Now Maurice's feet could reach the treadle, and he tried to start the machine. But the treadle was too stiff, and its worn joints too creaky. David got down on all fours under the table and cleared the dusty cloth clippings and cigarette ends away from the treadle. 'You can put a drop of oil on it to make it easier,' he said to Maurice, pointing to a little metal oil can. 'But, Maurice, whatever you do, never get any oil on the cloth. The boss'll kill you. And me.'

In the end Maurice got the treadle started, and the needle started to jerk up and down in uncontrollable fits and starts. In a moment the threads were tied in a knot. The machine was made for a man. Maurice's nose hardly reached the table top, and only by standing up could his arm reach the driving wheel.

David had watched all this carefully. 'Now,' he said, 'Start again,' and he took a pair of scissors and cut off the knot Maurice was trying to untie.

Slowly Maurice worked at the various tasks, until in the end a slow, wobbly seam appeared in the cloth. 'We won't show the boss that one,' David said, smiling. 'Now remember. Don't touch the belt while it's moving. It has a sharp metal clip that can tear your fingers off. And above all, always keep your fingers well away from the needle. We've got to get through all these orders as fast as we can.'

Maurice sat patiently at the machine. All around the room was filled with the intermittent roaring of machines as they raced through trouser seams, and many heated conversations, generally in a whispered tone, which Maurice could not follow, but where one of the most frequent words was 'horse.' At one end of the room Maurice noticed long shiny wooden tables, and tall standing men with shiny waistcoats and silk straps hanging at the back. Their lit cigarette ends were perched at the edge of the tables, among burn holes where they had been neglected in the past. The cloth was held together by innumerable pins, securing coarse white linings and silk facings. The tailors marked out the cloth with little white triangles of chalk, measuring from time to time with a rapid movement of a measuring tape they kept round their necks, or with straight wooden rulers with steel edges. Then they rapidly put in white coarse basting stitches by hand, and sliced the cloth with huge metal shears clacking loudly on the tables.

David noticed Maurice watching with admiration. 'They are tailors,' David told Maurice.

'Aren't we tailors?' Maurice asked, in surprise.

'Us!' David laughed. 'We're trousers machinists. They make jackets. But you're lucky. The boss could have given you vest machining. That's a job for real has-beens. Look over there,' David said in a hushed voice, 'That's a master tailor.'

The master tailor at that moment was holding a jacket up under his nose, and whistling with concentration as he sewed a fine line of tiny stitches into a lapel. As he reached the end he raised the cloth to his mouth and bit off the end of the thread. 'That's hand stitching,' David went on. 'It's just for decoration. But the most skilled part for the tailors is fitting the sleeves into the armholes.'

The din in the room never stopped. Young girls came in carrying half made orders and queued up silent, in front of the foreman. In no hurry, he examined each buttonhole carefully, opening it contemptuously with his fingers. Then he rapidly totted up the number of buttonholes, growled a few words of complaint, made a quick calculation, and grudgingly counted a few small coppers into the girl's hands. From time to time he glanced along the queue. 'Stand still,' he said. 'In a straight line. And don't lean on the wall.'

Behind the room, through an open door, large men sweating in white vests were working on high trestles with huge fluted steaming irons, to press the finished suits.

By mid-afternoon Maurice's back ached, and his eyes were smarting. Suddenly he gave a little squeak, and started to cry. Not surprised, David had been waiting for this. He jumped up at once, and put his left arm round Maurice's shoulders. 'Don't move!' he ordered. 'Don't move! Don't pull! And for God's sake get your feet off that damn treadle!'

The steel needle had gone right through Maurice's finger nail, and on through his finger. It was deep in the shuttle. There was not a drop of blood. But the nail was slightly dimpled where the needle went in. Maurice was pinned to the table. He couldn't possibly have got his right hand out, and there was no way he could ever have reached the driving wheel to raise the needle.

Standing behind Maurice, David clasped the little boy tightly with his left arm, and swiftly flicked the driving wheel with his right hand. The steel needle flew up out of Maurice's finger nail, followed by two black threads, a flash of white cartilage and a gush of blood. 'Here,' David said, taking a not too clean scrap of cotton cloth out of his pocket. 'Wrap it up. It's clean. You'll be OK. No one learns to sew until they have put the needle through their finger. Make sure there are no threads left in it. And, whatever you do, don't let the boss see.'

They finished late. 'You can sleep under the machine,' David said. 'No one will mind you being here. Use that sack of clippings to sleep on. It's quite warm,' and he kissed the boy briefly on the forehead before leaving.

Black Bread

Now Maurice didn't need floor space in the immigrants' room in Imperial Street, and while he was bringing in some money, Moshy had time to find a room in a hollow block of buildings, inserted into the corner where Quarry Hill met Templar Street, and I shall call it the Templar Street Fortress.

The point of the Fortress faced the fearsome heights of Quarry Hill, the heart of the Irish quarter, beside which towered the smoke-blackened Church of St Patrick. But along the side of the Fortress, the Lady Beck served as a kind of moat. The houses built into this edge of the Fortress looked straight out over the Beck. They had no entrances of any kind along this side, and their sheer brick walls, towering 40 feet above the water, were pierced only by square windows protected with iron bars. The Leeds City Council used to list how many carcasses of dogs and cats and putrefying pigs were cleared out of the Lady Beck to keep its foetid waters flowing.

Hoshy and Moshy's first home in Leeds was here, in the heart of the Templar Street Fortress. It was reached from Templar Street by a narrow passage, half obscured by a huge brick midden and overhung by the upper storey of the houses making up the outer wall of the Fortress. The entrance was surmounted by a square wooden beam, like a portcullis, pierced on either side by cast-iron tie-bars ending in great concentric iron medallions. The home itself was very tiny. Over the top was Tilla Goodman's slipper factory and in the basement was Israel Gibson's herring curing establishment.

On the pavement in front of the entrance to the passage stood a horse trough of speckled yellow granite. The trough was dry now and filled with rubbish, but under its overall layer of grime, patches of the original shiny surface still showed through. The new inhabitants of the Fortress would look at this horse trough, much the grandest object in any of these streets, and imagine that it must have been set up in a bygone age for the horses which drew the fine carriages of the English gentry up the hill out of Leeds towards Tadcaster and the county town of York.

Maurice was a complete contrast to his father Hoshy. Hoshy was a religious man with a full beard. His son Maurice was clean-shaven. Hoshy had not a word of English, while in no time, Maurice spoke English faultlessly, and played the English game of cricket outside their house in Templar Street. The large, irregularly-shaped area enclosed in the Fortress walls was called Metcalf Yard. Criss-crossed by half-ruined brick walls, and surrounded by dilapidated house backs and haylofts, Metcalf Yard was a playground for the children. Here, behind the safety of the Fortress walls, Maurice could study the varied new aspects of life in Leeds.

The entrance was flanked by a cabinet maker's, a rag and paper merchant's, and a fruit and potato merchant's. In the centre was the herring curer's office, and a huge communal rubbish heap, whose aroma mingled with that of a tripe merchant's, a grease extractor's, a sausage skin manufacturer's and an undertaker's.

After the failure of the pit-pony business Hoshy got a job replacing broken window panes. Moshy got the use of a small brick shed in Metcalf Yard. This shed was joined to the back of the Central Synagogue, deep in the heart of the Fortress.

As soon as enough people had come from a particular town to assemble a congregation of ten men, all they now needed was a Scroll to be able to set up their own synagogue, usually in someone's attic, or bedroom, or in a hayloft. The biggest town in Suwalki was Marienpol. It was about 15 miles south of Shakee, and had a railway station. Between Marienpol and Shakee was a dense forest. 'Marienpol wasn't a very big place,' said one Marienpoler. 'You drove up the main street, and turned right, and you were out of town.'

The Marienpolers were the first group of immigrants sufficient to muster a quorum of ten men. And so they set up the Marienpoler Synagogue. But who can tell whether the pious Marienpoler synagogue congregation might not have found this name somewhat blasphemous to use if they had known that their town had received its name from the Teutonic Knights, who called it the Fields of Mary, in honour of the Virgin Mary, the patron of their knightly order? The Marienpoler Synagogue must be one of the few synagogues in the world dedicated to the Virgin Mary.

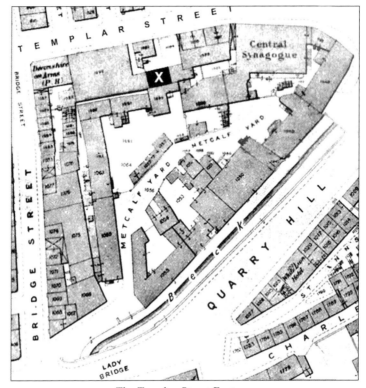

The Templar Street Fortress

In the shed by the Marienpoler Synagogue was a revolving oven of the kind used to bake the unleavened bread required for Passover. And now, the enterprising Moshy had the good fortune to marry one of the most formidable ladies of his day. Chayie was 14 years older then Moshy. People called her *Chayie die Shvartsy* (Black Chayie), some said because of her black hair, others gave less complimentary explanations.

Chayie set about making an everyday oven, and to later generations, Chayie was famous as the woman who first introduced the baking of black bread in the Leylands. Flavoured with the aromatic seeds of caraway, rye was made into the hard, dark, eight-pound rounds that the Leylanders called black bread. Leeds people called it Russian bread.

Standing beside the hot fragrance of the oven, Chayie took the order for the weight of bread the housewives could afford. It cost a penny a pound. With a practised eye, Chayie would size up the chunks already cut, and try them out on the scales. If they were not enough, with one brawny arm, she clasped a new great round against her floury pinafore. Then, seizing a bread knife whose blade was already razor thin through innumerable whettings, she turned it towards her own generous paunch, and with the gesture of a Japanese warrior about to disembowel himself, she sawed off a larger piece of bread, put it in the scale pan, and added the brass weights. Then, standing back, 'There!' she said, with satisfaction at her judgement, as the scale balanced out.

With the success of the black bread, Chayie could start to bake the little plaited rolls of white flour covered with poppy seeds in the Lithuanian fashion, and the soft white special bread made from wheat flour, glazed with egg and used on the Sabbath. The family now had income, and, with Chayie's determination, Moshy could move across Templar Street to a house at 1, Livery Street. This was the very heart of the Leylands, at the cross roads where Templar Street running from east to west, crossed Bridge Street running from south to north.

Bridge Street was the main thoroughfare of the Leylands, lined by shops, and full of life. Livery Street was a short street parallel to Bridge Street. Livery Street was short because it ended abruptly in a short flight of cracked sandstone steps leading down into a mass of lavatories, and beyond them a valve chamber which, at times when it could be released, allowed the sewage to flow into a huge festering ashpit-cum-midden which occupied all the space between here and the neighbouring Malt Street, where the mash was prepared for the brewery across the road.

Almost all the houses in the Leylands were back-to-back, one room above, one below, called a but and ben. They were regarded as particularly unhealthy, and medical opinion at the time was that they caused consumption. Moshy's house at 1 Livery Street was one of the very few Leylands houses that was not a back-to-back, but a through house. The living part of the house actually led through a step to the back of the shop at 34 Bridge Street, opening directly out on what the Americans might call the Leylands' main drag, and it was as far away as possible from the ashpits at the bad end of Livery Street.

Here Moshy opened a wine and spirit shop, and soon became rich enough to buy the next house at 2 Livery Street, the only other through house in the row, which opened to the shop on 36 Bridge Street. Moshy rented it out to his older brother Hoshy and his family. Moshy was rapidly becoming a man who could rub shoulders with Maishy Goodman.

The growth of the Leylands community was rapid. Forty years earlier, in 1841, there had been only ten Jewish families in Leeds. They worshipped in an attic in Bridge Street. Nine years later they opened the first synagogue. It was in Back Rockingham Street and was maintained by the subscriptions for 18 seats. But by 1860 they had built a synagogue in Belgrave Street on the hill to the west of the Leylands. Its official name was the Great Synagogue, but its members, aspiring to Englishness, called it the English Synagogue. In 1878, already prospering from the sweated labour of the new immigrants to the Leylands, they rebuilt the synagogue to hold 600 and maintained its exclusiveness by high subscription rates for membership.

The English Synagogue was a simple rectangular building with its long axis running along Belgrave Street. At each corner of the reading desk were lamps with elegant covers of pale, milky-blue blown glass shaped like candle flames, and the lectern was lit by two small lights shielded from the congregation by cylindrical shades of polished copper. The roof was supported by slender columns of cast-iron, the material of the new industrial age, and, as in the new Leeds Parish Church on which the English Synagogue was modelled, the wealthy patrons commissioned stained glass windows to commemorate themselves, their wives, and their generosity.

The newer immigrants were called greenhorns. Excluded from the English Synagogue, the greenhorns soon took steps to build a synagogue of their own. Under the leadership of Maishy Goodman, they clubbed together to start a synagogue in the fashionable quarter near the English Synagogue in St. Alban's Place. In 1869 they moved across the road and built the Greenhorns' Synagogue at the back of St John's churchyard, and Moshy Raisman became the first president.

My father described the Greenhorns' Synagogue: 'It wasn't like a Gothic cathedral, you know. It was a square, gloomy building. It was impious to have anything showy or ornate. A synagogue couldn't have towers, spires, flying buttresses or stained glass windows.' But even in the

Greenhorns' Synagogue, strict class distinctions were maintained. There were two separate synagogues. Moshy and the better-off members bought seats to worship in the upstairs. The poorer classes, which included older brother Hoshy and his family, prayed in the cellar.

Years passed, and Maurice continued to work in one tailoring workshop after another, grew out of short trousers into long ones, of which he made many, reached his barmitzvah, and took his place in synagogue cellar next to his father Hoshy.

At first the Leylanders had nowhere to bury their dead. The religious laws regarded corpses as unclean and required them to be buried outside the confines of human habitation. The authorities of the city of Leeds also had rules about where dead could and could not be buried. Caught between these two sets of rules the earlier Leylanders sometimes in desperation sent their dead back to Hull to be buried. On occasion they also buried them in various Leeds churchyards, such as the churchyard of St John's in Briggate, where the Greenhorns' Synagogue was built.

Soon, however, the Leylanders were put out of further difficulty by James Thomas Brudenell, seventh Earl of Cardigan, the man who led the charge of the Light Brigade at the battle of Balaclava in the Crimean War, and gave his name to the knitted woollen jacket. He sold the ruins of Kirkstall Abbey to Leeds in 1889, and for the peppercorn sum of two pounds he gave the Leylanders a couple of fields on the ridge of Gildersome to use as a cemetery.

Marble monuments: Tomb of Rabbi Moses Abrahams

Naturally the superior *Englishers*, separated from the greenhorns in life, would not wish to be mingled in death with hoi polloi. So the greenhorns' tombs were dug on the bleak hillside whose flanks are gashed with bare outcrops and broken layers of sandstone rocks, where the wind forever ruffles the grass. The more expensive *Englisher* plots were in a sheltered spot beneath the hill where, in the inclement weather in which people frequently chose to depart this life, the mourners' spiritual afflictions would not be further aggravated by the rude buffetings of an unkind Nature.

And so the *Englishers* stand apart to this day, and if the visitor doubts, he can see that on the hill nearby, all the tombstones are made of the rough local sandstone, obviously the cheapest material, with simply incised inscriptions, whereas below the tombs of the rich are marked by shining black or white marble monuments with elaborately carved lettering filled in lead or even marked with gold leaf. While on the hill, the local Yorkshire moulds and lichens, the humblest of all plants, lovingly encrust the soft sandstone tombstones, extracting nourishment from the moist, porous surfaces, and in return adorning the monuments with gaily coloured stars and rosettes and patches of white, gold and rich brown, obliterating the inscriptions on the now crumbling masonry. Yet they  disdain the glittering marble of the *Englisher* dead, finding no sustenance in those smooth, hostile surfaces. Thus the stones of those who wished so much to be accepted as even to take the name English, were rejected, and the humble greenhorns who didn't even know how to ask, this Yorkshire mould accepted as Yorkshire stone.

The Ice Cream Sermon

The Maggid of Yurberick had six daughters. Year by year he saved what money he could, till as soon as he had enough he sent or took one of his girls to seek fortune in the great world beyond the frontiers of the Russian Empire. By the time Hoshy and Moshy passed through his house, the three older girls had already travelled across England, not stopping at Leeds but continuing over the Pennines to Liverpool and over the Atlantic to America. The next two girls, Rachel, who had looked after Ada in Yurberick, and Annie, soon left Yurberick, and were now living in England.

By now the Maggid was getting old and tired. His wife had died long ago, and now only one daughter was left, Ada, a little girl of 14, bright as a button, with glossy black curls. The Maggid began to feel lonely. 'I want to go,' said Ada.

'Not yet, you're too young,' said her father. 'I need you to look after the goat and milk the cow.'

But Ada insisted.

When she first came to England Ada stayed with her sister Annie in Sheffield. Annie was a sad figure. She had no children, a terrible disgrace in those days, got divorced and remarried, and committed suicide at the age of 28. Ada, now 15 years old and entirely on her own, left Sheffield and came to Leeds to stay with an older cousin, Shroll Maishy, who had a grocer's shop and bakery on Bridge Street. And here she fell in love with Maurice, whom she had first seen six years before, on the night he had passed with his father through the Maggid's home on his way to England.

Shroll Maishy objected to Ada's choice: 'He is a worthless man. The whole family are gamblers. You are a Maggid's daughter. Don't throw yourself away on him just because he's good-looking.'

But Shroll's words could make no impression on the iron will of the Maggid's daughter. Ada and Maurice were determined to be married, and in 1886 the Maggid came over specially from Yurberick for their wedding. Ada was just 18, Maurice was 20. Shroll was not the only one who objected to this wedding. Maurice's older sister, Rebecca, felt deeply jealous that another woman would now be the one to cherish her precious kid brother.

By his profession, Maurice's father Hoshy was able to become one of the 15 members of the Glaziers' Synagogue, a special congregation made up entirely of glaziers. The Synagogue was a former hayloft on the roof of Granelli's ice-cream factory at the bottom of a yard off the lower end of Bridge Street. It was entered by climbing a sort of de luxe ladder, decorated with a wooden handrail. The services were taken at a leisurely pace, as the members of the congregation rarely had anything else to do with their time on Saturday and the ancient Hebrew litany was enlivened by the grinding sounds and colourful Italian curses of Granelli's ice cream makers percolating up through the rickety wooden floor boards. On the way up to the synagogue and down again, the children would pause and look wistfully at the Italians working away with their pincers and ice blocks on the stone floor.

The Glaziers' congregation was too poor to afford a rabbi of its own, but occasionally a wandering preacher came round to give a sermon in Yiddish. At Ada and Maurice's wedding, the Maggid addressed the congregation, his remarks punctuated by the rumbling of the ice-cream machinery from below:

> People wonder why it is that in Russia, we keep every detail of our religious law. There is a story of Rabbi Akiva:
>
> *The Romans had forbidden Judaism, and Rabbi Akiva helped to organize many small synagogues in secret.*
> *'Why do you do this?' his friends asked.*
> *The Rabbi answered with a story.*
> *There was a river, in which the fish were darting to and fro in great alarm. A fox passed by and noticed.*
> *'Why are you so afraid?' asked the fox.*
> *'Because of the fishermen's nets,' said the fish.*
> *'So come on to the dry land with me and be safe,' said the fox.*
> *'You are said to be the wisest of creatures,' the fish replied, 'but you are really the most stupid. If we are in great danger in our own element, how much greater if we were in yours.'*

'A good sermon,' Hoshy said to his new daughter-in-law. 'Your father's a very clever man.' Hoshy was very proud to have his son marry a

Maggid's daughter.

The newly-wed Ada was a beautiful young woman, with regular, strong features, a square face, prominent cheekbones and a high forehead. Her eyebrows were smooth elegant curves, her eyes were firm, but above all intelligent and full of the same deep compassion as her father's. In her way, Ada was to become as admired and respected in the new world of Leeds as her father the Maggid had been in the old one of Yurberick. And well might her sister-in-law Rebecca taste vinegar at the thought of the lost kid brother who had once been all hers.

Unlike Hoshy and Moshy, the Maggid's family were forceful. Their outstanding characteristic was their analytic, mathematical intelligence. 'Your grandmother could read and write Hebrew and Yiddish fluently,' my father told me. 'And that was a great deal more than her husband Maurice could. Obviously the Maggid had taught her.'

When she was young Ada had had smallpox. At the height of the fever she was blind. Her sisters had tied her down on the bed and tied her arms so she couldn't scratch the spots and leave permanent marks on her skin. Ada survived with a faultless complexion.

When my father was a little boy, Ada had told him that he didn't need protection against smallpox. She said the reason was that when she had been a dairymaid in Yurberick she used to look after cows. Cows suffer from cowpox, which can be transmitted to humans and make them immune to smallpox. So Ada had gained the view that immunity to smallpox might be transmitted not only from cows to milkmaids, but from milkmaids to their sons.

Listening over the years to such stories about my grandmother, I got the feeling that the unbounded admiration that Ada's children had for her obscures Ada for me, as the shining of a bright light obscures its source.

By 1887, the year after their wedding, Ada became pregnant for the first of 15 times. Out of respect for their grandfather Louis, the famous Rabbi of Shakee, both Hoshy and Moshy had called their first born sons Louis. This became the family custom. And so it was that when Ada bore Maurice his first son, the young couple dutifully called him Louis. He was to be one of five cousins. All of them were called Louis, all were the first-born sons of their families, all were left-handed and all were to become gamblers.

While she herself was still a teenager, Ada had started what was to be her family of eleven surviving children, all of whom would live to ripe old ages, and who would account for the combined millennium of Raismans whose exploits will span the long century ahead, and fill the remaining pages of this book. But in 1888 it was only by the narrowest of hair's breadths that that first son survived what was to happen next.

In 1850 a novel by Charles Kingsley had introduced the word 'sweating' into the language. One of the sweat-shop workers described the cloth to a reporter in 1896:

> *The cloth is made of anything and everything except cast-iron. It is sized with pig manure, so that when we put the irons to it we get choked with stinking gas. String, cork, feathers, wire and stones are found in quantities in this kind of cloth. A circular steam-driven knife is used to cut 20, 30, 40, or 50 double thicknesses of cloth according to the pattern chalked on the top piece. When the knife comes into contact with either stone or wire, the danger of its breaking is very great. And when one of these endless band knives does break, as happens very often, you never know where it's going to fly to.*

Like Fortune, tailoring is very seasonal. Spring, the six weeks between Easter and Whitsun, is a great rush. Suits can't be made fast enough. For the rest of the year, the Leylanders said, 'You can put your teeth on the mantelpiece.'

The first Leylands tailoring strike had occurred in the Spring of 1885 while Ada was still in Sheffield. For her it had been only a distant rumour, to which she paid little attention. Maurice was a young lad working in Hope Street at the time. In great secrecy Itchky Morris called a meeting of workers' representatives in an upstairs synagogue in Templar Street. The workers published a demand, a reduction of one hour in the working day (13 or 14 hours) with no extra pay. The strike was perfectly timed, the first week in May, the height of the Whitsun rush. Taken by surprise, the masters gave in after one week and conceded the shorter hour, with no extra pay.

But the strike victory had no effect on the workers' conditions. Destitute greenhorns continued to pour in from Russia, desperate for work on any terms. Agreements with masters could not be enforced. But the Jewish tailors persisted. The union slowly accumulated funds by a subscription of two pence a week, and by 1888 they had over £80. In that year Spring began early, with a spell of exceptionally fine sunny weather, the tulips were in full bloom, and the teenage Ada, with one baby at her breast, was pregnant again.

On the last day of April (reported the Leeds Mercury and the Leeds Times) the men sent a letter to the members of the Jewish Master Tailors' Society:

> *We, the workmen, wish you to attend a meeting, appointed by our committee, for them to lay down their reasons why we want society shops in Leeds, and to discuss this matter properly. We beg respectfully for you to attend this meeting, to be held at the Smithfield Inn, North Street, Leeds, on Wednesday, May 2nd, at 7 o'clock p.m., hoping you will kindly oblige us and attend. Again respectfully asking you to consider the above and attend this meeting, we remain, on behalf of the Leeds Jewish tailors, pressers, and machinists.*
>
> *Yours respectfully,*
> *The Officers of the Joint Management Committee*

The employers (the newspaper reports continued) in reply declined to meet the men but said that if the latter would send a written statement they would consider it, adding, however, that they would 'stubbornly resist any dictatorship.'

In 1888 Shevuas (Whitsun) fell in the third week of May and the tailoring workshops always closed for the festival. Thus, the strike leaders calculated, the masters would not be able to withstand a strike in the second week in May. They must capitulate quickly, while the strikers were still buoyant with the spring sunshine. Without coal bills the money needed for a short, sharp strike would be so small as not to reveal the fatal weakness of the tiny strike fund.

The masters held a meeting at the King William the Fourth Inn in Briggate. The chairman was Maishy Goodman. They were prepared to give the men shorter hours, they said, provided they accepted less pay. The masters knew, of course, exactly where the strike's weakness lay. If the masters could sit the strike out for a few weeks, starvation would drive the men back. But they had to work out how to complete the Whitsuntide orders before the festival of Shevuas closed the workshops. The masters could do this if they could bring in enough 'imported' seasonal labour. If the masters could get it, they could break the strike, and starve the men into submission. And of course there was an endless supply of men desperate to get out of Russia on any terms.

May 5th was a Saturday. The workshops had closed as usual on Friday night for the Jewish Sabbath. The Leylands were tense with anticipation. On Sunday, when the Leylands working week usually began, the men didn't turn up for work. Sixty-eight workshops were idle. Once again Maurice was bringing no money home. Helpless, Ada watched, listened, and wondered what the future held for her and her little one, and for the family she would bring up in this new, strange country.

The strike was to last three weeks, and although 2,000 men and more than that number of women came out on strike, most had only just joined the union, so that all got a share of the £80 fund so painstakingly built up by the few over the years. The strike fund never had a chance of keeping 5,000 people.

On Monday, May 7th, the Leeds papers reported:

Probably with the view of exciting greater public interest in the dispute, the workpeople on strike held a meeting yesterday morning in front of the Town Hall. Headed by a brass band, they marched in procession from the Leylands to a patch of waste ground known as 'The Muck,' and from thence through the principal streets, and by way of several of the large clothing houses, to Victoria Square. At the head of the procession was carried the red and yellow banner of their trade society. On reaching the square the men formed in a ring, in the centre of which was placed a stool, and from this the various speakers delivered their remarks. A prominent object in the centre of the crowd was a board, bearing in chalk the words, 'Down with the sweating system!'

Mr Morris Kemmelhor presided, and, in commencing the proceedings, denied that the object of the strike was to drive the

Christian work-girls out of the trade. 'It would,' he said, 'be disgraceful on the part of any Jew who came to a nice country like this to attempt to do anything of the kind. They desired the personal regard rather than the hatred of the English people. The employers and workmen were all supposed to belong to the Jewish race, but he would not like to be related to any of their masters.' (Hear, hear, and applause.)

With strikers all over the town, and colourful threats being reported in the courts, the national press descended on Leeds:

Among the Jews in Leeds (by a rambling reporter)
A Great Problem - The Jews - The Leylands

The great problem of the day which is persistently forcing itself upon the attention, and which is perhaps one of the most serious which either this or any other nation has had to face, is the immigration of foreign pauper labour and the emigration of the bone and sinew of the English race. The loss incurred by our country in sending forth its most able and enterprising children is aggravated by filling their places with the weaklings of inferior races crowded out of other old communities.

The Jews were once a favoured people, but, like the Lady of Shalott, the curse has come upon them and they are scattered throughout the world, no more a nation, though a people, in most countries despised, in many persecuted.

The influx of Jews into Leeds in unusually large numbers dates from the rise of the ready-made clothing trade, something like twenty years ago. At first they do not seem to have congregated in any particular locality; but when the better-class population deserted that part of the town known as the Leylands the Jews succeeded them in the large, many roomed houses in and about Trafalgar Street; which served their purpose admirably, a number of families living and working in one house. The English and Irish residents retired before the Jewish invasion of the locality, like the black before the grey rat, until the Leylands has become more Jewish, perhaps, than any part of Palestine, and is recognised as the Jews' quarter.

The Jews' quarter well repays a visit. Whatever language is spoken, the Hebrew is almost exclusively used in writing. Hebrew characters are chalked by the children on the walls. Notices in shop windows and price-lists in the public-houses are all in the same character. A view of the butchers' shops is about sufficient to make a Gentile turn vegetarian, and bread is baked in great round loaves apparently about a stone weight, and cut off in smaller pieces and sold by weight.

The mysteries of the Jew clothing trade are not generally understood, although it is clear that it depends for its existence upon the Jew tailors doing more work for less money than the native population around them, and that otherwise there was no need to gather the scattered remnants from all parts of the continent of Europe. It is not surprising that once fairly settled here, these downtrodden people should seek to obtain at least some of the advantages arising from residence in a free country where race persecution is, fortunately, no longer known.

Visiting the Leylands when the strike was young and the excitement was at its height, the quarter presented an animated appearance. The weather was fine, and the whole population seemed to be out of doors. In every street groups discussed the situation with considerable animation, and it was clear that remarkable unanimity prevailed, and the only danger of failure lay in the fact that very many of the tailors are not financially in a position to hold out long, while there was no mention of a fund upon which they might fall back.

Keeping an appointment, we proceeded to a rendezvous at Gower Street School, and not being promptly met, opportunity was taken to obtain an outside view of the question. The landlady was certainly not partial to the Children of Israel, whom she charged with making the locality too hot for English residents. She even went the length of bewailing the good old times when the Leylands were notorious for houses of ill-fame, and expressed the opinion that such gentry were at least preferable to Jews. She somewhat naively observed that she supposed that there always had been, always would be such, that they were a necessary evil, and that they were at least English. She said that the idea of the Gentile population with regard to the action of the Jews was that it was an ill-disguised attempt to drive Christian labour out of the trade.

Proceeding to a place frequented by the operatives, we questioned one of them of more than average intelligence. Asked to read some handbills, presumably in the Hebrew character, he did so with ease, but, questioned as to the language spoken, he seemed far from clear. Tried with some common phrases of French, German, and Spanish, he seemed utterly ignorant. He said that whatever language it might be, he believed there was no ground for claiming that it was the classic Hebrew, since this was no longer spoken anywhere; that, using this language, Jews wherever they came from could converse pretty freely together, and he left the impression that it was some lingua franca without a literature, something like the Romanny of the gipsies.

Other interviews did not elicit any fresh facts or interesting information. On all hands we were met with the greatest courtesy and candour, and an earnest desire was generally expressed that the case should be fully and fairly represented to the public, so that they might obtain the sympathy and support which, in their opinion, the justice and reasonableness of their cause entitled them to receive.

Leeds Times Saturday, May 12th

The Strike of 1888

Gradually over the warm days of the first week of the strike a pall of damp, heavy air had built up over the city. By the beginning of the second week the sun had disappeared. In the countryside the white morning mists were daily thicker and thicker. In the city they were brownish-black, charged with the smoke of smelting works, coal-tar refineries, burning rubber, sulphur dioxide, nitrogen pentoxide, and all the effluvia of the chemical factories of a great industrial city snuggled in a deep river valley, tucked under a warm and poisonous blanket. Beneath it no one could escape, and there was no corner it could not penetrate. Tree-trunks and green leaves were blackened. Every day the condensation etched another layer of black on to the bricks, and excoriated another layer from the lungs of the inhabitants. Remorseless and incurable, in the end it would cause more sickness and death than all the strike could bring about. And meanwhile, there was no sign of any improvement in the strike. The masters were sending work off by train to be made up in London. The strikers were now going hungry. There was no money left; the hole-and-corner grocers and bakers of the Leylands were giving food for nothing.

On Sunday, May 20th, two weeks into the strike, the British Isles were covered with thick cloud. Then, suddenly, far out over Greenland, the wind veered. By Monday morning it was blowing over the tip of Scotland. Icy winds raced down from the north-east, from Iceland and the arctic wastes. They drove the Mexican moisture ahead of them, tearing its protective cloak off the land. Howling down the mountainous spine of Britain, it took them less than a day to reach Leeds.

In the Leylands the Tuesday morning had been even warmer and foggier than before. The Leylanders could hardly see from one side to another of the narrow streets. The sounds of coughing floated in the opaque air. But by midday the sun, which had not been seen for weeks, appeared ghostly thin for a few moments high over the Parish Church. Then the storm began. First, huge outriders of warm rain lashed the city. The rickety window frames trembled, doors were hurriedly closed. After less than half an hour there was a break, and for the first time the sky cleared. Extraordinary clouds now began to appear, monstrous banks of inky blue-black, hanging over low vistas of clear orange sky. The sun came and went in flashes, raising angry red inflamed edges to the blistery storm clouds.

Chill winds began to blow. Then the vast bank of accumulated cloud flung itself furiously against the Pennines. Rain, then hail poured into the Yorkshire Dales. In the narrow streets of the Leylands, the people could hardly open their doors. It turned bitterly cold.

By about 5 o'clock the storm was all over. Despite all its raging, the thick moist air had been driven out of Leeds. Victorious, the arctic front settled its icy reign over the city. By next morning its advance guard, already speeding south towards London, would have ripped the cloak off the entire island. Total silence hung over the occupied city of Leeds. The air was clear as glass, the cold as sharp as a knife. To the Leylanders every brick of the church of St Patrick could be as clearly seen as if it were drawn in pen and ink. And the temperature fell and fell. Before dusk the last raindrops, which had not had time even to roll off the walls, were ice.

At night Leeds looked unreal, the yellow gas-lamps glittered bright and sharp. There was a deathly calm in the city. Breath came out like a white cloud. Not a soul in the Leylands was warm that night.

Early on the Wednesday morning Ada and Maurice huddled together in their draughty room in Livery Street, the baby between them, trying to keep warm. Ice from their night breath frosted the inside of the window-panes. When Maurice opened the door to go out powdery snow, which through the night had silently piled against the lintel, flew everywhere in the room. Overnight the red brick terraces had gone. Wonderful soft white mounds had appeared in their place, and the Leylands rang with shouts and screams of delighted children. The view across Livery Street had been completely transformed. The great midden was filled to overflowing with snow. The horse trough had disappeared entirely. The customarily gloomy entrance to the passage leading to Metcalf Yard sparkled with a mysterious light reflected through the nooks and crannies from a morning sun still so low as to be hidden behind the battlement-like rooftops of the Fortress. Under the arch long gleaming icicles hung from the bosses of the iron medallions at either side of the wooden lintel, but Ada, quite accustomed to the great frosts of the Lithuanian winter, was unimpressed by the picturesque scene outside. She knew what snow meant. Already pregnant with her second child, and without a stick of wood or a piece of coal to put in the grate, she hastily shut the door to retain what little warmth was left in the house.

For their part, the strikers were aghast at this change in the weather. They had not calculated the heavens would fight against them, that here, to Europe's western islands, scattered in the edge of a wild ocean, the tireless pirouetting of the Atlantic weather fronts, capricious as gilded youth, could bring now sun, now rain, now heat, now cold at any season of the year. Back in *Der Hame* they were used to the grim predictability of continental weather. For half the year the great Russian land mass froze; then suddenly, in summer, irrevocable heat poured like a furnace out of the deep belly of Asia. Snow in May was something unheard-of in Lithuania. Now the houses needed heat again, and there was no money left to buy coal. It was obvious the strikers' gamble had lost, and by the end of the third week, the Yorkshire Post could report, 'the greater number of the 1,200 Jewish tailors who struck a fortnight ago returned to their work yesterday on the old terms.'

Apart from the sudden change in the weather, an entirely new ally had appeared on the masters' side. In the columns of the Lancet, Mr Smith, reporting for the Special Sanitary Commission on the Sweating System in Leeds recorded:

In the district where the present outbreak of small-pox commenced there are several very important sweaters' workshops. The first cases of smallpox occurred in a very large common lodging-house. There were altogether nine cases in the lodging-house, and three other persons who had stayed in the house fell ill after removing to other parts of the town. Very energetic measures were taken to disinfect the place, to isolate the sick, and watch those who might have contracted the disease. Yet there have been since then more than 100 cases of smallpox in Leeds.

Just across North Street there was a hospital, maintained by public subscriptions, and called the Leeds Public Dispensary. 'I am a little bit of a subscriber to the Leeds Public Dispensary,' said Isaacs, a Leylands jeweller. 'During the strike, one of the working men's wives fell very seriously ill, and they called for an assistant of the surgeon of the Dispensary. Because the men were on strike, they used every endeavour even to prevent one of the assistants of the Dispensary going to assist this poor woman when she was very ill. They said "Oh, if the man can afford to be on strike, he must have plenty of money to pay for a doctor. He's not entitled to ask for help from the Public Dispensary. We can't use public funds to support the strike. Let him pay for a doctor himself."'

For their part, some doctors were not inclined to help the strikers. Evidence of this was given the next year to a House of Commons Committee by Dr William Clayton. 'I am a medical man, and my place of business is on the edge of the district in which they live. We adopt a different line of treatment in a Jewish case. That is to say, before we go, we either expect payment or a promise of payment. Before we go. My partner and I will not go unless we are paid.'

Clayton didn't only earn money as a surgeon. He owned many houses in the Leylands, and collected the rents from them. He was able to give the Committee a first hand account: 'Landlords do not like Jews as tenants; they avoid them if they can. I have some Jew tenants, and I would rather not have them, because they drive away other people from coming into the district.'

Apart from his business as a medical man and a landlord, Clayton had yet another source of income. He drew a salary as Chairman of the Leeds Board of Guardians. This put him in charge of the workhouse of St James, where the destitute could go as a last resort.

St James' Workhouse occupied a series of huge, ornate Victorian buildings on the hill overlooking the Lady Beck from the north side of Burmantofts. But, despite its closeness, none of the strikers went to St James' Workhouse. 'The Jews,' Dr Clayton told the House of Commons Committee 'object to go into the workhouse because the food is against their religion.'

'Are there any Jewish inmates of the workhouse now?' Clayton was asked.

'I believe not,' he replied 'but we have a difficulty when they come, for they do not understand English, and we do not understand their language, and it is their object to get out from us as much as they possibly can; it is our object to give them as little as we can.'

As in most conflicts, the combination of cold, starvation, and disease hit the youngest hardest. Babies and young children who had not reached the age of 13 were regarded as not yet having joined the congregation, and so they could not be buried within the cemetery walls of Gildersome, even in the greenhorns' section. They lie side by side in close ranks immediately under the outer brick enclosure wall. Narrow as they were, the graves of the children who never grew up still run for over 100 yards down the hill. Few families could afford a tombstone, some cobbled up a makeshift memorial themselves out of discarded pieces of stone, others had a simple triangle of stone with the Yiddish name roughly cut out in Hebrew characters. But for this time Ada's baby was spared. Fate is patient. But has a long memory.

Towards the end of the third week of the strike, the Leeds Mercury wrote, 'To-day Miss Beatrice Potter, who, though a lady of means, learned the trade of a machinist, and worked six months in a sweater's den in the East of London, in order to gather from experience the hardships that had to be endured, will visit Leeds, and will have interviews with deputations from the employers in the afternoon and from the men in the evening.'

Now Maishy Goodman, founder of the Greenhorns' Synagogue indicated that 'a member of the strike committee should wait on the masters.' They met at his premises, the sweat-shop of 31 Back Rockingham Street, known to posterity as 'Goodman's Buildings.'

The Lancet reporter described Goodman's Buildings:

It so happens that immediately opposite the door of the common lodging-house from whence nine smallpox patients were removed, separated from this door only by the width of a narrow street, is the entrance to an old abandoned mill, where there are now no less than five sweaters' workshops. Here altogether from 300 to 400 people, for the most part women, are engaged in tailoring. All these five workshops, which we carefully inspected, drain into a great shaft. It might have been the place formerly used for a hoist. There are no pans, no pipes, and no water. The closet seats are suspended over a vast deep opening made of bricks, and looking something like a huge well. Of course anything approaching to cleanliness is impossible, and this huge aperture, with its soiled sides, throws up its gases into the workshops. This huge well, some yards square, may be daily soiled by some 300 to 400 persons. The gases therein generated pass freely into the workshops and mingle with the atmosphere breathed by the workpeople as they handle many thousand different garments. To have a huge brick shaft running from the summit to the bottom of a lofty building is one of the most extraordinary cases of utter disregard for sanitary law we have ever seen.

We now entered the workshop of a sweater who had been described to us as one of the worst employers of the town, and we were certainly received with but scant courtesy. He (Maishy Goodman) complained that because he was a Jew people were always coming up to look at his premises. He had received 'von big letter' from the House of Lords, asking him how many hands he employed, but he was not going to answer. In fact he had burnt the letter. He did not know the House of Lords, he told us, nor did he care for the House of Lords, and concluded by protesting that the 'House of Lords vonn't give me anytink if I am 'ungry.'

It was in these surroundings that, at the end of May 1888, the final capitulation of the strike took place. 'We had to leave the union,' said Maurice, 'and tear up our contribution cards in front of the masters' faces to show them that we didn't belong to the union any more. That was the only way they would be satisfied.'

The strikers' leaders were summoned to the English Synagogue in Belgrave Street, and told they would never again be offered work in Leeds. So ended the Counting of the Omer of 1888. When some of the defeated strikers appealed to the Chief Rabbi in London to help them get their jobs back, his Holiness Dr Adler replied that 'he would only consent to do so if the masters would also invite him.'

After her visit, Beatrice Potter, whom the local paper had so admiringly described as a 'lady of means,' summarised her impressions: 'The Jew, engaged in a ruthless pursuit of individual profit without any concern for the public good ... a race of producers with an indefinitely low standard of life and apparently without the capacity for combination.'

Ordered Mon 13th Feb 1888, Westminster:

> *That a Select Committee of the House of Lords be appointed to inquire into the Laws existing in the United States and elsewhere on the subject of the Immigration of Destitute Aliens, and as to the extent and effect of such Immigration into the United Kingdom, and to report whether it is desirable to impose any, and, if so, what restrictions on such Immigration.*

Their Lordships began by taking evidence from David Isaacs, the jeweller:

'I know of a case where they had a lad (they call him a runner in the workshop, I believe), and a man was standing pressing, and he said to this lad, "Now go and fetch me a drink of water."'

'The lad fetched that drink of water. The master caught the lad on the steps with the drink of water. "What is that for?"'

'"That is a drink of water for So-and-so."'

'The master began cursing and using very bad language, and he took the drink of water out of the lad's hands, and he said "He must do without."'

'I am speaking of what occurred. I convinced myself to my sorrow that it really was true, and I can still scarce believe that a brother Jew, one to another, would be so harsh and unprincipled. Instead of being driven,' Isaacs concluded 'the men should be led, with a humane feeling towards them.'

'We are talking,' the Chairman interrupted, 'about what could be done by Act of Parliament; an Act of Parliament cannot compel a master to be humane. Do you know what the law is as regards the hours of labour?'

'If I understand it right, it is from seven till half past five for the tailor working; I may be wrong.'

'In these shops, are there men, women and children employed?'

'I suppose so,' said Isaacs.

'But do you know?'

'Yes, men, women, and children.'

'Do you mean that they work later hours than they ought to?'

'The men certainly, some of them, work till 11 o'clock at night.'

'But the women?'

'I never watched them; but they do not work proper hours according to what I understand the law of the land to be; I may be mistaken.'

'If you tell the committee that they do not work proper hours, and at the same time cannot explain what you consider the law of the land says are proper hours, then we do not understand your evidence.'

Westminster, 1889:

> *Ordered that a Committee be set up by the House of Commons. The House notes that United States Government had introduced laws to prevent the immigration of foreign paupers. The Committee is 'to contemplate the possibility of such legislation becoming necessary in the future (in Britain) in view of the crowded condition of our great towns, the extreme pressure for existence among the poorer part of the population, and the tendency of destitute foreigners to reduce still lower the social and material condition of our own poor.*

The Committee started by interviewing Alderman Scarr, the Mayor of Leeds:

'Have you noted the habits of the immigrant foreigners in Leeds?'

'Yes; I have noted their habits.'

'Are they good workers?'

'They are considered excellent workmen.'

'As to their habits, you do not think that they have done any harm to the morality of the town?'

'No, I think their morality is most excellent.'

The interrogation was taken over by Captain Sir John Colomb, Knight Commander of the Order of St Michael and St George.

'Do I understand you rightly to express the opinion that it would be a misfortune if the supply of foreign labour was limited?'

'I do think so,' said Scarr, 'a very great misfortune.'

'But the whole of the increase of foreigners has been in the direction of competition with English labour, has it not?'

'Yes; but you know, the increase in business is something wonderful during the last 25 years.'

'Do you consider that the class of foreigners that are coming to Leeds in the tailoring trade are useful and intelligent?'

'Yes, I do.'

'More than our own people?'

'I do not want to put it that way, if you will excuse me.'

'Do you or do you not think that a large and continuous influx of foreigners from Europe, looking for work in this country, would lower the wages in England?' the interrogator insisted.

'I will take Leeds as an example. Leeds has risen in population continuously; the working population and the foreign element have both risen, wages have improved, and the work has improved. The clothing trade of Leeds has become the most prominent in the kingdom, and therefore I draw the inference which I have drawn.'

'Could you tell the Committee who first introduced the Jews to Leeds, or how they were induced to stay in Leeds?'

'I should say that they were induced by the same motives that induced me to stay in Leeds; I came to Leeds, and stopped there; I was not sent for by anyone.'

'Did you come from abroad?'

'No, I came from Lancashire.'

'Perhaps you can see a slight difference between your settling in Leeds, and the foreigner coming from thousands of miles across the ocean?'

'I cannot see that there is any difference.'

'Where were you born?'

'I was born at Burnley in Lancashire, 40 miles from Leeds.'

'You have stated,' the questioner continued 'that Burnley is 40 miles from Leeds. Forty miles. Do you know how far away Russian-Poland is?'

'No, I do not know; I cannot give you that.'

'I am merely trying to ascertain what facilities you had in Burnley for getting information as to the advantage of settling in Leeds, as compared with the difficulties which, with a distance of 2000 miles, they must have experienced. I am trying to ascertain the difference between the facilities for getting information in Burnley with regard to Leeds and those in

Poland?'

'I happened,' Scarr said 'to have a relative in Leeds, and we were very poor and doing very badly, and we were induced to come there. I had not a shilling in my pocket when I came, neither had my father and mother. At length, one of my relatives wrote 'If you come to Leeds you may do better.' So I came.

'And,' Scarr went on 'I should apprehend that those foreigners have come in the same way - more or less. They may have had relatives who have come and done better than they were doing, and they have written back accounts, and they have been induced to come.

'That was the reason I put it that way. I did not wish to give you that history of mine, but since you have pressed me, I have done so. I think it is pertinent to the point.'

'Yet you stated,' the questioner persisted, 'that the same reasons which prompted you, a well-to-do merchant and Mayor of Leeds, to settle in Leeds also prompted those foreigners to come from Russian-Poland and settle there?'

'Yes,' said Scarr bluntly. 'I do say so, and I maintain it.'

There now began the examination of the last witness, the Rabbi Moses Abrahams, Minister of the *Englisher Shul*:

'What of the habits of your flock in general? Are they clean or dirty?'
'Generally clean. Some are less so,' replied the Rabbi.
'This committee has heard evidence that they are very dirty.'
'They observe strict religious rules about the cleanliness of food and the utensils for its preparation,' said Abrahams. 'They are as clean as they can be, given the very primitive sanitary arrangements in some of their houses.'
'We have heard evidence that their houses are kept in a filthy condition. Do the Jewish population in this country marry early?'
'Not so very early.'
'What is the average age at which they marry?'
'The average age would be twenty-one.'
'You do not consider that an early marriage?'
'I consider it an early marriage,' said the rabbi, himself a life-long bachelor.

'I would maintain,' the questioner asserted, 'that it is a very young age. Now, is it not the case that the Jewish population in Leeds must be increasing at a much faster rate than the native population?'

'I do not know,' replied the rabbi, 'what the rate of increase is in the population of Leeds.'

'You mean that you do not know at what rate Leeds - as a town - is increasing in population, and therefore that you could not answer my question?'

'I do not know precisely what the rate of increase is.'

In their final report the Committee wrote:

> *The immigrants' physical condition is inferior to that of the British workmen; but their health appears to be good, notwithstanding the neglect of all sanitary laws. They are quick at learning, moral, frugal, and thrifty, and inoffensive as citizens, but generally very dirty and uncleanly in their habits.*
> *It appears clear from the evidence that some of the results of foreign immigration on trade are bad.*

The government committees went on for over a year. There were more than 20 sessions. They produced over 2,000 handsomely bound and printed pages of evidence about the Leeds Jewish tailors' strike. Not one of the striking tailors ever gave evidence. The final outcome was the Aliens Act of 1905, whose effect was to restrict the flow of Jewish immigration from Eastern Europe.

END OF PART ONE

PART II

Myer's Kingdom

The miles Myer treadled away, making trousers he couldn't see, and the miles Harry stitched in his silent world, led to a dreamed-of place that they would never reach. The children and the children's children would get there and be saved.

We worked,' said my father 'so that you could go to school and have a better life - not to have the horrible life of drudgery to which we were exposed, not to have to work in the horrible conditions we experienced.'

What Ada Saw at the Gate

No I wouldn't like to die, sir,
For I think the good Lord's hard
On us common working women;
An' the likes of me's debarred
From his high, uncertain Heaven,
Where fine ladies all go to.
So I try to keep on livin',
Though the Lord knows how I do.

Machine Room Chants, Tom Maguire, 1895

 Although the Maggid had come to Leeds for the wedding of his daughter Ada Rosainsky, he soon went back to Yurberick. With the departure of his last daughter, he felt his life's task was over, and after settling up his few meagre affairs, he set off to go to Jerusalem. His goal was to reach the Valley of Jehoshaphat (whose meaning in Hebrew is God Shall Judge), which carries the brook Kidron. He wanted to be buried there, and lie, awaiting the Day of Resurrection on the western slope of the Mount of Olives, looking towards the Dome of the Rock on Mount Moriah, the Temple Mount. For, according to the prophecy of Joel, The Judgement Seat will be on Mount Moriah, which is opposite ... *and in those days and in that time when I shall gather all nations, I will bring them down into the Valley of Jehoshaphat; And I will enter into judgement with them there.*

But the journey across the Pale of Settlement was too much for the Maggid of Yurberick, and he only succeeded in reaching the southernmost end of the Russian Pale. Here, in the romantic sounding *Giberrny* of Bessarabia, he died. He had been within sight of the Black Sea, the gateway to the Ottoman Empire which then included the Land of Palestine.

A letter arrived in Leeds. The 19-year old Ada was pregnant, which was to be her usual state for the next 20 years. Maurice, who didn't want to shock her with the news of her father's death, said nothing. Two weeks later Ada told Maurice of a dream.

51

'I saw father dragging something after him on the ground. It looked like a shroud. When I went to run after him, he raised his hand and said: "No no, my child."

'I think he's dead.'

'Yes,' said Maurice. 'It's true.'

The Leylanders had a saying: 'One in, one out.' A baby could not be named after a living person, but had to be named after a dead one. This rule was sacred. So, when her father, Reb Meyer died, Ada reverently passed the name Myer to the new boy of 1889.

And with the passing of the Maggid, the ties with Lithuania were finally broken. The teenage parents and their two little babies were now on their own. There was no way but forward. From now on the Raisman's story will be a Leeds story. And though she could never have guessed it as she gave birth to the Maggid's namesake, Ada had produced the champion who would deliver them from the gambling demon that held in thrall her husband Maurice and the first-born Louis. The story we now begin is that of Myer's Kingdom. But the battle for it would be long, the costs grievous, and many a twist in the tale.

Two years after the strike of 1888, the tailors' union re-formed. Another strike was called, and it too was broken. The flow of refugees from Russia continued to increase. In the 1890's 10,000 came to Leeds, double the number already there. And in 1890 the tailoring boom came to an end. Trade slumped for over ten years. Only the Boer War at the end of the century brought relief. It also saw the heyday of the music hall songs from the Leeds City Varieties:

> *Underneath the gaslight's glitter*
> *Stands a little fragile girl*
> *Heedless of the night winds bitter*
> *As they round about her whirl.*

> *While the millions pass, unheeding,*
> *Seeking Pleasure's pleasant bowers,*
> *Still she cries with tearful pleading:*
> *Won't you buy my pretty flowers!*

Leeds' first workers' parade took place on May Day 1890. The bands played the Marseillaise. There was a street procession of 6,000 people.

The Jewish tailors' and the slipper-makers' union were in front. They alone were 2000. Each union had its own banner, and everyone had their own songs, but the most popular was the 'Song of the Sweater's Victim,' which Tom Maguire had composed specially for this occasion when Jewish tailors and Irish navvies marched shoulder to shoulder, and the Leylanders took it up enthusiastically in their broken English:

Every vorker in every trade
In Britain ond everyvhere
Vezzer he labour by needle or spade
Shall gazzer in his rightful share.

The demonstration caused quite a stir. The revered Friedrich Engels personally sent a copy of Karl Marx's *Capital* to the gasworks strikers. Many of the police sympathized; a good proportion of them were Irish. The city council didn't dare to call them out. Instead they called out the city garrison from Barrack Street. Like Cossacks in Russia, mounted hussars with drawn swords patrolled the streets of Leeds that day. But the Leeds hussars stood discreetly by, taking no part, and the meeting disbanded peacefully. Queen Victoria's empire was greater than that of the Tsar, and kinder.

Now Ada had two sons, and she celebrated the peaceful withdrawal of the hussars by getting pregnant again. But Heaven never forgets a debt. The new child of 1891 was a girl, who Ada called Khankerly (Hannah), to keep alive the name of her older sister Annie, who, despairing of having children, had committed suicide in Sheffield. It was a dutiful act, but inauspicious. The new girl was very sickly. Ada tried a new patent cough medicine. Khankerly grew daily weaker and more ill.

At night, after she had settled the two healthy boys to sleep, Ada took the fretful baby into her own bed. On her pillow the little head floated limply on the sea of Ada's bobbing black curls, its hot cheek resting against the young mother's still unwrinkled skin. Ada's full breasts felt the restlessness of the desiccated body gradually giving way to lassitude. As she breathed the warm, moist breath, its sweetish odour turned ever more foetid, and Ada, taking the tiny shoulders in her hands, whispered over and over again: 'Khankerly, Khankerly, Give it to me, Give me the sickness, Let me take the sickness away.' Then, with drooping lids, she veiled her eyes and to the invisible spirit who tuned the harmony of the universe Ada prayed 'Take me, Take me instead.' But Ada had not averted the divine purpose. Hannah died, and Ada conceived again. She was now 20, and next year, in 1892, it was twins, a boy Abraham, called Jeremy (for Lamentations), and a girl. The girl lasted 6 weeks, the boy 80 years. In 1894, both the Tsar Alexander III and Hoshy's mother Frada died. Alexander's son, Nicholas II became the new and last Tsar of Russia, and Ada's next child was yet another girl.

Struck by this, Ada, whose intellect never tired of trying to understand, developed another theory. 'I can't keep girls.' The cough medicine had failed, and now she tried a remedy described by Israel Zangwill in his book *Children of the Ghetto*, published the year before. Following this advice, Ada did indeed call the new girl Fanny (after her mother-in-law, Frada), but kept the name secret. Instead, Baby Fanny was simply called 'The Old One' until she had grown up. In this way, as Zangwill had explained 'Heaven would not be incessantly reminded of the existence of their dear one, and would not go out of its way to castigate them.' And in this way Ada at last succeeded in placating the transcendental powers and completed the first third of her pre-destined family, three boys and a girl, and her first-born, Louis, was now old enough to be enrolled in the INFANTS section of Gower Street School.

Victorian England was one of the world's leaders in education. In 1870 the Education Act had set up compulsory education for all children. The Leeds School Board had the duty of providing education free of charge for all children. The 'Board' school was built in Gower Street in 1875. Officially it was called the Leylands School, but the Leylanders called it Gower Street School. Outside the schoolyard, mothers and grandmothers would stand peering in, but not daring to enter the new Board Schools which their children were compelled to attend. At morning break they would hand cups of hot tea and bagels through the railings to their embarrassed offspring. But Ada looked at the school and wondered. She had never been to a school. Her father, the Maggid, had taught her all she knew. He had taught her to have an open mind. And now this young woman, whose own childhood was so soon over, realised there was something which could offer her children the opportunities she had never had. Beyond those gates lay a fortune that could never be gambled away, a treasure that could never be lost. Ada saw it, her husband Maurice, did not.

To teach the children how to be thrifty, the school used to collect bank money of a penny a week. It was entered in a bank book, and if it reached £1 (240 pence) it was deposited in the Yorkshire Penny Bank. Some families prospered early. By the time Edward VII's head decorated the sovereigns, Yules the butcher's five children each used to bring along two to deposit every Monday. Louis usually managed the penny on Monday, but long before £1 had accumulated his mother told him to withdraw the money on Friday. It was needed to help buy food, or coal, or clothes, or shoes, or to pay the rent.

Little Louis knew that when he came home his father would be away. The workrooms never stopped for lunch. After coming home and eating his own lunch, on his way back to school Louis would join the other boys and girls taking sandwiches to the workshops, so their fathers did not have to stop. All through the day, and well into the night, Maurice would be machining at top speed to earn as much money as he could, and during the remainder of the night he would be losing it as fast as he could at the card tables. Indeed, so fierce was the gambling demon that the machinists and pressers had developed a system to gamble without even needing to stop work. A bookmaker's 'runner' use to race round the workshops every half hour during the afternoon to take bets on each of the day's horse-races in Wakefield, or Pontefract, or Wetherby, or the Knavesmire at York.

It had taken no time at all for Shroll Maishy's direst predictions to be confirmed. Ada had wed a lifelong and incurable gambler. And in the years to come, Ada would need all her brilliant intellect to wheedle out from Maurice's gambling kitty enough to buy that bit of bread, or coal, or clothes, or shoes, or pay the rent. But never for one moment did her love for Maurice waver, or her tenderness cool. Somewhere inside that young woman lay the hidden strength to be, for that weak man, over half a century his true and faithful wife, and for all his many sons and daughters, the ever-loving mother.

Maurice was a popular, outgoing fellow, with a fine singing voice. But he never got to like English food. 'Chippertayters,' he would say, in disgust. He had a sweet tooth. Behind his back, people called him

Treacle Moses, a name he greatly resented. Throughout the Leylands gambling houses, he was known as a 'good sport.' Everyone had nicknames, and Maurice enjoyed the company of Charlie, known (from his habits when betting) as Charlie Who Implores the Lord, Itchky Lazer, and Aby the Corpse.

'My father,' said his son Sam, 'would bet on two flies crawling up the wall.'

Tailoring workshops rose and fell. Men became masters, and masters became men. Whichever master happened to have work at any one time, the men went there. When there was work they worked night and day. When there was not, they hung around, and Maurice had lots of time to spend at the miners' game of pitching (tossing two coins) on the piece of waste ground off Plum Street known as The Muck. When he was not pitching on the Muck, Maurice also found time to become a good billiards player.

One evening in the Harewood Arms near Kirkgate Market he challenged the billiards champion of South Africa. Most people laughed and backed the South African. Maurice backed himself and made a lot of money. Everyone took this as a sign of Maurice's great skill at billiards, unaware that the South African had also put a lot of money on Maurice.

Mr Marks had once asked him to go into partnership with him in his Penny Bazaar in Kirkgate Market. The sign over his stall read: *Don't ask the price: it's a penny.* Mr Marks admired Maurice's command of English and thought the eloquence of this good looking young man would be an advantage for sales. Maurice, however, refused Mr Marks' offer. With his gambling obsession, my grandfather had no time to stand around extolling the virtues of penny wares.

In 1890, two years after the disastrous strike of 1888, the government had introduced what now became secondary education. Leeds specially built a vast new school for over 2,000 pupils, Leeds Central High School. The new city was very proud of this new school. Under its first headmaster, Dr Forsyth, it was one of the country's leading secondary schools. There was a fee of a ha'penny a day, but the city offered a series of scholarships to enable poor boys to attend it. In the same year, Louis came to the end of the course at Gower Street School, and won one of these prized scholarships to the Leeds Central High School. All the remaining ten

Raisman children in turn were to do so.

Louis had a flair for mathematics. Throughout his life, people were amazed at how he could solve mathematical problems without any training. But Louis never learned to be thrifty. Instead he became a genius at calculating the odds. His father Maurice was his model, and Maurice could imagine no advantage in secondary education. Later his younger sons Myer and Jeremy taught their father to read and write. But Maurice never troubled to teach his children anything. Most of Maurice's children rarely saw him.

'He was a stranger to us,' my father said.

Maurice needed his first-born son, Louis to earn money at once. So Louis was unable to take up his scholarship of one pound ten shillings a year. In Louis' class at Gower Street School, John Gittelson, the son of their neighbour and later landlord, did. Instead Louis went out to work. And with his wages and his mathematical genius he began his lifelong career in gambling.

Louis' gambling had flair. There were many times when his wages were the sole income for the whole family. On more than one occasion on his way home on Friday night he had staked all his earnings on the turn of a single card at Faro. On Thursdays Louis used to stay up late, talking about how he would spend his wages, and what luxuries the family would enjoy from his anticipated winnings. Uncle Myer described it to me:

'Louis - oh, what a gambler! He'd work all the week from morning until night. He was a good worker, earned a good wage ...'

'Did people like him?' I interrupted.

'Oh, hail fellow well met! Oh, yes! Very popular. Very popular with everybody but us.'

Myer chuckled at his own joke and went on, in a low, conspiratorial tone. 'He'd have been working for a couple of years. He would work all the week - he would work all the week and draw 30 shillings - 30 shillings in those days was a lot of money - a lot of money - and he'd go into the gambling house and put that 30 shillings on the one card, up or down. Just like that. Whether it won or lost. In one punch!'

As he re-lived this experience, Myer's voice had got higher and higher, until finally he paused and spluttered in exasperation: ' ...that a man should work a whole week...' and spluttered himself into silence.

After another long pause, he drew a long breath, sighed, paused again, and continued, flatly. 'In the morning he'd ask me for a Woodbine. What could I say? I didn't say a word. Woodbines were five a penny...' Myer again became speechless with indignation.

'Did you give him one?' I asked helpfully, hoping for more.

'Well of course I gave him one,' Myer said disgustedly. 'What difference did that make already?' and he fell again into a period of silent rumination, from which I could think of no way to rouse him.

Myer's next utterance was preceded by a few low grunts, and several pauses. 'Jeremy and I once set about him. He was in bed. We both went up to him. What could we do? I'd have been eleven. Jeremy was eight. We threatened to tear him limb from limb. Of course he could eat us both up, I'll tell you. He was broad...'

I waited, but Myer lapsed again into silence, seeming to have decided to say no more.

'And,' I persisted 'were you afraid?'

'No,' said Myer expansively. 'We weren't afraid. We knew it was no bleddy good. We did attack him.' Again a long silence.

'And?' I said, helpfully ' … was he annoyed?'

'No,' said Myer, broadly. 'No. He didn't bear malice. He knew we were right.

'On a Thursday night, Louis would come home on a Thursday night and plan what he was going to do. All the wonderful things he was going to buy. He was going to buy a piano! That was always on the Thursday night.' Myer laughed again, briefly, a short, throaty sound, a cross between a chuckle and a snort. 'It was going to be so good. He was going to do such wonderful things. Not gamble. Oh no! Not his wages.'

Much as the first-born Louis, resembled his father, Myer the second son, resembled his mother. He would be the one to implement the vision his mother had seen at the gates. From his mother's side of the family he had acquired the Maggid's restless intellect. In his search for knowledge his youthful brain grappled with an architectural puzzle which he encountered in his very own bedroom in their home in Little Bridge Street. At this time the family lived in the back of a shared house for which they paid rent to the family of the Gittelsons, paperhangers.

'I can't understand it,' said Myer. 'Our bedroom was really an attic, but in the centre there was like a round tower. I can't understand why they had such a thing. It had no outlet at the top, but it had outlets at the side, and we could look in - and down - into the bedroom of the Gittelsons who lived in the front of the house. I'd have been about twelve. I used to throw pellets down. They used to play hell. I can't understand what sort of a structure it was.' We shall probably never know. The entire block was demolished and the proud portico of the Elim Pentecostal Church now rises over the spot where once stood that strange round tower.

Myer might as well laugh about their house in Little Bridge Street. They were so crowded they had to take turns at sleeping in the beds.

Myer told me about his first lesson in his Hebrew school. The bearded rebby strode into his class:

> *Vat is die fest ting ve do on die fest morning ven ve get opp fom die bet?*

The question ended with a triumphal ring, as though the teacher was pleased to have managed so much in English. The children dutifully intoned the answer in unison: 'Nailwater.'

This was a teaching of the first religious duty to be carried out on waking up in the morning. In the *Zohar* (Illumination), the chief work of the mystic Cabbalistic sect founded in Spain by Isaac the Blind, it is explained that during sleep the holy soul leaves the body, and an unclean soul takes its place. On waking, the unclean soul leaves all parts of the body except the fingers, from which it must be purged by washing the hands, first the left and then the right, three times alternately in running water.

From the north of our city, two small streams approach the centre. They are the Meanwood Beck and the Gipton Beck. They meet at Sheepscar. In the Yorkshire dialect, Sheepscar means Sheeprock, where the fields began. Between these two becks, Chapeltown Road climbs a small rise, on which commanding view of the city stands the long two-storey building - for men above and horses beneath - that was the barracks of the cavalry garrison. Seen from this vantage point, the adjacent low hills are completely covered by row upon row of houses, the terraces of red brick, blackened by continuous exposure to the smoke-laden air. But the black is not deposited evenly. Due to long exudation of moisture from the mortar between the bricks, it has gradually formed a delicate interlacing lattice of spidery, black fissures, as though encasing each individual brick in a filigree box of fine Victorian iron work.

South from the meeting of the becks at Sheepscar lay the dense mass of back-to-back houses that made up the Leylands, and through it the Lady Beck flowed down to the River Aire. In former times the Leylands had been a rough marshy pasture, a ley. The ley was about half a mile wide. It extended for not quite a mile north of the river, and was drained, only imperfectly, by the Lady Beck. The Lady Beck took its name from the long-gone Chantry Chapel of Our Lady, which used to stand at the street corner where the mediaeval traveller to York could bless himself and pray for a safe passage on the perilous 21 mile journey across the highwaymen-ridden plains to the county town of York. But the people living in the Leylands would not be able to trace the course of the Lady Beck, since they only got glimpses of it here and there over a broken parapet, or where it crossed a street. The rest of its tortuous course through the labyrinth of streets was shadowed by narrowly enclosing walls.

Every community has its initiation ceremonies. For Jewish boys, the barmitzvah at the age of 13 requires a ritual public recitation of holy scripture in the Sabbath service. But the Leylanders had another, far more basic test of manhood. On its way down from the heights of Sheepscar, the Lady Beck, after winding through their little world, under the bridges of North Street and Hope Street, lapped the southern wall of the Templar Street Fortress, and took a final turn before leaving their land for the big river. Here, like dying Hindus to the Ganges, the youthful initiants flocked to the bank.

Applicants for manhood must jump the Beck

It was at the entrance to Metcalf Yard, just by the Lady Bridge. The stream here was too deep to be fordable, too wide to be stepped over. Applicants for manhood must 'jump the Beck.'

Louis, the first-born son, had much of his father's fine physique. With no difficulty he passed the test. So well indeed, that he became a leader among men. But to his dismay, the next son, Myer, was small and mild. His friends called him Kets, meaning kitten, soft, weak and lovable. He was well named. Louis was deeply troubled in his after all only recently manly soul. What to do about his brother Myer and the Beck? How to avoid disgrace? Finally Louis hit on the successful plan. Louis taking one arm, and another stout friend taking the other, they physically jumped Myer over the Beck.

The kids did not dally on the other side of the beck. This was hostile territory for them. Here Mabgate (which name, like Leman Street in London, means the street of the prostitutes) wound its way into the Irish district of Burmantofts.

The Plan

By the end of the century, Britain was expanding its empire in South
Africa, and no one was more patriotic than the Leylanders. From the City
Varieties on the Headrow, Maurice had learned all the songs of the
Crimean War. He loved to entertain his listeners to the great duel of Ivan
and Abdul. Now he enthusiastically extended his repertoire, and like
him, all over the Leylands streets and schools, as the Boer War ground
on, the kids excitedly took up the songs of each new event:

> *One, Two, Three, The relief of Kimberley*
> *Four, Five, Six, Capture of Ladysmith,*
> *Seven, Eight, Nine, The relief of Bloemfontein,*
> *What Ho! What Ho! It'll be Mafeking next time!*

Myer was still only a child of ten. 'Mother was a weeping willow,' he
recalled. 'Father didn't work. He said his health was bad. Instead, he
became President of the Lonsdale Club. He was playing for £5 notes
when the weekly wage of a machinist was 30 shillings (£1.50). The
weekly rent was only one and six (one and a half shillings). But we
couldn't pay it. Louis gambled all his wages away. Every year there was
a new addition to the family. Mother was never without a child in her
arms. She used to say: "What will happen to me? Where can a person
find the strength to go on?"

'On Thursdays, there wasn't a bit o' food left in the house. Mother
used to put her hands in the air and say "Lord of the Universe!"'

But at such times, the Raisman family had a mysterious angel, pock-
marked Sarah Dagutski. No one knew why she looked after Ada. 'She
was mother's cousin,' Myer said. 'She was always very charitable to the
Raismans.' Sarah seems to have been somehow related to the Maggid of
Yurberick, perhaps the daughter of one of his brothers or sisters. No one
ever said what this precise link was, and Sarah herself never said what
was the reason. Sarah married a tailor's presser, Joe Fox, and had two
daughters of her own, the first a simpleton, and the second a beggar.
Sarah's family themselves were desperately poor, and 'very charitable'

could only mean sharing the odd loaf of bread. But it was enough for survival.

And now, with a father who produced nothing but children and his older brother a gambler, little Myer did his best to face up to the problem of how to bring some money into the house. The family needed iron, and iron it now got in the third son, the survivor of the twins, Abraham Jeremy Raisman.

The Boer War was on, but the English had little respect for the Boers. The Leylands kids sang:

> *Lords Roberts and Kitchener,*
> *Lords Bullen and Clyde,*
> *Will hang the flag on Pretoria*
> *And Kruger we'll hang on a tree!*

But they had great respect for another people the English troops encountered in South Africa. The proud, tall, warlike Zulus, who had so bravely resisted the British redcoats at Rorke's Drift, were the fiercest fighters in South Africa and the English schoolboys were fascinated by their magnificent physique, long spears, oval shields and picturesque kraals.

Thus, as Jeremy grew up, and his black hair set itself in tight curls, his admiring classmates called him Zulu. All his life he was to be blessed with magnificent bodily strength. His bearing was regal. His aquiline nose gave him an air of nobility. Jeremy seemed born to be an aristocrat, and in later years, his scant, greying hair would form a crescent of short curls round the back and sides of his head, like the laurel wreath of a Roman emperor.

As a child Jeremy soon began to assume command in the family. The older Leylanders did not feel English. The teeming, gloomy lands of the Tsarist Russian Pale, where they had lived, were what they called Our Home. Here in the Leylands they were hemmed in on all sides by people whose language they did not understand. But for Jeremy, the British Empire then at the height of its glory, excited him. Jeremy set about anglicizing the Raismans. Yiddish versions of names were changed into English. Jeremy himself abandoned the use of his first name, Abraham, although his mother continued to call him Vremky, and Myer and Harry never converted from Abe.

In their hour of need, iron had come to the Raisman household. Abraham called Jeremy was to cast them in a new mould, a mould which would irrevocably decide all their futures. This mould was what Myer and Jeremy called 'The Plan.'

The Plan was both realistic and visionary at the same time. 'It was useless,' as Harry ruefully said later 'to give money to the gamblers. Even if they were starving they would go and gamble it away. They couldn't stop gambling while they still had money in their pockets. However much money they had, they would go on gambling till they lost it all.' Jeremy saw that the Raismans could never succeed in business. It would be impossible to accumulate capital. They could never become capitalists. And after the disastrous tailoring strikes it was clear to everyone that the working class was on a hiding to nowhere. Myer would become a lifelong socialist, he never forgot the struggle of the working men, but he and Jeremy sought a way out of the working class. And that way was what their mother, Ada, had glimpsed at the gates of Gower Street School, gates she could never enter but her children would, the gates of education.

At school Jeremy began to encounter hints of a great culture beyond the narrow confines of the little Leylands world. For him it seemed somehow to come from ancient civilizations, from Greece and Rome. 'You must be ambitious,' said Jeremy.

Myer had offered himself willingly. He would go out to work, and his salary would come back, ungambled, every penny intact. While Louis' 30 shillings a week was lost in *der shpeeler* (the gambling house), the family would live on Myer's 18 pence. That was what Myer's intellect was to be used for, despite his winning the Senior City 'Schol.' He said he would eat as little as possible, and he was as good as his word. He ate only bread and jam or bread and butter, never all three. Once a week he had herring and potatoes.

Meanwhile Jeremy would go to school, learn the mysterious Latin and Greek and try to discover how these seemingly irrelevant languages had made Britain great. And he too was as good as his word. As long as Myer's money and frugality could be stretched, Raisman children would be educated into the professions. But the meagre gleanings by the one had to support the many. They only served to educate Jeremy and the next son, John. 'What could we do, Geoff?' said Myer later. 'We had no choice. That's how it was.'

The plan was steely but not inhumane. The anticipated success of the educated Raismans was to bring money to support the family and to elevate those who had sacrificed their education by working. For 70 years Jeremy was to keep his part of the bargain. He would see to it that his parents, his brother Myer, and finally Harry, never went hungry again.

And there were to be many more mouths to feed. By the time Myer had reached the age of 13 and taken his barmitzvah, Ada had three more boys, John, Harry and Jack, and now Fanny was big enough to help her mother with the ritual of bathing all the little boys. Kettles of water were boiled and gradually the large tin bath in the kitchen was filled. Towels were warmed on the fireguard in front of the fire. Standing side by side with aprons on and sleeves rolled up Ada and Fanny bathed and dried the boys in order. The kitchen was awash with water and splashing and little boys shouting and playing.

But the family were now so crowded that Myer didn't have a place to sleep. Louis, Jeremy and Harry were sleeping in the bed and John and Jack under it. So Myer was sent off to his aunt Rachel's family in Newcastle. After all, for Ada Rachel was as much a mother as an older sister. 'Rachel can't have a boy herself,' said Ada in justification, referring to the fact that her sister's three children were all girls.

Ada arranged to take him up to her sister Rachel's house in Newcastle. The railway excursion fare was three shillings and six pence. Myer was dressed in his new short Norfolk jacket, the type known in Leeds as a bum freezer. As they left the house in Leeds the baby Jack ran out into the street after him crying, 'Myer, Myer,' like a lamb bleating as its mother was led to the slaughter.

Myer stayed only three months in Newcastle. The relatives there were far too orthodox for him. His aunt Rachel shaved off all her hair and wore a wig. 'Her husband,' said Myer simply, 'was a religious maniac.' But Myer did conceive a great liking and admiration for his cousin Jinny, ten years older, and the oldest of his aunt Rachel's three daughters. Jinny and her sisters hated their father because he was, as Jinny put it, 'a bearded Jew,' and she used often to say how she wished she could have had an anglicized father like Myer's.

In Leeds, Ada's heart was heavy. 'You've plenty of children,' her friends told her. 'I've got ten fingers,' Ada said. 'That doesn't mean I want to give one away.'

Maurice also pined for his son. 'Well,' he said, 'I can't stand it. Whenever I go out I'm thinking of the boy.' Maurice had a friend going up to Newcastle for the races. 'Will you bring my boy back?' he asked. 'And listen, put a tanner each way on the second favourite in the four o'clock for me.'

When Myer got back to Leeds he started work as an errand boy for Rufus, a money-lender who lived on Camp Road. Camp Road was then the wealthiest street in the district, but even so, people considered that Rufus lived considerably below his means. Rufus was called Ruffky the Monkey because of his extreme ugliness. 'You have to take a swig of brandy before you can even bring yourself to look at him,' Ada said. 'He looks like someone who has escaped from the other world.'

Ada met Ruffky's wife one day in the grocer's shop. 'My daughter's just back from a holiday in Blackpool,' said Ruffky's wife.

'Well,' asked Ada 'How is she?'

'Ugly she went, and ugly she returned,' said Ruffky's wife glumly.

Myer only stayed a few weeks with Ruffky and then he started to work

How she wished she could have an anglicized father...

66

as a tailor's machinist at Olbrecht's workshop. Louis and his father taught him the trade. From his father's point of view, Myer was the best investment he ever made. As soon as Myer could use a sewing machine he went to work for Fat Simon in an upstairs hole-and-corner master's workshop in Templar Street. Officially he worked the usual twelve hours from eight in the morning till eight in the evening. In practice it meant no work for weeks, then working all night when work came.

And with the Boer War it came. Maishy Goodman made a trip to South Africa and came back with a huge batch of orders for uniforms, for both sides. This was the beginning of Myer's contribution. From the time Myer started to work, his father Maurice, then 39 years old, declared that he was too ill to work. He never worked again for the remaining 44 years of his life. His sons kept him. 'Father'd gambled before,' Harry said. 'But from now on he didn't dilute his gambling with work.'

Myer's is the powerhouse of this story. His work supported all that the Raismans were now to do or achieve. When Myer started work at 13 he had only a third of a century to work. At the end he was penniless and blind. 'Out of children that hadn't enough to eat, he made doctors and lawyers. That,' said his brother Harry 'was Myer's family ambition.'

After school in the afternoon Harry would go home and collect a jug of tea and a 'bit of a sandwich' and take it to Myer, who had been working since early morning. Myer worked for three years at Cohen's. There were two machines. The other machinist was Myer's friend Benny Goldman. After three years the boss was arrested for illegal overtime and the shop shut.

Now Myer worked for Samuel Henry Lyons in a firm that was to become Alexandre the Tailor's. One night, after only three weeks there, the pressure was on, and Myer got tired. At one o'clock in the morning he refused to work any more. 'Don't come back,' the boss said.

'What did you say?' I asked Myer, when he told me this story. 'I didn't say a word,' he replied. 'Not a word. What could I say? I might have said 'May you go with a crutch under your arm.' Myer chuckled. 'But I didn't. What was the point, already? I slung 'im a deaf 'un.'

'A spit on him,' said Myer's mother when he told her next morning. 'May he have an interesting end. Smoke should come into his bones.'

Myer found a job with Enoch, the Angel of Death. From his habit of keeping his own family hungry, the money he made was called belly gold. For a while Myer moved on to the attic of Raphael the Madman, then to Left Handed Moses, and so on, from hole to corner, and from corner back to hole, machining into the night. Lighting was bad. Sometimes the hard steel needle passed through his finger on its way to the cloth. 'You can't learn to sew till you've put the needle through your finger,' said his father, meaning to be reassuring. Myer was disdainful. 'It's only fools and horses that work' he said:

Work, work, work,
Till the brain begins to swim,
Work, work, work,
Till the eyes are heavy and dim!

Seam, and gusset, and band,
Band, and gusset, and seam,
Till over the buttons I fall asleep,
And sew them on in a dream!

The Jewish tailors came from a background of social ferment, and they took in socialism with their mothers' milk. Myer went to the workers' meetings in Tarnish's back rooms at the Star Inn, and listened to the pocket revolutionaries breathing fire and tobacco smoke. Myer joined the tailors' union, and immediately became a shop steward. He would go from workshop to workshop collecting the penny union dues.

Myer's union activities opened a new world for him. 'I remember Keir Hardie,' he said, with deep respect, 'talking to a meeting on Woodhouse Moor, a big, imposing man with flowing white hair, a huge white beard and a strong Scottish accent.' Myer became a member of the infant Independent Labour Party.

After the first Labour defeat at the elections Keir Hardie had predicted it would be three elections before Labour could get seats. In 1906 the predicted third election took place and 29 ILP candidates were returned to Parliament.

'Tell me what it was like.' I once asked Myer, years later.

'Ehh!' he said dismissively. 'What is there to tell? They're all gone now, all kickin' daisies in't boneyard.'

'Well,' I persisted 'where did you work?'

'Where did I work?' Myer chuckled. 'Where didn't I work? Every hole and corner in Leeds... and then some more.'

He paused.

'I started to work in the year nineteen hundred and starve to death. 'We worked for flompence a week. Whatever the employers would give us. Often they had no money themselves. From a pig even a hair is good.

'The four main occupations were tailors, cutters, machinists and pressers. I was a machinist. At that time there was a notorious scandal in the papers. An international criminal gang, led by the Messina brothers, were kidnapping young girls and selling them into the white slave trade. It didn't happen in Leeds, but police detectives came and questioned people. One time they cornered an old man who could hardly speak English.

'"Are you a Messina?" they asked sternly.

'"No," he replied mournfully, "I'm a presser."'

The Luftman

But now, for the desperate, struggling Raisman family, Fate was preparing its final weapon, that which would in the end, lay low Myer's noble Plan.

It was when Ada was starting on her second batch of three boys, that she realised that she had produced something unusual: 'He was born talking,' she said, and she gave him the name John, whose meaning in Hebrew is 'Gift of God.'

Behind the high foreheads of the Raismans were mighty intellects. All the children of Ada Rosainsky were exceptionally bright, even in a community which as a whole prided itself on education. In Leeds, the Raisman brains were a legend in their own time. But among brilliant peers, John was outstanding.

Jeremy used to study in the upstairs bedroom, calling his juniors to order when they became too noisy below by banging on the floor. 'Jeremy'd get up,' his sister Fanny said in admiration, 'at 4 or 5 o'clock in the morning, in winter and he'd put on an overcoat and sit and study. He did it from when he was only 12. He used to study hard, and he'd say, "I wish I had John's brains."'

More often Jeremy simply escaped the noise by working in the reference room of the public library, and John remembered it years later in his poem:

The nondescript and vagrant crowd which haunts
Our public reading rooms you deem to be
Citizens driven from their domiciles
By the conventions of society.

Times without number Jeremy climbed the resounding stone stairs with their brass handrails punctuated at the turns by grotesque marble effigies of kissing dogs, and many hours he spent in the majestic, echoing, wood-panelled reading room in the Central Library. But while Jeremy was industrious and determined, John was idle. John's laziness was proverbial in the family. He was naturally left-handed. Nor did school help. Hymy Pessakovitch was a few months older than John and they shared the same double desk at Gower Street School. 'They wouldn't let him write with his left hand,' said Hymy. 'They used to rap his knuckles. In those days they thought it would be a disadvantage to you when you grew up. They thought you wouldn't be able to use the tools. It was no use telling them John was left-handed. They were very strict in those days.'

To the early, unsuccessful pressures of trying to make him eat and write rightly right-handedly, various people ascribed John's various ills. My father believes it gave John tuberculosis. John believed it made him a gambler. John's writing was always illegible, his speech mumbling and difficult to hear. Between his mighty brain and his fellow men, not a few difficulties were to be interposed.

'I knew all the Raismans at Gower Street School,' said Hymy. 'Jeremy, Jack, Harry, Fanny, a stout girl she was, stout. John was very well liked. He used to be a good actor, in school plays. He started the first Jewish scouts in Leeds. He'd've been about ten years old. Always a very popular feller.'

When he was a boy John fell ill with tuberculosis and was sent out of the smoky city to a sanatorium in Gateforth, just outside Wakefield. Jeremy and Myer went to visit him. They walked the ten miles to Gateforth, chatted with John and set off back. Myer was worn out. 'You go on,' he said to Jeremy. 'I'll follow later.' Jeremy didn't bother to reply. He picked his older brother Myer up on his broad back and carried him home.

John had great difficulty with anything practical. His clothes were always what Myer called a 'ragshop,' and he never learned to ride a bike. Harry, whose only relaxation was cycling was amused: 'John tried cycling - just once. He decided to go to Adel Woods. He got as far as

Long Causeway, and then on the steep hill he got out of control. He ran into a wall and nearly killed himself. He didn't try to get on again, just walked the five miles home. I'm surprised he ever managed to get on the bike and steer it in the first place.'

From the beginning John was totally impractical. His mother used to say that he couldn't cut himself a slice of bread. John's younger brother Sam marvelled at this as he later recounted John's experiences. John never learned to cut bread. He never wielded a knife for any purpose in all his eighty-odd years. He could never eat meat, never strike a fellow man, never countenance cruelty in others, never bear to hear a baby's natural crying.

John never needed to learn to cut bread. Somehow, in the nick of time, and it was only just so at times, others always cut it for him. He was indifferent to material things, could not handle money, and accumulated no possessions, only knowledge.

I once asked Myer 'Where did uncle John learn gambling?'

'He learned it at the university, I suppose.'

Myer avoided suggesting any connection between his brother John's gambling and that of their father and oldest brother, Louis.

'When John's circumcision was due,' said Harry, 'father was hard up as usual. He was at his wits' end to find a few bob to make a circumcision. Well! a circumcision you had to have. So he went through the lists, and there was a horse called St John, and he backed it and it came up. And that's how he got the money. I've often wondered whether that affected John and made him a gambler.'

My father had a special way of saying the word John. It is soft and vibrant, and the sound no sooner starts out than it seems to fall back into a deep warm hollow in his chest. To hear my father say that word, says all that lies between the covers of this book, betrayal, dashed hopes, a struggle wasted, a lifetime of drudgery and, in the end, compassion for a man who wandered through the earth, bearing his guilt like Cain, whose forehead was branded with the murder of his brother.

The Visionary

Queen Victoria just managed to outlive the nineteenth century, by which time Ada had five children and was pregnant with the sixth, my father Harry.

Like Hoshy, Moshy the Wine Merchant also had sons who needed feeding and could soon help bringing in money. But he also had two daughters. To keep up his new social status they needed dowries. Moshy's first daughter was also called Fanny, after her grandmother Frada. His second was Rose. When she was 22, Rose was engaged to a brutal man from Albert Grove called Moshe Kelerovitch. Moshe not only wanted money for Rose, he wanted a house and a business and he calculated he could get both out of the wine merchant father.

Just after midday on Saturday, as the service ended in the main hall of the Greenhorns' Synagogue in Belgrave Street, President Moshy Raisman waited for his older brother Hoshy to come out of the slightly longer poor-man's service in the cellar.

Together they walked down Belgrave Street towards the Leylands.

'So?' Moshy said.

'So?' replied Hoshy.

All around little groups of people in trilby hats and raincoats were walking peacefully down the street, some on the pavement, some in the roadway, all involved in quiet, earnest Sabbath conversations, carrying red velvet bags embroidered with wide gold stars of David, and containing prayer books, or black and white prayer shawls with their knotted tassels hanging out. The womenfolk, in their best hats and coats, following behind in even more animated conversations.

The brothers reached North Street, waited for the electric tramcars to rattle on their way to Sheepscar, or back to Briggate, then crossed into the Leylands.

'Rose has made a good match,' Moshy said.

Hoshy nodded.

'But he needs somewhere... and he wants to set up a drapery shop...'

Hoshy gave the slightest nod.

'Can you manage?'

No reply from Hoshy. They soon reached Bridge Street. Moshy went into Number 34 and Hoshy went into Number 36, not even bothering to reply to the customary, 'Good Sabbath' from his neighbour Left Handed Moses, who was just going into his trimmings shop at Number 38. Moshy sat down at the table. 'Ehh khh!' he said and picked up his spoon. Chayie brought his plate of chicken soup. 'Ehh khh!,' Moshy said again, putting the spoon down and shaking his head.

Maurice was away at Wakefield racecourse. Hoshy came in to Number 34 and gently put his hand on Ada's arm. 'I'm sorry,' he said. 'We can't stay here. Do you think you could ask Shroll Maishy?' By now, Shroll Maishy owned six houses, just round the corner in Plum Street. Ada had to swallow her pride, and go the man who had so strongly disapproved of her marriage.

So Hoshy and his wife, and Maurice and Ada and their brood of kids moved out of Moshy's house-cum-shop at 36 Bridge Street and into Shroll Maishy's back-to-back house in Plum Street. It would be 20 years before they were able to live again in a through house.

Moshe Kelerovitch changed his name to Matthew Kelly, moved into 36 Bridge Street and proudly hung out his drapery shop sign next to the Greenhorn President's wine and spirit store at Number 34. It was not to be a happy marriage. 'Rose,' people said, 'was a weeping willow.'

A few weeks later Ada was already in bed awaiting the delivery of her fifth boy, Harry. Moshy, still feeling guilty at his treatment of his older brother, said to Chayie, 'Take them something.'

Chayie went up to see Ada in the bedroom in Plum Street and on her way downstairs furtively left a black bread on the mantelpiece. Ada didn't notice until the Chayie was half way on to the street. Struggling out of bed, she grabbed the bread and threw it out of the window after the capacious retreating form of her would-be benefactor. Powered by all the

Matthew Kelly: Moshy Kelerovitch's shop sign at 36 Bridge Street

force of Ada's indignation, the bread bounced all the way down Plum Street and into Gower Street, finally coming to rest in the gutter by the row of curb stones where Sun Street and this book began, and Harry, the next boy, was born.

Harry was the middle one of the middle three sons. He was a weakly child and the family never expected him to survive till manhood.

An article in the Lancet described Plum Street and Gower Street School. But far from the rain-washed emptiness of the modern, desolate streets which I had seen, the Lancet described a scene full of life, the Paradise Alley of my father's words:

> *Within a stone's throw of the spot where the small pox broke out, there is a court inhabited by a number of Jews, who are constantly seen bringing clothes home from the places where they work during the daytime. They will carry home two or three coats, fell them during the night, and take them back to the workshop in the morning all finished.*

76

The Jews' quarter is only separated by one comparatively broad street from the district which suffered principally from the typhus epidemic. It consists of a number of small streets with red brick cottages. The sanitary accommodation is altogether inadequate, and in some cases the most revolting consequences ensue. In one street, where a great number of tailors live, we found only two closets for seven houses. These were placed back to back in a little passage between two houses. The door to this passage opened on to the street. Anyone could enter, and complaints were made concerning drunken men from a neighbouring public house who made use of this place.

The houses on this side of the street have no back yards or back windows; it is therefore no easy matter to supply proper accommodation, and the construction of a street on such an unsuitable plan should not have been sanctioned. As a result the whole passage leading to these two closets is one mass of filth. People come here and empty utensils outside the closets, being fearful to approach such foul places. The flagstones are covered with soil, the liquid is seen oozing from under the stones, where it contaminates the subsoil and, passing out into the street, stains the pavement of the causeway until it reaches the gutters.

Immediately opposite there is a large Board School, and on the other side of the street another closet in bad condition. Thus, swarms of children have daily to pass by these places to reach their school.

In a cottage on one side of the passage in question we found that the inhabitants could not open their windows. Yet the little room thus deprived of ventilation contained, when we looked in, no less than nine persons huddled together; one of them was a tailor, and there was a child suffering from whooping cough.

The Lancet reporter offered no medical advice, and Harry's parents did not know what to make of his cough. Both Ada's girls had died of coughs. Ada called an old woman, who came and stooped over the bed. She drew her hand three times across his forehead, at the end of each stroke shaking her fingers as if to shake off drops of sweat. Then she

turned her head and spat three times over her left shoulder. As a result, Harry survived, but was never a healthy child. During his many childhood ailments he would only accept his older brother Myer, ten years his senior, to look after him. At first he shared a bed with Myer and Louis, but as Louis had to gamble all night and Myer had to work at night, often all night, then Harry slept with Jeremy and John.

Harry grew up to be dark and handsome. He had dark eyes and black, tightly wavy hair, keeping a lot more of it than any of his brothers. Throughout his life he was unworldly, as if the old woman had only half called him back from the other world. His serious, shy exterior conveyed few of his emotions. Indeed, he rarely spoke. Harry was a visionary. His earliest recorded vision was of a house. He described it in great detail. 'That,' his father told him, 'was Plum Street, where you were born. We left it when you were only a few months old.'

When he was five Harry was sent to Gower Street Infants School where each morning he joined the neat lines of boys and girls marching in to the notes of Blake's Jerusalem tinkled out on the school piano. The sound of the school hall echoing to the words:

And did those feet, in ancient time...

Bring me my bow of burning gold,
Bring me my arrows of desire...

and the rustling children's voices straining to reach the high notes of:

And was Jerusalem builded here.

gave Harry his first glimpse of the visionary world of the outcast, a world which he was to make peculiarly his own.

In Harry's childhood one event in 1906 determined his future. As a boy of seven he was dressed in a white shirt, grey flannel shorts and a red, white and blue belt and he was playing on the corner of Gower Street, swishing at pieces of orange peel with a stick. He was waiting to go on a school outing. He fell on his nose. By some unlucky chain of nasopharyngeal events, combined with his previous illnesses and abetted by surgical mismanagement he became gradually almost completely deaf.

Oddly enough, for such a crucial event, Harry later gave two completely different stories, asserting both equally strongly although, it must be admitted, at different times. According to the second story he was walking to school one frosty morning with his sister Fanny and his older brother John. It was 1905 and they were coming from their house in Sheepscar Place. As they entered Bridge Street from Byron Street just opposite the Polish Synagogue, he slipped on the ice, fell on his nose, got up and went on to school.

'After the fall I was ill,' said Harry, 'very ill. For a long time. Then one day I was sitting at the table and I turned round. Mother's face was aghast. "The child is deaf," she said in a tone of such utter dismay. She must have been talking to me. She was the first to realise it. I didn't know I was deaf.'

But deaf he certainly was, and as he sat in what was now for him a silent classroom high up in Gower Street School, idly watching the rats play on the roof of the Melbourne Brewery across the street, could he have guessed that this disability would deprive him of his education?

Shortly after Harry had been born the family left Shroll's house in Plum Street and moved to Little Bridge Street. To help pay the rent of one shilling and sixpence a week they took in a lodger, Morris Cohen, a rivetter. Hoshy also moved into a house, only five feet away, on the other side of Little Bridge Street. He was now totally dependent on his younger brother Moshy. At Passover Hoshy looked after the *matsy* ovens. *Matsy* is unleavened bread. To preserve its sacred unleavened state, the flour and water, once mixed, must be baked instantly and rapidly, lest some fermentation occur and leaven the dough. To do this specially constructed rotating ovens were used, and as Hoshy tended them the children would cluster eagerly round him, waiting for a glimpse through the oven door of the jets of flames as the circular baking plate rotated.

Maurice's growing family of children used to sew the paper bags for packing the crumbs (*matsy mell*) used for frying fish. Jeremy would load a gross of these bags on to a handcart and push them through the streets from the house in Little Bridge Street to the *matsy* oven in the Templar Street Fortress. In return the family were given 120 one pound bags of *matsy* for the ten days of Passover. It was generous, and would have cost ten shillings to buy.

Maurice and Ada Raisman occupied ten residences in their move from the Leylands to the suburbia of Chapeltown. Eleven of the children produced in them were due to reach old age. As the family expanded, houses became too small, landlords pressed for rent, or the non-humans who shared the house, rats, mice, dogs, cats, lice, bedbugs, fleas, cockroaches and crickets, multiplied too fast. Though it had few plants, the Leylands was popular with the animal kingdom. Lesser creatures contested the human sway. The human denizens occasionally adopted a nocturnal migratory pattern. It was called the moonlight flit.

With the end of the hungry nineteenth century, Queen Victoria died, and an era died with her. The restless Raismans had abandoned Little Bridge Street and moved to St. John's Square just behind, and here Ada produced her sixth son, Mad Jack.

Throughout Edward's reign the Leylands were on the move. The twentieth century could not be avoided, and the Raismans set off north. Their sixth residence, half way to Sheepscar, was in Myrtle Street. By this time, by virtue of his age, had passed to my father the task of coming down first in the morning to sweep up the sleepy cockroaches from the still warm hearth in the kitchen. 'It was a hot summer,' Harry said. 'Instead of going to bed people would be sitting out in the streets in their vests, talking. The lice were nothing. You got used to them. And the bedbugs were under the wallpaper. But the fleas! The fleas made it impossible to sleep. If you got one flea in the bed it was bad enough. Two, and it was absolutely impossible.'

Myrtle Street was beloved of gamblers. A large crowd frequently gathered in the street. It was a school of pitch-and-toss. The game was illegal and 'doggers-out' stood guarding either end of the street ready to signal the moment the police arrived. Pitch-and-toss was a local Yorkshire game. It was played behind the colliery slag heaps by the miners in Barnsley, and my grandfather sometimes went the twenty odd miles there by electric tram when a game was not available in the Leylands. Two pennies were tossed. The 'spinner' was not the banker. People backed either two heads or two tails. Bets were taken until the money was equal on the two sides. 'Two ones', one head and one tail, counted as nothing, and the coins were tossed again.

Myrtle Street was convenient for gambling, but the house defeated the family. 'We were flooded with crickets,' said Myer. 'and Uncle John fell into the midden.' It was the last straw. After only two weeks the Raismans turned tail and fled, leaving the field to the invertebrates.

That the family should have been vanquished by a midden was not necessarily a sign of faint-heartedness. In 1872 it was recorded that a man had fallen into a Leeds midden. It was seven yards wide, and its contents six feet deep. The body was not recovered for several days and the coroner recorded suffocation as the cause of death.

The family continued north, reaching Number Two Sheepscar Place. Their migration was following the route of the Lady Beck. Here Ada was ill for a long time, had a miscarriage and lost her hearing. Her youth was gone. It was only in 1905 she resumed reproduction. It was her final fling, only three more boys were to come and the 3-1-3-1-3 symmetry of the family was to be completed.

Sheepscar Place was a small blind alley opening on to the north side of Skinner Lane. Skinner Lane was an old road. For a long time it had been the only way across the north end of the marshy Leyland pasture. Between it and Sheepscar the beck had run past mills and tanneries, and the name of Skinner Lane recalled the leather trade. The back-to-back slums of Sheepscar Place were erected at the time of the French Revolution by a land speculator called Richard Paley. Even though he built at the absolute minimum cost, he went bankrupt ten years later. These houses could only stretch a short distance towards Sheepscar before encountering the Beck (here called the Sheepscar Beck) and so Sheepscar Place ended blindly with a high sandstone wall overlooking the sunken course of the beck below.

It was the nearest to the Beck that the family had lived. Its foetid vapours permeated the house. On rainy days its restless waters, rising indignantly, reclaimed some of their old, lost territories and stood triumphantly three feet deep in the cellar-kitchen.

Sarah, the younger girl, born in this unhealthy spot, was a sickly child. Unlike all the other children, her hair was fair. Although her older sister Fanny the Old had survived, Ada had never stopped grieving over her previous two lost daughters. She was worried that she couldn't raise girls. Now here was another girl looking very poorly.

Soon after Hoshy had arrived in Leeds, his daughter Rebecca had married a man called Notty Wolf and had gone to live in Lydia Street, just beside the Templar Street Fortress. Rebecca had never forgiven Ada for taking away her treasured kid brother Maurice. She was known to the Raisman children by the respectful title of Aunty Wolf. She had 16 children of her own and so she could taunt Ada, at that time with only 8 children, as being a barren woman, a serious fault which had been the cause of Ada's older sister's suicide.

The baby Sarah's mysterious illness got worse. Ada was afraid Sarah wouldn't be able to see. And the child's legs dangled uselessly. 'Like lumps of candle grease' Ada said to the Chinese doctor who came to the house. Now Ada was sick with worry about Sarah. One loss, Ada later told Sarah, she could accept better because the child was only a little baby when she died. 'The other,' Ada said, 'was a real child. Ooh, they were lovely little girls. Long life to you!'

Ada's sister-in-law Rebecca appeared just as the Chinese doctor was leaving. 'Ask him,' said Ada, who hadn't heard all the doctor had said. 'Run after him and ask him what he said.' But Rebecca declined to run after the doctor. 'Do you want to raise a cripple?' she asked Ada.

Ada was not in favour of Darwin's thesis of the survival of the fittest. She never spoke to Rebecca again. Meanwhile, Rebecca went all round Leeds telling people about how her sister-in-law was trying to raise 'a white-haired cripple girl.'

Spared any further medical interventions, Sarah recovered, although for years she couldn't walk. One day her brothers came home to find that their alarmed mother had lost Sarah. Much to her brothers' amusement it was found that she had shuffled on her bottom all the way down Skinner Lane as far as the Army Barracks on the corner of Regent Street. This was where the beck crossed the road and ran towards the Irish district of Mabgate.

Here, in the damp ground beside the Lady Beck, two adjacent streets were called Lilac Grove and Lilac Terrace. Lilac Grove was fully housed, but Lilac Terrace had a row of houses on one side only. The other was too narrow. The builders of our city did not want to waste the valuable space so, using their standard red brick wall and slate roof construction, they filled the other side with a neat row of tiny but beautifully constructed privies. By Edwardian times, the houses of Lilac Terrace had become brothels. The Leylanders didn't like to mention the brothels directly, but they were always amused by the idea of a street of lavatories.

...beautifully constructed privies

Lilac Grove wasn't a grove of lilacs. In fact, there were no gardens anywhere in the Leylands. The houses were too closely packed, and the streets too narrow for trees or flowering shrubs. The earth here grew no grass. Yet the vegetable world regretted the loss of this former pasture, and every Spring, in the odd corners and crevices which the hasty builders of the houses and streets had never quite covered up, delicate green columns of coltsfoot appeared. At first the young shoots, thick with soft, downy hairs, were bent over like shepherds' crooks, but as the sun shone they straightened out, and the bright yellow flowers defiantly spread their petals towards the sky.

At the end of Lilac Grove, the water formed a little pool, called Benson's Pond, and on the waste ground beside it grass and coltsfoot covered the rubbish heaps. The kids called this natural playground the Tushky Fields. No one knew the origin of the word *tushky*; some thought it meant rhubarb, which was quite likely, since this had been the crop of the Meanwood Valley in Victorian times.

Here they could watch mysterious religious ceremonies performed by the more orthodox of the old Leylanders, who beat each other with shoelaces in synagogue on the Day of Atonement. There were times when they came and waved chickens round their heads. At other times they stood leaning over the banks, muttering prayers and emptying crumbs from their pockets into the water.

Louis visited Lilac Terrace for non-religious purposes. The houses here were made of a special type of shiny brick, with an unpleasant white sheen above, rather like tiles in a public lavatory, and leprous green below, as if sweating out an unhealthy miasma seeped up from the Lady Beck below.

One morning the six-year-old Harry picked up a letter that had come through the box. 'What's an affiliation order?' he asked his older brother Myer. It was a court order requiring Louis to pay maintenance for the child. It could not be escaped, even though Louis pleaded in court that he was only one of many who had had access to the lady.

Louis' father had by now despaired of his first-born ever doing anything useful in life. 'Why doesn't he join the army?' Maurice used to ask plaintively. Louis didn't join the army, but while the family lived in Sheepscar Place there occurred an event which was to shape Louis' life.

Like Ada and Maurice, Rebecca and Notty Wolf had also piously called their first born Louis after their common great-grandfather Rabbi Levi of Shakee. This name brought to Louis Wolf and Louis Raisman a further common bond, both first-borns gambled. Their destinies were to be interwoven.

Louis Wolf had just managed to bankrupt a small grocery business in Goole. His father Notty was so angry he refused to have anything to do with him. My grandfather Maurice, on the other hand, had the virtue of not attempting to judge others. So he helped his nephew Louis Wolf to find a place to live, opposite the pub and his own house on the other corner of Sheepscar Place. And while he was here Louis Wolf's fortunes began to look up. Someone arranged a marriage for him. The dowry was generous and he used it to get out of Sheepscar Place and go to Canada.

Meanwhile Jeremy too had a lucky break. In London some wealthy Jewish families had set up a fund to provide a pound a week to help the most promising sons of the struggling immigrants obtain an education. The scheme was country-wide, and the standard of competition fiercely high. Only two bursaries went to Leeds, one to Jeremy and the other to Jacob Kramer.

Jacob Kramer was born in the same year as Jeremy, but in the southern Ukraine. His father had studied with Repin, the Tsarist court painter in St Petersburg. The family came to Leeds in 1900, when Jacob was eight. Jacob was determined to be an artist. He never learned to speak English properly, but as a teenager he wrote a theory of art in Yiddish, written in Hebrew characters. His charcoal and ink sketches of Leeds people became famous. Kramer's picture of an old woman standing, mouth open as for a scream of agony, was entitled 'My Mother or Pogrom.' One critic, echoing an anti-semitic criticism of Mahler earlier that year, accused him of indecent displays of emotion.

When Kramer was given the bursary, his impractical nature was recognized, and the trustees asked his co-recipient Jeremy to look after him. Kramer's bursary was intended to send him to the Slade School of Art in London, where he did eventually go, although he completely ignored the then fashionable trends in art. His pictures never lost their Ukrainian background, even though he had left when he was so young. Masquerading under quite non-Russian titles, huge Russian peasant women suckled babies in fields of yellow corn.

But the hallmark of Kramer's work was that he painted not what was, but what was to be. His *Head of a Young Man* is old, bald, and seedy. 'Kramer painted my sister,' Louis Teeman told me. 'We were all terribly upset. She was only a young girl, and he painted an embittered, middle aged woman. As the years went by, that was what she became.'

Kramer never took the trouble to learn how to handle money. Week after week he would go to Jeremy to borrow a half-a-crown against the next week's pay. It was in return that he once drew a magnificent sketch of the young Jeremy in 1913, a pipe clenched determinedly between his teeth. Kramer's sketch clearly shows what Jeremy would, in fifty years, become.

What little money Jeremy managed to keep together went on books. Throughout Edward the Seventh's reign, Everyman were issuing a uniform edition of classical works at a shilling. The frontispiece was a jungle of fruit-bearing arabesques occupying two facing pages and emanating from the flowing robes of a wise virgin. In these books, Jeremy acquired the great historical works, such as the Historical Essays of Lord Macaulay, a former Member of Parliament for Leeds, and the man who had pioneered the Act for the Removal of Jewish Disabilities in 1838. Jeremy read everything systematically, marking his favourite passages with a neat pencil line closely following the left margin. In the Life of Burleigh, Jeremy was thrilled with Macaulay's picture of the sturdiness of the English people in Tudor times. They seemed to have all the virtues the Leylands lacked.

After the Central Library closed Jeremy used to take his books back to read by candlelight in the little Leylands bedroom. And on hot summer nights the street noises of the gambling Leylanders loudly cursing in Yiddish wafted like an unholy litany through his open window, strengthening and nourishing his growing admiration of the solid English yeomanry he was reading about. Jeremy was acquiring knowledge he would later use himself. In the Lives of Lord Clive and Warren Hastings, he read of the founding of British imperial rule in India. He imagined poor boys going out to discover honour and fortune in Madras and Bengal.

All around the Raismans now families were gradually becoming more prosperous and moving out of the Leylands into the adjoining, less

Kramer's sketch clearly shows what Jeremy would, in fifty years, become

crowded areas on the other side of North Street and Sheepscar. The Gittlemans, bound for greener pastures, moved to Pasture Road. The Raismans were not yet to share in this new prosperity. Myer's machining did bring in enough to keep Jeremy at school and then at Leeds University. But however hard Myer worked he could not earn enough for the whole family. Once when Jeremy came home from university he knocked on the bolted door and shouted to his mother, 'Don't open the door. The bailiff's here.'

In the end, however, the bailiff did get in and it became impossible for the Raismans to stay in Sheepscar Place. Maurice's family had to retreat south, back towards the centre of the Leylands, the original home of the immigrants. They fell back as far as Trafalgar Street, only two streets away from the Templar Street Fortress at the heart of the Leylands. They were bitterly disappointed. Sheepscar Place itself had still been in the Leylands but the family had at least enjoyed the sensation of moving gradually north and had cherished visions of the next move being an escape. To go back down south when everyone else was moving up north was an admission of defeat.

'It was *The Return to the Leylands*,' said Myer.

The Return to the Leylands

O Luck, like the moon changeable in state;
You are always waxing and waning.
Fate monstrous and empty,
A whirling wheel you are
Now at the gaming table,
My bare back I bring to your villainy

Orff's Carmina Burana; transl. William Mann

A ginnel ran from Nile Street to Back Nile Street and in the passage operated a book-maker's runner. This was Myer Esman who had been the secretary of the ill-fated Jewish Tailors' strike committee in 1888. Of all the strike leaders only he had managed to stay in Leeds, and that was only by accepting that he could never work again as a tailor. Myer Esman was a little stocky man. He had no known relations anywhere and no family in Leeds. He lived in lodgings in Glover Street. His job was to take illegal bets for bookmakers. But as Myer Esman grew older and stiffer this profession became ever more precarious. So, at either end of the ginnel he commissioned two small boys for a ha'penny each to 'dog-out' for the police. If a policeman came they all ran away. But in the end he wasn't fast enough and the police caught him. For the second time in his life (the first was in the strike of 1888) Myer Esman's name appeared in the Yorkshire Evening News. He was fined a small sum.

The morning after he was convicted Ada Raisman was buying bagels in the little baker's shop on Nile Street when she overheard someone say 'Myer Esman's been pinched for taking bets in the ginnel.' At that time, there was no difference in the pronunciation of Myer Esman and Myer Raisman. Ada rushed home to find out whether her second-born had also succumbed to the family disease.

Myer was highly amused.

Myer Esman died not long after. His tombstone is very plain. He had no family, so no one wrote, 'Deeply missed,' or other such things. The inscription just says, 'Myer Esman, aged 68,' and gives the year. Perhaps the money for it was put up by some grateful old trade union members. In a way he had no name. Myer was so common, it meant little more than Mister. Esman, which sounded so grandly oriental, like a pasha in the Ottoman empire or a caliph in Baghdad, meant no more than he had stood in the immigration queue in the place in front of Myer Teeman. Because he had no family, he was the first and the last to bear the name Esman.

The bookie for whom Myer Esman worked was called Chaim Heshky, and he had a kosher butcher's shop on North Street, just by the top of Nile Street. Although he was much esteemed by the Leylanders for both his services, he too came to suffer disgrace when it was discovered that the meat he was selling was not kosher.

And now it was that Ada was to complete the third and final cycle of her creation. She gave birth to three more boys, Ralph, Sam and Sidney. She was by now quite accustomed to delivery, and didn't even need the neighbour to help. 'The last one,' she told Myer 'just fell out when I was on my way up the stairs.' For 21 years Ada had never had a year when she was not pregnant.

The three middle brothers, John, Harry and Jack, slept in one bed like sardines head-to-tail-to-head. Bed lore arose. John ate in bed. Crumbs disturbed the brotherly repose. Long afterwards Sarah was to give the evidence of bed-eating as an early sign of her brother John's madness. Sarah was a repository of bed-lore. For the little sister the mundane task of filling the stone hot water bottle to put in her big brothers' bed was a sacred ceremony which approached in solemnity the placing of the scrolls of the Law in the Sacred Ark on the Sabbath.

And all these grandchildren were a source of unending delight to their grandfather Hoshy. To the end Hoshy remained a cheerful, ineffective, friendly little man, full-bearded and so broad-shouldered he looked almost as wide as he was tall. As he walked down the street his squareness was emphasized by a square wooden frame he wore on his back for carrying plates of glass. 'He spent all his time,' said my father, 'wondering how to convert his grandchildren into orthodox Jews. He used to haunt us. When we came out of school in Gower Street at four in the afternoon he'd be waiting for us - the three middle boys - John, Jack and me. He'd give us a ha'penny to bribe us to go to Hebrew school.'

Hoshy was quite unlike his younger brother Moshy. Through Chayie die Shvartsy's baking, Moshy had become quite successful. At first he had set his older brother Hoshy up in a wine and spirit shop. But Hoshy was quite unable to be a business man, and in the end the prosperous Moshy gave up trying to help Hoshy along. Apart from getting Hoshy to look after the matsy ovens at Passover, Moshy left Hoshy to his own devices, and Hoshy resigned himself to a life of glazing broken window panes and playing cards.

Sarah was growing up, and finally she had learned to walk. She knew her grandfather Hoshy as an old man with a peaked cap, who came to the front door with one piece of glass under his arm, and another in the wooden frame on his back. She knew that he worked in a bakery, and that her big sister Fanny and John used to go there and get sweets. So one day she set off with her brother Jack to go to Hoshy's matsy place in Metcalf Yard.

'I remember,' Sarah said later, 'my grandfather coming out to see us. Then he picked up my pinny and filled it with matsy crumbs. Then he packed Jack's pockets with them. We were so excited. 'Then Moshy came. At least, I guessed it was him. He was Hoshy's younger brother, but he was bigger, and taller, and wealthy, and the matsy factory belonged to him. He shouted at Hoshy, "You're giving away all the profits!" Then he took the matsy away from us. We ran all the way home as fast as we could. As we ran we could hear him still shouting at Hoshy. Mother was furious. "With all the money the pig's got," she said.'

Hoshy had never moved from his two room, back-to-back house in Little Bridge Street. The lower room was about ten feet by fifteen feet. Opening to the street was a door and a window, but all the other walls were solid, adjoining the three identical houses, one on each side, and one behind. Upstairs, the 'one-up' room was the same size. Water came from a tap in the street. Inside the house, there was no water, no bathroom, and no lavatory. 'It was not really a house,' said my father, 'just a shelter to get out of the rain.'

Hoshy's wife Rachel spent her last years an invalid in bed. To look after her upstairs became too much for the ageing Hoshy so he had her in a bed in the downstairs room. My father remembered her, sitting up in bed, 'a huddled old woman wearing a wig'. Myer remembered her devoutness, and how, when she was dying, she repeated over and over again a Hebrew phrase from the service of the most solemn of the Jewish Holy Days, the Day of Atonement, 'For behold I am like clay in the hands of the potter.'

'Hoshy,' said my father, 'was very fond of playing cards. His old cronies came and they played *klabbiyash* for the smallest possible sums - ha'pennies. At the back of the room his wife sat up in bed watching. In summer the door was kept wide open. In those days playing cards, that is to say, gambling, was a criminal offence. Little Bridge Street was on the regular beat of the coppers from Millgarth Police Station. They invariably stopped at the door to watch Hoshy and his friends playing. They liked the old man and used to pass the time of day with him.'

My father obviously had a soft spot for his grandfather Hoshy. 'He was more a father to us than our own father,' he said. 'Much more. I hardly knew my father. Very rarely saw him. He took no interest in his children.'

And now, with the completion of Ada's family, the stage was set for the next act of history, and the older generation began to disappear. 'Hoshy died of torticollis,' Harry said. 'It was in 1911, just before Passover. I remember Hoshy's funeral. In fact I got quite a thrill out of it. It was because I was able to sit next to the driver of the horse drawn hearse all the way to Gildersome.'

The hearse was a four-wheel cab of the commonest type, called a growler. Growlers were very different from the more expensive hansom cabs which had two high wheels and carried only two passengers willing and able to pay the price of this status symbol. The more working-class growler was like a square box on wheels. It carried four passengers, completely enclosed. The driver sat, exposed to the elements, on the top at the front.

'The funeral,' said Harry, 'started off at a slow march and then the driver whipped up the horses and travelled as fast as he could.' Following the hearse, about twenty mourners travelled to Gildersome in an open cart with big wooden wheels, and no tyres. The cart was drawn by two or four horses with plumes of black painted ostrich feathers. The cart went through the city centre, by the magnificent bronze statue of the Black Prince on horseback, the horse about to charge, the prince's mail-clad right arm, still holding the bridle, raised, about to bring destruction on England's mediaeval French foes. This imposing statue was erected in front of the main station where it could impress the traveller entering the city. Few knew of any very obvious link between Leeds and the Black Prince, but it was a stirring subject.

The Black Prince was indeed jet black, blackened by the smoky air, and he was attended by statues of local men of note, such as Doctor Joseph Priestley, standing outside Mill Hill Chapel where he was the non-conformist Minister and holding the magnifying glass with which he concentrated the sun's rays to discover the existence of oxygen. But the reverend doctor was eclipsed by a bevy of eight slender young girls. Their naked bodies, also jet black, glistened in the rain. Their firm bosoms and shapely legs were tastefully but completely revealed by spare, delicate bronze rags. The bronze girls were of two varieties, four Morns with their eyes looking upwards, and four Eves with their eyes cast down. Their bodies writhed upwards and their upstretched arms held street lamps, a lame attempt to find a decorous excuse for their existence. Lame or not, a later attempt to remove them caused a public outcry, and they stand there still, the only proviso being that when the corporation's workmen wash them, their bodies must be concealed by screens, lest the spectacle of their various parts being publicly scrubbed should elicit unseemly comments from the passers-by.

Should anyone today look closely at these eight bodies he would see that when he made them Alfred Drury used the same model for each. And if his eyes examined that face the stranger might wonder who was

*The discovery
of oxygen...*

*...spare
bronze rags*

that girl, and what happened to her, whether her story was sad, or romantic, or whether she became old and fat and matronly, and perhaps with a secret smile strolled unrecognized across City Square beneath those statues of her preserved youth.

Leaving City Square, the mourners crossed the river Aire west of the city by a Victorian arched bridge of delicately carved sandstone. The paired supports of the bridge projected above the level of the roadway at each end of the bridge and proudly bore the city arms deeply incised in their most elaborate possible form: the coat of arms was split into two roundels, one with a crowned owl, the other with a woollen fleece.

After crossing the bridge the journey became more adventurous for the mourners in the open carts. As they passed the locked gates of the great star-shaped prison in Armley, they had to run the gauntlet of kids throwing stones from the narrow factory workers' streets of the non-Jewish areas west of the city. Then came the problem of whether to get out and push, so as to help the horses get up the steep hill at Gildersome. When they finally reached the crest of the windy ridge they could look back over the whole of Leeds, where the river Aire flowed majestically through its ever-widening valley down towards Hull. And if, holding tightly on to their hats, they turned to look west with streaming eyes into the teeth of the wind, they could see ridge upon ridge of hills rising in the distance to the summit of the Pennines and the Lancashire border.

All around, ragged fields were enclosed by crumbling walls of a poor quality sandstone, quarried in Beeston, just south of the river. This yellow stone has a warm orange tinge, and is so soft that it can be frittered away to sand by a rub of the finger. Over the years, the surface of the stone walls, like the house bricks, also became encrusted with a black deposit from the smoky air. But the underlying stone, continuously eroded by the weather, repeatedly flaked off revealing ever new fissures and rounded cavities of unexposed yellow stone beneath.

The tops of the walls were capped by a row of blocks of black millstone grit, roughly decorated with spiral chisel cuts and here and there fallen, their space at once filled by eager spires of thistle or of willow herb. Unlike the sandstone, this millstone grit is so hard that it is untouched by even the harshest weather. It had lain on the Pennine hilltops since the retreating glaciers of the Ice Age had left it there and it now sits grimly on the sandstone walls, obviously determined still to be there when Leeds and all its sandstone has long since turned to sand.

A little track turned off to the cemetery. No human or animal representation was allowed on the tombstones. The only adornments were an occasional few leaves on vine-like twining branches in the corners of the stones. But the tombs of the Cohens, the hereditary members of the priestly cast, had a pair of hands carved over the inscription. These ghostly hands were put together in a curious configuration, like the letter 'W'. This is the position in which the priests hold them when they bless the congregation. Because of the danger of the Evil Eye this ritual may not be directly observed either by the blesser, who covers his eyes with his prayer shawl, or by the blessed, who are required to avert their gaze. The blessing travels in straight lines radiating out from the hands. Like a light ray or the glance of an eye, it cannot turn corners or go through opaque things. Thus those who wish to be blessed must not stand behind the blesser since the blessing cannot penetrate the blesser's body.

And here, within blessing distance of the ghostly hands, Hoshy lies not far from his mother Frada, beneath a cheap stone, rough-carved from the sandstone quarries of south Leeds, and standing on the very crest of the ridge at Gildersome, exposed to the fiercest winds. His memorial is cut

in the soft stone of Yorkshire and not in the expensive Italian marble gracing the tombs of the well-to-do *Englisher* dead who lie in their sleek cemetery below the ridge.

The week after Hoshy's burial it was Passover, and

Harry had the job of taking the live hen, which had been kept in the coal-cellar, down to Jinny Ruben's, the ritual slaughterer's on Lower Vandyke Street. He held the bird closely. For most of the time it was deceptively quiet, but every so long it let out a loud squawk and struggled violently to open its wings, deluging Harry with chicken fleas. If it escaped it would provide one of the three main diversions for Leylands children, the others were a horse slipping on the ice, and the dancing bear.

The slaughterer placed the razor-sharp holy knife between his teeth, grasped the hen firmly, stretched out its neck, and idly plucked a few feathers from its throat, as unconcerned as if that was all he was going to do. As he took the knife from between his teeth, the little boy closed his eyes. It was a single clean, rapid cut. But death does not come that easily. The dying bird's feet wildly clawed the wooden trestle, more and more incoherently. The hen's life blood spurted from the gaping wound in its neck. No change of heart could save it now, Harry thought, but it seemed to him the agony would never end.

Harry handed over the slaughterer's fee of a ha'penny, and, with his teeth still tightly clenched, carried the limp but still warm body out into the street. It seemed heavier. On his way home a woman darted out from a house at the corner of Byron Street and, without so much as a 'By your leave,' plucked a couple of large feathers from the dead bird's tail. Their purpose was to sweep the crumbs of unleavened bread into a matchbox to purify the house for Passover.

The year before, John had been persuaded to take the hen to the slaughterer's. It had made a deep impression on him. He never went again, and in all his life never ate chicken or any form of meat again.

Harry was beginning to play his part in family affairs. When he was ten he started delivering milk for Steinberg, their next door neighbour at 43 Trafalgar Street. 'It was just a half-hour before and after school,' Harry said. 'I used to go to Steinberg's shop at 53 Bridge Street to get the milk. Milk was delivered twice a day. There were no refrigerators in those days. Milk went off. I had a metal milk churn with two measures, a pint and a gill. Milk was only a penny a pint. It was nearly all water anyway. I can still remember what a struggle it was carrying that big heavy churn up Grafton Street, how glad I was when I got to the top. I was only ten. My wages were one and six a week. It was a small fortune. I took it home to mother. My pocket-money was threepence. Once I found a little yellow coin in the street. I didn't know what it was. I picked it up and took it home. It was a gold sovereign. You can imagine what a sensation it caused.'

Harry's only escape from the Leylands was his bicycle. He loved solitude. The countryside never failed to reward him. Here he discovered for himself the visions of Blake's *Songs of Innocence*, which he had heard marching into school, the clouds unfolding, and the chariots of fire, and as he free-wheeled down the steep Yorkshire hills he sang:

> *Piping down the valleys wild,*
> *Piping songs of pleasant glee,*
> *On a cloud I saw a child,*
> *And he laughing, said to me...*

To the amazement of his family, Harry liked nothing better than to be on his own, to wander alone all day and return refreshed. When he cycled beneath Lawnswood's avenue of sycamores, the wind gusted the dried leaves that danced round him in the autumn sun, snatching at his legs as he pedalled on in solitary exhilaration, as if swimming in a whirlpool. One type of sky especially impressed him. He liked its name, a mackerel sky. Due to some strange atmospheric disturbance, the clouds are occasionally fretted into fold upon fold of delicate regular pleats. This phenomenon always fascinated and disturbed him with ever increasing intensity as he got older.

Because Harry was too deaf to hear the teachers at school, Myer and Jeremy taught him at home. At school Harry was the star pupil of his year. When the Board Inspector came the teachers used to show off his prowess at mental arithmetic. They would bring him out to the front of the class and make him stand with his back to the blackboard. Then they would write a long string of figures on the board, turn him round and ask him to add them up. He would do this instantly. 'That was nothing,' Harry said later. 'Myer could do cube roots.'

While Harry was at school, a pen-pal system was introduced, and Harry exchanged letters with his American cousin, Ideal Sybil Cohen in Cleveland, Ohio. Like Harry, the Ideal Sybil Cohen was a grandchild of the Maggid of Yurberick, although Harry never knew the name of her mother. 'Ideal Sybil Cohen,' Harry said, '- at home we called her The Ideal Sybil Cohen - told me that when she showed my letters to people, they didn't believe I had written them. And even when I showed people in Leeds, they said, "You didn't write that." Later I heard that Sybil Cohen got married, and divorced and then she married the same man again after 18 years.'

In the summer of 1911 Harry took the scholarship examination at Gower Street school. It was the same 'Schol' all his brothers had won. Only a handful were awarded for the whole city of Leeds, and Gower Street School usually only got a couple a year. The first question was an easy one for him, arithmetic. The second was 'Explain why the time in London is different from that in New York.' The third was 'Explain why the day has different lengths at different times of the year.' The last question was an essay on a subject of your own choosing. Harry wrote about the sky. These questions confirmed Harry's lifelong and unshakeable view that education was about mathematics and astronomy.

Shortly after the school broke up for summer holidays, Harry was informed he had won a 'Schol.' Scholarship boys would now go on to secondary school, while the rest would return to Gower Street School for a final year, before being given the School Leaving Certificate which they needed so as to be legally entitled to work. By this time Jeremy was enjoying his first summer vacation from Leeds University. Jeremy and Harry decided to go out for a cycle ride. 'Apart from Myer I was closest to Jeremy,' said Harry. 'When I was poorly, and it was quite often, Myer was always busy working, and so it was Jeremy who used to take me to the infirmary. Only Myer, Jeremy and I went out cycling. After his first experience, John never tried again.

'One day Jeremy and I set off to Knaresborough, one of our favourite rides. Jeremy had just had a long argument with John over some translation. Anyway Jeremy had won. That was very rare, to get the better of John in an argument. Jeremy was cock-a-hoop over it. He kept repeating, " I've beaten John, I've beaten John in an argument."'

However, on that day, despite this initial elation, Jeremy soon became very quiet and pensive. Harry noticed but didn't ask. The cycle ride from Leeds took the two boys through the mildly undulating lower reaches of three dales. Leaving the Leylands, they crossed the Lady Beck at Sheepscar and set off up Roundhay Road. They pedalled the five miles uphill out of Airedale, and paused to catch their breath at the Dyneley Arms. A vast landscape spread before them. Jeremy pointed to an elegant country mansion. 'One day,' he said 'I'll have a house like that.'

From this point the road descended the Chevin to the valley floor, and then followed the river through Burley-in-Wharfedale to the Cow and Calf Rocks on Rombald's Moor. The two boys had remounted and were about to ride off. They took one last look at the high moorland horizon on their left, and Harry, putting his hand on Jeremy's handlebar, quoted:

Yet shall your ragged moor receive
The incomparable pomp of eve
And the cold glories of a winter's dawn
Upon those barren hills be drawn.

Jeremy nodded, and the two brothers freewheeled down into Wharfedale, bridged the River Wharfe at Wetherby, climbed once again, this time out of Wharfedale, and finally, with their ineffective brakes creaking, descended the steep bank into the town of Knaresborough in Nidderdale. Here, they stopped, and at the bridge over the River Nidd, Jeremy hired a boat, and Harry lay flat in the bottom as they punted leisurely down the river beneath the ruins of the castle, behind whose walls, fifteen feet thick, Richard II had been imprisoned and kept from sleeping by having trumpets blown in his ears all night. As it didn't kill him he was taken to Pontefract Castle, just south of Leeds, to be stabbed to death.

After punting for an hour, the boys walked on to the bank opposite the castle, where thick woods conceal the cave in which lived the prophetess, Mother Shipton, who prophesied the end of the world:

In nineteen hundred and eighty one
The world to an end will come.

By her cave, in near darkness, the boys came to the wishing well. Over this well is a huge rounded overhanging rock, worn smooth by the water which drips over it like a curtain. This water has the property of slowly turning to stone any objects kept in it, and in the curtain of water are to this day hung all kinds of things at various stages of transformation. They included gloves, socks, cups, teddy-bears and small dead rabbits. Harry put his hand in the ice-cold water to wish. 'Cha,' he said. 'It's cold. Cha.' Jeremy neither put his hand in, nor replied. He seemed very sad, and turned away from the scene, stepping out under a wooden sign inscribed with Mother Shipton's lines:

Beside this petrifying well,
I first drew breath, as records tell.

The brothers climbed the castle hill, and wandered through the narrow streets of the old town. Here and there as they turned, they would catch, between the houses or at the street ends, a glimpse of the wooded banks of the river far below them. They passed in front of an antique shop. '*Pauca sed Bona,*' said Jeremy, reading the sign. 'It's Latin. It means *Little but Good.*'

Jeremy caught a glimpse of his own face mirrored in the window against the dark interior of the shop. He stroked the stubble of his jet-black beard, already visible despite his morning shave. 'Well,' he said, 'it's permissible for a dark-haired man to look a little dingy towards the end of the day,' and Harry smiled at this elegant sample of the way he imagined English was spoken by men of quality. Already Jeremy was known in the Leylands as 'the dark gentleman.' No one called him *Zulu* any more. His rise was already foreseen.

When the brothers got home from Knaresborough, Jeremy waited impatiently for Myer to get back from work. 'Your trouser bottom's torn out,' he said to Harry.

'You didn't tell me when I was lying in the boat,' Harry said reproachfully. Jeremy once again turned away thoughtfully and didn't catch Harry's eye again.

Myer came home at nine and the three brothers finally sat together. Harry suddenly felt cold. 'We can't manage,' Myer said. 'It's no good.'

'Will you go to work?' Jeremy asked Harry. 'Myer and I've talked it over again and again. There's no way out. We've got to choose between you and John.' Myer and Jeremy looked helplessly at Harry.

'Yes,' said Harry, and that was the end of the matter.

'The school,' my father told me later, 'were horrified when I came back.'

'What are you doing here?' they asked. 'You should be at the High School.'

'Well, I've come back to school,' I said. 'I need my School Leaving Certificate and here I am.'

But by some bitter joke of Fate Harry was allowed to go to Leeds Central High School for one half day before being sent out to work. He was even allotted a desk. So he gained one peep at that strange astro-mathematical world of education which had always fascinated him and which was never to be his.

Escape from the Leylands

Harry's first full-time job was in 1912. He was thirteen. The family were too poor for him to have a barmitzvah. On his first day he was greeted by the boss: 'Well, have you got a thimble?'

As was the custom he started working for no wages as an apprentice learning how to use the tailor's shears and needle.

After six weeks his employer was sent to jail for raping his eight-year-old daughter. Harry moved on to the tailoring factory of Olbrecht and Olbrecht, where he worked next to Ringworm Hymie. Hymie would scratch under one armpit and say 'England scratches here,' then under the other one, 'Russia scratches there...' Then he would ease his jacket back off his shoulders and scrub it from side to side across his itching back and say, 'The whole world is turning round.'

His neighbour at the workbench pointed with reverence to one corner of the room, where a man was carrying out the most skilled process, shaping the collar and lapels. Gradually Harry learned all the steps.

The foreman, a white-haired old man of sixty called Greenberg, used to pick up the work and, spluttering with rage at the untidy stitches, he would say, 'People are dying everywhere. Only not here!'

Harry's brother Myer used to scoff at this self-important little man, and say, 'His soul is not a raisin.'

'I worked next to two men, called David Fryfish and Saucepan of Peas. There were six races in an afternoon,' Harry said. 'The first race began at half past two in the summer, half past twelve when the days were shorter. When it was half past two, they'd send the errand boy out to the nearest bookie. "What's won?" This sort of thing would go on over and over again right through the afternoon with appropriate expressions of disgust at the results.

'This feller Aby Passman had a pressing shop. He used to take in pressing. He pressed to the trade. He'd take in work from small master tailors who hadn't a presser of their own. Every half hour in the afternoon you'd see him. He'd come out of his shop door and look both ways, and then dart across North Street to Brunswick Street. His shop was opposite the bookmakers.

'There were half a dozen editions of the paper - one was sent out after each race. Every half hour they'd send out a new edition with the latest results. In the morning the men in the workshops used to consider the horses' performances on previous occasions, weighing up form, "Well, that's the form horse of the race." The only subject of conversation was gambling, either what bad luck they'd had at cards the night before or what horses they were going to back.'

Wages were not large, and Harry took them all home. Summary sackings were common. The foreman would get in a rage and shout, 'I'll throw you down the steps.' Often the masters were themselves in such difficulties they couldn't pay the wages. 'I'll pay you when I've been to the bank,' they'd say. Usually it was the race-course. Workers changed jobs often.

The Lancet had reported:

> *We entered a workshop which seemed to be crowded by very young girls; and thence to one where an effort was made to conceal the number of workers, and we found that there was no Factory Act notice paper on the wall, though many girls were employed on the premises.*

'You rushed the children out,' Harry said, 'when the inspector came. On one occasion, I was working in a bedroom shopky at the top of Villiers Terrace. When they heard the inspector was coming, they said, "Hop it," and when the inspector came in I was sitting at the table in the kitchen, meant to be having a bit of a meal, like one of the family. 'I remember hearing them say, "Grease him up." How much do you think an inspector was paid in those days? Ten bob would've been a lot to give him. They probably only gave him five bob.'

Like Myer, Harry became a lifetime socialist and was filled with admiration and pride when his older brother came through the shops collecting the union dues. 'We could only get work in the tailoring trade,' said Harry. 'All other jobs were closed to us. Apart from tailoring, if you saw a notice VACANCIES, it would say underneath JEWS NEED NOT APPLY.

'We wandered around for weeks with no work. When it came, Easter and Whitsun time it was, the seasonal rush in the trade, it was all night. When I was coming home one night along Bridge Street I saw three or four old greybeards holding a candle and reading a passage from a prayer book. I wouldn't have dared to disturb them. I asked a passer-by what they were doing. "It's the New Moon," I was told. Then I noticed there was a moon in the sky. Moon worship is very common in primitive religions.

'There were no apprenticeships in tailoring. No one was interested in training you. They started you off as an errand boy. They gave you what jobs were useful to them. And that's all. They'd keep you on menial tasks as long as they could. It's only when you got fed up and wanted a little more wages, or your father said, "What's going on here?" After all, there wasn't any distance between masters and men in those days. Not like now. They all knew each other, came over from *Der Hame* together, sat next to each other in synagogue. You taught yourself by watching. Now and again some kind-hearted feller might give you a tip. What to do. And so you did it.'

Myer and Harry worked and worked. With their combined earnings there was now enough money for the others to stay at school and go on to university. Jeremy completed his degree at Leeds University, and applied to go to Oxford. He was accepted, but he needed to find the matriculation fee of £2. No one in the family had such a sum of money. Finally, Myer managed to borrow it from Benny Goldman, the machinist who worked next to him at Cohen's. And so Jeremy was at last launched on his career.

'While he was at university,' Harry said, 'Jeremy used to go out camping with his fellow students on King Lane. They were mainly medical students. They were all skint. If they had a shilling between them it was a lot of money.'

Jeremy was impressed by his first close contact with Nature. 'While I was trying to sleep in the tent,' he told Harry, 'a bee hovered over my nose. I think it was trying to fertilise me.'

'At this time,' said Harry, 'Jeremy had started to associate with the wealthier section of Leeds Jewish society. He got a book on etiquette from the library. From it he discovered that if you have black or blue or grey clothes you mustn't wear brown shoes. In fact, it's a dreadful thing to be seen wearing brown shoes unless there's a positive reason for it. It was also a dreadful thing if you wore a made-up bow. You have to tie it yourself. That set him off trying to make a bow. Some of his wealthy friends had given him a bow tie, and he brought it home. He was desperate to learn how to make a bow according to the standards of the upper class. He asked me to try to tie it. We all tried, Myer as well. None of us could do it. I suppose later on in life he had a valet do it for him.'

One afternoon Jeremy had returned hurriedly from university and rushed upstairs to change for a visit to Alwoodley. Within a minute he was pounding downstairs again, purple with rage. 'Who's been wearing my white shirt?' he asked furiously, casting his eye angrily over the innocent roomful of younger brothers and sisters.

'It must have been Louis,' someone replied bashfully.

'It's ruined,' exploded Jeremy, 'All crumpled.'

Jeremy impatiently awaited Louis' return from work.

'Gerraway! It's not ruined,' Louis said contemptuously, 'All it needs is ironing - if that. What are you worried about? Do your friends wear new shirts every day?'

'We younger children were terrified of Jeremy,' Ralph told me later. 'You couldn't talk to him.'

The shirt row went on for some time, with increasing bitterness on both sides. Finally Jeremy stormed off up the hill to Alwoodley, and Louis left for his card club. And it was much later than Jeremy that Louis returned that night, added his jacket to the pile hung on the back of the door, and crept off to bed. But John returned even later, hung his coat up, and started to rummage through the pockets of the vast pile of brotherly coats on the door. Reaching Louis' pocket, John discovered a last remaining cigarette in a crumpled packet, took it, and lit up contentedly.

At breakfast it was Louis' turn to be indignant. 'My last cigarette!' he shouted across the table at John.

At 6 o'clock on the morning of the first Sunday in the August of 1912 Myer set out to take his younger brother Harry to see the source of the River Aire. It had been a cool night outside the city. Early morning mist hung over the fields. The rising sun picked out spiders' webs hung with shining dew drops. As the day warmed, the brothers cycled up through Otley and Ilkley and past Skipton Castle. Sandstone walls disappeared and were replaced by limestone. All around white walls snaking over the landscape joined and rejoined, dividing the hillsides into squares and diamonds and polygons of brilliant green sheep meadows, glistening in the sunlight. Meadow cranesbill opened

shining petals of a delicate powder blue, translucent as saucers of the finest porcelain. When they stopped by the roadside for their first sandwiches, laying their bicycles down and perching on a pile of stones, Myer pointed at a newly-shorn sheep. 'Shaved like a sheep,' he said laughing, as the skinny, black-faced source of Leeds' wealth took a few delicate steps up a rocky slope.

After cycling through Settle, Myer and Harry crossed the River Ribble at Giggleswick and struggled up Buckhaw Brow by the Ebbing and Flowing Well. Their route took them over Buckden Pike and Buttertubs Pass to Keld and Muker in remote Upper Swaledale where from the heights of Castle Bolton they were able to gaze over lonely Semerwater and the Aysgarth Falls. In the afternoon they cycled into Malham. 'Now,' said Myer, 'I'll take you to see the famous Gordale Scar.'

Leaning their bikes against the dry-stone walls, the two brothers climbed a stile and followed the crystal clear water of the river upwards over a pavement of glistening white limestone slabs. Gradually the valley swung to the right, narrowing and deepening all the time until a sudden further right turn took them into a narrow cleft in the rock, so narrow that to stay on the path by the river bank they had to crawl cautiously along, bent double to prevent bumping their heads on the overhanging cliff. Here the polished limestone flags of the path were wet and slippery with spray and as they progressed, the brothers held unsteadily on to each other to avoid slipping into the river with which they shared the ever narrowing space and the river, which had seemed so peaceful and jolly further back, now churned powerful and menacingly in a deep cauldron. Then, suddenly they found themselves able to stand up

again. Bracing their shoulders back with relief and looking around they saw that they had entered a deep echoing chamber which had been invisible both to and from the world outside, sealed off in sound and over-mounted by precipitous walls encircling high above a tiny patch of sky. Speech was impossible. The air was filled with the roar of crashing water and all around, stretching high above their heads, the spray forever trickling down the rocky walls nourished a hanging emerald garden of fern-like fronds and flowers. Here, the path they had been following ended blindly in a pile of fallen rock, stones and tiny pebbles, all white and all polished smooth by the rushing waters under a high rocky promontory which, like a magic wizard's wand, turned the river into a single slender shining pillar of water. In the narrow space before it, their faces bathed in the fine misty spray, the brothers stood a long time in silence, over-awed, as if in a Holy of Holies, where the worshipper may fancy that if he put out his arms he could encircle that entire slender column of virgin crystal, holding in momentary, statuesque embrace the endless quivering mother of the River Aire.

Then, retracing their careful steps under the overhang that guarded the entrance to the chamber, the brothers scrambled up the grassy slopes on to a desolate, marshy plateau, and finally gazed over the shallow, reed-fringed mountain lake called Malham Tarn. All around on empty, purple moorsides, black-faced sheep grazed as if they had grown out of the ground. There was not another human being in the whole vast landscape. Limestone rocks encrusted with lichen stuck like teeth out of the meadows, and above them rose the pile of crags called Parson's Pulpit.

For years the source of the River Aire had been a mystery. It was only after putting dyes into the water it was confirmed that this lake is the source of the stream that comes out in Gordale Scar. 'And now,' said Myer proudly, 'I'll show you a river disappearing into the ground.' And silently from the Tarn they followed the course of the River Aire to where it trickles out in a dry bed. Here the brothers stayed for a while, crouching here and there on the white boulders, putting their ears to the ground and trying to imagine the disappearing waters, like Alph the Sacred River, tunnelling through hidden limestone caverns measureless to man, down to Leeds. Still crouching close to the ground Harry raised his head and glanced shyly around, but he couldn't hear the river nor the wind sighing in the encircling hills nor the *peewit* of the peewits nor the screeching of the gulls as they wheeled over the ripples of the lonely mountain lake.

Towards evening as the weary brothers gratefully free-wheeled down the winding roads, the dark shadow of the mountain fell across the upland moors. The narrow stream-filled gullies had long been in twilight, and as the sun fell low over the moor its final, almost horizontal rays picked out only the bobbing wispy heads of the cotton grass which glinted eerily, as

if dancing over the acid peat mosses, like a cloud of tiny trolls from a long-gone Nordic past when Vikings first rowed their war boats up the Yorkshire rivers and gave these Dales their name.

Jeremy's career was an unbroken series of academic successes. He got a first class degree in Greek from Leeds University, and then won an entrance scholarship to Pembroke College, Oxford to study 'Greats' - Latin and Greek - the language, literature, history and philosophy of their civilisations, and the inspiration of the glorious British Empire.

Pembroke College, Oxford

The family had only just been introduced to the new Gillette safety razors. Jeremy had one to take to Oxford; the rest shaved with the other. 'What a boon and a blessing it is,' he said as he packed his safety razor, 'what a wonderful invention!' Jeremy shaved himself especially carefully on the day he left. Harry, not yet needing to shave, stood at his elbow watching. 'Like scorching the hairs of a hen,' Jeremy said, laughing. He was referring to the last stages in the ritual purification of a chicken.

On vacation from Oxford, Jeremy brought the family three samples of the wonders of the outer world. He took the first out of his suitcase. It was a bag of chocolate biscuits. The family had never seen anything like it. Jeremy then sat down at the table. 'I'll show you how they eat bread in Oxford,' he said. Then he cut a slice of bread, spread butter on it and to Myer's horror, put jam on top of that. The younger brothers were delighted with the discovery. Butter and jam together was the second wonder.

Jeremy sat back, preparing his third revelation. And much though his first two had appealed to his father Maishy Treacle's sweet tooth, the third far excelled them. 'Sit down,' commanded Jeremy. 'I'll teach you a new game. It's called bridge. They play it in Oxford.'

'We never heard of such things,' said Harry. 'Jeremy was showing us how people lived. Father took to the new card game like a duck to water. He must have been one of the most extraordinary card players that ever lived. Father and Myer - what a pair!'

But on this and every future visit, the first thing Jeremy did when he got home was to sit at the kitchen table with Myer and one by one ask about each of the children in turn. How were they getting on at school? What were their interests? What did Myer think about their prospects? The two brothers never rushed this conference. It could go on well into the night. No detail was too small to be considered. After they had gone over each child Jeremy would carefully ask Myer's opinion, offer his own advice, and again check what Myer thought of that. Overnight each ruminated alone on this conversation, and in the morning they again went over all the points together.

Jeremy was to get a Double First in Ancient History and Philosophy from Oxford, where he won the John Locke Scholarship, the University's major prize in Moral Philosophy. He was beginning to make quite a name for himself and was highly indignant when he received a begging letter from one of his gambling cousins. What made him most angry was that the envelope was backed 'H.M. Prison' and sat visible to all in his mail-box in the porter's lodge in Pembroke College.

Meanwhile Leeds, restless as ever, was beginning to reconstruct itself. A tide of demolition swept from the city centre. The owners of the demolished houses were compensated for their lost property at what was estimated to be their value. Since the houses were almost all the same size, compensation was assessed at one pound per house. And with their houses, the older generation of immigrants was also beginning to disappear. In addition to setting up the Greenhorns' Synagogue, Maishy Goodman had been back to Lithuania, married again, this time to his orphan cousin, raised a family of ten children, travelled to Jerusalem, set up Leeds' first Zionist organisation in Brunswick Street, acquired a pub in Holbeck called the Moulder's Arms, and a cinema called The Grosvenor in Oatland Road.

His house had been one of the first to have electric light and a telephone. He admired Disraeli and the Conservative Party, and was proud to wear a primrose. His restlessness was not satisfied by his frequent chess games at the Young Men's Club of the Jewish Institute in Albert Grove. He had pleasant memories of South Africa where he had picked up the Boer War uniform orders that made his fortune. Now he planned to emigrate there and allow his lungs to retire in its gentler climate. But Fate intervened and in 1914, at the age of 69 and still full of vigour the great pioneer had a fatal road accident in Leeds.

It was while the family lived in Trafalgar Street that my grandfather had a good idea. Since he had always lost at gambling, why not join the winning side? Let others lose to him. 'There was a bookmaker,' said Harry, 'called Harry Sutcliffe. His real name was Suckall. He was the founder of the Lonsdale Club of which father later became president. He'd come over from Russia together with father. When Sutcliffe died in 1920 he left half a million. Well, Father tried to follow his example and be a bookie. Just once. It was at Doncaster on Saint Leger Day. During the race for the Leger he'd been taking a lot of bets. Just before the off a man rushed up to him and put £300 on the last shout, a horse called Caligula at a hundred to eight, and it took every ha'penny out of father's bag to pay him. Father was just unlucky.'

After this Maurice decided to start a gambling house at home. An illegal club was set up. His wife Ada, deeply upset by the whole thing, had to stand at the door with a baby in her arms acting as a dog-out for the police. Myer and Jeremy were so horrified that more than 60 years later they still couldn't bear even to mention this episode. Only once by persistent questioning I got it out of Myer. 'Who told you that?' he said furiously. 'How do you know about it? I never told you,' and fell silent for a long time. Finally, uttering a long, theatrical sigh, he said 'Yes, Geoff, it's true. It wasn't much, one night a week it used to be, one night a week. So we had something to pay the rent. That's all. And buy a bit o' food.'

Poor Myer relived it in his mind as he recounted this to me later. He was in a terrible dilemma. His plan for the family had involved education, years of study and finally an entry into the professions, law, medicine, government. His brothers were to be respected men, contributors to the rich life of the society they lived in. And here was his father, the begetter of the family, indulging in a disgusting, illegal vice, whose discovery would ruin all Myer's plans, and disgrace the family forever.

Myer was prepared to work as hard as he could, to sacrifice himself totally, and give everything to his plan. But obviously his earnings were not enough. The family his father had begot was just too large for Myer to keep, especially with his father and Louis' perpetual gambling losses. Myer had already sacrificed the education of his deaf brother Harry to supplement the family's earning power. Now he simply could not refuse to accept the extra income from the gambling house even if it was just to 'pay the rent and buy a bit o' food.'

And naturally his father would want to make more than that if he could. The less successful the gambling den, the more his father would gamble. The more successful it was, the less his father would be prepared to abandon it.

All Myer could do was to try to work so hard at tailoring that in the end his income, supplemented by Harry's, would be enough to keep the family. It must have seemed a forlorn hope. The family were restricted to living in the half-underground cellar-kitchen. The upstairs rooms were converted into a gambling saloon where Faro was played, and the children attempting to study or sleep were disturbed by the noise of the card players gambling loudly in Yiddish right over their heads.

At this time Louis got married and went to live with his wife's family. That at least gave Myer a little break, reducing the family costs he had to find. Both Louis and his wife now worked for a time next to Myer at Pierce's tailoring factory. Then suddenly the First World War was upon the family, and it brought them prosperity. The army ordered khaki, as much as could be made. Tailoring boomed in Leeds. Overtime was continuous, and Myer seized the chance. By working overnight he managed to scrape together enough to buy himself a ramshackle old sewing machine, 'a right old contraption,' he called it, and was able to start to take in work at home.

Given this slight respite the combined indignation of Myer and Jeremy finally forced their father to abandon his gambling house in Trafalgar Street. With one great leap forward the family finally crossed North

Street, the western frontier of the Leylands. They left the Leylands, this time never to return.

The family usually looked back on the gambling episode with shame and disgust. As a business venture it seemed so unlikely to have succeeded. Whatever Maurice gained by others' gambling in his house he at once went out and lost by his own gambling on horses. But strangely it was my father who once put the other view: 'Pity he wasn't left to his own devices. With his knowledge of gambling he may have become a millionaire casino-owner. Many did.'

The Mackerel Sky

The Raisman family had long traditions of non-violence. When I was too ebullient as a schoolboy my father would say, 'Enough of this horseplay. Do not as other children do, who on the slightest grounds, will imitate the kangaroo, with wild, unmeaning bounds!'

'A noise annoys,' Myer used to say. Nonetheless, Myer told me, the family did have the distinction of producing two of the Leylands boy heroes. Louis, before he became fully occupied with gambling, had taken part in one of the night-time retaliatory excursions across Regent Street into the wild Irish district of Burmantofts. He didn't get far. When his friends brought him home on a shutter they tried to reassure his mother. 'Don't worry,' they said, illogically 'the other feller's in hospital.'

At this point in Myer's story I interrupted: 'What's a shutter?' I asked, imagining it must be some kind of medical instrument.

Myer tried to explain this unfamiliar object to me, and paused. I pressed him to continue with his story, and learned that the second of our family heroes was Mad Jack. Jack was the third of the middle three Raisman brothers. Like his grandfather Hoshy and his oldest brother Louis, Jack was a short, thick-set, broad-shouldered creature. He had rather straight, bristly hair and a fierce temper. 'He shared with John,' said my father 'the prize for being the most slovenly and tramp-like of the brothers.'

During one of his childhood escapades Mad Jack's physique was modified by a fall from the roof of a half-finished synagogue building in Upper Templar Street. He too was brought home on a shutter. Mismanagement of a broken collar bone added a further, asymmetrical twist to his already hunched, squat frame. This contraction did not diminish his strength, nor abate his ferocity. He began to have an alarming resemblance to Quasimodo, the hunchback of Notre Dame, and the gentile kids skirmishing in the Leylands streets gave him a wide berth. Later, when the family moved out of the Leylands, to a more genteel area, the adolescent Jack positively terrorised the neighbourhood.

Traditionally, the Russian peasants regarded the village lunatic as sacred. Wild and uncontrollable children in the Leylands had a similarly high status. 'His brain was too big for his body,' people used to say. 'Genius,' said Myer 'is akin to madness.'

114

In the family plan John was trained as a solicitor, my deaf father designated to be a worker ant, and mad Jack was to be a doctor. Doctors were highly respected in the Leylands. The first Jewish doctor in Leeds was the son of Herman Friend, the pioneer of the divisional system of tailoring. Friend's son had a surgery in Chapeltown Road, and although he had a wealthy clientele, he also gave his services free to any Leylander who could not pay. Jack, however, was indifferent to all this possible honour. He always hankered after the Latin and Greek his older brothers Jeremy and John used to study together and discuss over breakfast, and he never wanted to be a medical student.

'I don't want to be a doctor,' Jack said. 'I'm no good at practical things, and I don't like chemistry and physics. I don't understand them.' But before Jack could start on his medical course, warlike events far exceeding his exploits took a hand in the proceedings.

When the family moved out of the Leylands they lived on the side of a little hill. Camp Road, its glory now faded, was once one of Leeds' first class streets. It was called Camp Road because it led to an ugly stone building on the crest of the hill. This was Carlton Barracks, in appearance something of an architectural hybrid. The sprawling lower part resembled a stable, and the taller, upper end, with its little barred windows resembled a prison. Between these two incongruous parts, was

Carlton Barracks

115

a squat stone gateway of the type one might expect at an abattoir.

The Jewish streets didn't quite reach to Carlton Barracks. Around it, from Reuben Street onwards, was a cluster of narrow streets where Leylands children didn't go. When the family moved to Villiers Terrace his father pointed up at this area and said to Harry 'That's Little London.' It sounded impressive, quite a social step up. Maurice didn't imagine that soon four of his sons would be trudging up the street on to which the gateway of Carlton Barracks opened, nor how many of the Leylanders would be swallowed up by it.

In the heat of August 1914, the Grand Duke Nikolai Nikolaievich, Commander-in-Chief of the Russian Army, ordered the attack on Germany. The Russian High Command chose the very roads which the Leylanders had used when they crept so fearfully out of Russia. Fourteen divisions of the Russian First Army crossed the river Niemen at Kovno, rolled up the high road through Marienpol and Shakee, and flung themselves at the German Eighth Army which was stationed at Gumbinnen, the first German town across the frontier. The German resistance broke, and next day General Von Prittwitz ordered a retreat. From all sides Russian soldiers poured into East Prussia.

'At that time I was working with Myer at Hipps,' Harry said. 'The August Bank Holiday week of 1914 was very fine weather. Myer and I cycled to Bridlington for a holiday. It was 64 miles from Leeds. I'd have been fifteen. I'd already been working for some years. On the way, we stopped at York. There's a ruined abbey there, and underneath it is a sort of cellar they call an undercroft. It's very ancient, much more than the abbey itself. It's said to go back to Roman times. In it I noticed a number of tombstones with the letters TTSL on them. Later I found out it was Latin. They used to put it on the grave of a child. It means *Terra tibi sit laevis - May the earth lie lightly on thee*.

'After York it was a doddle across the Plain of York and through the avenue of pollarded willows between the villages of Pocklington and Warter. Then we had to climb Garrowby Hill to Fridaythorpe on the Yorkshire Wolds. From here the road dips down into the Hole of Horcum, and then goes on to Whitby. Whitby is the home of Captain Cook, the Pacific explorer on whose voyages they discovered the prevention of scurvy. At Whitby the ruins of St Mary's Abbey look down over the little harbour, where we saw the ships of the Icelandic fishing fleet moored in the mouth of the river Esk, and the shops here have bits of jewellery and trinkets made of a local shiny black semi-precious stone, called jet. After climbing out of Whitby, we struggled over Sleights and Ravenscar to Scarborough with its castle jutting far out into the North Sea.

'On the first day in Bridlington we walked out to a little place called Danes Dyke, and then seven miles on to Flamborough Head, and went up the lighthouse there. The lighthouse keeper told us the light could be seen eighty miles out to sea. It's a simple matter to verify. You can calculate it easily enough.

'I came back on the Tuesday. Myer stayed for the rest of the week. And all along the roadside on the way back I kept seeing notices stuck on all the telegraph poles calling up the reservists.'

Louis enlisted as an engineer, Harry was called up as a private, but John, with his university degree, was enlisted in an officers' training unit, where he instantly showed convincing signs of insanity. Myer, as the sole breadwinner for the family, was exempted.

The average life span of enlisted soldiers was not long, and in that pressing time official humanitarian considerations were few. However, to ensure that any mortal remains were not exposed to inappropriate funeral rites the enlisted men had to fill in a form showing their religion. *None* or *Atheist* were not acceptable states for sending people to the next world, and such candidates were automatically registered as 'Anglican.' To avoid this John filled in his religion as *Tychist*. As a devoted gambler he explained he was a worshipper of Tyche, the ancient Greek goddess of Chance.

Shown to his new quarters, a tent, John immediately asked where he could find a shoe horn and a clothes hanger, and the next day he turned up on parade in carpet slippers. During his first drill he insisted on breaking ranks and picking up scraps of litter while meant to be standing stiffly at attention.

Due to military planning, the Leylanders were largely kept together in War, and a more unsoldierly regiment can rarely have been raised. Harry was sent to Blackpool where it turned out that Moshy's son Harry, inheritor of the now failing matsy business, lived. This Harry's wife eased my father's passage into the army. 'Don't eat the army pig food,' she said. 'Come to our house whenever you want, and have a chicken dinner.'

Sharing the same tent, Harry met his first Scotsman, a very friendly youth of the same age, who, by dint of constant repetition, taught Harry his first words of Scottish. To Harry's ears they seemed to be, "*A war'n gear sell up tither poleys*" (Away and give yourself up to the police.) For some time after he finally learned to repeat this phrase Harry took it to be the Gaelic equivalent of 'Good Morning.'

My father's first night under canvas was not a long one. A gust of wind blew his tent off the cliffs at Blackpool and far out to sea. The recruits were drilled by fierce drill sergeants who sought to make them warlike. Harry's deafness spared him the sergeant's obscenities but made marching under orders a problem. One day he experienced a feeling of solitude as he marched. The rest of his platoon had

Harry

A more unsoldierly regiment can rarely have been raised

turned right. Clearly further training was a waste of the army's time. So Harry was consigned to the medical corps as an orderly, and sent out at once to the front line in France. In his pocket was a little book of Thomas Hood's poems that Myer had given him as a leaving present. His favourite was *The Song of a Shirt:*

> *With fingers weary and worn*
> *With eyelids heavy and red,*
> *A woman sat, in unwomanly rags,*
> *Plying her needle and thread.*

'My first job was as an orderly in charge of a ward of fifty men,' Harry said. 'They were a Gloucester Regiment sent back to France from Salonica. They all had dysentery. There was no effective treatment. I don't remember a single one of them surviving. Most of the time I was on my own with them. There was nothing I could do for them. They were a pitiful sight to see. When they started hiccupping that was the beginning of the end. The doctor used to come round once a day and tell me to wash my hands very carefully.'

Meanwhile, Flanders was producing its own casualties. After each battle the flag of truce was raised, the Royal Engineers removed the pieces that didn't move, and Harry those that did. One night Harry was assisting a major in a post-mortem on a suspected case of meningitis. Harry failed to hear an order to move the lantern he was holding, and the major ordered his immediate arrest and court-martial. Failure to obey an order in the front line meant death. Fortunately, Harry was examined at his court martial by a surgeon who was in fact a specialist from Leeds. 'This man can't hear,' he declared.

'Actually,' Harry said later, 'my deafness was an advantage. The shellfire never bothered me very much, because I could hardly hear it. I once slept through an air raid. They told me in the morning that the enemy'd dropped 150 bombs and I didn't even wake up. Even when I was under very heavy shellfire it didn't bother me much. At that time, however big a shell was, if you lay flat on the ground you were all right unless it actually fell on you. Even if the shell falls next to you it won't hurt you. That's why so many people survived.

'People used to tell me they could hear the shells coming. What happens is that the nose of the shell screws off, and it screams. I couldn't hear it, but they told me they could hear it scream as it came. The shells came over day and night. They never stopped. If the nose didn't come off the shell didn't explode. It was a dud. I've never heard one scream, but they assured me they could hear it miles away. They used to grab my arm and say, "There's one coming. Get down!"

'They'd developed these weapons. They're terrible. I don't know how anybody lives against these weapons. Machine guns: a great belt of bullets. They'd feed the belt into the gun. It fired dozens a minute: Ack, ack, ack ... At night we could see the flashes of gunfire all along the horizon, a constant line of flashes where the front line was. And different kinds of bangs, some guns made one kind of noise, some another.

'There was a gun called a Big Bertha. It was a German invention, made by Krupp's Ironworks, and it fired the biggest shell yet known. One came over about every half hour. It was an inefficient kind of a thing. It fired three or four shells and that was it. It sort of blew itself up. It damaged itself every time it fired, and had to go back to the factory for repair. So after three or four shells you knew that was it.

'One thing used to surprise me about these big shells. Where one fell it used to make a hole in the ground, so big that you could sink a house in it, a big house. So a shell would fall, say, on an open field. During the night the hole would fill with water, so deep you would drown if you fell in it. And in the morning the water would be full of frogs, big frogs, jumping about. I saw it often and I never understood it. Where did they all come from? A great big hole would fill with water and the frogs. It always surprised me.

'I was stationed for a while at Etaples on the coast. Eeltaps we called it. It was well behind the lines. For the first time in weeks I took my singlet off. It was brown with lice. You had to hold it down to stop it running away. Soldiers used to take their singlets off, pick off the lice, and put them back on.

'They'd formed the Women's Auxiliary Army Corps to help relieve the soldiers of some of their duties. We were under strict orders that no soldier was to go near them. I was one of the guards that was meant to keep the soldiers off, and report any that did get in. Despite all their precautions, however, they kept having to send the girls back to England with little souvenirs. A great many of them that came in ones went back in twos.

'The army soon posted me back to the front. Now I wasn't allowed to tell anyone where I was.' So when Harry wrote home in the censored mail he said that the place where he was stationed reminded him of the river at home. Myer and his mother, anxiously searching the map of France realized that he was at Aire-sur-la-Lys, just behind the front line. 'We live,' wrote Harry 'in a stone building, a former prison. It has a row of four stone cells hewn out of rock, and the bed I sleep on is stone. There's no light in the cells. They open on to a little yard. We use it as a cookhouse, but I imagine that the little cubby-hole where I sleep was formerly a cell where the condemned men waited for their execution in the courtyard.'

The building was the fifteenth century *Manoir de Criminil*. It and everything old in France was, for the impressionable Leylands boy, full of strange imaginings and the menace of ancient evils.

In the Middle Ages the northern French port of Calais had been for two hundred years in English hands. At that time, the town was defended from recapture by a chain of forts on the surrounding ring of low hills. Because of these low hills no major river can get to the sea at Calais. The River Lys arises near the town of St. Pol, just inland to this ring of hills, and flows hopefully north towards Calais. Encountering the hills it bends eastwards, wending its way sleepily across froggy pastures in its search for the sea. Soon it passes through the town of Aire, where the tall brick walls of the houses hem it closely on either side as it runs under the main street from the market place to the Collegiate Church of St. Peter. Here it looks very much like the Lady Beck running under the walls of the Templar Street Fortress in the Leylands, and if Harry had been able to understand the local dialect he would probably have been surprised to find that the simple people of Flanders used the same word, *becque*, to describe the innumerable little water courses that meander in every conceivable direction across their flat land.

Inconvenienced by the absence of navigable waterways from Paris to the port at Calais, the French had long ago constructed a canal, the Canal du Nord, which went from the River Somme in the south, northwards through the coastal range of hills to Calais. This canal crossed the River Lys at Aire, and in the Middle Ages the town had clearly been important. The huge black stone building of St Peter's with its massive square tower in the decorated Gothic style looks, even without its spire, more like a cathedral than the church of a little country town. St Peter's was the centre of the famous pilgrimage to the miracle-working statue of Our Lady of the Breadbasket. The statue is carved from a single oak trunk, and the Airois call it the Black Virgin. They call the Infant Jesus 'the imprudent' because of the way the child is shown in the act of bursting forth from its mother's arms. In one hand the child holds a wooden ball, which the sculptor intended to represent the orb of the world but which the villagers consider to be a loaf of bread.

'Almost every day,' wrote Harry, 'I go into the town. There's a church that fills me with horror every time I pass it. I associate it with a kind of dream I have. First I have to tell you one of the pleasant little habits of the Spanish Inquisition... But not now. Whenever I pass the church this particular little dream always comes into my mind. It has such a forbidding aspect, this dark, blank wall. I go by the side of it. I've never been inside the church.' And so he never saw the miracle-working statue of Our Lady of the Breadbasket.

'In town,' he went on 'there's an estaminet, a café, called *Le Chat Botté* - the Cat in Boots. You can get egg and chips - *deux oeufs pomfritz*. There's a canal, just like the Lady Beck at home. I have the job of carrying sacks of coal on my back across the bridge. It's terrifying as the planks of wood go up and down. I think it's called the *La Bassée Canal*. It was said that, in one battle further up the line, it ran red with blood.'

From Aire the Lys enters a wide flat plain. Innumerable sluggish streams, covered with green pond-weed infiltrate the marshy pastures and on the left bank is a dense and boggy wood, the *Forêt de la Nieppe*, where the Lys itself splits into two, one stream finding its way through the heart of the forest before rejoining the main river again at the next town of Merville. And from Merville the Lys flows on to Armentières, where it peacefully crossed the front line into German occupied territory, skirted the enemy-held city of Lille, and meandered on through Belgium.

One morning, solitary as usual, Harry took a walk into the flat Flanders countryside. It was a fine day as he left the town by the rue du Halage (the Street of Barge-Towing). Along the street, the housewives in their black skirts and black stockings stood in the doorways, one hand leaning on the doorpost, chatting to their neighbours or merely watching the world go by. They smiled maternally at the sixteen-year-old English soldier boy walking self-consciously by in his webbing gaiters.

Crossing the high bridge over the Canal de Neuffosse, Harry left the town. He felt more at ease on the empty tree-lined lane leading from Aire through the Nieppe Forest to the neighbouring village of Merville. Beside the road, at almost every field path, were little shrines of the Sacred Heart. At regular intervals he passed farms, with their red roof tiles sloping almost down to the ground, and supported or half-supported by twisted tree trunks roughly fashioned into pillars.

Soon Harry's walk took him into the edge of the forest. The trees were still well-spaced here. Harry noticed with a shudder that there was a mackerel sky. The old feeling of part-pleasure, part-fear, a sense of contact with a not unfriendly supernatural came over him strongly. It became almost insupportably strong and then suddenly he saw himself, a small furry animal, like a squirrel, half-afraid, at the mouth of a cave on a hillside. He could see his paws holding the edge of the cave. In front of the cave was a field of high grass with the wind billowing it. Instantly he recognised that its surface was the mackerel sky. That was what it had represented all along. He realized that at last the vision was complete. Glancing behind he could see his great furry tail, and he was aware of a shadowy being behind the dark entrance of the cave. He knew it was his mother, reassuring him to go on down the hillside. Harry later interpreted this as an evolutionary memory, recalling his past existence.

At this moment a tremendous German artillery barrage started. Such barrages were common. They went on, sometimes for several days, before one side or the other decided to mount an infantry charge out of the trenches. Harry flung himself into the ditch and waited. There was nothing else to be done. Fortunately, this was a short barrage. When it was over he marvelled at the great holes where the once tall trees had stood, and resumed his country walk, alone down the road. He was always an acute observer of Nature. But from that day on, whenever he saw a mackerel sky it caused him no sense of unease, only a great peace.

Hymy Pessakovitch, the one who had shared John's desk at school, was shot and taken prisoner. 'I was in the West Yorkshire Regiment - The Prince of Wales' *Own* Regiment,' he said, with a special intonation on the word *own*. We were in trenches at the Somme. The Germans were just sending shells over. There were no protection. You'd just about enough time to say *Shema Yisroel*. You were lucky that you came out alive.

'They took us out on a midnight raid. It was the Battle of the Somme. It was too dark to see anything. They got us out of the trenches and told us to quick-fire. Well, the enemy had machine guns. They just mowed us down. My best friend was killed just beside me. He'd been with me all through the war. They lived in the next house. They were nearly all done in. I were shot in the shoulder and the ribs - two machine gun bullets. I were laid there for dead, just wondering how long it would be before I passed out for good. Then I heard someone

Hymy Pessakovitch

moving about on the top. I had an idea they would be Germans. I called out in Yiddish. "Help me, help me!" I could understand German. I heard them say "We'll be back soon," and they went away. After a short while I heard them coming. They said "Where are you? Where are you?"

'After a while they managed to find me. Two of them came. They asked me where I was wounded. Between them they managed to get me on my feet. "Don't worry, dear brother, we'll see you well buried."

'The irony of it - here's the enemy trying to kill me, and here they are trying to save my life!

'They took me to a German military hospital. I were the only Englishman. I could speak German. I could speak to them. I was surrounded by Germans. The sister could speak English. She called me Tommy. She thought all the English were called Tommy. In England I was reported "Missing, believed killed." My people didn't know if I were alive or dead. And it were three months before I could get a postcard home from Hanover. My mother said it was as though I was born again.

'The Germans weren't friendly, but they didn't ill-treat me. When my wounds started to heal they transferred me to prisoner-of-war camp. The first place was Hamelin. That's where the Pied Piper came from. There's the river Weser. The Pied Piper was supposed to have drowned all the rats in the Weser. Don't you believe it. We used to try to smoke them out. The Germans used to try to drown them. They blocked up one end of the drains and let water into the other.'

The Royal Army Medical Corps, having trained Harry as a medical orderly, decided to make him a jailer. A detachment of Uhlans had been taken prisoner. These were the crack cavalry soldiers of the Prussian army, specially selected for their size, martial bearing and ferocity. To improve their appearance they had in the past worn corsets. Uhlans were meant to symbolize the peak of German militarism, the savage Huns who were to strike terror into the Kaiser's foes. Harry had never been trained in the use of arms. 'They were the pride of the German Army,' he said. 'None of them was under six feet tall. They were in field grey uniforms.'

'Didn't they try to escape?' I asked in amazement.

'Escape?' he said. 'They were young teenage lads like me. Only too glad to be out of the fighting. They weren't in any shelter - just in a barbed-wire fencing. They could have got out of it easily if they'd wanted to. I was the night-watch. Just me and them. Any one of them could have finished me off easily. When it came to night-time they said, "*Gae shloffen* (Go to sleep)." I could understand that much. I was happy to get some sleep. They hadn't the slightest intention of escaping. Where could they have gone? Back to the trenches? And they would have had to cross the British lines. They were quite safe where they were.'

The many exploits of the Leylanders in the Great War could fill a book and, indeed, five years after the end of the war W.H. Scott wrote a stirring account of Leeds' contribution to the war, a Book of Remembrance:

> *The first great day in the history of the Leeds Rifles after their arrival in Flanders was May 5th, when the Seventh Battalion went into the trenches for the first time...*

'I can remember,' said Celia Narunsky (Harry's future wife), 'when we went to see my father off at Leeds Station. I remember my mother holding this baby. It was Teddy. And giving him to my father. This baby, I remember him holding the baby.'

> *One may imagine (the book continued) the pride of the Leeds Riflemen when they found they were to relieve so magnificent a unit of the Old Contemptibles as the Second Scots Guards.*

'In the morning,' Harry said, 'they used to send someone up in an observation balloon. They could see over the enemy trenches and send back information. You had to volunteer for it. They didn't stand a chance. The balloon was shot down after a few minutes. I had to attend to the casualties. They never survived. Every single bone in their bodies was broken by the fall.'

The main technique of trench warfare was to send waves of men out of the trenches so suddenly that the enemy could not shoot them all down quickly enough. Unfortunately, machine-gun technology was so advanced that, even stimulated by patriotic poetry, the warring motherlands could not produce enough young men quickly enough. There was a continual demand for more men.

One by one, as the Raisman brothers became old enough, they were enlisted. In 1915, early in the war, Jeremy had just qualified from

Oxford. He made two attempts to enlist, but was rejected each time because of his short-sightedness.

'While Jeremy was at Oxford,' Harry said, 'he had an affair with Blanche, cousin Jinny's second daughter. She was by no means a beauty. Afterwards she asked me to marry her.

'Actually it was very difficult for Jeremy to stay at Oxford in those days, even though he supplemented his allowance by his winnings at bridge. Myer hadn't enough to send anything to Jeremy. So after the first term, Jeremy was threatening to leave. You had to live in college, and you had to eat in. When the bill came he couldn't pay it. He was at his wits' end about it. So he went to the Master and told him he was going to leave. So the Master asked him, "Why?"

'So he told him, "It's impossible for me to stay here. I can't pay the bills."

'Well, he was the college's star pupil. So the Master said, "Never mind the financial aspect. I'll attend to that. You stay."

'Jeremy's tutor impressed on him, "For a man in your position the best thing is the Indian Civil Service. That offers the greatest prospects. If you've passed the Civil Service Exam, whatever they offer you in the Civil Service, take it. With your qualities you'll be a great success there." It was his tutor that persuaded him to enter the Indian Civil Service.'

After completing his degree, Jeremy entered a course at the Indian Institute in Oxford. 'When they were appointed,' Harry went on, 'they'd got to learn to ride a horse and they'd got to learn to speak a language called Urdu. Urdu is a sort of mixture of one thing and another. It became the official language of the British Government in India. They were given twelve months to learn that. They didn't go out for twelve months. They stayed twelve months in England to learn Urdu and practise horse-riding and other things like that. It seems that the Indian native was greatly impressed by a man riding a horse, and if a government official didn't ride a horse it was sort of debasing the government.'

Although Jeremy could not enlist for the war in France, he was expecting Myer to be called up, and Jeremy's last action before leaving was to raise a loan which was to encumber his salary for a long time to come. With the considerable sum of money he went to Zermansky's jewellery shop and bought a gold cigarette case. He gave it to Myer.

The Indian Institute in Oxford

The little cigarette case had a simple striped decoration. Slender and smooth, it nestled in the palm, its hinge perfectly rounded off so as to fit into the contour of the case. Even after sixty years, the case, highly polished by continuous use, sprang open at the touch of a little bead of sapphire, and snapped shut, with a satisfying click, and with the same ease that its maker had so carefully built into its design. It slipped easily into a left waistcoat pocket. These cigarette cases were given as good-luck keepsakes to soldiers about to leave for the front. If a bullet was directed towards the heart of the wearer they would stop it.

In fact, Myer's poor sight and the fact that a family of ten depended on his income, spared him being conscripted. 'There was a feller called Sam Lublinsky,' said Harry. 'Myer and I both knew him well. We were the same age. I'd worked with him for years. Myer and Lublinsky were both machiners. Lublinsky lived opposite where we lived in Villiers Terrace. His father was a cobbler. He only had a few words of broken English.

'The moment he knew he was conscripted he was in a state of terror. "I've stark terror," he said. Usually we said that as a joke. Once he was standing next to Myer working and suddenly he put down the work and said "Ehh! I haven't got the heart to work." That was when he knew that he was conscripted.

127

'Lublinsky'd only been in the army about six weeks. The recruiting officers were scraping the barrel at that time. That war was very costly in manpower. He'd been in France only two to three days. When there was a great demand for manpower they just shipped them straight across to France and bunged them into the front lines. I used to watch them going up.

'It was a terrible time. They were simply hawking commissions. If you wanted one you could be a second lieutenant. Any day. A lieutenant's chance of heaven was greater than anyone else's. They usually lasted about six weeks, and then they were on a Roll of Honour. The second lieutenant had to lead his men out of the trenches. Previous to the war the officers were a special class, and there was a very marked class distinction between men and officers. But that war broke down class distinctions. All classes of men were officers. So many people were killed, they had to have more and more men, and if they had to have men, they had to have officers:

It was from this position of the line (wrote Scott) that the British attack on the Aubers Ridge was launched on May 9th...

'Well, they were marching up to the front line when Lublinsky sat down in the road and refused to go any further. He was terrified. As they approached the front line he'll have heard for the first time the continuous thunder of the guns. I myself could hardly hear it, but I knew it was going on from the way the ground never stopped trembling. It's indescribable. If you were anywhere within five miles of the front line there was a continuous barrage. Day and night, it never stopped. You'd do anything to get out of the noise. And at night you could see the line of flashes on the horizon.'

The actual attack (on Passchendaele)... took place on October 9th, under the worst of weather conditions, and it speaks volumes for the grit of the men that such a good advance was made in such difficult circumstances. The Brigade was congratulated by the Corps Commander on the work done 'under the extremely adverse conditions.'

Under very heavy shelling the battalion moved forward splendidly and their steadiness undoubtedly saved the

128

situation,' (wrote the General Officer Commanding the Sixty-second Brigade in his report on April 11th.)

'The soldiers,' Harry went on, 'developed a condition called shell-shock. When they had shell-shock they developed a tremor. A man suffering from shell-shock had to be sent back to base to recover. It was a complete nervous breakdown. I've seen scores of them. Men never really got used to shellfire. They were breaking down all the time. They had a continuous tremor. They flapped their hands about and shivered. They could respond if you spoke to them. More or less.

'Actually the worst case I saw was a suicide. We used to have a communal bath-house where we went in to get washed and shaved. He shaved very carefully and then looked closely at himself in the mirror, carefully examining his shave and stroking his chin. Then he practically cut his head off with one stroke of the razor. He fell on the floor at once. The doctor came and pressed on his vessels but it was useless. This fellow was under orders to return to his unit, and rather than go back to the trenches he'd sooner be dead, and he was stood next to me when he did it.

'Men often ran away. Our commanding officers often dragged us out at 7 o'clock in the morning to hear the sentence of death passed on two or three men. That was a frequent occurrence, reading the sentence out on parade. *Court-martialled for desertion or cowardice.* It was an example to the rest of us.

'Well, Lublinsky sat down in the middle of the road. The officer was probably a second lieutenant, or he might have been a lieutenant. He'd have been a young boy like the rest of us, not twenty-one. Remember, anybody could get a commission if only they'd accept it. Second lieutenants were going begging.

'"Well," the officer said "If you get up you've got some sort of a chance at least. But this way you've no chance at all. If you don't go I've got to shoot you."'

On an extended front (wrote Scott) they encountered the full force of the enemy attack on the morning of the 16th and fought most gallantly until overwhelmed by superior numbers... There were practically no stragglers. What remained of the battalion was formed into one company...

'I doubt if Lublinsky knew his surroundings,' said Harry. 'His state of terror had set in as soon as he heard he was going to be conscripted. He got into such a state he couldn't control his fear. He must have been a pitiable object.'

> *The morning (Scott continued) was so very foggy that it was difficult to distinguish friend from foe… The enemy (whose discrimination seems not to have been affected by fog) got round in the fog, and captured or killed twelve officers and 450 other ranks.*

Presumably the number of officers is exact, but the 450 is just, so to speak, a round figure.

'When I hear,' said Harry, 'what was written afterwards about the war I realise that it was the generals won the war. We were just there to see fair play.'

> *The weather was bad, the trenches were soon in a terrible condition, but the men kept up their spirits in a wonderful manner… Christmas Day was spent as joyously as possible… The battalion went into the trenches again the same night, and remained there until December 29th when their long term of six months in the Ypres Salient came to an end. They left with no regrets…*

After the war some demobilised Leeds soldiers were walking along a grassy ridge in Roundhay Park. 'It's just like Hill Sixty at Ypres,' they said. The ridge has been called Hill Sixty ever since. And the fields behind it are called the Soldiers' Fields.

Pig's Trotters

The stars in their courses fought against Sisera,
The river of Kishon swept them away.

Judges V, 20,21

In 1916, when the war was at its height, it happened that both Harry and
John were home on leave at the same time, and Jeremy was on vacation
from Oxford. It was the first family reunion since the war began, and
their Passover dinner was to be the last time the whole family were all
together.

Maurice was reading through the newspaper. 'To hell with Lloyd
George,' he said. It was one of his favourite sayings.

'As it happens,' Jeremy said coldly, 'some of my friends from Oxford
have already been killed in this war.'

Harry and John both began to speak together. 'In our platoon,' said
Harry, 'there was a man who wanted to go to the toilet. We were out in
the country. So he went to the farmhouse. Well, the French country is
rather primitive. The farmer said, "Go through that gate and into the
field. Turn right and go along the hedge to the corner of the field. There
you'll find a shed with a bucket in it."

'Well, the man went to the field, and almost straight away he came
running back. 'Well,' said the farmer, "did you find the shed in the corner
of the field?"

'"I found the shed and the bucket," said the soldier, "but there's no lock

Harry's arm on John's shoulder in 1916

131

on the shed door."

'"Don't worry about that," the farmer told him. "All the years I've been here no one has ever tried to steal it."'

John, stretched out on the sofa, with his hands clasped behind his head, looked at the ceiling through all this conversation. Sensing a pause he broke in: 'When Rupert Brooke wrote *There is some corner of a foreign field that is forever England*, what sort of England did he know? *Washed by rivers, blessed by suns of home*. Green fields, country villages, grand houses? He didn't know the Leylands. Heh! Heh! Heh!'

'What if,' John continued, 'the only England he knew was Lilac Terrace? Eh? One half of the street is outside lavatories. When Rupert Brooke wrote "There shall be in that rich earth a richer dust concealed," what would a person who only knew Lilac Terrace think? He'd fertilise the corner of the field all right. Heh! Heh! Heh!'

Jeremy turned away bitterly from the spectacle of his unpatriotic brothers. 'Once I get away from all this,' he thought to himself, 'I'll never come back!'

Harry returned to the front and the war rolled on.

As it happened, Jack almost escaped the war but as it dragged on into its fourth year and more and more soldiers were killed, he reached the end of his schooling and was called up. Myer and the whole gang of younger Raismans saw him off at the station. Jack was still wearing his school cap. Such was the hurry to enlist men, the army hadn't had time to issue uniforms and a school cap was the next best thing.

Harry's little sister Sarah had now started at secondary school and Harry wrote to her from France:

> *The moon shines uncomplainingly*
> *Out of a cloudless sky*
> *And all the world writes letters,*
> *And I wonder why can't I...*

'Because I hadn't been to school, no one ever believed that it was me who wrote the letters,' Harry later said, wryly.

Meanwhile Myer worked on at home and ate himself up with worry. More than thirty years later, in his bed-singing for me, he sometimes tried to sing 'Keep the Home Fires Burning,' but he could never control his

132

emotion sufficiently. Communications were bad. Death was signalled by the telegraphic words 'Missing - presumed dead.' Years later John was to incorporate this idea into his poem. But none of the Raismans went missing. Chance brought them together in a curious way.

One night, Harry's unit stopped in the centre of the small village of Estaires, and the soldiers camped for the night in the churchyard. The evening was convivial, the French wine plentiful, and the soldiers caroused in the church. Harry, who never drank alcohol, tired of the noise and smoke, and decided to go to sleep early in his tent outside. In the early hours of the morning an artillery attack began. Shells rocked the churchyard. During a lull in the crashing and flashing the fragments of another British unit fled up the street through the village. Harry, startled, looked up. By the flickering light from the burning church, he saw his brother Jack, driving a mule team pulling a limber.

'Hello Jack,' he said, simply.

'Hello Harry,' said Jack.

It was the only time they met in the whole war.

'Can't do anything with the horses,' said Jack apologetically, completely unable to stop. 'One's half-blind and the other's mad altogether.'

The shelling resumed, Jack and his horses sped off into the night, and Harry took cover again. In the morning light he saw that the churchyard was surrounded by potholes. A direct hit had brought down the church steeple, crashed through the roof of the nave, and destroyed most of Harry's unit. Only by retiring early to the churchyard had he escaped.

People differ in what they wonder at. My father, who marvelled at where the frogs in the shell craters came from, never saw the strangeness of the image he imparted to me as he described the apocalyptic figure of Mad Jack driving his mules through the murderous barrage of that weird night.

Jacob Kramer also went to the front in France, and his experiences tormented his work. He produced a vast canvas of misty soldiers, which he entitled 'Russian Peasant Funeral.' The strands in him were mingling. From the funeral scene he began to develop a great, gloomy crowd picture, with mourners surging under a black low sky towards a thick, stunted cross. Kramer sought frantically for a model of Jesus. One of his ideas was John. But he never satisfied himself, and in the end only a dark, shrivelled creature writhes on the cross in the picture.

Quite late in the war American troops began to appear in the lines. The planners expected them to fight the enemy. According to Harry they were indeed fighters. They fought the English and the English fought them. The front line became a patchwork of nationalities. Little patches were inserted here and there in an attempt to separate the more incompatible contingents and encourage them to direct their warlike attentions away from each other and towards the Germans.

For their part, the German High Command knew that they must act quickly before the new influx of American soldiers completely turned the balance against them. Ludendorff responded by moving in a million troops, fresh from victory against the Russians on the Eastern Front. A massive offensive, called the *Kaiserschlacht*, was prepared.

In the spring of 1918 Harry was moved up to the front line at the point where it was crossed by the river Lys, considerably forward of the village of Aire, where he had previously been stationed. Just behind the line was the large town of Armentières.

This point was the junction between the British First Army to the south and Second Army to the north. It was the key to the Lys Valley and was held by England's oldest allies, disparagingly called by the British soldiers, the Pork 'n Beans. In reality Harry did not remember the food preferences of the Portuguese. But these swarthy southerners certainly hated the Flanders climate. It happened that the unit occupied a small square, surrounded by low walls. On these walls our oldest allies sat sadly, no doubt dreaming of their native land. In the morning they sat on the western wall, to catch the early sun. As it rose in the heavens they gradually shifted to the north, finishing their day dejectedly on the eastern wall to catch the last few warming rays of the weak westering sun as it disappeared beneath the horizon on its way to happy Portugal.

In the early morning fogs of the last week of March 1918 the Great German Offensive had taken place far to the south and had now been checked. April began with an abnormally dry spell of weather and the Flanders mud had dried up. This opportunity for mobility made the conditions suitable for a German assault on the northern sector. They called it the Georgette Offensive. In front of Armentières the First

Portuguese Division had been withdrawn from the line on April 5th, and the Second Division was left holding the whole sector. It was due to be relieved on April 9th. It had no such luck.

At four o'clock in the morning of April 9th, the German High Command commenced a bombardment along the whole front from Armentières southwards. Suddenly in the darkness the whole eastern sky became a wall of fire. The Portuguese had never experienced heavy artillery.

'We had been warned they couldn't stand shellfire,' said Harry. 'The men had actually made themselves comfortable in the trenches - undressed and gone to sleep, if you please! It was unheard of. They had no idea what they were in for. When the barrage began they came running out of the trenches naked.'

Sunrise on that morning was a totally insignificant event compared with the unceasing German artillery barrage coming out of the east. Four hours later, a little after eight in the morning, the shellfire stopped and through dense fog the German infantry appeared. By 9 o'clock the German High Command had flung nine divisions into an all-out frontal assault on the line junction held by one weary Portuguese and two British divisions.

The Portuguese, totally unused to war, gave way, and the Germans poured through, rolling up the Allied lines on each side of the gap. Armentières, its eastern defence line shattered, was flooded with poison gas. The Germans occupied it on the next day, April 10th, and continued their advance along the river Lys. From Armentières no geographical feature held up the German advance along the plain of the Lys. Merville fell on April 11th. The gap widened unremittingly. Trenches could not be defended from the rear. The static trench warfare of four years was mobile again. After four years of moving a few hundred yards back and forth, the Germans poured through the smashed Allied front line, racing towards the Channel.

The defeated soldiers hurried back through the deserted streets of Armentières. Men in no order, detached from their units, fled in twos and threes. Climbing walls, running across the flat fields, as far as the eye could see, the British Army was fleeing in utter disorder.

'The Germans,' said Harry, 'broke through and got round the back of the trenches. Then they had a fine old time murdering everyone they could lay their hands on. I had the pleasure of sitting on a little stone wall and seeing the British Army in full retreat.'

When the anti-imperialist Harry got home, it was this part of the story that he most relished as he recounted his experiences to his brother Jeremy. Jeremy, who worshipped the British Empire, was speechless with horror at the lack of deference in the impudent phraseology chosen by his brother to describe his undeniably eye-witness account. 'Men and officers came up to me,' Harry went on, 'asking, "Had I seen such and such a regiment?" In the end somebody came and told me, "You'd better move on, the Germans are just down the road." And I did.'

'The 99th Siege Battery of the Royal Garrison Artillery was gassed. It was the most horrible sight of the war. The men were burnt on the inside and on the outside. We took them back to Boulogne with us. They all died. If you go to Boulogne you can see row upon row of their graves in the Boulogne cemetery.'

The men ran for days. Despite their destroying the river bridges nothing could stop the German advance up the valley. One after another the Lys villages fell.

In front of the Germans, the villagers of Estaire and Merville had fled along the river roads to Aire. Night after night in the packed houses, the people of Aire and the refugees listened to the thud of shells falling on the other side of the Nieppe Forest. When the refugees had told them how the retreating British had blown up the Aire bridges, the Airois realised what it meant. For four years, the Allied front line, had stretched from Ypres in the north to Béthune in the south, a shield between them and the Germans. Now it was broken. Glumly the townsfolk peeped through the shutters at the spectacle of the British soldiers scurrying about the streets, and the wounded pouring into the town.

The German advance up the Lys valley had entered the narrow defile where the Nieppe Forest on their northern flank came down to the river. And here, at this crucial moment, like the River of Kishon in the Song of Deborah, the River Lys, unaided by British, French or Portuguese, fought single-handed against the Germans. The marshy wood, wet even in the height of summer, bogged down the German advance. Armed men sank to their waists, their boots sucked off, tanks, cars and gun carriages floundered and stopped. In the coolness of the shady wood sphagnum moss clogged the axles of the great war machine.

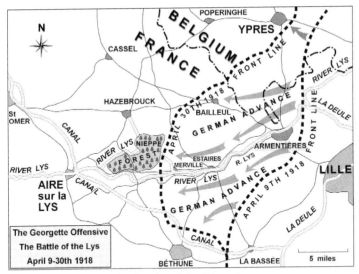

The Battle of the River Lys

At last, far back, the Allied lines began to re-form. The British Fifth Division was rushed into the Lys Valley. On April 18th the Battle of the Lys died down. By April 30th, the German front had reached its furthest point. It lay broken on the eastern edge of the Nieppe Forest where Harry had previously walked and had his last vision of the mackerel sky. In all, the Germans had penetrated to a depth of about twelve miles over a twenty mile wide front, and they had taken 30 000 prisoners. Merville had fallen, but the town of Aire remained in British hands. The Georgette Offensive was the last fling of a spent war effort. Harry encountered a British major in a lane. 'Who are you?' the major demanded, somehow not unkindly. Harry identified his now irrevocably dispersed unit.

'Join these men. I constitute you the Fifth Army Operating Theatre,' said the major. And so it remained till the end of the war.

The British Army had re-grouped, and when it started to advance, it was only to stop when Germany surrendered. Harry left Aire with his new unit. Despite his deafness he had learned some French in the little estaminet of the Cat-in-Boots. He had found how to ask for '*deux oeufs pomfritz,*' and as he left, someone wagged her finger at him and admonished (to his imperfect hearing) '*Ecrirez! Ecrirez!*' He never did

137

write.

'Once the Germans started retreating,' said Harry, 'they were going so fast we couldn't catch up with them. I never saw a German, they were so far ahead of us. I never heard a shot fired. On the advance, I saw Armentières. We had to stop there for the night. It was a ghost town. It had been utterly destroyed. It'd been shelled over and over again. In the morning we had to go into the houses to look for bodies. They had cellars, dug-outs. When you got anywhere near them the smell was horrible.'

In front of Armentières, the Germans had abandoned their famed line of fortifications, called the Hindenburg Line. 'At one point,' said Harry, 'we found the Germans had built a complete underground. In it, there were lots of little trinkets, watches and so on, booby-trapped. We were warned very seriously not to pick anything up. We picked up the bodies. If they weren't quite dead we brought them up and they were examined. If they had any chance we sent them up the line. If they'd no chance, we just gave them a lump of morphia and they'd go quietly. All we had to give them was something to kill the pain.'

By autumn the British advance had carried the Fifth Army Operating Theatre all the way down the Lys valley and past Armentières. Now they approached the city of Lille, capital of Flanders, and four years in German hands. There was no sign of enemy troops. Lille appeared to be deserted. The men of the little mobile Operating Theatre were the first Allied soldiers in Lille. They cautiously entered the town. They saw no one. The doors were barred, the windows shuttered. There was not a sound in the streets. The men were not sure whether the Germans were all gone, nor whether the citizens would be still there. After four years of German occupation the local sympathies were not clear to the English force.

The English column, non-combatant and unarmed anyway, warily threaded its way along the ghostly streets. The soldiers kept glancing apprehensively at the shuttered windows frowning over their heads. Then someone peeped around a shutter, and suddenly there was a woman's voice crying, *'Les anglais, c'est les anglais!'*

The town seemed to explode with people, and the cry was taken up from house to house and street to street. Elated, but at the same time terrified, the men of the Fifth Army Operating Theatre sped to the railway station in the town centre and locked themselves in.

The population were starving. Relief trains brought loaves, and the soldiers handed them out through the bars of the station gates to the people milling around.

'There were no French young men in the town,' said Harry. 'The Germans had occupied Lille for the whole war. They hadn't left a bit of bread in the town, but they'd left lots of little souvenirs. There were lots of little kids of three or four years old running about the streets, speaking German. For some time after the war, the population of Lille was pro-German. Probably it still is.

'I was stationed in this hospital - the *Hôpital Saint-Sauveur*. There were Roman Catholic nuns running this hospital and they didn't seem too pleased about the German retreat. They just scowled at us and scurried out of the room if we went in. In a drawer in the hospital I found some photographs. Somebody'd been playing tricks. I saw a photograph of a little baby with the legs of a pig - you know - pigs' trotters instead of legs. They were composite photographs that had been made of monstrosities. I had nightmares about them for years. The bottom half was a pig and the upper half was a little baby.'

But now, after four years, the war had spent itself. The Nieppe Forest returned indignantly to its centuries-old silence but to this day, where the narrow country lane winds through the shady woodland, the marshy ground has old bomb craters full of stagnant water, still deep enough to sink a house in, and the ground is littered with the remains of rusted pieces of cast-iron shell cases and fragments of artillery. Encrusted with moss, they look like clods of earth; only when you pick them up they are heavier, and have crumbling metallic cores.

On the German side, an obscure, moustachioed little Austrian corporal went bitterly home. The three years before the war he had spent in a doss house for homeless men in Vienna. During the heady days of the advance on Merville he had been a regimental messenger, scurrying dutifully about with dispatches. Now, in defeat, he returned to Germany with a new idea. It was the Jews who had brought about the defeat of his Fatherland. In his mind was growing a monstrous vision that was to outdo all the destruction so far.

But the havoc of this first war was still very far from over. The flu epidemic which began in 1918 was to kill even more millions than the fighting. Harry caught the flu and was invalided home. When he arrived at the Channel port he saw soldiers dancing in the streets. 'What's happening?' he asked.

'Don't you know?' they replied 'The war's over.'

Back at home, Ada awoke from a doze in the chair and said to Myer: 'Harry's coming home.'

The next day Harry arrived. The flu didn't kill him, he burnt his louse-ridden army singlet, drowned his lice in a hot soapy bath, and never left England again.

Beyond the Leylands

After the war the map of Europe had again been redrawn. When the Raisman brothers and sisters heard their parents say they came from Yurberick, a town on the German frontier of Russia, they would search the maps in vain. Nowhere could Yurberick be found. In fact, Yurberick was now the Lithuanian Jurbarkas. It was, moreover, neither on the Russian nor the German frontier. Nor was there any frontier between Germany and Russia. Between Russia and Germany no less than four states had sprung up - Poland, Lithuania, Latvia and Estonia.

'There is no Yurberick any more,' Harry said. 'It's been completely wiped off the map.' Maurice didn't answer. He accepted what his sons told him. It was more than forty years since he had left Yurberick. For him the past was over.

After he left the army, Harry decided to try his fortune in London, working in a bedroom tailoring workshop in Whitechapel. 'I remember six of us young lads going to the victory celebrations in Trafalgar Square,' he said. 'They went on all night. We stayed so late there were no buses, so we walked back to the East End. We stopped in Brick Lane to get some bagels at four o'clock in the morning.

'While I was in London I went to see Matthew Kelly. After the drapery business in Livery Street, he had become a picture faker. He used to make portraits from old photographs. One of his portraits was the Maggid. I'd seen it in cousin Jinny's house in Newcastle. Jinny probably destroyed it later.

'Matthew Kelly was a big, coarse, unpleasant man. He had three children, Freda, born in 1898, the same year as me, and two younger sons. They were all friendly with our John. When one of Matthew Kelly's sons got engaged to be married, his father actually stole his own son's dowry. Everyone said Matthew Kelly was doomed to end either as a millionaire or in jail. By the time I saw him, he'd done his time in prison and now he was a millionaire. He kept a Mercedes and a chauffeur, and used to boast he did 75 miles an hour. They lived in a big house in Cromwell Road, and when he heard I was in London he invited me to a party there. The first thing they did was to stick a huge tumbler full of whisky in my hand. They were all drinking the stuff. I didn't touch a drop. Even the smell of it made me dizzy.

'The place was full of CID men. He said, "Come whenever you like."

'I didn't go back again. Later Matthew Kelly's son became a solicitor in London, and he too went amiss.

'I stuck it out in London for six months. London made me tired, endless streets, not a bit of green anywhere, great blocks of tenements. It depressed me. In Leeds at least I had a bicycle. I could get out of it. So I went back to Leeds. The family'd moved into a house with lots of room, and I started working in the house with Myer.'

As they stitched away, Harry reminisced: 'I heard that Morris Rooms was blown to bits. A shell fell directly on him. They couldn't even find the pieces.'

'He was a wonderful pianist,' said Myer.

When they moved out of the gambling den in Trafalgar Street, the family also moved out of the Leylands and up the slight rise in the land to the west of North Street. Their house in Carr Road provided them with hitherto undreamed-of luxury. Here was their first bathroom, and a flush toilet. 'I remember, said my father 'how surprised I was to see hot water coming out of a tap. In the whole of the Leylands there wasn't a flush toilet. You were lucky if a house had a tap - and that was only a cold tap. There was no hot water anywhere in the Leylands.'

But here, on the good side of North Street the houses were no longer lit by gas, but by electricity, and beside the front door was a little button which, when you pushed it, rang an electric bell. Maurice was so thrilled by it he nearly forgave the family for the loss of his gambling house. For the first time in Harry's life, the house he lived in was not a back-to-back.

Maurice and Ada when they moved out of the gambling den

Here, the houses were all in terraces, joined to each other only at the sides. As a result, each house had two doors, a front door opening on to the front street, and a back door opening on to the back street. The front doors were always slightly more elaborate. Usually at eye level they had a little window with tiny panels of different coloured stained glass a few inches across, set in lead frames and arranged in various geometric or floral designs. The windows of the front rooms had lace curtains.

The people who lived in the houses in Carr Road kept their front doors locked. But the back doors were always ajar, and in the openings the old people would place a chair and pass the time of day. Behind them, the comforting heat, noise and cooking smells of the kitchen; before them, the whole world. And as they gazed over this rectangular microcosm of the universe, where cats enthroned on mounds of soil gnawed old chicken bones, they sat for hours, warmed even in the coldest weather by the heat from behind, sustained by unasked pots of tea and buttered bagels, shutting the door for only the heaviest showers and seeing who knows what of their old lives in *Der Hame*.

The Leylanders had no conception of any form of horticulture. The rare expert among them might proudly grow rhubarb. The commonest plant was the humble privet. Planted by earlier occupants, the privet plants had originally been restrained by regular clipping so as to make neat hedges. But the Leylanders did no violence to plants, and allowed them to grow as freely as Nature intended. Of all the delicate plants which may once have decorated these gardens before the Leylanders arrived, only the hardy privets survived. They became rambling small trees with thick, branched trunks and bark blackened by the smoke of the polluted Leeds air. Unlike properly trimmed privet hedges, they flowered profusely, clusters of tiny, off-white, bell-like flowers emitting a penetrating, rank fragrance.

Because the family's house was no longer a back-to-back, it had two addresses. Sarah, studying history, made a discovery about them. Some whimsical, historically-minded, now-forgotten member of the Leeds City Corporation Planning Department had named two adjacent streets after two favourite bedfellows of King James I, Robert Carr, Earl of Somerset, an inept Scot, and the notorious George Villiers, Duke of Buckingham, who (until his assassination) was also favourite of Charles I. So the front of the family house was 56 Villiers Terrace and the back was 14 Carr

Road. Naturally the family quoted the front address, the one to which the postman delivered letters, but always spoke about living in Carr Road, where they played.

John was now at Leeds University, where he started a debating society. The fashion for Greek letter clubs had just been imported as a novelty from the United States, and some of the students in Leeds formed a club called the *Alpha Phi*. Amused by this, John decided to found his own alternative club. He called it the *Beta Gamma*, meaning second-and third-raters. Its motto was *Quieta Non Movere*. Usually translated as Let sleeping dogs lie, John preferred to translate it as *Leave it alone*. All his life John deliberately assumed an air of childlike innocence.

Carr Road had a famous poet, called Raskin. 'Raskin,' said my father 'thought of himself as a poet. He was a sanitary inspector - what we called a closet-rammer. He carried a long stick. I don't know what he used it for. I never went with him on his rounds. He must have been the only Jew in Leeds to do such a job. No other Jew in Leeds ever held such a job. Mind you, in those days if a man earned a living it was quite something. You didn't sneer about it. People used to sing Raskin's most famous poem, and while they sang, they danced about and made with their hands:

> *God is right in His judgements*
> *We dare not say God is bad.*
> *God knows what he is doing,*
> *And all that he does is good;*
> *And He doesn't punish anybody for nothing.*
> *God is right in His judgements...*

'Raskin's manner was very earnest. He was a tall, straight feller, with a military-style moustache and no beard. He was so very serious about it all, and that always amused our John. Raskin used to walk about with such an air of seriousness and authority. He carried his stick more like a walking stick than anything else. As well as his closet-ramming stick, he carried a couple of iron rods. I don't know what he did with them either. He was a sanitary inspector and that's all there is to it. No need to go into the details of his life, what he had for breakfast and what he didn't have.

'Everyone knew he was addicted to writing rhymes, but the idea of Raskin being a poet struck John as very funny. John couldn't get over it, and couldn't resist the obvious rhyme for *mishpot* (judgement). Mother used to tell John not to be so scurrilous about it. As a matter of fact, while John only made fun of his verses, other people treated Raskin with real scorn, a mere closet-rammer, they would say. Raskin's daughter was very annoyed with John. She knew what he said about her father.'

Later on Raskin went to America, where his poetic talents were finally recognized, and the up-till-then unacclaimed rhythm of *God is Right in His Judgements* gave great pleasure to certain literary circles, who named Raskin the *Ghetto Poet*. His diploma from the Royal Institute of Sanitary Engineers became transformed by the compilers of an American encyclopaedia to a degree from the (non-existent) Royal Literary Institute of Leeds. No one put it better than the famous novelist Israel Zangwill who, while little appreciating the Leylands reality of his phrase, wrote: 'There is an aroma in Raskin's poems...'

By this time Myer and Harry's workshop was so busy that they also recruited the full-time help of Fanny. Without Fanny's help in the house, however, looking after the large house and family became too much for the ageing Ada alone, and the family now had enough money to get occasional help from cleaning women. Thus began the succession of family servants.

The first was the 'fire-lighting lady who lived at the top of Reuben Street.' The second was only known by her confession 'Tell her what I done.' There was one called Georgina, a name the children could only manage as *George Rina*, or *Joe Jinny*. One 'came with a black cat.' Another 'smoked a pipe and drank a pint.' Amused at the way she scurried about, Ada used to say 'She runs about like a poisoned mouse.'

The children enjoyed the excitement of the servants' lives. One girl came from the distant suburb of Morley, south of the river and got married in the Workhouse at St James after she had had a child of her brother who 'had to go into the army.' Finally, they got 'Alice the Deaf'. Sam said she secretly drank the wine, but Myer insisted she was so honest she asked for a glass of water. Both were probably true.

'My mother,' said Harry, 'knew every grandma's tale that had been perpetrated since 5000 B.C. and earlier. She had a fund of them. She could bring one out to suit any occasion. She disbelieved them all. I have the opinion that she was an atheist, despite the fact that she observed all the rituals. "Well," she used to say, "you live in a Jewish community, you can't help but go along with them."

'My older sister, Fanny had acquired many of the superstitions. Fanny could interpret all your dreams. Mother used to scoff at her for believing all this rubbish. Mustn't cut a child's nails, you have to bite them. Mother was disgusted.'

According to traditional Leylands' views, a mistress of the ancient wisdom could bring many unusual outside influences to bear on the human body. When a housewife in Livery Street was seen secretly emptying her chamber pot into the street drain (instead of carrying it, like everyone else, all the way down the street to the valve leading to the ashpits), the children placed hot coals on the grate. The purpose of this was not to sterilise the grate, but to cause blisters on her backside.

One day Ada cut her finger, and it festered. In the end she had to go to the Public Dispensary for a very painful treatment. 'How could you bear it?' asked her younger daughter, Sarah.

'You have to be brave,' said Ada, 'brave to live, and brave to die.'

Fanny was a fast buttonhole hand. She made eighteen an hour. In the trade at that time a buttonhole hand was paid sixpence a dozen. To earn a pound you had to sew 480 buttonholes by hand.

Sarah always had a passion for history and a phenomenal memory for all kinds of dates, ancient and modern. Now Myer had enough money coming in from the workshop to allow her to go to Leeds University to study the economically useless subject of history. But for him to be able to manage this, Sarah still had to spend her evenings in the workshop, sewing on buttons.

Ralph was going to Leeds Grammar School, and Myer would ensure that he too would soon go to university. Ralph was the most polished of the brothers. 'He's the only gentleman of the family,' his mother said. But to Harry's dismay, the family were now beginning to produce Conservatives. To counteract them Myer and Harry acquired a dog, and their mother called it Trotsky in honour of the overthrow of the hated Tsar of Russia.

'Mother liked the dog to be white,' Harry said. 'It was an off-white dog. So she used to bath the dog. The dog hated being bathed. At the first sign of the large tin bath being prepared and the towels, it would rush out into the street and not come back for a long time. A very long time. So the first precaution in bathing the dog was to lock the door.'

Observing Trotsky introduced Harry to the amazing world of dogs, so utterly different from that of the loathsome cat. Dogs, unlike men, could smell water. In fact once they had smelled something - a place, a person, or an object - they could remember that place, that person or that object forever. Like elephants, dogs never forgot. They had extraordinary powers of navigation, and could return infallibly over incalculable distances to the place they regarded as home. A dog can always tire a man at walking. For every mile a man walks, a dog walks four or five. Only George Borrow, wandering about Spain selling the Bible, was able to walk so far that he could tire a dog.

Ada liked to be with students. It was well known throughout the Leylands, and when they'd nothing to do on a Sunday afternoon, university students from many of the neighbouring families often said, 'Let's go to Mrs Raisman's.' A couple of them would bound hungrily into the kitchen unannounced and ask, 'Are there any of those Raisman kippers?' They used to love to sit and talk to her. And when the Raisman children came home they often found their mother sitting talking happily with the students all about their courses.

At this time Myer and Harry managed to raise enough money to buy the piano that Louis always used to talk about, and the family would all cluster round it. Everyone had their own favourite songs, the ones that expressed their own deepest desires.

Myer specialised in the music hall songs which told of the soulful romances of working people, *The Honeysuckle and the Bee*, and his favourite character was the shy *Joshua:*

> *Joshua courted Miss May.*
> *To be correct I should say*
> *She courted him, for he was so shy...*
>
> *Joshua, Joshua*
> *Nicer than lemon squash you are,*
> *Yes, by gosh, you are,*
> *Josh - u - osh - ua!*

Jeremy had quite a different favourite:

> *Take a pair of sparkling eyes,*
> *Hidden, ever and anon*

In a merciful eclipse,

Take a pretty little cot,
Quite a miniature affair,
Hung about with trellised vine.

Furnish it upon the spot
With the treasures rich and rare
I've endeavoured to define.

For him, the little cot hung about with trellised vine was a symbol of that England he so admired.

For Fanny it was the sailor's wife, waiting for her husband to come home:

Blow, blow, breeze and blow
Wind of the Western Sea
Blow him again to me
While my little ones
While my pretty ones
Sleep...

Harry's favourite song also told the story of how he felt:

The minstrel boy to the war is gone
In the ranks of death you'll find him.
His father's sword he has girded on,
And his wild harp slung behind him.

As he sang it, utterly out of tune, he must have bitterly envied the minstrel who at least had a father he could look up to. Harry had a lot of trouble with Commandment 5a.

By this time Myer was too busy to go out cycling with Harry at weekends. Jeremy was away in India. So now Harry started to go with his friend Charlie Blass, who lived two doors away in Villiers Terrace. Charlie was a thin little man with an adenoidal voice and a wry sense of humour. He worked with Harry as a tailor. Charlie's family had only recently come to Leeds from Galicia. This was in Austrian Poland, and hence enemy territory. At the start of the war, the whole family had been briefly arrested and interned as enemy aliens.

While Charlie's father was alive, Charlie went with him to synagogue every Saturday morning. He did it, he said, 'out of respect for his father.'

But Charlie saved his socialist soul by going cycling with Harry every Saturday afternoon. To cycle on the Sabbath broke so many important religious rules that Charlie felt it neutralised his synagogue attendance in the morning.

Unlike Jerusalem, or Rome on its seven eternal hills, Leeds is a valley city. Whether the cyclist chooses to go north over the Chevin, or south over John o' Gaunt's Hill, he faces a long and weary climb out. But at the end of the day his return is glorious. Pedalling between the folds of land by Morley or Bramhope he is given a momentary vision of the entire city sprawling before him, its shot towers and factory chimneys and smoking wharves crowding the meandering banks of the River Aire.

One early spring day in 1920, Harry and Charlie rode over the ridge of Gildersome and out to the black, stone-built village of Howarth, the birth-place of the Brontes. At the top of the steep cobbled street, stood the church, and beside it the parsonage where the Brontes lived. During the night there had been a light snow fall. It hadn't even settled in Leeds, but here it mingled, powdery, with the white blossom of the blackthorn hedges and dusted the tops of the dry-stone walls. Harry and Charlie surveyed the view, and read Charlotte Bronte's description of it:

> *A little and a low green lane*
> *that wanders o'er a common wide*
> *The distant and the dim blue chain*
> *of mountains circling every side.*

Then they went into the village shop and bought the local gingerbread, called parkin. Seagulls swooped over the frozen fields. 'It's the sign of a hard winter,' Harry said, pleased to be able to show off his knowledge of the mysterious countryside to Charlie, 'when the seagulls come inland in search of food.'

On the river-banks the mist had not risen all day and now the winter sun sank into an icy pink milkiness. Long before they got back home the short day was over. Charlie was feeling pleased that he had managed to mend his last puncture before it got too dark. They were on the downhill home run into Leeds. 'You know,' Harry said, straining his eyes to peer into the gloom, 'even on the darkest nights there's always some light in the sky. However little it is, the sky never gets completely dark.'

Harry lit his acetylene lamp and periodically replenished its water by the usual means dictated by necessity and the scarcity of water taps on country roads. Charlie didn't bother with a lamp at all.

Late in the evening they reached the outskirts of Leeds. In ancient Greece the city limits of Corinth were marked by statues of Pegasus, the winged horse. Leeds, which might as well have borne this motto as far as the Raismans were concerned, was marked by the wise owl. On each road entering the city a tall pole carried a varnished wooden effigy of the city's heraldic bird. But just as Harry and Charlie passed the owl, a policeman, only half visible in navy blue, stepped out of the shadows: 'Stop!' he commanded.

The cyclists showed no sign of stopping, so the policeman stepped out into their path. 'Lights!' he roared. 'No lights! Stop!'

The cyclists swerved suddenly to the other side of the road, put their heads down, and flew past, pedalling furiously. The policeman tore off his navy blue cape and threw it at Charlie. Charlie deftly caught it on his right arm, slung it over his shoulder, and rode on, thinking of the *Charge of the Light Brigade:*

> *Guns to the right of them,*
> *Guns to the left of them*
> *Volleyed and thundered.*
> *Into the Valley of Death*
> *Rode the Six Hundred.*

The furious blasts of the policeman's whistle gradually faded in the distance as the two friends disappeared down the hill, into the darkness and the safety of the city. Charlie treasured his trophy in secret for many years.

By this time, Louis was in the state of *essen kest*. This means living with his in-laws. The nearest English expression may be something like 'to eat the bread of affliction.' Louis used to come back to his family at Villiers Terrace and describe it. 'The other day I broke a cup. You know how greedy they are. So to stop any argument I threw the saucer down after it. I said "You won't be needing it now." When I come home from the club for breakfast I'm dizzy with their pestering. My mother-in-law always refers to Chaymky Cohen who is so wealthy. She says, "He has a great gold watch chain." Then she points at my chest and says "Well, where is the watch and chain?"'

'For breakfast I can have a banana. Or I can have an egg. But I can't have both. If I have a banana I can't have an egg, and if I have an egg I can't have a banana.'

'At that time,' said Harry 'Louis tried to be a bookie. It was at Wetherby Races. So he started taking bets. It was a two-and-a-half mile race. And there was a horse in this race called Only One, and it was fifty to one. And someone came and bet on this horse with Louis and finished his career as a bookmaker.'

For his part, Maurice was never happy that his offspring had compelled him to give up his gambling house in Trafalgar Street. What he considered to be his delicate state of health precluded his going back to work as a machinist. In any case Myer, Harry, Fanny and Sarah were all now working in tailoring and Jeremy was sending a regular small allowance back from his salary. Maurice resigned himself to a life of gambling. His children could keep him now. As Jeremy put it bitterly, 'Other men live on their income, father lives on his outcome.'

What Maurice won from the bookies by his skill at cards each evening he had given back to the same bookies by the end of the races on the following afternoon. He had an unlimited ability to lose at horse-races. He once went to the Manchester Handicap and picked from the card the winners at all six races, but he himself didn't back a single one of them.

'Back my horse,' said his friend David Fryfish at the club one day.

'I wouldn't back your horse with used tram tickets,' Maurice replied.

The horse, White Bud, won the Lincolnshire Handicap at 66 to one. In the same race the next year, the members of the club had a hot tip. It came from no less a person than a co-founder of the club, one of the Goodman family, a man who was himself both a bookmaker and a racehorse owner. His jockeys wore his colours, gold, silver and copper. The tip was his own horse, Valentine Vox. Maurice and everyone else in the club backed it.

The day after the race someone innocently asked Maurice how his horse had done. 'It's still running,' said Maurice in disgust. 'Everyone in Leeds backed it. One man was so heart-broken he went to Roundhay Park to throw himself in the lake; but he couldn't because it was already full of people.'

The flat racing season starts on the nearest Monday to March 21st and ends with the November Handicap in Manchester. The rest of the year there are only 'jumpers,' and punters regard these races 'over the sticks' as too unpredictable for serious betting. November to March was the dead season for Maurice. One winter's day, in the depths of this doleful time, he was sitting by the fire and consoling himself by reading the newspaper. He always read the paper through religiously from beginning to end, as though he was reading a novel. Like a novel, the climax for him was at the end, the racing pages. Suddenly he reached an item that made him explode with indignation, 'These horses we've been betting on, they're selling for fifty pounds! A racehorse should cost thousands! They're just scrubbers.'

Maurice had become obsessed with his health, and used to walk around with his pockets full of nuts and other health foods which he obtained on credit. He ran up quite a bill for them at the grocers. On one occasion Jeremy had given his father £12 to settle this health food account. Maurice went out and at once lost the entire sum at gambling. Jeremy swore he would never again give his father money. All future remittances went to Myer.

For the first few years that the family lived in Villiers Terrace, Myer and Harry made up tailoring orders in a workroom in the house. 'Myer,' said Ralph, 'spent half his life at that treadle sewing machine.'

Of the original two Raisman brothers who had come to the Leylands from Lithuania, Hoshy, the elder, had died at the time when his son Maurice was still running the gambling house in Trafalgar Street. But although Hoshy had never been prosperous enough to leave Little Bridge Street in the heart of the Leylands, his well-to-do younger brother Moshy had come to live in Ramsden Terrace on the good side of North Street. Moshy was quite a patriarch. His son and daughters brought their families and came to live nearby.

Moshy's son Harry had taken over the matsy business. He was a gentle, ineffective, soft-hearted man, like most of the Harrys of the family, and it was not long before the matsy business went bankrupt. The process was accelerated by his gambling. 'Moshy's family,' my father said 'were riddled with gambling. That, and the large protruding jaw that was their hallmark.'

In 1920 Chayie die Shvartsy was 93, and her husband Moshy, 79. Both became ill. Together, husband and wife took themselves to their huge, curtained four-poster bed, preparing to leave the world in state.

The bedroom was always full of their children and grandchildren. Of these alone there were over fifty, not to mention more distant relatives or simply acquaintances who had come to pay their last respects to the revered first president of the Greenhorns' Synagogue, and to the famous woman who had introduced black bread to Leeds. All could not get into the bedroom at the same time.

The front door of the stricken house was always open. Knots of people drank tea and talked in the kitchen. Others queued, talking in quieter tones in the hall, on the stairs and on the upstairs landing, as they waited their turn, exchanging brief notes and meaningful glances with those coming out of the bedroom,.

Little Nina was one of the countless great-grandchildren. Just old enough to get about on her own, she was put on the huge bed of state where she amused herself by crawling all over and in the bed of her fading ancestors. So while the sad relatives circulated outside the four-poster bed, peeping mournfully from time to time through the bed curtains, Nina circulated within. In the end she took to pulling the august Moshy's beard. It was too much for the weary old man.

'Take the little girl away,' he said.

The King of Spain's Beard

One Saturday evening in the early spring of 1927 Ralph, persuaded his older brother Harry to go with him to a dance at the 'Institute' on North Street.

Although Ralph and Harry looked very much alike, their personalities made a strange contrast. Ralph had now qualified as a solicitor at Leeds University. He was confident, cheerful and talkative, a fund of jokes and tall stories, the soul of any party, and much in demand as an after dinner speaker. Harry was serious and quiet, using his deafness to shield himself from small-talk. He had never been to a dance before, and couldn't dance anyway.

Celia Narunsky, just 21, was a tiny slip of a girl. She hated eating and she was so thin her friends said she could fall down a water grate. She wore a veil and a rounded, close-fitting hat, secured to her thin hair by two huge hat pins ending in cloth-covered balls. Bernard Burton, head of her office at the Burton tailoring factory used to give her tickets to go to the dances so she could meet nice eligible boys. She had gone to the dance with her friend Beattie Goldberg.

Ralph asked Celia to dance, and then invited her back to his table. On the way she met another friend who had the next dance with her. Then, as she was going through the door, she bumped into Harry. The two brothers looked very much alike. 'Its hot in here,' Celia said to Harry. 'Let's go and sit down.' She took him familiarly, by the arm.

At the best of times Harry was reserved. Addressed in this way by a girl he had never seen before, he was amazed. Celia thought it was funny how his manner had changed. Then, as Ralph came up, she realised her mistake. 'Oh,' she said, 'I'm sorry I thought you were him.'

Ralph and Harry laughed. 'He's my brother,' Ralph said.

Celia, as if driven by some strange sense of her destiny, went to her

154

friend Beattie, and said 'This is Ralph. He's a very good dancer. Wouldn't you like to dance with him?' She had made her choice.

Beattie and Ralph went off to dance, and Celia and Harry's lifelong relationship began. Celia wasn't bothered about Harry not dancing, and used the opportunity to sit down at the table with him and tell him about her family.

'My mother and father came over from Kovner Giberrny in 1904. My grandfather had died in Russia. They didn't have enough to eat in winter. He knew the Russians used to break the ice and fish in the frozen river Niemen. So he decided to do it, and the ice broke and he fell in. His brothers brought him home and put him in the oven. They used to sleep on the oven. But it was no use. In Russia, my father used to go from town to town with his father. He carried a sewing machine on his back. Between towns they took off their shoes and wore them round their necks to save wearing them out. When there was work in a house, they came and lived there. The people gave them to eat and put them up. They stayed as long as it took to do the suit.

'My father was an anarchist. When he got to be eighteen he was called up for the Russian Army. There was a war with Japan. He got engaged to my mother. They were both 17, and they ran away. They'd saved up a dowry for my mother. She was a lady's companion. She was a right pretty girl when she was younger. My father insisted he had to come and see her before he'd have her. She just did what she was told. She didn't know any better. They used the dowry to get to England.

'When they got to the border the soldiers tried to stop them. Father ran for three miles. Even though they were on horses they couldn't catch him. He hid among the reeds of the marshes on the river bank, pushing his face in the ground and trying not to breathe.

'My mother, trust her, fell, and the soldiers caught her. She gave them all her jewellery and they let her go. But she managed to keep her heavy kitchen mortar and pestle and her chopping knife hidden in her bundle of clothes.' Celia paused. She wasn't sure whether Harry was listening, but he smiled in a vacant sort of way, so she went on.

'They stayed with Mrs Jackson at the corner of Byron Street. She had sixteen children of her own. I don't know where my father and mother slept. I suppose they slept on the floor.

'My father's brother was a hunchback. When my mother and father got some money they sent over to bring my grandma to Leeds. When my grandma got to Leeds the first thing she did was give my mother a wig. My grandma always wore a wig - a right fancy one. She looked right funny without it - her hair was cut right short. Well, father wasn't going to have my mother wearing a wig. He grabbed the wig out of her hand and threw it straight into the fire, shouting "No wig! No wig!" My grandma was right upset. She shouted, "Hey, Murderer! murderer!"

'After they'd been married a couple of years my mother still had no children. She went to the rabbi and said "I can't have children. What'll people say? You've got to have children."

'The rabbi just said quietly: "Go home, my child. You'll have children."

'So she went home, and, what do you think? - she fell on! And the next year she had me.

'We lived first in Lower Brunswick Street,' Celia continued. 'Later we moved to 25, Vandyke Street. After I was born my mother had no more children. She went to the rabbi again and he said it was the Evil Eye. So he said prayers to drive out the Evil Eye.

'Mother then had five boys. Let no Evil Eye see... This year she asked me what I would like the next to be, whether I wasn't tired of brothers. "Ooh No!" I said. So she had another boy, Bless him, called Ronny. So I've only brothers, no sisters.

'When I was little, Father used to take me everywhere. We used to walk round the lake in Roundhay Park. We noticed a pretty little girl about my age - I'd have been about twelve. My father said "Come here."

'I was right embarrassed. I said "Ooh, don't! don't!"

'Father said "My daughter hasn't got a friend to play with. Will you go out with her?"

'The little girl said "I haven't got a friend either. I'd love to go out with

Little Celia and her family

156

her."

'After that I used to go with her. Father thought she was a right pretty little girl. She was called Eva Levy. They lived in Glover Street. Her father was a tailor like everyone else. I used to go to their house and sit in the middle of the floor telling stories. There were five little children sat all around listening fascinated.'

Celia had finished her life story, and Harry had not had to dance. The evening ended with 'God Save the King,' and after it the Jewish National Anthem. There was not yet a State of Israel. The anthem's name *Hatikvoh*, means *Hope*. It was full of yearning. 'Still in every heart...' it began. The tired dancers stood proudly to attention. The violins played plaintively. At the second repeat of the chorus, 'Not yet has it come to pass, our hope, the hope of two thousand years...' the dancers sang, not understanding the Hebrew words, only the feelings. '...to be a free people, in our own country, in the Land of Zion, in Jerusalem.'

Celia didn't catch a word of the Hebrew, but Ralph heard her sing clearly, and perfectly in tune with the last soulful phrase, a classical Jewish recipe in Yiddish, '... and then she added some pepper to the chicken fat.'

The first time Celia went to Harry's house was when she had a holiday from work on the Day of Atonement. She arrived pale and hungry, since all her family and everyone in Vandyke Street fasted on this holiest day of the year. She found, to her amazement, a large number of brothers and sisters all gathered round the piano in the front room, not in the least solemn or religious. Sam was playing and the others were dancing and singing and generally messing about. 'All those naughty children,' Celia said. 'I thought it was right lovely.'

Celia went into the kitchen and found Harry sitting at the table, quietly, on his own, reading, with a mug of tea in front of him, and a half eaten bagel. Celia was amazed. 'It's the Day of Atonement...' she stammered.

'Never mind that,' Harry said, simply. 'If you're hungry, eat!'

'You daren't eat on the Day of Atonement,' Celia said, confused.

'Don't be silly,' Harry said. 'If you're hungry, eat!'

At this Celia looked shyly towards Harry's mother, who smiled at her, encouragingly.

Harry's mother couldn't imagine any girl would be interested in him.

'Which one do you belong to?' she asked Celia.

'Oh,' Celia said, 'I belong to all of them.'

On a Saturday afternoon two weeks later, Harry left the Raisman house in Villiers Terrace and walked down to North Street to meet Celia. Together they crossed to the poorer side of North Street and walked together down Byron Street. They were descending into the Leylands where Celia lived. Celia was terribly nervous that her family might make a bad impression. Harry was pleased about the noise of the tramcars since it meant he could give up even trying to hear what was being said to him.

'That's our school,' said Celia as they passed Darley Street School, quite a step down from Lovell Road School on the other side of North Street. 'We only spoke Yiddish at home. When I went to school they looked at me right funny when I spoke. I didn't realise. I thought everyone spoke like that.'

They had come to the top of Vandyke Street and stepped off the pavement to cross the cobblestones of the slightly wider Byron Street. Celia pointed out a house. 'I went to Hebrew school there,' she said. 'It was a private Hebrew school. My grandma used to pay a ha'penny a week for me to go. She thought I should marry a rabbi and be a rabbi's wife. So I had to learn Hebrew.'

By this time they were beside the house. It was at the end of the terrace and slightly bigger than the others. Harry glanced through the window into a square kitchen-living room. Celia carried on chattering. 'It's not a Hebrew school any more. The teacher's dead now. He lived on his own. He used to have a little shoe repair business downstairs. Upstairs was our classroom, and his little bedroom. He didn't charge much for the children to go to his classes, not enough to manage without any other work.

'All my brothers went to Hebrew school, to learn to say their barmitzvahs. I was the only girl among the boys and he taught me how to read and write. My father used to get letters from his sister in Russia and I had to read them to him. They were in Yiddish, but written in Hebrew letters. I used to spell them out letter for letter. They were always asking if we could send them anything, saying how poor they were, how so-and-so was poorly, how they had nothing to eat. We used to send them a few shillings when we could.

'I used to write the letters back,' Celia continued. 'It took a long time, spelling the words out. My father was right pleased with me. They gave me a ha'penny for writing the letter. It was so unusual for a girl to go to Hebrew school. I was the teacher's pet. The boys were right wild and he used to bang them on the head and all sorts with his ruler. He was always shouting at them and I was very quiet. The teacher used to like me because I was a little bossy ha'porth.'

Celia and Harry turned away from the house and meandered on into narrow Vandyke Street. Celia continued her story.

'The teacher used to say, "You're the best girl of all the boys." He used to say, "Well, well, well… Read, read, read..." and he'd stand over me patting me on the head with one hand and stroking his beard with the other.

'"Well," he used to say. "You're the best girl of all the boys," and pat my head.

'"But I'm the only girl here," I said. So he laughed.

'"That's why I said it," he said.

'People said he had a son who was killed in the war.'

Harry listened as best he could to all this, but didn't choose to tell Celia the story of Rebby Lublinksy's son, Sam R. Lublinksy. Rifleman 39321 of the 7th Battalion, the West Yorkshire Regiment, the Prince of Wales Own, whose name appeared in Scott's Roll of Honour for Leeds, followed by the letters K. in A. (Killed in Action).

Celia slipped in through the half-open door of Number 25, Vandyke Street and Harry was about to follow. 'Come in,' a welcoming voice said from inside.

Harry stepped over the threshold and stopped dead in his tracks. 'Ugh! Ugh!' he said, shuddering violently. Two big fat black cats were disporting themselves in the room.

'You must choose between me and the cats,' said Harry agitatedly, adding no further explanation, and stepping hastily back into the street.

'Mam, get rid of the cats quickly!' Celia almost sobbed in fright.

When the cats had gone, Harry entered very gingerly, looking suspiciously at the floor round his feet, and finally sat at the very edge of the table. Celia's mother and father looked on, amused.

'We have to have a cat for the mice,' said Celia apologetically. 'The other one, the right fat one, belongs to my grandma. She lives in the next street with my Uncle Reuben. The two cats are friends. When my grandma comes to see my mother, the cat comes to visit her friend and they play together.'

Celia's father Isaac Narunsky was a big man with a square forehead and a strong triangular nose and a thick mass of wavy hair, brushed well back from the corners of his temples on each side. He had a gruff voice, almost a bark and he used it little. Celia kept glancing nervously at her father hoping that this bear-like man with his rough uneducated speech would not make a bad impression on Harry who was so softly spoken, who said such incomprehensible things, who came from such a learned family and who lived on the good side of North Street.

Celia's mother set about entertaining her daughter's guest. Everything happening in the room was dominated by the two brothers, Eddy, aged eleven, and Teddy, a year younger. Eddy was a paler, slightly-built version of his father. There was a faintly angelic cast to his delicate features. Teddy was more full-blooded and his little face bubbled with mischief.

'Teddy,' his mother said, 'go and get some eggs.'

bubbled with mischief

Teddy ran off with Eddy quietly following.

'Eggs,' grunted his father in disgust. 'Who she sends for eggs!'

In a few minutes Teddy reappeared at the open door, still running. Unfortunately, he didn't remember to look where he was going. He slipped and dropped the bag of eggs. 'Oh Dear!' said his mother, glancing nervously at her quick-tempered husband.

'I can't live,' he growled, 'I can't live from him!'

'Go and get some more,' said his mother. 'This time take a bowl.'

Teddy soon reappeared carrying two eggs in the bowl. He held the bowl in both hands at the level of his face, and proceeded carefully, almost ceremoniously, through the door. He was just about to put it down on the table, under his father's nose, when his attention was somehow diverted. He slipped, and the bowl fell. Once again the eggs were lost. The father stood up in rage. 'Don't hit him, don't hit him!' said his wife. They couldn't help laughing.

160

'He's a gift from heaven,' growled Teddy's father, sitting down again.

It was already dusk and the light from the half-open door flooded into the street. It was a mild evening. Celia's mother cut slices of black bread and placed them before the family and guest. 'Eat, eat,' she encouraged them and brought out a dish of rendered chicken fat.

Celia's father spread the fat on the bread and sprinkled it thickly with salt. He looked up at their guest. 'Well, take a piece,' he said gruffly.

The two little brothers sat unwillingly at the table. They were used to running around while they ate but Celia had warned them to behave properly in front of her guest. They fidgeted. Their father frowned. There was much kicking under the table. Teddy giggled. 'Be quiet!' said their father. 'How much more of this do we have to put up with? Have you findished? Stop sniggering like a horse!'

Teddy tried to suppress a giggle, and nearly choked. Then they were silent for a while. Serenely, the angelic little Eddy, always his father's favourite, manoeuvered himself into a suitable position to land a kick without seeming to move. 'Ow!' said Teddy, and began to giggle uncontrollably.

His father made a move. 'Rascal!' he said threateningly.

'It wasn't me. It was him,' the innocent Teddy protested in a high-pitched voice.

Now, the two little boys, still sitting in their seats, had actually secretly lifted themselves off their chairs and were supporting themselves on their hands. When the adults' attention was suitably averted, they completed this complicated manoeuvre and wriggled down under the table. Harry felt a slight tug at one shoelace, and involuntarily moved his foot. The boys were trying to undo his shoelaces and tie them round the table leg.

'Where are the children?' asked their father suspiciously. Reluctantly the two brothers wriggled back up into their seats, their faces red with exertion.

'Got to go to the toilet,' said Teddy suddenly, seeking an escape.

Teddy and Eddy got up together. They took the metal key. It was over a foot long and fitted the doors of the communal lavatory in Bushfield Street at the back of Vandyke Street. They looked appealingly at their father for matches.

Their father knew this was one of their favourite places for tricks. 'Three, and that's enough...' he warned, holding out the matchbox but not letting go of it. Teddy fumbled in the matchbox and managed to extract four matches. Then he raised the long metal key in his right hand. He saw himself as a knight in armour, carrying a standard and leading his comrades into battle.

'Charge!' roared Teddy, and with Eddy following he galloped his imaginary horse out of the door. A cold blast of air replaced him.

'Teddy,' barked his father 'Door!' Eddy briefly reappeared and closed the offending door.

The outside lavatories were a row of cubicles. Each one had a key and was shared by a group of four adjacent houses. In each cubicle the occupant sat over a stream of water about six inches deep and a foot wide which flowed continuously about eighteen inches below the seat and ran from one cubicle to another. They were unlit and at night the users would illumine them briefly with matches stuck into the crumbling mortar between the bricks of the walls.

Naturally, matches presented many possibilities to the kids. That week at Darley Street School the boys had learnt about Elizabeth, that most English of queens, and her gallant sea-dog, Sir Francis Drake. In 1587 England's enemy, the King of Spain, was assembling the huge galleons for the Spanish Armada which was to sail against England the next year. The vast ships of this supposedly invincible force were being gathered in Spain's natural harbour at Cadiz. Outside, in the open Atlantic, sailed Drake with his fast squadron of heroic little English ships.

One night, under cover of darkness, Drake's little squadron edged up to the harbour mouth of Cadiz. Inside, the tall galleons were packed close together, bristling with guns. Drake ordered a few of his ships to be packed with timber, pitch and other inflammable material, and had them silently sailed into the crowded harbour. Once in, they were lit. Fire spread rapidly from one ship to another. The galleons were too closely packed to be manoeuvred in the confusion. Many were still only half-constructed. In that one night without a single shot being fired, a large part of the dreaded Spanish Armada fleet was destroyed. Drake sailed off exultantly as the Spanish fleet burned. In England the incident was called 'The Singeing of the King of Spain's Beard.'

The two brothers reflected on this amazing story as they wandered off to Bushfield Street. When they were in the toilet they heard someone enter the next cubicle downstream from theirs. From her mutterings, they recognized the voice of the six-fingered woman. This was the *nextdoorinky* (the woman from next door). They didn't like her. Quietly they constructed several boats of folded newspaper. Each boat was filled with a load of crumpled paper, and set down on the stream, just eighteen inches below the seat. When all was ready and they could hear that their neighbour was seated, they lit the contents of the boats and, using the long toilet cubicle key as a punt-pole, sent them down the stream, like Drake sending his fire-ships into Cadiz Harbour to singe the King of Spain's beard.

The boys slipped out and ran silently back home. It was time for them to go to bed. They shared the same bed. Their mother went off to see them settled. Unlike the grand houses in Villiers Terrace, the Leylands homes had no electricity. Downstairs the rooms were brilliantly lit by a delicate gauze mantle heated to white incandescence by a hissing gas-jet in the ceiling. But upstairs a simple gas-pipe ended in the wall over the beds, and the rooms were lit uncertainly by its smoky, yellow flame.

'Put your hands under the blankets,' said Celia's mother as she tucked in Teddy and Eddy; and she told them her nightly story, which she had had from her mother when she was a girl in Lithuania. And even though the two boys in Vandyke Street knew nothing of Lithuania, they caught, hardly knowing where it came from, a glimpse of the chill and the terrors of the Russian night:

There came a little bear
It gave a knock on the little door
It broke the door down
And ate up all the little children.

The brothers waited tensely under the blankets, ready:

Where is little Teddy?
He's here, he's here, he's here!

And his mother's hand dived in under the blankets and under Teddy's pyjama jacket and tickled his tummy while the two little boys wriggled about squealing with laughter.

After this first visit, Harry began to see Celia regularly, but he could never get her to enjoy the countryside he so loved himself. 'She always remained unimpressed,' my father told me.

'She's dead to natural beauty. She finds it boring. She says, "What is

there? There's only green grass. I'd much rather sit in a cafe in town."
That's her idea of a good time.'

My mother, who had listened to this impassively, now repeated with
some emphasis. 'Well, what is there? There's only green, green grass.
It's the same everywhere. And all those horrible old houses, just like the
Leylands. I'd much rather see a lovely modern house. And what if
you're out there and it starts pouring with rain? I'd much rather sit in a
right nice cafe in town and talk with all the girls.'

For his part, my father was more at home with the saying 'where every
prospect pleases, and only man is vile.' It was the vast, brooding
solitudes of moorland that pleased him. He was not particularly attracted
by picturesque villages or country cottages, or colourful local people.
'Every little village,' he said, 'however small, has a pub and a church,'
and he shuddered. 'Cesspits of the body and the mind.'

Over the years Harry and Celia had come to a perfectly amicable
agreement to differ on this matter of green grass, although for a short
time after they had first met, he had persisted in trying to convert her, and
for this purpose he bought a James motorcycle and sidecar. This
extended the range of his excursions into the countryside. He could even
get beyond the Dales and into the Lake District. That was when the
machine was working.

Despite his own impractical nature, Harry was not against machinery.
On the contrary, he treated it with undue respect, always thinking things
were much stronger, more powerful, and more efficient than they really
were. At that time, motorcycles were such that even able enthusiasts
spent far more time repairing than riding them. Somehow, Harry's
persistence got the machine on the road. Getting the engine to start was
itself a triumph. The bike rarely managed more than twenty miles an
hour, and frequently shed its exhaust pipe, which deafened everyone else
around, but Harry said, gave it more power. To stop the bike Harry would
look for a hill to drive up since the brakes didn't work on a downward
slope.

Myer used to be amused by this unreliable machine. He little guessed
that one time when he was enjoying a ride in the sidecar and the bike was
accelerating to 70 miles an hour, its highest speed ever, his brother Harry
was actually trying to stop it. Myer used to tease his brother by singing
a popular song:

He had to getunder,
Getout and getunder,
To fix up his automobile.

The bike was short-lived but its last day glorious and sunny. Harry took
it down to Vandyke Street to pick up Celia. 'No cars or motor bikes ever
came down Vandyke Street,' said Celia. 'It caused a sensation. People
came out to look at it. They kept talking about it for ages, saying what a
wealthy man I must be going out with. And here he had nothing.'

Harry and Celia set off early in the morning, crossed into Wharfedale,
drove up through the riverside towns of Otley and Ilkley, and climbed
over Addingham Hill to descend again into Upper Airedale. It was
around midday when they drove through the crowded market-place in
Skipton. Harry noticed that the warmth of the sun seemed to be coming
from below as well as above. Petrol had leaked from the carburettor and
the engine had caught fire. Flames came from between his legs. Harry
leaped off the saddle, and hauled Celia out of the sidecar. An amused
passer-by kindly threw a blanket over the engine. It was apparently
unharmed, and it arose, like a phoenix, from the ashes. Harry and Celia
continued at twelve miles an hour into Malhamdale where the bike easily
climbed a small rise and started off on a slight downward slope. The
James seemed to have been stimulated by its recent roasting. It gathered
speed. The fresh Dales wind was in Harry's face and the blue sky
sparkled. In the exhilaration of the moment he recited:

Come fill the clarion, sound the fife
To all the wondering world proclaim
That one hour of crowded life
Is worth an age without a name.

Unfortunately, at that moment a cow decided to cross the road a few
hundred yards ahead. There should have been plenty of time. Harry
pulled fiercely at the brake lever. The bike rolled on inexorably. Then
he applied himself vigorously to tooting the little rubber bulb of the
pipsqueak horn mounted on the handlebars. The cow was unmoved,
obviously determined to contest its right to cross its own road at whatever
pace and place it chose. Harry looked around desperately. The road was
flanked by dry-stone walls, and there was no escape route. With its horn
honking like a forlorn duck, and its brakes squealing, the bike juddered

on down the hill. It hit the cow full amidships.

'The cow,' said Harry, 'uttered a loud belch, and walked off in disgust. The bike stopped at last. The cow went into the field and started to graze indignantly. I noticed that in the heat of the moment I had forgotten to close the throttle. That was the end of the James.' They caught the bus home. It was late. 'The end of a perfect day,' said Celia.

Harry saw Celia back to Vandyke Street. 'And even the weariest lover,' he said 'winds somewhere home to tea.' He was too tired to notice Eddy and Harry fussing round his feet. He didn't stay long. The night sky was clearing and it was getting cold. They stood outside the door and he looked up at the stars. 'They all have names,' he said. 'The Pleiades, Andromeda, Cassiopoeia. The stars have colours. Through a powerful telescope you can see them, red, blue, green. There are 85 constellations altogether. A lot of them we never see, they're in the southern hemisphere. It's a pity we never get a cloudless sky. I'd point out to you the Great Square of Pegasus, you can't mistake it, and the Great Bear, the Lesser Bear, Cassiopoeia, Andromeda, and the Pleiades, the daughters of Atlas. You can see six or seven stars, they form a white patch in the sky. Actually there are several hundreds, but they're so far away they just form a white patch in the sky. With a telescope you can see them all clearly.' His voice was full of longing. The strange names of the constellations reminded him of the Greeks and of the education he could never have. Wistfully he savoured the words, full of wonder.

'The distances to the stars,' he said 'are so great that you can't measure them in miles. They are measured in light years. A light year is the distance that you can travel in one year if you travel at the speed of light.'

Celia didn't try to follow all this, but she felt it was the way educated people talk, and she was thrilled. She looked at the stars.

'I always wanted a bedroom of my own,' she said 'with a dressing table suite, like my friend Beattie Goldberg. When I was at your house your mother asked me what I wanted, and I told her a boy. Your mother's a very clever woman. Very clever, and very kind. She looked at me and said, "Do you want him to be like your father and brothers?"

'"My father!" I said, "my father's a tailor, his father was a tailor, his brother was a tailor. We're donkeys. We work with our hands and our feet. I want to have a little boy and I want him to be clever, like your Jeremy and your boys." She just smiled.'

They were both silent for a while.

'What would you do if you had a lovely house?' Celia asked.

'I'd have a billiard table,' Harry said, 'and an observatory in the attic, with a telescope to look at the stars.'

Celia and Harry both fell silent again. They had spoken of their dreams. A tired little wind curled down Vandyke Street. It had come a long way from Mexico and the final crossing of the Pennines had chilled it. Harry turned up his collar and trudged off up Vandyke Street towards North Street, not noticing his unfastened left shoelace trailing along as he walked.

Celia went back inside and closed the door.

Alfonso Spagoni

Jeremy's career in India was a determined rise. When he arrived in 1916 he had started out on the lowest rung of the Indian Civil Service ladder, as a district officer in the eastern provinces of Bihar and Orissa, where he learned both of the local languages so as to be able to act as magistrate in the court cases that were brought to him. For this purpose Jeremy's training in horsemanship may well have impressed the natives but it had a much more important function. A horse was the only way a district officer could get around the rough tracks of the large district he was responsible for. In his spare time Jeremy learned Persian so as to be able to read the *Rubaiyat* in the original.

After several years in this posting, where he rose to be Under-Secretary, Jeremy was transferred in 1922 to Customs and Excise in Bombay, where he lived in a *chummery*, a bachelors' shared flat. From its earliest days, young recruits to the Indian Civil Service were expected, like Roman Catholic priests, to dedicate their entire attentions to the needs of the Indian Civil Service. To ensure this there was a strict rule that they were not allowed to marry until they had been in India for 6 years. In 1925 he married. From Bombay Jeremy and Renée went to Calcutta.

Replacing the innumerable local and corrupt methods of money gathering with a fair and open central taxation system was one of the main concerns of the Indian Civil Service. An essential element, as envisaged 100 years earlier by Macaulay, was the training of a generation of salaried Indian officials who would replace the venal court favourites of the many States, and provide a future independent India with a strong central government able to look after the welfare of the entire country and carry out large-scale effective public works.

For this role, Jeremy must have impressed his superiors. In 1928 he was made Commissioner of Income Tax for the entire region of the North-west Frontier Province and the Punjab, where the British were constructing barrages on the five great rivers. In 1929 Jeremy and his wife produced Ada and Maurice's first grandchild, John Michael and later, a second, Jer. And throughout his long and incredibly busy life, Jeremy would be to his sons everything that Jeremy's father had not been to his. After 5 years Jeremy was transferred to the Central Board of Revenue in Delhi.

In ancient Greece, the Spartans had the custom of exposing their newborn infants on the rocks to ensure that only the fittest survived. In the British Empire, it was the long established custom that members of the imperial foreign service, scattered over the globe, sent their children back to school in England. For Jeremy, sending his son back to England had another purpose, to ensure that John Michael would receive the world class education that Jeremy himself had

BY APPOINTMENT
TO HIS EXCELLENCY THE LORD WILLINGDON
VICEROY AND GOVERNOR GENERAL
OF INDIA

received. But the early separation was a wrench for a father who could look back on his childhood as a boy sardine sharing a bed with four brothers, and a family life as close as the four close walls of a Leylands back-to-back house. And all the more so when John Michael, who had been sent away at only six years old and was staying in England at the Manor House School in Horsham, caught mumps.

26th November, 1934

Dear John,

Ask Miss Rob to read this letter to you. I got your letter all about Marseilles and Gib. You're a lucky fellow to have been to so many places in the world, aren't you?

You have been a Mumplestiltskin once, so now the dumplings have bumped your face you can never be a Mumper again. Miss Rob has sent us a photograph which she took of you in your football kit and white sweater with your mouth open showing where the teeth had dropped out. We thought your toothless face was quite funny enough without mumplets as well, and what it must have looked like when Grannie wrapped the stocking round we cannot imagine. Grannie says it made you laugh like bilio, so it must have been very funny indeed.

Well here we all are in Simla at last, back in old Chislehurst in the house where you romped and climbed and jumped and shouted. We all came together in the Humber, we left Delhi very early in the morning at five o'clock and we saw the sun rise when we were driving along. There were thousands of monkeys all along the road sitting munching and chattering and making funny faces at us. When I sounded the horn the tiny ones all scampered away but some of the old ones just sat and blinked at us as we passed, and looked as if they had mumps! Jer was very good indeed, he slept quite a lot, and sat and played and was very happy, and had his meals very nicely out of the lunch box. Once he put his hands on the steering wheel and tried to drive the car. When we reached Chislehurst he would crawl all over the floor and into all the rooms exploring the strange new house, and his hands and knees got so black that it took Mummy and Nanny a long time to scrub all the dirt off before they put him to bed. Pip is very happy here and full of beans, dashing all round the place. He now sleeps in my room at night.

Well that is all our news but we do hope that your mumps are better by now and that the Doctor will say you are out of quarantine before very long. It really is awfully unlucky and tiresome for you but you must be brave and cheerful and make the best of it. Give my love to Grannie and Grandpa, we are terribly sorry for the trouble they have had and very thankful to them for looking after you.

Bye-bye, God bless.
Lots of love from Daddy

Coming back to India, after his first year away, John Michael described the journey from Delhi to Simla. 'I remember going from Delhi by train to Kalka at the foothills of the Himalayas. Then we continued by car. The drive up into the hills from Kalka to Simla was very winding, and we used to sing songs. Alfonso Spagoni was Papa's great party piece. Very often at parties they were called on to recite a poem or sing a song, and Alfonso Spagoni was his great party piece. He sang it. He had enough of a singing voice to sing that. It doesn't take a lot of a singing voice.'

List to me while I tell you
Of the blighter who blighted my life.
List to me while I tell you
Of the man who ran off with my wife.
'Twas at the bullfight that I met him
He was doing his daring display.
And when I went out for some nuts
*   and a programme*
The dirty dog stole her away.
Yes he did, yes he did
And tonight I will have my revenge.
If I catch Alfonso Spagoni the toreador,
With one mighty blow I shall dislocate
*   his bally jaw.*

But soon John Michael was off back to England again. In India the pressure for independence was growing. The Viceroy, Lord Willingdon, speaking for the British Raj, proposed to Gandhi that India should be raised to dominion status, on a level Canada and Australia. The Indian Civil Service was involved in tense negotiations over the status of the Indian Native States.

3, Queensway, New Delhi, 3rd December 1935
Dear John,

It is Daddy's turn to write to you this week. I am sorry I have not written for such a long time, but I have been rather busy in the office. You know, India is a member of the League of Nations, and because Mussolini won't stop fighting (in Ethiopia) the League says that none of her countries should send Italy anything to fight with or lend Italy any money or buy any of the things that Italy wants to sell to get money. So I have to send

171

orders to the chief men in the ports of India such as Bombay and Calcutta and Madras where the big ships come with passengers and cargo that they must not allow any cargoes from Italy to be taken off the ships and landed in India. And we all hope that if Italy can't sell her things to any other country she will soon have no money left to buy guns and ammunition and aeroplanes or even to pay the soldiers and then she will have to stop fighting whether she likes it or not. And that will be one in the eye for old Musso and perhaps he will stop thinking himself the greatest man in all the world and go off quietly somewhere and sell ice cream!

You must be feeling quite excited getting so near the end of term, and with Christmas coming along so soon now, I hope you will have a jolly good time at Sutton with Grannie and Grandpa and Mike, and then at Tedfold Farm with Richard. I see you have thought of the things you would like Father Christmas to bring you. Well I hope he won't forget any of them. But what are you going to do with roller skates at the Gallop? The pavement there isn't smooth or flat enough, neither is the Crossways. I expect you'll come lots of 'purlers' right down on the seat of your pants.

> *Mr Corkery on his skates*
> *Rolling swiftly down the Gallop,*
> *Whizzing past the people's gates*
> *At the bottom he goes –Wallop!*

> *Up he rises undismayed*
> *Once again upon his feet.*
> *See, once more too far he swayed*
> *And gone bump upon his seat!*

Master Jer is now the 'Chota Sahib' of this house. Nagina, the chaprassi, salutes him every morning and says 'Salaam, Chota Sahib,' and Jer smiles back. I think Mummy has written to you that we have arranged for you to have 'Brownie' to ride. She is an awfully nice pony, much bigger than Tinker Bell but very gentle and nice-mannered. Barbara de Burgh used to ride her, but she is big enough for grown-ups to ride if they are not too fat and heavy (like me!!) and she goes very nicely with horses. So I think you will have some interesting trots and gallops on her and Mummy or I will ride with you on Joan.

Soon after we get to Delhi, on the first of November, I shall have to go travelling for six weeks to see some of the great Maharajahs of India and discuss things with them. Although India belongs to the British Empire only a part of it is really ruled by us on behalf of the King. This part is called British India. The other part is a lot of States, each like a separate country, with its own Ruler or Prince or Raja. These Rajas are not quite independent, I mean they cannot rule their States just anyway they please, for they owe allegiance to the King and if they behave too badly to their subjects he can even remove them from the throne and put somebody else in their place. But if they are fairly good rulers the King does not interfere with them. But now there is a great plan for all the Rajas to join in British India and make one great Union, to be called the Federation of India. So several officers of British India are going to talk it over with the Rajas, and I am one of them. The chief States which I shall visit are Baroda (whose Ruler is the Gaekwar), Nawanagar (whose Ruler is called the Jam Sahib – not marmalade!), Hyderabad (ruled by the Nizam), Mysore, Travancore and Cochin (all ruled by Maha-rajas). I think it will be very interesting and if I can get some nice postcards of their palaces I shall send you them. I hope to finish my travels in the States of the Rajahs before Christmas, so I shall be in good time to go down to Bombay and meet the Moldavia when it arrives on January 14th. Won't that be an exciting meeting?

Aunt Maisie writes that you did not eat much tea because you want to get thin. We hope this is only a joke, because we don't want you to eat too little, and if you get thin you might not be so strong and healthy.

Bye-bye, God bless.
Lots of love from Daddy

In 1936 Lord Linlithgow became Viceroy of India and Jeremy was appointed secretary of the Finance Department. Two years after that he became Director of the Reserve Bank of India and in the next year Finance Member of the Government of India, one of the most important government posts in the British Empire. Now he was the man responsible for carrying out the economic policies of the entire sub-continent.

Myer's Tale

In this wilderness shall ye be consumed, and ye shall not come unto the promised Land. But your little ones, them will I bring in, and they shall know the Land.   Numbers 14

And this generation was known for ever as the Wilderness Generation   Ibn Ezra

Once it became obvious that the Labour Party was able to get candidates elected to Parliament Myer felt satisfied. 'Now the working class has a voice,' he said 'it can look after itself.' From now on Myer withdrew himself from trade union activities and from the meetings at the Star Inn, and devoted his entire attention to his obsession with the family plan.

No wand of Fate, and no one event was responsible for the Raismans' improvement, but for every one of those who experienced those days, the tale of the Raisman family will always be Myer's tale. Countless miles Myer marched on the foot treadle of a sewing machine, countless times, as he paused to turn a seam, his hand flew up to halt the shiny wheel, avoiding without a thought the sharp steel clip spinning in the leather drive belt. Myer could load the intricate little shuttles made of smooth shiny metal, even when he was so blind he couldn't see them; he could thread a needle in total darkness.

For the tailors hand sewing was the most tedious work. The cloths were dark and heavy, and the tailors bent over them with large, hot naked light bulbs hanging a few inches in front of their foreheads. After hours of concentration the herring-bone patterns of the tweeds seemed to be dancing of their own accord, and Harry found that when he looked up his eyes could no longer focus. 'My attic,' he said 'brought me no Attic salt.'

The miles Myer treadled away, making trousers he couldn't see, and the miles Harry stitched in his silent world, led to a dreamed-of place that they would never reach. The children and the children's children would get there and be saved. 'We worked,' said my father 'so that you could go to school and have a better life - not to have the horrible life of drudgery to which we were exposed, not to have to work in the horrible conditions we experienced.'

And even as Myer and Harry worked the other brothers seemed to be escaping. Their cousin Louis, who had lived next to them in Sheepscar Place, had not followed the family's move west of the Leylands. He had gone much further west, to Montreal, and had become a very wealthy man. Now he returned on a visit. He had made one fortune, he said, and lost it gambling. Then he made another as a stevedore and secured it by an annuity.

Cousin Louis' parents had died, his father of delirium tremens, and his mother of diabetes, after having an arm and a leg amputated. Louis wanted to show his gratitude for the help Maurice Raisman had given him when his own father had rejected him and he had lived in Sheepscar Place. He did so by trying to help two of the brothers. The oldest brother, Louis, he took back to Canada with him and set up in business there. Brother Louis never once sent any letter back to Leeds, and in fact the family never heard from him again during his lifetime. Later they learned that he had gambled all his life, dissipated all the money his cousin had given him, and died penniless.

The other thing the well-meaning cousin Louis did was to put up money to set John up in business. Without knowing it, by this act he set the stage for the ruin of all the Raisman hopes, and all Myer and Harry were working for. Cousin Louis had lavished his help on the two most feckless of the Raisman brothers.

By this time Jeremy had stopped coming back to stay with the family. When he came to Leeds he associated with his great friend Jeremy Frais, grandson of the first Marienpoler immigrant. The Frais brothers' huge tailoring factory was a great, ugly square building in Millgarth, towering over the section of the railway line that ran on rubber sleepers through the old cholera graveyard. 'We woke up one morning and found we were wealthy,' Jeremy Frais said, and with their new-found prosperity the Frais brothers reconstructed their grandfather's simple grave as a miniature domed mausoleum in the Marienpoler part of the cemetery, right at the top of the greenhorns' plot at Gildersome. The dome overlooked the little dilapidated brick wall which separated this part from the adjacent Yurbericker plot, just as the River Niemen separated the two little towns in Lithuania.

From the time he had won his Oxford scholarship, the Frais family had been filled with admiration for Jeremy Raisman, and they had given him a pound a week to help him over his difficult first years. Now Jeremy was well on his way to becoming Sir Jeremy Raisman, and his reputation spread in Leeds. 'Jeremy told us,' Harry said 'that they had to give him a knighthood. It wouldn't do for a plain mister to be in charge of all those titled people. Just think of the dinner announcements when he came in first.'

After the war, Jack had, despite his complaints, gone to Leeds Medical School. Jacob Kramer, who knew all the Raisman brothers, had become obsessed by the idea of the corpses in the dissection room, and he persuaded Jack to let him sketch one. From the sketch Kramer developed a strange plastic, wasted object, glowing with a phosphorescent light of putrefaction. 'I was fascinated with its beauty,' he wrote later, a similar preoccupation to his more famous counterpart, Chaim Soutine.

At this time Kramer began work on what was to be his life's artistic ambition. The most mystical moment in the Hebrew calendar is when the priestly caste, the Kohanim, covering their heads with their prayer shawls, process round the synagogue on the Day of Atonement. At this moment the congregation are required to turn away, lest the Evil Eye enter into their eyes. Kramer was fascinated by this moment. Gradually he began to amass studies of heads in half profile, bearded old men, with prayer shawls. Over the years the pictures began to assemble in ones and twos. Eventually he produced a complete procession on a small canvas. This was followed by another and another. The canvases became larger and larger, and the heads and shoulders more and more stylised and geometric. In the end the Kohanim were assembled into a rhythmic, pulsing pattern. By now the picture was too big for him to afford the canvas, and Kramer carried out the final version on three vast wooden doors, covering more than half a room. It was to be his final effort at the procession. He never again attempted such a large scale project.

The Day of Atonement

Gradually now Myer's Plan was working itself out. Jeremy, John, Jack, Sarah and Ralph were all qualified. Fanny got married and moved with her husband to Sunderland. Only Myer and Harry were left working. And now, to Myer's horror, the two youngest brothers refused to go to university. 'They were impatient,' Myer said. 'They thought it was easy. They wanted to get rich quickly. They didn't want to have to work.' The opportunity Myer and Jeremy had had to deny to Harry was being flung back in their faces.

In truth, the last of the brood had a hard time at school. 'You're not as bright as your brothers,' the teachers said. The heroic days were over. They would get up late, not dress and idle around in the house all day in brocaded dressing gowns. The family was becoming bourgeois.

John, despite his idleness, had an outstanding university career. In the intervals between gambling he qualified in Latin and Greek, then Law.

His professor later told Jeremy that John might have had even better results if the examiners could have read his writing. His early teachers had failed in their efforts to make him right-handed. Now his left hand, once perhaps prepared to serve him well, was not happy as second choice.

Using his cousin Louis' money, John set up as a solicitor. The family now formed the plan to concentrate the younger members in John's law office. Ralph, also a solicitor, joined him, Sidney became a solicitor's clerk, Sarah helped with the office work, and Sam started to form a related business for building houses. With this family consortium, the pattern was set for a family leap to fame and fortune. The Leylands were firmly behind them. The family had a doctor, three lawyers, and an imperial civil servant with a knighthood. They lived in a house with two addresses. The future must have seemed indeed bright.

It was for so many other Leylands concerns. The Leylanders were at that time producing what were to become the major tailoring firms of our country. Montague Burton had started a retail clothing shop with £100 in Sheffield in 1900. Six years later he set up a factory to make the clothes in Concord Street, a narrow Leylands alley parallel to Byron Street. It opened on to North Street just past the Smithfield Iron Works, where a hundred years earlier the world's first lawn mower had been invented, and opposite the Sheeny Park.

With his new found wealth Montague Burton had spearheaded the migration northwards out of Leeds to Harrogate, where he built a sumptuous new home. 'One day,' Burton said, 'I'll employ all the Jewish tailors of Leeds.' But he was not antagonistic to other Leeds Jewish tailoring firms, and when Lubelski's small factory had a fire, Burton wrote him a sympathetic letter offering assistance to get him started again. In fact, the production of Burton's suits was to ensure that the Leeds Jewish community would never again have paupers.

Burton's idea of both manufacturing and retailing was immensely successful, and when the factory moved to new premises in Hudson Road in 1921 it was the largest tailoring business in the world. In the end its demand for cloth even outstripped the available supply in Leeds and the firm sent buyers to the Australian cloth market in Sydney.

Mr Marks' Penny Bazaar, which Maurice Raisman had disdained in preference to his gambling, had stood in the covered market at Kirkgate, just across Lady Lane from the Leylands. Now it was on its way to becoming the gigantic firm of Marks and Spencers'.

Not everyone did so well, and at about this time Myer and Harry's home tailoring workshop started to run seriously out of orders. Trade was seasonal but the family's needs were not. It was impossible to save money. The big firms like Burton's, with nearly 900 outlet shops all over the country, could smooth out the seasonal aspects of the work by building up stock in the slack time. Myer had hardly enough money to keep the family in food, while Harry wanted money to get married and set up his own home. Harry decided to go to work at Burton's.

Celia was already working as a secretary for Montague Burton's half-brother, and when Celia and Harry got married, Bernard gave them a gift of a magnificent clock. The clock was made of a marquetry of different coloured woods set together in a step-like form somewhat reminiscent of the pyramid of Zoser near Cairo. It had an extraordinarily complex mechanism, which could be viewed in action through a wooden door at the back. At the front a brass frame bearing the glass covering its square face opened like a bay window to reveal three round holes with little square pegs through which different parts of the mechanism were wound up weekly with a special key kept under the pedestal. The clock chimed the Westminster chimes on every quarter, and it was to serve many unusual purposes, as it chimed away the nearly 3 million quarters of a three quarters of a century marriage.

The gift did not modify Harry's socialistic disparagement of the Leylands capitalists. 'I doubt,' said Harry 'if he was 5 feet tall - a little dumpling of a man. I forget what Montague Burton's real name was. Probably Moses followed by some Polish surname with the usual unpronounceable conglomeration of consonants. People used to say that when he first arrived he went around with a pack on his back. He used to take elocution lessons to try and hide his foreign accent. But he was never successful. He spoke very slowly and distinctly, but it was still no use. He never got to say 'th' or 'w' properly. To annoy him one of the competing firms once published his real name.

'The factory's enormous. It was said to be the largest in Europe, and he was said to be the richest Jew in Europe. He loved to see his name everywhere. The factory had hundreds of drain pipes and on every available space they put his name. Where there wasn't enough space for the whole name, they just put the initials MB.

'One time Montague Burton had a very nasty set-back in his career. Someone had asked him to speak at a dinner in honour of the opening of something or other, and he didn't want to go. So he said, "Why don't you ask Lord Sieff?"'

'"We've already asked him," the man said.

'There was an author who, by chance, wrote about a person called Montague Burton. Burton called him to his office and asked him how much he wanted to remove the name from his book. And he gave him it.'

Burton's factory buzzer was so loud it resounded in all the houses in all the crowded little terraces for at least two miles across the valley at Harehills. It was thought to be a convenience for Burton's workers and their families to be daily informed of the factory's starting and finishing times. As for people who didn't work at Burton's, it would do them no harm to be reminded of the might of that great enterprise.

'Conditions,' said my father, 'were much better in Burton's factory than in the old days. In its day it was hailed as the most modern factory of its type. They were very proud of it. Altogether they claimed to employ 16 000 people. The total Jewish population of Leeds was 25 000. One in four men in England wore Burton's suits. At Passover they gave out free matsy to anyone who needed it. No questions were asked. If a family needed matsy, it didn't matter whether it was a pound or a hundred pounds, they went to the office, told them how much was wanted, and it was delivered to their homes. Even so there were many unofficial strikes and stoppages at Burton's. They were mainly about the arrogant way the foremen treated the tailors. The men regarded me as something of an unofficial leader. Apart from mother and Myer, I was the only one in the family that had left wing tendencies.'

May Velinski's little grocer's shop in Harehills occupied what would have been the parlour of the house. The workers passed there on the way to Burton's factory. 'When there was a strike at Burton's we fed 'em,' she said. 'Families wi' kids, we couldn't let 'em go hungry. Herring, bread, potatoes. We never made anything. They'd pay a pound for a week's food and we'd give 'em two pounds worth.'

After Harry had been working for a while at Burton's, the trade in Myer's home workshop in Villiers Terrace began to pick up again, but Myer found he couldn't manage the costs of sending the work out to other tailors. 'Will you come back and work for me?' he asked Harry. 'I'm not sure we can make as much as you get at Burton's, but there's the whole family to keep.' Harry left Burton's and went back to work with Myer.

As the home trade continued to expand, Myer and Harry looked around for a place to rent. They found a small workshop in Back Rockingham Street. With the help from Jeremy's remittances, they scraped together £30, and bought three second-hand sewing machines. Two hands were hired. For Myer, it was a major business venture. He had reached the peak of his career.

The cluster of dilapidated brick buildings and rusting corrugated iron sheds in Back Rockingham Street was known as Goodman's Buildings. They had been the hub of Maishy Goodman's empire, and they had a long history. Forty years before, in 1881, Maishy Goodman had gone back to Lithuania, intending to retire. But he found conditions there too harsh, and decided to come back to Leeds. Before leaving Lithuania he had recruited a pack of penniless young men, eager to get out of Russia, and desperate for work at any price. Among them were several members of his own family, including a young cousin who later became his second wife.

To employ all these people Maishy Goodman opened a tailor's workshop at 23 Back Rockingham Street. All this willing labour made Goodman rich. Five years later his workshop had expanded into 9A Rockingham Street. At Number 11, his friend Moshy Raisman was running a grocer's. By 1894 Maishy Goodman owned the grocer's and within three years his tailor's workshop had got into 10 Rockingham Street. Four years later he acquired another, even larger workshop at 26 Hope Street, and now made 11 and 13 Rockingham Street into a baker's.

Everyone in the Leylands knew Goodman and his Buildings. Celia described her experience of it to Harry. 'I remember when we hadn't anything to eat. On Friday afternoon we boiled an onion in water and left the window open so people would smell it and think there was food in the house. There was an Irish couple who lived next door. They were called

Joe and Elly. She used to come in and light the fire on Saturday morning, and we'd leave her a ha'penny on the mantelpiece. When we had no money we used to leave a piece of bread, in the end not even that. One day she came and lit the fire and we found she'd left us a ha'penny.

'Father was only too thankful when he could get work. He used to go round to Maishy Goodman's in Back Rockingham Street and wait. Every day. In the end they gave him work. I used to go there to bring my father's dinner, a few sandwiches of black bread and egg or chopped herring. It was in a little passage. I went up this old staircase. They were right thin rickety stairs, a right lot of steps and I had to get to the top. Oh, heck, I was right frightened of falling through. The boss has a right big stomach, 'cause he had plenty to eat. Father was always working when I went in. They didn't dare to open their mouths, they were so frightened of losing their jobs. They never stopped working. No dinner hour, no tea break, nothing. They were quite happy. They thought it had to be like that. Then trade got slack, and father had no work again. We had a few pounds in the Yorkshire Penny Bank at the bottom of Regent Street. Father kept drawing it out. After he'd been a few times, the man said "What's wrong with you?" In the end people came in and brought us what they could. Sometimes it was only a piece of bread. Then someone told him there was a job at Burton's. Ooh, and what joy! And jigger Maishy Goodman!'

Once you got a job at Burton's you were made for life. Celia's father could keep his family, and play billiards for threepence a tap in the union building in Cross Stamford Street. For the rest of his life, even much later when he was incapable of any useful work, Burton's ensured that Isaac Narunsky was never again out of a job.

In their workshop in Goodman's Buildings in Rockingham Street Myer and Harry tried to make a go of their tailoring workshop. 'It was a ramshackle building,' said Harry, 'nearly falling down. Goodman's Buildings, Eh! We called it Goodman's Yard. All Rockingham Street was in a state of decrepitude, advanced decrepitude. As for Back Rockingham Street... We rented the workshop from the Goodmans. It was conditional on us making up their orders first. In the cellar there was a baker's. They employed a baker. We used to get hot bagels early in the morning as we arrived at work. At street level there was Goodman's grocery shop, and above that was the workshop Myer and I rented.

'We started making up waistcoats for a family in Brunswick Terrace. They were enormous creatures, all of them. If you saw them you'd think they were cows wandering about on two legs. One of the women was so fat they had to get a car door modified for her to get through.'

'It was hard work,' said Myer, 'very hard, but we made a good screw out of it. We kept the family.'

The Crash

*As to murder, I never committed one in my life. It's
a well known thing amongst all my friends. I can get
a paper to certify as much, signed by lots of people.
Indeed, if you come to that, I doubt whether many
people could produce as strong a certificate. Mine
would be as big as a breakfast tablecloth.*

de Quincey: Essay on Murder as One of the Fine Arts

The Plan was simple. The money from Myer and Harry's tailoring had
been able to keep the family while the others were at school, then
university. When they were qualified, the family had combined in a huge
business venture which would now enrich them all. But now, for the
bustling brethren, who had wrestled in the Leylands with crickets and
cockroaches, cosily coping with bedcrumbs and bedbugs, the last act was
about to be enacted.

The Plan had only one weakness. It depended on all the family
working together, not an unreasonable expectation in the villages of
Russian Lithuania, or even in the early Leylands. But time was passing
and such family unity was everywhere falling apart. The Maggid's
sermon was to be prophetic.

The family had always expected Myer to marry his older cousin Jinny
whom he had seen regularly although at long intervals, ever since he had
been sent as a boy to stay at his aunt Rachel's house in Newcastle. Myer
and Jinny seemed well-matched. Both were progressive thinkers, and
Myer especially admired Jinny's forceful providence, so like that of his
mother. But by the same token Myer did not approve of marriage while
there was the stern business of the Family Plan to carry out. In Myer's
view a wife was a Victorian luxury, to be kept in idleness and in
expensive, unnecessary clothes.

Nonetheless, Myer did once send Jinny a present.

'What did you give her?' I asked.

'Brush,' said Myer, softly, self-deprecatingly dropping into the broad Yorkshire accent he always used when he felt a bit embarrassed. '...a hair brush... it's a personal thing.'

In the end Jinny married a master tailor, Barney Burlovitz, in Newcastle. He was twenty years older than her. 'Jinny's husband may have made the trousers,' said Myer, 'but Jinny wore them.'

Jinny

Jinny's marriage was neither long nor happy. 'Her husband,' Myer said, 'was coarse, drank, and was an adulterer and associated with loose women.' But he soon died, and Jinny had to fend for herself. She started her own very successful business selling drapery in all the little mining villages around Teesside, and setting up her own credit business. Like her mother, Jinny had three daughters. In Newcastle Jinny soon became, like Myer in Leeds, the undisputed head of her family. Her authority was respected even by her own mother, herself a tall imposing woman, totally blind with raven-black hair who lived to be a hundred and well nigh survived her redoubtable daughter.

Jinny had restless energy. She was the first genealogist of our family, and she travelled to America and Canada to visit the family of her aunts, the older daughters of the Maggid. A portrait of the Maggid hung in her living room.

So Myer and Jinny each carried out their separate, parallel plans. They were too similar to have married. Each was absorbed in the grim, historical struggle to drag their families from degradation into that invisible, bright future which only the next generation should enjoy.

But even as Myer's plan advanced, some of his younger brothers impatiently began to break ranks. Ralph took £400 from the office of the family business, gambled it away and disappeared.

'Mother was very ill at that time,' said Myer, 'and I wanted to get him back before she found out. I went to look for him in London, if you please. I took the train to London. Well, I thought that he might get in touch with their solicitor's agent in London. So I thought that I'd contact the London agent and leave a note for him. I did go to them. I hung around in the hope that he might come in but he didn't. That was on the

Ralph

Friday. I hung around all blooming day after getting into London. I hung around. No sign. So that's when I decided I'll go to the Strand Corner House in Trafalgar Square. I don't know what made me think of going to the Strand. I waited overnight. No I didn't go in. I waited outside. I stood and waited. I waited and waited and waited. Hours. Time seemed... Just imagine what a fool's errand it was to go on. How foolish of me to do a thing like that.

'And yet I met him. And I met him with a girl. Apparently she was the cause of his flight. And I told the girl he was not for her. He was very pleased to see me, I'll tell you. He was only glad I'd come. I said, "Come home and forget it." He was pleased to come home, I'll tell you.' Myer paused. 'Don't you think it was a marvellous thing to have done?'

Still, the flesh could not be gainsaid and after a seven-year engagement, Harry and Celia married.

'We got married,' my mother told me, 'at the synagogue opposite Gower Street School. It's the Salvation Army now. The day we got married, it was terrible weather. It was raining so hard the rain was bouncing up again off the ground. The rabbi said, 'You see the rain. Your life will be like that. At first it will be very hard, but later it will grow higher and higher. Then the sun came out. And that's how it was.'

But it was John's marriage that was the final straw. John had given way to his vanity. He seems to have become quite a fop. He posed for his photograph, pipe clenched in his teeth, looking

Harry and Celia

187

straight forward at posterity, his trilby at a rakish angle. His left foot took
a step forward, and his right hand rested nonchalantly. Myer spoke
disapprovingly of John carrying around a pair of white gloves. More
ominously he bought a pair of greyhounds.

John's mother Ada spoke with his intended wife. 'Don't marry him'
Ada said. 'He's a gambler. He'll lead you a very unhappy life.' No
doubt Ada didn't mention that her cousin Shroll Maishy had given her the
same advice. John's wife took no more notice of Ada than Ada had done
of Shroll. John left home. And here we can let him tell his wife's tale,
as he did, years later in a place no one in Leeds could ever, in their
wildest dreams, have imagined:

I delve into the past
And conjure up in orderly review
The separate stages of his tragedy,
That you may fully understand how he
By one rash action took the fatal step
That led to his destruction,
Plunged us both into the lowest depths of misery
And though I managed to survive, henceforth,
My days were spent in dreary drudgery.
Gone were my hopes of reaching out beyond
The Road of Chapeltown, our Appian Way,
And in the lowest bounds of this same road
My tale begins:

I dwelt in Evelyn Street
Which, as you know, is but a stone's throw from
Law's bastion, the station of police at Sheepscar
Where our Appian Way takes rise.
When I first met him at a students' ball,
Given when I was in my eighteenth year,
Full of a girlish modesty, all agog
To let my heart be fluttered by a man.
The dresses lent enchantment to the scene:
Georgette and Crepe de Chine and Marocaine
Were then in vogue. The gown I wore was red -
My favourite colour. The music played;
Gaily I tripped on light fantastic toe,

In blessed unawareness of the lot
Reserved for me by the relentless Fates.
The Cyprian Goddess played her wonted tricks,
The boy who never for a moment leaves his mother's side
Completed the fell work; the shaft struck home.
We entered on the long and customary round
Of lovers' trysts. Then for a time we parted.
But he returned
And a protracted courtship
With frequent interruptions for five years
Pursued its course till we became engaged.
As Enlil, Anu's son, ravished Ninlil
In various guises on his journey down
To the infernal regions,
So the man of law, the earnest student of the classics
Changed into the gambler...

'Whilst John was at home,' said Myer 'we could control him to some extent. But when he was out of our hands. That was it!'

Changed into the gambler

189

But now at least, despite these ominous signs Jeremy and Myer's plan seemed to be working and the family could afford to move up Chapeltown Road, north of the meeting of the becks at Sheepscar. 29 Mexborough Avenue was the last of the ten Raisman residences. Close by, the congregation of the former greenhorns were beginning to build a huge synagogue in the shape of a mosque with minaret. The synagogue combined the Moslem style with that of ancient Egypt. A broad and imposing flight of entry stairs flanked by huge ceremonial Egyptian urns ascended to a massive cream marble portico in the style of a pharaonic temple and led into a great vaulted entrance hall with massive fluted columns crowned by papyrus heads of multicoloured marble.

'It was easy to set up a synagogue,' Harry said. 'The synagogues didn't all have a rabbi and an eternal candle flame over the Holy Ark and the whole caboodle. Only the bigger ones had that. They didn't need a rabbi. Among the orthodox Jews at that time any one of them could have conducted a service. They knew the damn stuff off by heart just like we know the alphabet.'

When the Indian Government first set up a public broadcasting service it was looking around for material, and the director asked Jeremy to talk on any subject of his choice. Jeremy chose Bridge:

My first piece of advice is: Don't play bridge. Bridge is a pastime, an indoor pastime, at best a mental recreation. But why should you merely pass the time, while the short and precious hours of your numbered years are fleeting away? And are you sure that you exercise your mind sufficiently to deserve a mental recreation? If you become a regular bridge player, you will not be able to read one fiftieth of the new books on every subject which are daily poured forth on a bewildered world. You will probably never become an authority on Assyriology, or the fourth dimension, or the ultimate constitution of the atom. If you refrain from playing bridge, you may perhaps acquire a great stamp collection or master the Basque language, or read all the works of Goethe. Think then, before you cut the fatal pack, how much of your heritage you are relinquishing.

For bridge is not even an elevating pastime. You start with the handicap of your own incompetence and you pursue a chequered and hazardous course towards a series of goals, at one moment raised to the heights of self-congratulatory achievement, at another dashed down to the nadir of self contempt. And luck comes in at almost every stroke.

My next piece of advice is that if you want to become a good bridge player, don't play for love. Love is too high or too low a stake to play bridge for. The best as well as the most exciting bridge is played for the highest stakes the players can afford.

After Jack had qualified as a doctor, he had set up in practice from the house in Mexborough Avenue. Within a year, Celia's three oldest brothers fell ill with rheumatic fever. Celia's mother tried the usual fever remedy, a handful of salt was thrown into the fire, and the flames closely observed. As soon as the flames burned up blue, the fever would depart from the patients. It didn't work. Celia's mother sought advice.

'I hadn't known Celia five minutes when I was taking Jack down to see her brothers,' said Harry. Jack came to see them. Apart from making wise statements, he wisely offered no treatment. As Jack had predicted, the first boy died. While the body lay in the front room in Vandyke Street, Mrs Lipman organised the honorary professional mourners of Vandyke Street. Khaffky and Mrs Levy wailed and screamed and tore their hair outside the door.

'They took quite a pleasure in it,' Eddy said later.

As the second boy lay close to death, Celia's distraught mother summoned all the ancestral wisdom from *Der Hame*. She went to a Jewish chemists on North Street and came back with a small round block of special wax, shaped like a little cheese, about two inches across. Following the chemist's instructions, she melted it in a pan and poured it on to a metal plate held over the sick boy's head. As the wax foamed and set, she studied the pattern of the bubbles, mumbling 'I know who it was - it was Mrs So-and-so from down the street who put the Evil Eye on him.' Then she intoned three times, 'All evil, Get out! All good, Come in!' and carefully threw the wax away.

Nonetheless, the second boy died. Once again the holy body-washers came into the house, laid the body on the floor and carried in the huge board on which to lay it out, and basins of water to wash it. 'I thought I heard a dog barking,' said Celia. 'It was my father howling after his two sons.'

Meanwhile, the third boy lay close to death. Celia's mother, ran to Harry's mother Ada for advice. 'Open the window and take the coffin out that way, feet first. Don't take it through the door. Then there will be no more deaths,' said Ada.

Harry's arm was round Celia's shoulder as they followed the coffin into the street. The professional mourners performed vehemently, having recruited the additional shrill voice of Mrs Quaite. This final descent to barbarism was the last straw for Harry. 'Shut up!' he said to her, and she did.

For the week's period of mourning after a death the family sat on low stools and during this week all mirrors in the house had to be covered, or better, turned to face the wall. This was because the devil might look out through them.

The more prosaic Leeds Corporation had also been alerted to this outbreak of fatal fevers. Seeking a more worldly cause of disaster, they sent Raskin, the poetic closet-rammer, to scour the drains for possible sources of epidemic infection. He found none. However, Ada's window advice had worked, and Joe, the third boy, survived.

Celia's mother decided that the boys had caught their fevers while on a camping expedition on the Yorkshire moors. She told the younger brothers never to go there and never go out in the rain. This also meant that Eddy and Teddy couldn't go swimming. To be sure of this, their mother burnt their swimming trunks.

Teddy found this restriction intolerable, so he quietly went off and bought another pair, and secretly went to the public swimming baths in Meanwood Road. When he got back to Vandyke Street he had the problem of how to hide the wet swimming costume. In the house wall beside the kitchen door was a little metal trap door, covering a small opening for the coal man to deliver coal into the cellar. Teddy gently raised the flap, flung the tell-tale, wet swimming trunks inside, and went into the house as though

Teddy gently raised the flap

nothing had happened. To his horror, the first thing that met his eyes was his mother coming up the cellar steps with a shovel of coal in her hand and the wet swimming costume draped round her head.

Soon after this, Jack married, and he was able to use the dowry to buy a medical practice in the Lancashire textile town of Burnley, just across the Pennines on the Leeds and Liverpool Canal. He moved into a rambling old house, whose front windows looked out over the desolate moorlands which led back east to the Yorkshire town of Howarth.

At this time Harry himself became severely ill. The dreaded rheumatic fever was diagnosed. There was no known cure. To arrest its progress he had all his perfect, even teeth extracted. Harry's doctor was called David Livingstone, but it wasn't in admiration of the famous explorer of Africa. He came from Sunderland and his original name was David Levenstein.

In his surgery Dr Livingstone used to sit at his desk with a drawer open. Invisible to the patient at the other side of the desk, lay the sporting paper with the afternoon's race lists uppermost. He was a gentle and kindly doctor, but he didn't know what to do for Harry, so he advised his patient to spend some time taking the waters in the pump room of the medicinal spa at Harrogate, fifteen miles north of Leeds. The regime consisted of drinking pints of the stinking sulphur water which issued from the ground there. There were also religious observances in the pump room. Before evening cocoa the sick were gathered to sing holy hymns. Harry, relying on his deafness to shield his Jewish purity, stayed apostatically on, waiting for the opportunity to get rid of the ghastly sulphur taste by drinking cocoa. He learned all the hymns, and often sang them to himself later. This spiritual improvement, however, had no bodily counterpart. He became gradually more ill. He returned to Leeds.

Myer became alarmed and took him to see Jack in Burnley. Jack's wife was horrified at the accumulation of three Raisman brothers in her home, but Harry appeared to be dying and Jack and Myer both thought so too. 'Harry's condition is v serious,' said Jack. Jack was always conscious of how precious time was to a busy doctor, so he never wrote or spoke the full word very, but used *v* instead. For greater emphasis he would say *unco* (uncommonly). So his speech always sounded like someone reading a medical student's notes, or a scribbled message from one busy physician to another.

'First,' Jack said to Myer, as they looked at Harry, 'there will be crisis, then lysis.' Myer was impressed by these Greek words, and felt reassured by the presence of such specialized knowledge. Harry was accommodated in the spare bedroom, and Myer slept on the couch in the parlour. Harry's fever got worse, and his joints became so painful that he could no longer tolerate even the vibrations caused by footsteps on the floor. For four days Myer watched him, only leaving the room when he could arrange a substitute. Harry became comatose.

Now Myer not only stayed with him all day, but by night he crept into bed with him, hardly daring to move in case he caused pain to his brother's agonised joints. Another three days and three nights passed in this way. Through those long nights, Myer's own body must have been aching and tired. As he lay there, timidly trying not to move, and feeling the fierce heat of Harry's fever, Myer must have wished that by his very contact his body could have infused some of his own health into his brother's hot frame. Finally Harry could not be roused. Myer rushed downstairs to get Jack.

For only a moment Jack considered the unresponsive figure of his older brother who had so often lain beside him in bed. Then, seizing the bedposts with both hands, Jack vaulted his bristly, Quasimodo-like body high into the air and landed with his shod feet hard down on the motionless ankles in the bed. The soul may well have been floating on the brink of the great void, wondering whether, as Harry used to put it, 'to join the great majority.' But after the exquisite agony caused by the vibration of a mere footfall, this insult was not to be tolerated. The soul returned indignantly and Harry let out a very earthly yell.

The body to which that soul returned had more than half a century of life ahead but the Family Plan was within a year of its end. That noble plan, which now looked so rosy, was actually not all that secure. Legal business was hard to get and John played ruthlessly on the family's reputation, on the Raismans' impressive academic records in Leeds. But mainly he played on his brother Jeremy's success.

John's brilliance was well known in Leeds, and other solicitors rang him up to ask for advice on difficult legal points.

'You can look it up,' John would reply.

'I wanted to save time.'

'Oh, all right then,' John would say, and tell them.

John's reputation was finally established by the Frais case. One of the Frais brothers, a close friend of Jeremy, was a very keen golfer, and had gone to stay at a hotel in Scotland where only very wealthy golfers could stay. While he was there he committed suicide, apparently because the family were pressing him to marry a girl he did not like. The news of his suicide was published in the newspapers, and the hotel sued the family for damages because of the bad effect of the publicity on its trade. The family retained John to defend the case.

The Frais case was a cause célèbre in Leeds, and John's successful defence made him a popular hero. John had become self-indulgent. With his fee, he bought a car for the immense sum of £150. He acquired an office in the centre of town, right opposite the front of Leeds Town Hall, where the law courts sat. This office was on the second floor of the pink stone building of the Jubilee Hotel behind an ornate 1904 facade of appropriately decadent style. The previous occupant of this office had also been a solicitor but to satisfy his expensive tastes, which included a mistress in a hotel in Harrogate, he had done 'dishonest dealings' and had been 'sent down' for a spell.

Leeds Town Hall

The narrow Park Cross Street ran by John's office, under the windows of Lubelski's former tailoring workshop, which still bore his name, and down to Park Square. This was the professional centre of the city. On three sides of the square the elegant Georgian houses had been taken over as offices for lawyers working in the law courts in the Town Hall opposite, or as consulting rooms for fashionable doctors from the Leeds General Infirmary just behind it. These men were known as the Forty Thieves of Park Square. The fourth side of the square was entirely filled by the impressive Moorish facade of Barran's factory, now a warehouse.

The centre of the square was taken up by a rose garden, with a striking bronze statue of the temptress Circe as an adolescent girl, completely naked. The sculptor had captured her body at the very moment of change, her breasts firm but not full, her thighs shapely but not voluptuous. Circe is frozen at the point where girlhood changes into womanhood. Having given Odysseus' sailors drugged food and wine, she has turned them into three wild boars that have forgotten their past, and now prance at her feet. The one behind her, rearing up on its hind legs, has just torn off her clothes, and her last flimsy garment was still draped over its tusky snout.

From his window John looked over the wide street where the statue of Queen Victoria had stood before its removal to Woodhouse Moor beside the University. John would sit at his desk phoning in his bets, and reading the 'Sporting Pink,' a racing paper known as 'The Tisher' (i.e. tissue, from the thinness of its paper). He had just devised a special system for backing horses by the rank of the owner. A horse owned by a

196

member of the Royal Family came first, then in order, a duke, marquis, earl, viscount, baron. It was a conspicuously ineffective way of selecting winners at the races. At weekends, unknown to the rest of the family, he would fly (then an unheard-of luxury) to the gambling casinos at the French resorts of Deauville and Le Touquet. The only useful thing he ever brought back was a copy of James Joyce's Ulysses, whose publication was banned in England at the time.

John was not selective about whom he robbed to raise his gambling money. His younger sister Sarah had just got married and her husband Wilf became John's articled clerk, the junior in the law office. At this time John offered this defenceless and unsuspecting articled clerk a reduction in his fees if he paid the next year in advance. John then successfully contested a motor accident claim on behalf of his brother Jack, but pocketed the money himself. To call it robbery is how unfeeling outsiders might see it, but John didn't regard money as private property. And in this idea of communal family wealth, wasn't Myer's vision partly to blame? The money others felt was their own was to John merely a transient essence whose true function, like the paper cash the Chinese burn on the tombs of their dead ancestors, was for him to dedicate on the altar of the Goddess he worshipped, Tyche, Lady of Chance.

Like a true *luftman*, John accumulated no material wealth. Things that came into his possession he treated roughly, as though disposable. 'Property,' said John 'is madness.'

The most celebrated master tailor in Leeds was Barney Bailey. His workshop was near the English Synagogue in Brunswick Street, and his name was spoken of in hushed awe. As a tailor it was said he hadn't an equal in England. He had been proud to supply Jeremy with his first outfit - on credit - when Jeremy went out to his first overseas posting. Now John ordered one of Barney's fabled overcoats, made up in the thick, heavy tweed which could repel the harshest winter. This overcoat saved John's life, but it did so in an equatorially hot place, and in a way neither John nor Barney Bailey could, even in their wildest dreams, have imagined.

'Yes,' said Harry later, 'and John never paid for it. John never paid for anything. He considered himself wealthy, and spoke contemptuously of the likes of us, who he said were too poor to buy on credit. He never paid for his car. When I got married he gave me a magnificent wireless set. It cost £30, equivalent to more than three months of my wages. Later the man who owned the shop, who was a personal friend of mine, came and told me. He said he didn't like to upset me by taking back a wedding present that my newly-wed wife so liked. He was very happy for me to pay off for my own wedding present in instalments.'

One drizzly October day in 1929 Myer set off from the house in Mexborough Avenue. He entered Chapeltown Road by Harris' fish and chip shop. After walking a hundred yards up Chapeltown Road, he passed the pastry shop that sold the gingerbread men, turned off east by Cantor's fish and chip shop, and went down through Potternewton Park. He was on his way to his brother Harry's house in the adjacent suburb of Harehills.

Potternewton Park spanned the dry valley between Chapeltown and Harehills. It was a disappointment, no streams, no woods, only grass. No mysteries. A friendly little horse lived behind a copse at the back of the park. It used to stick its nose across the broken fence and you could feed it grass as long as you kept your hand quite flat.

Myer went in by a small gate at the top end. At the summit of a grassy slope was a small wooden belvedere, painted green. The Leylanders called it the little booth. Within were two little girls of about ten or eleven soberly dressed in hats and coats and deeply engrossed in a serious conversation, exactly like grown-ups.

Myer, oblivious of everything around him, scurried down the path towards the main gates. Flanking the park's ceremonial entrance was a pair of magnificent flowering cherry trees, and at this time of the year their leaves had taken on the unhealthy, luminous colours of cherry trees in autumn, not reflecting, but as if themselves sources of a decaying light. Their shining bark gleamed as if they were encased in bands of highly polished copper. In the last few nights there had been frosts, only a brief, light powdering of the early morning grass. A late riser would never have seen them, and never have noticed the footprints round the horse-chestnut trees where the kids on their way to school had searched for the treasured windfall of shining conkers. The trees were still in full leaf, their branches heavy with rain. Had the sun come out now, it would have looked like a summer day, all the finer for a few orange tints.

But the frosts had given the trees that long-awaited secret signal. However much the sun shone now, it was too late. The mysterious inner chemistry of the vegetable world was set in motion. Unseen, the first swollen petiole dehisced. The leaf tottered for a moment on the twig, and then silently through the still air, with the side-to-side motion that little girls use when they pretend to rock a baby in their arms, floated down to the moist October grass.

Leaving the park, Myer crossed a couple of streets and entered Harry's house, unannounced, by the unlocked front door. It led into a narrow hallway, lit by the yellow light from the half-open kitchen door at the other end. Myer grasped the curved wooden back of one of the old kitchen chairs and sat down at the end of the table. 'A terrible thing has happened,' he said dramatically. Harry pushed his own chair back from the table, scraping its wooden feet noisily against the linoleum, and put his head on one side in the gesture that presented his slightly more useful left ear towards the head of the family.

Myer paused a long time before replying 'John has disappeared.'

'So?' Harry questioned.

'So!' echoed Myer, semi-indignantly, but didn't go on.

Harry waited. 'He didn't come to the office this morning,' Myer continued at last. 'He had a lot of business to attend to. There were documents needed his signature, things only he could do. Clients came in, and phoned. 'A lot of money has gone. A lot of money.'

'How much?' Harry asked.

'Too much. Thousands. Probably two or three thousand.'

Harry was silent. The unthinkable had happened. That was the sort of money that could buy houses. It was far, far more than all Myer and Harry's tailoring could ever, in their wildest dreams, recoup. John had done that from which they could never hope to rescue him. Myer got up and went out. Harry knew Myer had nothing more to tell. Harry wondered to himself what the law would do. John was a highly intelligent man, and a lawyer. Had he in some way protected himself against detection or prosecution? It seemed impossible. Anyway, what did that matter now? The business they had all hoped would bring them prosperity was wrecked.

Then Harry thought of Myer's sacrifice, a whole life, and of his own not small sacrifice of an education and a profession. The Song of the

Shirt seemed to echo mockingly in his deaf ears:

Work, work, work,
In the dull December light,
And work, work, work,
When the weather is warm and bright,

While underneath the eaves
The brooding swallows cling...
Oh! but to breathe the breath
Of the cowslip and primrose sweet.

Harry looked down at his fingers, the skin tough as leather where it had held the hated tailor's needle. To prevent the rough, calloused skin catching in the silk linings he used to file his thumb on a matchbox. Bitterness welled up. And behind him he thought perhaps he heard a sigh. Not so much a sigh as a soft exhalation of breath, as if someone was hastening up a flight of steps to catch a closing door.

All business runs on credit. Credit is other people's money. Giving money to John was like asking an alcoholic to drive a brewery dray cart. John had secretly run up greater and greater gambling debts, using all his legal skill to conceal them. Loan after loan was raised. When it was apparent to him that the end was near, he had taken all that was left, a last chance to recoup all, and fled to Le Touquet where he felt the odds were better. They were not, and with an ever-dwindling reserve he continued south to Monte Carlo. Still Tyche, the Goddess of Fortune, frowned. With his final few pounds he bribed the Portuguese consul in Nice to give him false papers to enter Brazil and left Europe by boat, not to return for a third of a century.

So ended Myer's plan. It had been born out of harsh necessity, and was not without nobility. But it had consumed two good men, and a third was in exile. Had it succeeded, our family might have been just another of the wealthy Jewish families of our country, and perhaps I would have watched the ideals of its self-sacrificing founders gradually debased by succeeding generations of increasingly vain luxury-seekers. But it was not to be so for my family. Their sacrifice yielded no wealth, only tragic heroes.

Just as the Maggid had predicted, the time-old customs of the Lithuanian *shtetlakh*, freed from Tsarist oppression, had fallen apart.

Only now Myer understood the fatal weakness of his lifelong plan. It depended on a family loyalty that existed no more. 'My tailoring business,' Myer told me, years later, 'was a family business. I couldn't do it without the family, without Sam and Harry. Well, it came that just at that period everybody'd finished their schooling. I'd nobody else to look after. It'd already got too late to do anything for myself. I was finished. I were only forty-three, but I was finished all right.'

'I'd no incentive,' Myer went on, 'I'd got them all where I wanted. That was all I worked for. I was played out. I were an old man then. Already my sight was bad. I couldn't work any longer at the tension that was necessary at that time. I used to work all night by myself. Many a time. It was a difficult life, but I did make a living at it. Look what I've done. I've kept the family. There were Jeremy, John, Jack, Ralph, Sarah, Sam, Sidney - all being kept at secondary school and university. Just imagine what it meant. Instead of them all working from twelve and thirteen as they did in those days, they were all being kept...' Myer paused. 'With pocket-money. We never took a penny from John's office. Not a penny.' Myer paused again.

'How can I explain it, Geoff? This blooming gambling bug they've got. How can I explain it?'

END OF PART TWO

PART III

All Roads Lead to Rome

Many years had passed since my autumnal excursion to the Leylands with my father. During the many interrogations I needed to get this story out of him, he would often ask me, in an amused way, 'Well, how is the booklet getting on?' And so, when all was nearly finished, I put a draft in my father's hands.

My father took off his glasses, and held the book close up to his face, tilting it to catch the sunlight streaming through the window, and screwing up his eyes. But almost at once, the resulting wrinkles on his face hardened into an expression of horror. After taking only a short time to detect the drift of the book, he closed it, put it down, and remained silent and unapproachable for the space of two and a half days. Then at last, in his careful, measured speech, and with great firmness, he said, 'I don't want any of this to be known.' But then, seeing how downcast I was, he relented a little, 'at least not while anyone is alive who knows about it, about John, I mean.'

Passovers

Oh talk not to me of a name great in story
For the days of our youth are the days of our glory

Byron

My body was travelling rapidly backwards through space when my right shoulder blade thudded into a large resilient protuberance. My feet scrabbled to a stop on the rough cinders. This was how it happened.

Shortly after the Second World War, alien invaders started creeping up through England. Like the Vikings, they first got a foothold in the estuaries and then, following up the rivers, year by year crept further into the heartland. The invader came under many names. Himalayan balsam was one description of this plant that botanists call Impatiens glandulifera. Furtively it spread along the waste ground by the river banks. It was a sturdy colonist, one of the first plants to reclaim the banks of the industrial river Aire. A clump of it grew in the yard of our Hebrew school in Cowper Street.

Our favourite childhood games were all battles, and now the battle raged to-and-fro over the low stone walls of the half-derelict houses in one of whose yards was built the long one-storey brick block which housed the six classrooms. My army had just been repelled from the heights, and was retreating down the uneven slope of broken walls. Alone I turned and faced the onrush of the yelling enemy. As a flag I waved a battered frond of touch-me-not, and shouted, 'Charge!' or, crossing the broken walls, 'Take the ramparts!' so absorbed that I failed till too late to notice that both the victorious enemy and my faint-hearted comrades had fallen strangely silent. Too late, because in that instant my right shoulder blade encountered the plump, resilient form of Mr Hayman, the head teacher.

Encountered at such breathtaking speed, the revered form, tightly girt in a blue serge waistcoat, had a curiously elastic feel, which almost seemed to echo with my feet trying to scrabble to a halt on the loose cinders.

I meekly followed the outraged Mr Hayman into the building with my eyes on the ground, and with the footfalls of a condemned man mounting the steps of the scaffold. Around me the awestruck class assembled silently. 'I vill give you die shtrapp,' said Mr Hayman as I stood fearfully before his desk. He was a short man, and he sat on a high stool behind a little wooden desk in front of the class. His clasped hands, fingers interlocked, rested on the desk, and he held his head tilted forwards at an angle. None of us had ever seen the dreaded shtrapp. It referred to an old sewing machine belt, which had, it appears, been much used in the Leylands Hebrew schools of the past, but like the Holy Grail, had long ago passed into legend.

Mr Hayman had never hit anyone in his life, but he said it with such conviction that we could never quite be sure. Mr Hayman's dark little moustache seemed to bristle with anger, and on his chin and neck the white stubbly hairs of his not-close shave seemed to bristle too. The round face with its deep cheek furrows and slightly pointed little nose, the soft furry white hair on his nearly bald head, and the dark little moustache made him look like a delicate little raccoon.

Our teacher paused. The whole class sat silent before him, a dozen young heads bowed apprehensively at their desks. Mr Hayman pushed his little black skull cap forward off his short white hairs and on to his bald patch. The usual skull cap was a simple, saucer-shaped piece of cloth, shaped as though skimmed off a hollow sphere. As such a thing could not easily gain purchase on Mr Hayman's smooth round head, he wore a specially adapted one with deeper sides, which clung to his head like a mountaineer on a precipice.

Mr Hayman surveyed the class, his mind working quickly. Here was a specific instance of waywardness, but from it he should draw an example to teach a moral principle. Waiting till the pupils were suitably attentive Mr Hayman, looking over my bowed head, addressed the class, 'You donn't shatt ond ronn! You donn't sing ond dance! The heart can't stand the strain. If you sing, sing, ond if you dance, dance, but donn't sing *ond* dance. If you shatt, shatt, ond if you ronn, ronn, but donn't shatt *ond* ronn.

'So!' Mr Hayman said conclusively, striking the desk top with his hands. Then, raising them slightly in a dismissive gesture, he sat back satisfied with his lesson on moderation. At last, noticing me, he paused again for thought. 'Ehh!' snorted Mr Hayman disgustedly, at a loss for further words, and waved me back to my seat.

The class began:

And ye shall take a bunch of hyssop, and dip it in the blood that is in the bason, and strike the lintel and the two side posts with the blood that is in the bason. For the Lord will pass through to smite the Egyptians, and when he seeth the blood upon the lintel, and on the two side posts, the Lord will pass over the door, and will not suffer the destroyer to come in unto your houses to smite you.

Mr Hayman could hardly speak English. Penicillin had just been discovered. He liked to give logical, preferably physiological reasons for the many apparently curious rules of Judaic law. Solemnly he explained to us children that the hyssop branches were conducive to the growth of penicillin, thus protecting the houses of the Children of Israel. Judaism is a logical religion:

And it came to pass, that at midnight the Lord smote all the firstborn in the land of Egypt, from the firstborn of Pharaoh that sat on his throne, unto the firstborn of the captive that was in the dungeon, and all the firstborn of cattle...

It always seemed a little hard on the captives, not to mention the innocent cattle. But no one questioned the magnificence of the act that could take in all of Egypt in one night. The Angel of Death had to work quickly. Under such pressure, it was not unreasonable that the Children of Israel should be required to mark their doors clearly, so as not to delay the course of the Wrath which, although Divine, still had a lot to do in a short time.

The knowledge gained at Hebrew school had practical as well as theoretical value. During the high and holy festivals, the different synagogues all started at slightly different times, and proceeded at very different speeds. The halls varied from large imposing marble halls, like the new Greenhorns' Synagogue, to small bedrooms with a handful of bearded men swaying fervently in front of an ornamented cupboard which served as the Holy Ark for the revered Scrolls of their former towns and villages. At the more important holidays sweet sanctified wine and cubes of dry sponge cake were given out during the synagogue service, and apples and fruit were distributed to the children, who wandering in groups from synagogue to synagogue, operated a sort of intelligence service, so that we could know the rate the services were progressing in different synagogues, that Francis Street was already up to such and such a place, but the Study House was really slow, or that the Camaraderie of the Psalm Singers had already made the sanctification. And so we could plan a route to take in as many as possible of the available delights.

Passover, however, was celebrated at home. The ceremony is called the *Seder*. It is the Last Supper of the New Testament. A text, called the *Haggadah*, is read at the dinner table. The *Haggadah* recounts the Passover story and the flight from Egypt. But for me the Passovers of my childhood had a very special function. They were the glass through which I glimpsed the dark story of my uncle John.

It was not easy for a would-be family historian. My family seemed to have a moral objection to all forms of looking back. My father would never tolerate what he regarded old-fashioned things, such as hats, moustaches, beards, walking sticks, umbrellas, and most unkindly of all, as it seemed to me, brocaded waistcoats, while my mother had our ornate Edwardian door panels covered with plain, modern plywood, and removed all ornaments from the mantelpieces. My Aunty Fanny had the candlesticks taken off the piano. Most often when I asked Uncle Myer to tell me what things were like when he was young, he would simply grunt and say, 'What do you want me to talk about? The other world?'

Passover was the only exception, somehow the lingering tradition kept open this one last window on a disappearing past, and I sensed this and seized my annual opportunity. Two strange dishes survived, like treasured dinosaurs. The first was 'home-made', a kind of jam, hours in the making, a seething cauldron of tiny beetroot cubes and almonds, filling the house with the scent of sugar and lemon, spitting scalding sweet droplets from its bursting bubbles. The second was a crystallisation of carrots, sugar and ginger. And those who had the privilege to taste them could understand how the peasants of Lithuania turned the coarsest vegetables of their poor land into sweetness.

On Passover evening I eagerly waited until the cooking was ready and the table laid. The celebrant, and indeed the king of that evening was my

Uncle Myer. Ten years older than my father, Myer was by this time an old man, short and comfortably plump. Uncle Myer grew hair as ineffectively as most of his other brothers, but he had a unique hairstyle. His round, nearly bald pate was surrounded by a fringe of pure white hair. But it did not grow in a complete circle, rather in the shape of a horseshoe, open at the front. Myer wore his hair cut very short at the back and sides, but at the front he allowed one tuft of hair to grow as long as it would. The resultant wisps he brushed or combed across the front of his forehead to complete the circle, like a monk.

As soon as I could possibly get the *Seder* started, I pressed Myer to read all the long service, omitting nothing. I loved to take on the duty of the youngest child to ask the Four Questions. The Four Questions are more or less an introduction to the Passover night service.

To ask them is a privilege given to the youngest male child as soon as he becomes old enough to learn them. In a large family, it obviously passes on every few years. One advantage of being an only child was that it fell to me to ask them over and over again year by year. The Four Questions were about the odd preparations going on in the home. The first question was: 'Why is this night different from all other nights?' The next question was, 'Why do we eat bitter herbs?' and so on.

Of course these were rhetorical questions. The answers were known to everyone. But despite this, the answers were complicated and oblique. The underlying idea was that the answer depends on the questioner. The text gives four examples. The first is the answer to the wise son. He is to be given the full details. For the simple son, there is a much simpler answer. There is even a kindly answer for the son who is so stupid he can't even ask, 'But as for him who hath no capacity to inquire, thou must begin...'

But my favourite answer was the one for the wicked son:

What says the wicked son? He asks, 'What do you mean by this service?' By the expression you, *it is clear he doth not include himself, and he hath excluded himself from the body of the nation. Therefore must thou retort upon him - set his teeth on edge - by saying, 'This is done because of what the Lord did for* me *when I went forth from Egypt,' - for* me, *but not for* him; *for had he been there he would not have been thought worthy to be redeemed.*

Myer entered into the spirit of this with a great sense of fun. No sooner had the last question left my lips, than he looked up, snorted, and said 'Now, this is the answer.' Then he tore into the Hebrew text with a gusto and at a speed commensurate with the general haste of the Passover story, but not too fast to prevent his voice rising and falling in the weirdly beautiful plainsong and cadences of the mediaeval liturgical chant.

After going through the text we ate the meal, and sang the four songs, and when it was finally over, Myer's voice would be totally broken by the hours of recitation and singing.  He would push his chair back, satisfied, brush a few of the crumbs off his waistcoat, and then leave the table and sit in a chair by the fire, with his arms folded over his ample stomach (which he called his 'future,' since it went in front of him), and looking down over his own generous form say: 'Let me have about me men that are fat and sleep well o'nights.

'Sufficient unto the day,' said my father, 'is the eating thereof.'

Myer seemed to have inherited his father's 'nervous dyspepsia.' 'To eat,' he would say, 'is human; to digest - divine!' After a while he would begin to doze, with his favourite battered old cap on his head, and now the younger brother, my uncle Sam, took the stage. Sam was renowned in the family for his story-telling. We sat back, and Sam told us about the Passovers of the family, when they were all together in the Leylands, and when Sam was, like me, a little boy, listening fascinated to his elders.

But if this conversation went on for any length of time - and I always did my best to ensure it did - my father soon tired of the effort to join in. From time to time his lips would move, and he might softly mutter or sing a word or two, purse his lips, or even frown. Like a child singing on a bus, he didn't notice others could hear him, and somehow it was strangely embarrassing to listen, as if eavesdropping on a private thing. Indeed, if ever I challenged him to reveal what he was saying, he would simply shake his head and smile blankly, obviously not wishing to speak and disturb the inner sounds he was so enjoying. He never once told me what he was hearing, but on occasions the wave of his inner experiences would crest above the line of silence into the outer world, and then I found he was reciting lines of poetry or song often, like *Auld Lang Syne*, with strangely changed and made-up words of his own, or even haughtily debating some courtroom point with himself.

Meanwhile, Sam talked about the old Leylands Passovers, when the doomed hen was imprisoned in the coal cellar until its ritual slaughter by the slaughterer for his ha'penny fee, and Myer, waking up, interrupted to describe proudly how his mother assembled the ingredients for the slow casserole to be baked overnight for a penny in the baker's oven. 'What else did grandma make?' I asked, never satisfied in my search for detail. 'She made mead,' Myer said solemnly. 'She made it every year. Only one year it went wrong. Mother said it was because Sarah went near the mead when she had scarlet fever.'

Sam then went on to speak of the long political arguments John used to have with Jeremy, when Jeremy, the older brother, supported state and empire, and the socialist John sprawled idly on the couch. I could never have enough of these stories, and it was in them, year by year, that I gradually pieced together the story of my Uncle Myer's Plan, of the spectacular career of my Uncle Jeremy, and of the fiercely guarded secrets of my legendary Uncle John.

But twenty years had passed since the Crash. The Leylands had been abandoned and of those who had been born in Lithuania only a few of the oldest people were left. The Second World War and the German occupation destroyed what had been *Der Hame*. To us sitting, our throats hoarse with singing and our stomachs full of roasted chicken around the Passover table in middle class Hilton Road in middle class Harehills, where the comfortable Number 44 bus with its cloth covered seats ringed the comfortable suburbs from Halton Moor and Osmondthorpe all the way through Meanwood to Stanningley on the borders of Bradford, it all seemed so long ago, like a history told, not like something that, unknown to all of us, was still going in a far continent, an unheard whirlwind racing towards us over the years, that would once again engulf the Raisman Family, every one.

My Uncle John had been long unheard of, assumed dead, and I belonged to a family whose first desire was to forget, and whose last desire was to recall any of these things:

> *For you believe Parmenides has erred*
> *And that between the living and the dead*
> *A tertium quid, a missing limbo, lies.*
>
> *In this Nirvanic other-world you trow*
> *The wraith-like image of the No-man stands,*
> *The Warden of the Marches of Negation*
> *Mid being and non-being interposed*
> *Obscured from vision by the veil of life.*
>
> Uncle John

Croquet at Peterhof

The second Lord Lytton and his Lady dismounted and stood on a green hill. All around, even in the height of the summer of 1876, the Himalayan peaks glittered with snow. While a cooling breeze refreshed Queen Victoria's plenipotentiary in India, Hoshy and Moshy, who were indifferent to the weather, were following a handcart from Leeds City Station to the doss house in Templar Street, determined to keep an eye on the bundles containing their entire worldly goods. Far to the south down precipitous winding roads through the foothills lay the Red Fort in Delhi, the old Mogul capital, sweltering in summer heat on the mud-caked banks of the Jamuna, and beyond that the dusty plains, the tiger forests and the bare mountains of the teeming Indian subcontinent, stretched to Kerala's swamps where Krishna had recited the *Bhagavad Gita* to Arjuna, and where Adam's Bridge led to the equatorial tea leaf of Ceylon over which, thousands of years ago, the Aryan hosts had carried the mother of our tongue and the Monkey God helped Rama rescue the virgin Sita from the clutches of the Demon King.

Most suitable, don't you think, my dear?' said Lord Lytton to his Lady, as they moved into Peterhof, the Viceregal Lodge in Simla, which had been named after the Tsar's fantasy palace outside St Petersburg and was where successive viceroys spent the summer months when the Government of India moved its locks, stocks and barrels up into the Himalayas to escape the enervating heats of Calcutta, and later Delhi.

A steep drive wound up to Peterhof from the road, and on the top the gleaming mansion stood in immaculate green lawns. From the icy roof of the world behind, melting in the dazzling summer sun, glacial streams drop by drop trickled, then joined, first chattering mountain brooks, then gathered strength in numbers, crashed over white water falls, cut their way through precipitous crags, wound and doubled back like the thrashing of snakes, now east, now west in their long appointment with destiny, ever more mighty and more holy, nourisher of age old civilisations, to the distant oceans.

But here, arriving at the hill of Peterhof, they divided. From the windows at the front of the house the westering sun sank over the Beas River, whose waters flowed down, joining the Sutlej and the Five Rivers of the Punjab to the Indus, the mysterious ancient city of Mohenjodaro, and the Arabian Sea, and in the morning rose again through the eastern windows, beneath which the Jamuna wound its way down to Delhi, and then on to the sacred River Ganges, past the burning ghats of Benares to enter the Bay of Bengal. From its towering vantage point, Peterhof stood at the watershed, a suitable site for the Lord of the Indian Empire.

Two years after his arrival in India, Lord Lytton's government oversaw the first British debacle in Afghanistan. In 1884 Peterhof became the residence of Lord Dufferin, Eton and Christ Church, the Viceroy who annexed Burma. Ten years later it was Lord Elgin, whose India endured the defeat of the British Army by the Afghans at Malakand. Of him, his more famous successor Lord Curzon remarked, 'I discovered he had not taken a single policy decision over four years.' The British Empire had reached its peak, and now a new, even grander Viceregal Lodge was constructed on the next hill to Peterhof. In 1936 when Lord Linlithgow replaced Lord Willingdon as Viceroy of India, Peterhof became the official residence of the senior member of the Indian Civil Service, the Finance Member of the Viceroy's Council. By the time the Second World War broke out, PJ Grigg, the then Finance Member was seconded to London, where he became Secretary of State for War in Churchill's cabinet.

Jeremy had been made a Companion of the Order of the Indian Empire in 1934, of the Star of India in 1938. In 1939 he was knighted, and replaced Grigg as Finance Member of the Viceroy's Executive Council. In 1941 he was promoted Knight Commander of the Star of India, and from now he will be known as Sir Jeremy Raisman. But this was only the first of the many imperial decorations he would wear. Later he would be raised to Grand Commander of the Order of the Indian Empire. His chest blazed with the sashes and great stars so coveted and treasured by the Indian princes and maharajahs. In later life he would add to these the Knight Grand Commander of the Order of St Michael and St George. From his start as a poor boy at the very bottom, he had now reached the summit of the Indian Civil Service, the cream of the administrators of the British Empire. He had entered the ranks of the 'heavenly born.'

Following his appointment as Finance Member, Sir Jeremy Raisman and his Lady and the two boys left Chislehurst and took up residence in Peterhof. The family were on leave in England in summer 1938. It was to be Jeremy's last leave. From now he would remain at his post without a break until he retired in 1945. Jeremy was about to start on the most challenging years of his life.

'I must have been 12 years old,' John Michael said. 'And it must be summer, because it's in Simla. The Viceroy came over unannounced. He's paying a friendly call. He may have come over to have a short chat. He wouldn't have walked over if he didn't want the exercise... and the society... to make a friendly call.

'From Viceregal Lodge to Peterhof is about half a mile. You go down a drive - there's a long drive the other side that goes down to the road at the bottom, and almost immediately you come to the gate of Viceregal Lodge, and then there's about a half mile drive up to Viceregal Lodge itself, through its grounds. So I suppose in total it's about three quarters of a mile. Simla town's a long way off.

'As far as I know he was unaccompanied. Certainly he was unannounced. He might have had a guard behind him.

'We were playing croquet on the lawn. It was about tea time. Or something like that, so he would have come down, had a cup of tea, and my father said: Would you like to join us in a game of croquet? And he said, "Yes."

'Of course I knew who he was. He was the most important man in India. Victor Alexander John Hope, second Marquess of Linlithgow, Earl of Hopetoun and Viscount of Airdrie - Lord Linlithgow as he was known - the Viceroy, the supreme figure in India, the King's representative, and a marquis. He was well over six feet tall, a commanding figure. I'd seen him come to dinner in our house. I remember the big dinner when the Linlithgows came. There must have been 16 or 20 people to dinner. I stood on the landing looking down as they walked into the dining-room. They would have dressed for dinner on that occasion, black tie certainly, liveried servants with white gloves. That was an official entertainment. We didn't do that often, once in a while.

'Linlithgow was the Viceroy who declared war on Germany in 1939 without consulting the Legislative Assembly. That was what Gandhi objected to – understandably. But he had a perfect right to do it – constitutionally he was in his rights doing it. But you could understand Gandhi objected, on behalf of the Legislative Assembly.'

'From Peterhof,' John Michael said, 'we used to go horse riding all round, and on long walks too. I have a letter from my father to me at school in England, when I was 6 or 7, to say that he had walked from Chislehurst which was a bit further into the centre of Simla, walked from there to Wildflower Hall which was Lord Kitchener's old house when he was on retreat. It was converted into a hotel which was 8 miles from Peterhof. He wrote and said, "Your mother went by rickshaw, but I walked there, and had a picnic lunch in the gardens." And then in the afternoon he walked back again. So it was a 16 mile walk he did.'

It was the same distance as Jeremy had walked to Wakefield from Leeds and back to visit his brother John in the Gateforth Sanatorium, although in the Himalayan walk he had not had to carry his older brother Myer home. And by coincidence, at the same time that Jeremy was walking to Wildflower Hall, Myer was walking the ten miles past the Dyneley Arms, over the Chevin from Leeds to Otley and back with his nephew Lenny. Those brought up in the crowded slums of the Leylands never lost their love of open countryside.

'I did a long walk with my father,' John Michael said. 'We stayed in an outpost of the United Services Club, called Carignano. It had only a few bedrooms, and facilities for men only. So I went to stay with my father, not my mother or my brother Jer. There's a funny little golf course, one of the two highest golf courses in the world. It was started up by Curzon. The place is called Naldhera, and Lord Curzon had called his younger daughter Naldhera because it was such a favourite place for them to go to. Carignano stands above the glacial River Beas, and has a marvellous view of Mount Shali. From Carignano it's about a 7 or 8 mile walk to Naldhera, and we had lunch and walked back. And why I remember it so clearly is that on that walk my father told me the facts of life.

'In the summer the nights were pleasantly cool. Of course in winter it would be bitter. Papa was bald. He wore a topee all the time. We all did. You didn't go out without your topee. It was made of pith. Light but strong. And for riding it was marvellous because if you fell off, as I did from time to time, it saved your head.'

By the start of 1940, Britain's war with Germany was at its lowest ebb. The British Army had been driven out of France, the heart of Europe lay under Nazi domination, and the German Army was at the gates of Moscow. Britain stood alone in Europe. India stood alone in Asia.

In June Jeremy was with his family in the great hall of Peterhof, in Simla, high in the Himalayas, when a telegram arrived. Jeremy read the telegram with an expression of disgust, and then threw it into the fire.

'It was the height of summer,' John Michael said. 'It must have been evening. At Peterhof it was cool enough in the evenings to have a fire.

217

We were in the big hall-sitting room. The chairs were drawn up closer together. All the family were sitting round and listening to the news. We listened to the news a lot in those days. It was the dark days of the War. Britain was alone. It was before America came in to the War. 1940 was grim. It was grim, and getting worse all the time.

'A chaprassi came in. He's the person who brings the post. If you were senior enough you had chaprassis who could carry messages. There was a post, but mostly you sent letters, messages to someone else in the vicinity, by hand of a chaprassi. And of course it was more secure.

'My father looked very serious, and then he tossed it in the fire. I could see it was a telegram. So I asked what it was. And he paused for a moment and then he said, "Well, it's supposed to be confidential, but you'll know in the morning. It says that Italy has just entered the war on the side of Nazi Germany." That was a black moment.

'"Shouldn't you keep the telegram" I asked, watching a piece of history going up in flames.

'"It's of no value," my father replied. "Let's get on with winning the war."'

On December 10th 1941, a Japanese air attack sank the two largest British battleships, the Prince of Wales and the Repulse off the coast of Malaya. Singapore fell.

'If the entry of Italy into the War was a black moment,' John Michael said 'the moment when Japan entered the war was even worse.

'The blackest moment was when the two capital ships were sunk and then Singapore fell. That was the blackest moment I can remember. We were in Delhi when that was announced. That was in the winter of 1941-42, 18 months after the telegram in Simla. The announcement of the fall of Singapore wasn't a telegram. We must have heard it on the news. By that stage it was becoming obvious that a disaster was on the way. The big shock was the sinking of those two ships. Those two ships were sent out by Churchill to give Britain command of the seas, the Indian Ocean, and the southern approaches. They were sunk by aerial attack.

'It was always known that those ships would be vulnerable to air attack, so an aircraft carrier was sent out with them. They had to go round the coast of Africa, round the Cape, because the Suez Canal was closed. And the aircraft carrier went aground through some failure of navigation, the most appalling humiliation for the Royal Navy. And they had to leave it there, and so the whole support and security of those two great ships was removed. Because there was no land based aircraft of sufficient strength to be able to defend them. They were off the east coast of the Straits of Malaya when they were caught. They'd already come to Singapore and then they were sent out by the admiral commanding. He decided they would put out to sea to try and stop the Japanese crossing over by sea - to interdict their advance. They were well down Malaya by then.

'It was a black moment, but on the other hand the attack on Pearl Harbour brought America in at the same time. So in a sense it was a relief. India was no longer on its own. But still that was a very black period.'

1941 was the last year the Government of India moved up to Simla in the summer. It was simply too remote and had too poor communications to run India's war effort from there. From now on India was ruled from Delhi. Petrol rationing was introduced.

'In Delhi, my father used to cycle to work in the winter,' John Michael said. 'He couldn't cycle in the summer, in temperatures of 110 or 115 degrees. He cycled as an example, and as an economy, not as an economy to him, as he had an official car, it wouldn't have cost him anything to go in the car. He wanted to set an example, and also because petrol was rationed at that stage. As Finance Member of the Viceroy's Council, what he did would have been very visible. And it had wide repercussions. He had to cycle about a mile and a half. But uphill at the end.

'Because of the war I couldn't go back to England to school. Although there were schools in India my father didn't think the public schools in India were good enough. It was really for the 10-15 age period that my father thought the British schools in India didn't have high enough standards. So he arranged for me to have lessons in India. We had a school in our house. In the house in King Edward Road in Delhi, and in Simla, in both places. It became known as the Raisman Academy. There were anything from 3 to 6 or 7 children in it. Some were the children of other Indian Civil Servants, some were the children of soldiers. Who were in a similar position to me, caught out by the war. Otherwise we'd have been back at school in England.

'My tutor was a marvellous Scottish missionary, called Jennie Copeland who taught me all the other subjects than Greek and Latin, including maths. She came to the house, every morning at 9 o'clock. We worked through till 4 o'clock in the afternoon with a break in the middle of the morning and a break for lunch. Between the ages of 10 and 15. My younger brother Jer went to a small school in Delhi and Simla for most of the time that I was there, and then he too had Jenny in the latter stages.

'Jenny, she was a marvellous person really. She was somebody who tried to improve the lot of poor Indians, particularly the coolies in Simla. She was a great supporter and defender of them. She came out to India as a missionary having been brought up in Glasgow, having been to Glasgow University, having got a first class degree from Glasgow University. She was a superbly educated woman. She belonged to the Church of Scotland. My parents got to know and admire her in Simla because of the work that she was doing there, and when they found that she was so remarkably well educated they recruited her to run the Raisman Academy. And she later got a Kaiser-i-Hind, which was a medal awarded to women who did good work in India.

'I found algebra particularly difficult, and my father used to do algebra with me when he was shaving. I would be standing by his elbow, reading out equations to him, how do I do this quadratic equation, or whatever it was, or simultaneous equations. He enjoyed being able to do that. I enjoyed algebra once I had made the breakthrough. Not that I ever went very far in it.

'Whereas Latin and Greek he was teaching me as a complete subject. It was because the classics were hardly taught, and Greek I don't think was taught at all in the schools in India at that time. Initially, my father had employed a retired Winchester housemaster, who happened to be in India, to teach me classics. But he quite quickly decided that his classics were not good enough and so he took it over himself, busy though he was. There was also a colleague of his in the Indian Civil Service who spent time up in Simla in the summer who I went to occasionally. He was another classical scholar who remembered enough of his classics. There were a lot of classical scholars. But most of his colleagues in the Indian Civil Service who were classical scholars had forgotten their Latin and Greek and wouldn't have been able to teach. But there was another, Sir John Thorne, who lived not far from us and I used to go to him occasionally.

'The Greek and Latin my father and I did in more formal sessions. I wrote verbs out and sentences and did translations and all the rest of it. And then we wrote passages and verses and composed verses. He was incredibly busy, but somehow or other he found half an hour or so in the afternoon and another half an hour or so in the evening so that I had an hour to an hour and a half of classics every day. And when he was in Delhi and I was in Simla, after the Government stopped moving up to Simla, but the families moved up to Simla, and some of the officials went up to Simla, he would send me exercises to do, post them to me by the government bag, I would do the exercises and send them back by the government bag, and he would then correct them and send them back to me corrected.

'We did not so much the philosophy, but the history, and especially the literature. We were doing Virgil, a bit of Ovid, Horace, Caesar of course, and Cicero. And we did some Sophocles, and Plato, started on Plato. We did Gray's Elegy in Latin, and the Jabberwocky of course. The Jabberwocky in Latin. In the case of the Jabberwocky someone had written it and he knew it. Gray's Elegy, he did himself. As far as I remember. And with me. He did it with me. As an exercise. And it was fun. It was something he enjoyed, and I enjoyed sharing it with him. Into Latin verse.

'I took my School Certificate in India when I was 15, based on the work I had done with Jenny, and in Latin and Greek based on the teaching of my father. And the interesting thing was that for my School Certificate I did the New Testament in Greek, and he taught me the New Testament in Greek. And the odd thing was that I was the only boy in India who was taking the Greek New Testament for my School Certificate. It was an option. I took the exam in Delhi in a big public examination hall. Nobody else in India had taken that option. They sent it out from England. It was part of the Oxford and Cambridge papers. In fact, I'd actually studied Matthew, and we made a mistake, my father and I, and when the paper was put before me in the examination hall I found that it was Mark that I was being examined on. Fortunately, Matthew and Mark are the two Gospels that are closest to each other, and I was able to construe the passages without difficulty.

'So when I went to Rugby, having got distinctions in Greek and Latin in my School Certificate, I was immediately put into the upper school. Thanks to his teaching.

'We had stables within our compound in King Edward Road, five horses on average. I rode Tiny Tim. Father mainly rode Charity, but sometimes Henty. We also had Titia. Mama used to ride. My younger brother had one. He took over one of mine. We had two *syces* (grooms), who brought the horses to the front of the house.

'As relaxation we often rode before breakfast together because it was cooler then. After the Quit India Declaration, and the ensuing violence, we had guards follow us everywhere. My father and I used to find that tedious. So, early in the morning we would give them the slip. My father rode a lot and played golf occasionally. There was lots of good riding country out near what was then the airport. Now its all been sort of built over, behind *Safdar Jang*, behind Humayun's tomb. And then down by the banks of the River Jumna, what he used to call *ripae Jumnaicae*.

'My father never went jackal hunting. I was the one who went hunting. He didn't have time. Our head *syce* would ride my horse out to the Meet. I would get a lift in a friend's car, or later go by bus when petrol rationing came in. I was mad keen on hunting. Jackal. We had marvellous gallops across country with hounds. With English foxhounds. Not in Simla, it was too steep there. But in and around Delhi. There were hunts in all the sort of key places. There were hunts in Lucknow, in Calcutta, in Bombay, Madras, Ootacamund, Peshawar. There was a Delhi hunt which used to meet in different places where there was good hunting country and where jackals could be found easily. They were the size of a big dog and they howled. And big ears. It was very popular. There was a Breakfast once a year, in the middle of the hunting season. In 1940 it was hosted by Lady Linlithgow. The Viceroy himself didn't hunt. He was too big.

'We didn't shoot jackals. It was exactly like fox hunting except jackal instead of fox. At first I was the youngest person in the field. But then four years later, the hunt had swollen. By that stage Lord and Lady Wavell hosted the Hunt Breakfast.'

A Lesson in Plato

You are, all of you, in the land, brothers. But
when God fashioned you, he added gold in the
composition of those of you who are qualified to
be rulers; he put silver in the auxiliaries, and
iron and bronze in the farmers and the rest.

Plato, The Republic, Book III

For Britain 1942 was the lowest point of the war. During the blitz, the night streets of London were deserted except for fire engines, air-raid wardens in tin hats and ambulances with sirens and tyres screaming between the blazing bombsites. All around Whitehall the streets were blocked by sandbags, barbed wire, and sentry posts. A little before 5 a.m, Leo Amery's driver turned into the Foreign Office. The upper semicircles of the car headlights were covered with black tape. Below them the pale yellow glow was already being eclipsed by the early dawn light. The tired sentry in khaki uniform saluted the car. Pin-striped double-breasted dark blue Amery in glasses, looking like a banker, strode through the corridors of power, already a legend in his time. From his first days reporting the Boer War for the Times, Leo Amery (Harrow and Balliol) had been so long with the British Empire, he was identified with it. He had been in parliament since 1911. In 1925 he created the Dominions' Office. After the humiliation of the Munich Agreement with Hitler in 1938, Amery had spearheaded the ousting of Chamberlain's government by his famous quotation of Oliver Cromwell's injunction to the Long Parliament, 'You have stayed too long in this place. In the name of God, go!' Churchill, succeeding Chamberlain, owed a lot to Amery. But Amery's first and last love was the Jewel in the Crown, India, where he was born, and throughout Churchill's term of office as war Prime Minister, Amery was Secretary of State for India and Burma.

Amery climbed up the ladder that led from the Foreign Office to the separate building housing the India Office. Here, among elephant's foot waste paper baskets, tusks, portraits of Tippoo Sahib, the Multan Campaign, camel cavalry, and imperialist generals with greying moustaches, the telegrams came in daily, or rather nightly, for Delhi time was 5 and half hours ahead of London, with the result that the shirt-sleeved telegraph officer would not come in with the glued strips of paper with their strings of capital letters all awry until the German bombers were nearly done with that night's destruction of London, and the skies were lightening and the all clear siren was sounding over the streets of Pimlico.

From the Viceroy of India to Leo Amery, Secretary of State for India at the India Office, Whitehall:

355 Linlithgow to Amery   Simla, 28 Jul 42
Raisman is in London.

'Reply,' Amery instructed his secretary, 'as follows:'

396 Amery to Linlithgow   London, 3 Aug 42
Important private and personal. Your private and personal telegram. The Prime Minister has agreed to Raisman attending War Cabinet in order to state Government of India's point of view.

I consider that it should not be publicly disclosed that he had done so as it is improbable that accredited Indian Representatives when they arrive will be admitted as of right. Winston is very curious and incalculable on questions of this kind.

435 War Cabinet minutes   London, 6 Aug 42
Also present for part of Item 2, Sir Jeremy Raisman.

Raisman then entered the meeting.

Sir Jeremy was asked whether India could not pay for the aircraft now being sent to India. In Sir Jeremy's view, any possibility that might have existed of asking India to accept a larger defence liability had been finally dispelled by India's entry into the war, which had already caused a heavy increase in India's own expenditure.

War Cabinet thanked Sir Jeremy Raisman for his statement and he then withdrew. The War Cabinet decided to take note of the views expressed but to record no decision.

On August 8th 1942, fresh from the War Cabinet, Jeremy appeared unexpectedly in Leeds.

'Can you put me up for a few days?' he asked Celia. 'I don't want you to do anything different from what you normally do. No fuss. And no one is to know I am here.'

'I've just been to a meeting of the War Cabinet in London,' Jeremy told Harry, 'and I've got a few days before I have to go back.'

Harry was delighted, and he and Myer spent every evening after work sitting with Jeremy, listening to him talk. And as always Jeremy did not fail to ask in detail about each of the family's children. His first question on meeting any member of the family was usually, 'Well, and how's Baby?' This part of his conversation was one he never hurried. He remembered all the children's names, their likes and dislikes, and what was hoped and dreamed for them. To all of which he would give a measured, considered response. Jeremy never became impatient with children, and he would ask what were the names of their toys and dollies, and what they did, and what they thought, and he ruminated over this information with as much gravity as when he was considering the fortunes of a vast empire, or the conduct of a desperate war.

'You'll have seen the headlines in the papers today, the arrest of Gandhi and Nehru,' Jeremy said. 'The morning before I left Delhi, the Government of India signed an order for their arrest. We've been negotiating with them for years. Britain is at war, but the people of India are not. The Congress Party was about to make a public declaration calling on the British to quit India. It required someone of the standing of Gandhi to influence them. We asked Gandhi to support us. After all, everyone knows that it's only a matter of time before India gets independence. And all along the aim of the Indian Civil Service has been, and is, to prepare India for it in the best possible way.

'"Look," we said to Gandhi, "if you support us we'll give you a written guarantee that when the war is over, we'll make India independent."

'"That guarantee's worth nothing," Gandhi said "The Japanese'll have the country in two weeks."

'And,' Jeremy grimaced, 'at that time it looked as though they would.

'"Well," we said, "We don't want to put a man like you in prison. If you give us your word that you won't oppose us, we'll just put you under house arrest."

'"Oh no," he said. "I must stick to my principles."

'Principles!' Jeremy grunted ironically, 'With the bodyguards we provide to protect him, it costs the Government of India millions to keep that one man in poverty. Anyway, now we have put him under house arrest in the palace of the Aga Khan in Poona.'

Harry smiled, and Jeremy continued.

'We've got together an Indian volunteer army,' Jeremy went on. 'We can put two million men into the field, but there's no money for arms. I've just come from the War Cabinet in London. I was there to persuade them to do something which is terribly important from India's point of view, which is not to insist on them retaining the money Britain owes India. And I can tell you this is something the War Cabinet did not expect the representative of the British Government in India to do. Because I was acting on behalf of India, not taking the part of Britain. You can't take this money away, was my argument. This money belongs to India. This is money that Britain owes India to cover the costs that India is incurring in supplying British troops in India, and in providing and equipping Indian troops to serve outside India. India is responsible for its own defence. Of course. Any money for that has to be generated in India. But any money spent supplying British troops which are in India as part of Britain's overall war effort elsewhere needs to be paid back. Money for the airlift to Burma and China. There's a big build up of British troops in India fighting against the Japanese.

'There's an agreement between the Government of India and the Government in London that India should pay for the costs of its own defence, but that India should not be required to pay for Britain's war in Burma or elsewhere. This is an agreement that the two governments negotiated with each other, and it is public knowledge in India that this is the basis on which finances were to be shared. Congress members know that, and the newspapers. The educated Indian public know about it. And that's why it is so important for India to win this battle with the British Government, and therefore with the War Cabinet.

'Obviously, from Britain's point of view, their financial reserves are very important because they're diminishing fast. They're having to spend vast sums buying equipment from America, and so on, destroyers and tanks and all the rest of it, to sustain their position in the war. They wanted to keep the money they owe India. And I had to tell them that that would be unethical and against all the agreements that have been worked out between Britain and India. It would be an immoral act.

226

'These are the principles of the Indian Civil Service. They are the principles on which members of the Indian Civil Service work. The Viceroy, Linlithgow, supports me in this. Before I left he discussed this with me. He'd said to me, "You better go back and explain this to the War Cabinet, and persuade them." Well, after a lot of telegrams to-ing and fro-ing between the Viceroy and the India Office in London, I got the right to present India's case at the War Cabinet in London. It's taken over two days to fly here, zig-zagging all over West Africa. At the Cabinet, Churchill was not there, he was seeing Roosevelt. Atlee presided, with Eden as deputy.

'Actually,' Jeremy went on, 'they had only agreed for me to attend to present our case. I had to withdraw immediately after. And it took quite something to get them to go that far, I'll tell you. Churchill is worried that if I am replaced by a non-European it will set a precedent for an Indian to claim the right to attend the War Cabinet.'

Jeremy paused, and Harry waited.

'No,' Jeremy admitted wrily, 'I don't suppose they'll take much notice. The War Cabinet told me they thought I should raise some money. I said "Well, get some of your financial experts to do it if you think it can be done."

'We're fighting on three fronts. We're fighting the cause of India at the War Cabinet, we've got Gandhi and Nehru saying, "Quit India, this is not India's war," and the Japanese are talking about the *Chalo Delhi,* the March on Delhi.

'The most damaging thing the Japanese do,' Jeremy said, 'is to humiliate the District Officers. They ride them out on horses and show them up to public ridicule. Up to now they'd have only seen our District Officers as distant figures on horseback. Their authority was unquestioned. Once they see them degraded and humiliated, it becomes impossible to govern the territories. It's a very clever tactic. The control of the British Empire rests on the respect that the native people have for the British administration. We don't have enough people to hold Burma and India by force.'

'Last month the American government sent one of their financial experts to discuss the supply situation with us. He arrived late in the evening, and he stayed at Peterhof. Well, the next morning, when he came to breakfast, he said "Hello" in Yiddish. Then he said, "Don't you recognise me? I'm Adler. We used to have the grocery shop in Templar Street."'

Harry nodded briefly, not to interrupt the story, and Jeremy went on.

'"Oh," I said, "now I recognise you. Why didn't you tell me when you arrived?"

'"I wanted to keep it as a surprise," Adler said. "I knew you were here, of course. I've heard a lot about you."'

This was followed by a long pause, during which Harry remained obediently attentive, and Celia brought in the tea-tray.

'You know,' Jeremy went on, 'in New Delhi we live in a house in King Edward Road. It's not far to the Viceroy's Palace. Our house in Simla is called Peterhof. It used to be the Viceroy's summer palace, but in the time of Lord Curzon they decided it was too small for them.

'Too small!' Jeremy snorted. 'The ballroom is big enough for two hundred couples to dance. There's a wonderful view from the balcony over the snow-covered Himalayas. It's like Switzerland. We have a staff of 36 servants. We need them to run the house and the gardens. The butler is the most senior. But in fact the head cook is equally important. Actually, he regards himself as equal to the butler. The dishes are always made from freshly ground spices. They have an intense fragrance. The servants are strictly separated from each other; they belong to different castes. Each member of the household has his own bearer.'

'Actually,' Jeremy went on, 'I felt proud of Leeds. When the Prince of Wales was sunk off Singapore there was a public appeal for £10 million to build a new one. The first donation was £1 million from Montague Burton, and he said that if they had difficulty in raising the rest they should come back to him. The last time I was here on leave Montague Burton offered me a job. He asked me what I would want. I said £40 000 cash and a percentage share in the business. He thought about it for a while and then said "No, we can't offer you prospects like you'll have in India."'

At this point my mother chipped in, 'I work for Bernard Burton. When we got married, he gave us that clock as a wedding present,' and she proudly indicated the mantelpiece, where stood the wooden step pyramid whose chimes had quarterly punctuated Jeremy's conversation throughout his visit. At this time in its life, covered by a folded doyley, the clock was the base for a chipped, cut-glass water jug that my mother used as a flower vase.

At the end of his stay Jeremy asked Harry and Celia what they would like for putting him up. 'I'd like a sundial,' Celia said. 'There's lovely ones in Schofield's.' Jeremy duly had one delivered. It was in stone with a lead pointer and dial inscribed, '(I record only) Sunny Houres.' Harry and Celia examined it appreciatively. 'Don't forget,' Jeremy said to Harry, 'you need to line it up accurately with the Pole Star.'

Harry mentioned that he was shortly going to be speaking at a political rally at the Town Hall. 'I hope you don't get into trouble, Harry,' Jeremy said, knowing his brother's inflexible left-wing opinions.

Myer saw Jeremy off at the station. It was milling with soldiers and civilians. Myer bought a platform ticket, and got on the London train with Jeremy, determined to see his brother get a seat. The corridors were packed with people and suitcases. Panting with effort and indignation, Myer got off the train and found a ticket collector.

'This man must have a seat,' he said, puffing out his chest and stomach. 'Do you know who this is? This is Sir Jeremy Raisman!'

The harrassed ticket collector, about to give Myer a sharp reply, seemed to notice something unusual about this ruffled little man, standing like an outraged hen that had just been pulled unceremoniously off its egg.

'I'll see to it,' he said, as if it were a privilege, and went off down the train.

Jeremy, not sure how to calm Myer down, seized the opportunity and said, 'Don't wait. I'll write to you. Love to the family,' and stood at the door as the crowded train moved off.

Myer, snorting with pride and excitement, scurried straight back to Harry's to compare notes. 'Did he tell you,' Myer asked, 'how he escapes his bodyguard? They insist on him having his own personal bodyguard wherever he goes. Well, he doesn't like it. In the morning he gives him the slip so he can go off riding.' Myer chuckled. 'He's the real ruler of India,' Myer went on. 'The whole Council defer to his opinion. The Viceroy won't say a thing without consulting him.'

For a long time after Myer had gone, Harry turned these things over in

his mind, and looked thoughtfully at the sundial. Celia joined him as he was trying to decide which way was north. 'When you talk of the time,' Harry said, 'what you are doing is in fact describing the relative position of the sun and the earth. The mathematicians divide the sky into 360 degrees. The astronomical degree is made up of 15 minutes. In fact, if you were to read the position of a ship at sea, it would tell you how many degrees, minutes, and seconds.'

Harry continued musing on the sundial, occasionally trying to explain his thoughts to Celia. 'From the first day of winter to the first day of the new year, the sun rises at the same time. December 21st is called the winter solstice because there's hardly any variation in the rising and setting of the sun for some days. But from September 21st to March 21st the sun never rises on the North Pole. If we had a clear night we could align the sundial on the pole star. You can't mistake it, and the Great Bear. The Great Bear's got many names, Charles' Wain, the Plough, the Pointer, Ursa Major, the Great Bear, the Dipper. It's also called Septentriones, the seven northern stars, sept is seven, and the Pointer, because it points to the Pole Star. The earth would appear to be attracted in some way by the Pole Star, because it spins round the Pole Star in a period of 19 thousand years and in doing so it describes the shape of a cone. Actually there are four separate movements of the earth. In addition to spinning, it wobbles, it undulates as it goes round the sun. What they do when they give you the calendar, they give you something that overrides all these different movements of the earth, its turnings, its tumblings...'

At that moment there was a commotion in the street. A platoon of soldiers had been drawn up in the main road, and an officer, swagger-stick in hand, was going from house to house. 'We need to billet the men,' said the officer. 'How many can you take?'

Celia called Harry. 'We'll take five or six,' she said.

'Will you be able to make them meals?' asked the officer.

'Yes.'

'We need some water now. Do you have a bucket?'

Celia rushed off. 'I thought she was going to poison half the British Army,' my father said later. 'In her haste, she took the same bucket she used to keep your nappies in.'

My mother told me how much I amused Sir Jeremy. 'We dressed you up in a little grey flannel suit I got specially at Schofield's. You looked lovely in it. In fact I've got a picture of it somewhere. You looked a picture, round face, jacket and short trousers.

'Well, you could understand everything. So we warned you, "You must be a good boy! You must be a good boy!"

'So you said, "All right, I will." Not that you wanted to be, but...

'"And you must keep yourself clean."

'How many times I washed you! I washed your hands, your face, everything. You kept running out into the street and every time you came back black bright. So, we watched you carefully then, and you hadn't to run out into the street or anything like that. But you wanted to go and enjoy yourself. Anyway, after Jeremy had been there a couple of days, he noticed you kept coming in and looking at him and then going out. Well, one time after you came in Jeremy said, "Come here."

'So you went up to the big armchair he was sitting in, and you stood up right straight.

'"Why do you keep looking at me?" Jeremy said.

'So you said, "How long are you going to stay here?"

'So he said, "Why do you ask?"

'So you said, "I'm sick of being a good boy. When are you going home? I'm sick of being a good boy."

'Well, he laughed so much. He thought it was right funny. He was right tickled pink by it. We all were. We screamed laughing.'

625 Linlithgow to Amery   **Simla, 24 Aug 42**
Raisman returning by air today.

773 Linlithgow to Amery   **Delhi, 20 Sep 42**
My Council are aware that Raisman also was invited by His Majesty's Government when he was home to pay for the campaign in Burma on the ground that India was interested in Burma's future.

Soon after his return Raisman made before Council a verbal statement of results of his visit to England in which he informed them of "offers" he had made to His Majesty's Government within the existing settlement, for example, that India would pay all rupee costs of the Air Forces in India and Burma. Council declined to endorse Raisman's "offers" out of hand and required a detailed written statement.

769 Winston Churchill to Linlithgow   London, 20 Sep 42
His Majesty's Government do not suggest that a new settlement or new account keeping should be negotiated at the present juncture with the Government of India. We are however also keeping our own accounts which may eventually serve as the basis of a counter-claim, in which such items as the naval, air and military defence of India by British forces will play a part.

781 Linlithgow to Amery   **Delhi, 13 Aug 43**
I am bound in terms to warn the War Cabinet that the Government of India and I cannot be responsible for the continuing stability of India now, or her capacity to serve as a base against Japan next year unless we have appropriate food help in prospect. You will be familiar from the Press with the critical situation that faces us in Bengal. I can only repeat what has already been said in my personal telegram of 29th July and convey to His Majesty's Government in the most formal means possible the considered warning given earlier in this telegram. If they are not prepared to modify their decisions we can take no responsibility for the consequences. And it is essential that this should be fully understood at this stage, and that what is at issue is not merely feeding India, but our capacity to wage war against Japan.

The View from Almscliff Crag

In the years since Uncle John had disappeared Leeds had been changing. Even the poorest of the Leylanders had now left the Leylands for more suburban areas. On the hills west of North Street, around Lovell Road School and Ramsden Terrace, where Moshy the Wine Merchant had kept his last court, the once-coveted streets now in their turn became the homes of the poor. Camp Road, in Ruffky the Monkey's day the height of elegance, now gave its name to a notorious slum. The Leylanders had moved up the hills north of Sheepscar, to Chapeltown, to Harehills, and to Roundhay. The wealthy had reached Moortown, at the edge of the city. People said they made so much money they had Rembrandts in the lavatory. Their wives were known as the Merry Wives of Moortown.

Further north from Moortown the road leads out of the Aire Valley to a place where the past is laid out like the scene of a drama. After passing Eccup Reservoir the road climbs up through the Wyke Cutting. The cutting is dark. On either side the road is flanked by rocks, tree-roots and rough, ivy-covered walls. The sky is overhung by tall elms, their winter branches encrusted with huge noisy rookeries. Once out of this cutting and over the crest of the hill the traveller has left Airedale and stands beneath the ruined stone keep of Harewood Castle. From here he surveys a new vista, the sweep of Wharfedale's fields and hedgerows dotted with stone farmhouses. But the clear waters of the River Wharfe winding along the valley give no hint of the prehistoric turmoil when the receding glaciers gouged this chasm out of the ground. Granite crags, torn from the crumbling summits of the Pennines, carried like pebbles on the ice floes, were strewn fifty miles along the valley floor. So now, to the children who scramble over summer sunbaked Almscliff Crag, the rustle of the wind in the stiff upland grass carries no echo of the grinding boulders, nor the accents of their grandparents carry any whisper of the times that tore the Leylanders from *Der Hame* and brought them here to Leeds.

And indeed far to the east, down the Aire and the Humber up which the Leylanders had come, far across the North Sea and the Baltic, all traces of the parent community in Lithuania and its culture were about to be extinguished.

Long ago the Lithuanians were a woodland people who practised magic, and preserved the legends of the mysterious spirits with whom they shared their forests. In the fortified palace of the Grand Duke Gedymin were kept the sacred green snakes and the perpetual holy fire of sweet-smelling Baltic amber. When they died the Grand Dukes and their nobles were dressed in their most glorious robes, mounted on their most prized horses and burned on pyres of oak logs in the sacred groves. And still in the remote villages and woodland clearings certain triangular shaped stones are treated with reverence.

Since recorded history armies have surged backwards and forwards across the fertile, low-lying land at the mouth of the River Niemen. Here was the furthest incursion of the Lithuanian Grand Dukes into the territory of the Teutonic Knights. This road was the main road from Kovno through the frontier town of Yurberick to Tilsit and the ports of Königsberg and Memel, the Hanseatic trade routes across the Baltic to the North Sea and the distant Atlantic Ocean. This tongue of German coast was also the goal for Hoshy and Moshy, fleeing Tsarist persecution, the lifeline of the nineteenth century deliverance from Russia.

In his novel, August 1914, Solzhenitsyn describes the amazement of the Tsarist Russian troops as the Tsar's ill-fated army crossed this frontier from the Russian Province of Lithuania into East Prussia. To this day, the traveller is struck by the way the ramshackle wooden huts and the unmade muddy streets on the Russian side are replaced on the German side by the paved roads of Smalininkai, with its neat rows of immaculately kept brick houses that satisfy the old Prussian passion for order and authority. Black, yellow and red bricks form a series of storeys, diamond courses, horizontal bricks, bricks at an angle, vertical bricks of window sills, roof layers, and even little turrets of brick.

In a field by the road a dead tree

Black, yellow and red bricks...

234

stands, long ago stripped of its bark, shiny and straight. At about 15 feet it forks into two equal branches, cut off, after another couple of feet, with German symmetry. And upon them, as on two fingers a waiter carries a vast tray, is balanced a huge nest of twigs and little branches woven by the stork to raise her luck-bringing chicks in the village.

The churches too change. The Roman Catholic confections of Lithuania, baroque in opulent Italian coloured plaster, here are replaced by severe, angular brick German Lutheran churches, all straight lines and geometric triangles and plainness, unpainted, unadorned, all in red brick with their roofs shod, like soldiers' helmets, in plates of shiny, galvanised iron, pale steely grey under which the harsh, unyielding tenets of a cruel faith for hundreds of years were preached.

Lithuanian church   *German church*

On June 22, 1941 the war between Germany and the Soviet Union began, and on that same day German regular army units marched up the river road from the border town of Smalininkai on the German side, crossed the Lithuanian frontier and entered Yurberick at 8 o'clock in the morning. Two days later they were in Vilna. Like Napoleon, whose armies had, strangely, crossed the River Niemen at the same point on exactly the same day of the year 1812, Hitler's attack on Russia was to fail but few of the Jews of the Pale were destined to know that. Yurberick was included in a part of a 25 kilometre strip, which the Gestapo in Tilsit designated for annihilation of all Jews. The head of the Gestapo in Tilsit, Boehme, at once started to plan the annihilation. Initially, the target date for completion was set for Thursday July 3 1941. After consultation with the mayor, Georg Hefner (or Jurgis Gepneris as he was known in Lithuanian), the Jewish cemetery was chosen as the location for the murder of the 2 300 Jews of Yurberick. Action against the Jews started on the Sabbath June 28 1941, with an order for all Jews to remove all the weeds from the streets. On the same day, they were ordered to bring their books at 4pm in the afternoon to the yard of the synagogue and the old Rabbi of the town, Rabbi Haim-Ruven Rubinstein was forced to bring his books and the articles that he had written on a cart. At 5pm the Lithuanians ordered that the Torah Scrolls be brought to the yard. The Maggid's work was put on top of the heap of books already piled up. Petrol was poured over the heap and then ignited.

But Mayor Gepneris still did not have in place the machinery for the killing of such large numbers of his townspeople. He could see that Boehme's target date for total annihilation was over-optimistic, but meanwhile, he stepped up the persecution. On July 25 1941 the Jews were ordered to tear down the wooden synagogue. They obeyed with trembling hands. A group of spectators quickly gathered near the

Rounding up Jews

synagogue; some of them shrugged their shoulders, being afraid to voice their protest or to show it by the look on their faces. Others looked intently at how the Gothic style roof, the wooden walls, the interior carved decorations were being torn down, and some more active spectators hurried to take parts of those decorations home.

On July 3 in the morning Boehme and his assistants came to Yurberick together with 30 to 40 Germans from Smalininkai. Small groups of Gestapo people together with Lithuanian helpers were formed; they were ordered to remove the Jewish men from their homes. The number of Jewish men was not enough, and they were sent out a second time and found another 60 Jewish men. Three women with their children, who did not want to part from their husbands, were included in the group. During the arrest, the Lithuanian doctor turned to one of the leaders of the Gestapo named Karsten, and asked that the Jewish doctor be freed. He explained that the Jewish doctor was a surgeon and the citizens needed him. After repeating his request to Boehme, the Lithuanian doctor was beaten by Boehme.

More than 300 Jews were arrested. They were led through the town towards the Jewish cemetery. There, they were asked to turn over all of their valuable things and also to remove their shirts. They were ordered to dig more pits, since the existing ones were not large enough for the large number of Jews. During the digging, the Germans ordered the Jews to beat one another with the shovels, and promised that whoever would defeat his friend, would stay alive. The victims were led by the Germans and the Lithuanians under terrible threats, shouts and beatings, and their outcries filled the air. They had to stand in front of the holes, facing their own graves. Some were ordered to kneel. The murderers went from one to the next, shot them in the neck and kicked them into their graves. Because of the large number of men, some had to witness the murder of their friends and family. Lithuanian citizens from two neighbourhoods adjacent to the cemetery watched the murders.

Among the victims was a Jewish customs agent who had fought in World War I and had been awarded the Iron Cross, Class A, for excellent fighting. He attacked Boehme and hit him. A deadly shot stopped him. Many tried to escape from the graves. The murderers and watchmen chased them and some Germans and Lithuanians were injured. In this action, 322 Jews were killed, among them 5 women and children. After they had completed their task, the murderers held a dinner, celebrated and drank a lot of vodka.

On the same day another 80 men who had hidden, were caught. At 10pm the policeman Botvinskis informed them that they will be shot at 3am. The writer mentions, that this information did not make any special impression on anyone. Nobody cried, and there was one who had *Jahrzeit* and all the prisoners stood and prayed *Maariv*. The information proved wrong, and the prisoners were not shot. Men who stayed alive and were aged 15-50 were commanded to work, and the elderly had to report to the police twice a day.

On July 21, 45 elderly people were arrested and were transported on three carts that belonged to Jews, to Raseiniai, as though to go for a physical check-up. Ten miles along the road towards Raseiniai, they were murdered together with the coachmen and the Jews from the nearby town. Before they were murdered, the old people were forced to write home that they were taken to work and would be treated well; many of the people back home believed what they read.

On August 1, an order was issued for all elderly Jewish women to appear before the commander. All were pushed into the yard of the Maggid's old school, which had been turned into the Women's Ghetto. Many women with babies in their arms were violently dragged towards the headquarters. From morning until night the women were kept without food and drink. In the evening Lithuanian activists came and ordered them to line up in lines of two. To speed the process they beat the women cruelly.

By now the killings had dragged on throughout the summer well beyond Boehme's deadline. The date of the fourth action was September 8, 1941. This time younger working women and hidden children who had been betrayed by local people were shot. Again the women were driven into the school yard. In the afternoon the building was surrounded by Lithuanian and German policemen. The waiting women were to be driven to work, but in fact their journey ended at the seventh kilometre, near Kalnenai. Their torment was the same. The women were ordered to beat one other, to kick and bite, to tear their hair. Questions of 'Why?' or 'Because of what?' were answered by automatic shooting or beating.

The Maggid had no direct family descendants left to witness the end of Yurberick. The last Raismans, Raphael, his wife, five grown up sons, daughter and daughter-in-law were shot at a pit in the forest. The final act of the retreating Germans in 1945 was to blow up the school house where the Maggid of Yurberick had taught. Before the birch leaves of 1941 had begun to turn silver and gold, mayor Gepneris was able to post a sign on the road to Yurberick:

THIS TOWN IS CLEANSED OF JEWS

What the Cossacks had tried, and the Tsar's government had wished, twentieth century efficiency had at last brought about.

But in 1941, as the blackouts were put up in the windows in Leeds, no one could have had the slightest idea of the enormity of what was happening in Yurberick. After the war, the Russian occupiers did not allow any investigations, and it was over half a century before the fate of the Yurberick Jews became known. And meanwhile, the war was coming closer for the Leylanders. On the western front, France had fallen, and Britain faced the German armies across the Channel. Barricades and pill-boxes started to go up in the Leeds streets. From time to time Ada, listening for news on the wireless, picked up Lord Haw Haw's propaganda broadcasts from Germany. The instant he found his mother doing it, Myer would switch off the set angrily. 'Don't listen to that rubbish,' he burst out. 'When they come even I'll find a way to take just one with me,' and he looked down ironically at his bulky, impractical, totally non-violent figure.

I myself was too young to remember anything of this. I had been born at the summer solstice of 1939, at the moment when the shadow cast by the sun stopped shortening and began to lengthen again, in the breathless interval between the betrayal of Czechoslovakia at Munich and the declaration of war when Germany invaded Poland. My father told me that my name was chosen because it meant God's Peace.

'Because of the bombing,' my mother told me later, 'I was evacuated with you as a baby to Poppleton. It's somewhere near York. I'm not sure where. Anyway, it was right out in the country, in the back of beyond. There was just a few houses and a big open space. They called it The Green. The Green,' she repeated with a shudder, seeing again in her mind all the green, green grass. 'And you cried all the time. You didn't have enough to eat.

Celia

'Well, after I'd been there a couple of days my brother Teddy came to see me on his bicycle and I said "I'm going home. Take me home."

'So we piled the baby and all the clothes on the bicycle and went to the station to get a train back to Leeds.

'When I got back Daddy wasn't at home. He was in the club, playing cards, of course. I was right annoyed. But I was so relieved to be back home. I said "I don't care about bombs, I'm never going anywhere again."'

Behind black-outs in our kitchen in Harehills I was told about the surrender of one of our allies and the exciting entry of another. I was never clear which was France and which America, but I knew both were on our side, and one was hopeful and the other disappointing, and I could remember the excitement of breaking up the old wooden chairs in the stone cellar (Can I really break it up?) and burning them for fuel, because even the small coal ration we could get was half stone, and going to bed with the windows cased in ice, and my father holding my cold feet in his hands and saying 'Wrap up your feet and then you'll get to sleep. You can't get to sleep if your feet are cold.'

On the kitchen table was a heavily patterned floral oilcloth, cracked and creased from wear, and on the mantelpiece was a row of blue-banded jars whose names I used to chant from memory, 'Salt, Sugar, Pepper etc,' and with the end of the war in 1945, the all-night street party, the amazing machines with huge hanging balls, like battering rams from a mediaeval siege, whose repeated swings destroyed the massive concrete air-raid shelters, the premature end of the sweet ration, and its re-imposition, and the appearance of an unbelievably exotic fruit my mother had told me was shaped like a hand, and was very sweet, and I was so disappointed when it wasn't either, of which I had only seen pictures, the banana.

No news ever came back from *Der Hame*.

My mother told me, 'Father lost all his family, his sister that I used to write to, and her little girls.

'He'd wanted to bring them to Leeds, but my mother said we had no room. Father was heartbroken. Mother never got over it.'

In 1948 there were a few days of unusual excitement at Hebrew school. It all seemed to hinge around appeals for money to buy dunams of land in Palestine and plant trees. Then one evening there was a short pile of slim new books with hard covers in light blue. Mr Hayman handed them out. 'There,' he snorted as he gave one each to the disciplined boys filing past his desk. I was disappointed to find it wasn't a new class reader, but we

Mother never got over it

were to keep it and take it home, free. It didn't have the large, clear Hebrew letters with pointing that I found so beautiful. Instead were pages of plans, and numbers, and maps with lines enclosing gradually increasing dunams of trees. On the cover was the word Homeland. The State of Israel had been founded.

I grew up to be a fat, shy child. On my way home from school, zig-zagging wearily through the back streets of Harehills, I often stopped to buy bagels at Mrs Bloom's shop. Old Mrs Bloom, with her grotesquely wrinkled face, used to point me out as a curiosity to her other customers, 'His uncle is a famous judge in India.' But the main attraction for me was a large black dog waiting impatiently outside, trembling with excitement. The dog was not hostile, but it was difficult to distract its attention from the shop door. 'It's waiting for its bagel,' said Mrs Bloom. 'It won't have

a plain bagel, it's got to have chopped herring on it.'

One day Myer unfolded a tattered sketch on brownish paper. An old tea stain spread out from one corner. It was a portrait of Sir Jeremy as a young man. Myer said it was by a famous artist called Kramer.

On the kitchen sideboard in Mexborough Avenue stood a photograph of Sir Jeremy in knee breeches, with tight, white silk leggings, buckled shoes open at the top, and a sword. But my father never allowed me to touch this photograph, in case by chance I knocked it over. For his part, Myer frequently pointed out the untouchable photograph of Sir Jeremy with great pride, and indeed held him up to me as a model. He repeated Sir Jeremy's stern admonitions, such as 'You must be ambitious,' and 'I could not love you dear so much, loved I not honour more.' I couldn't remember having seen my uncle Sir Jeremy. I had been too young when he stayed.

Still, Sir Jeremy was at least obviously alive, but my Uncle John... Uncle John was a romantic shadow, someone who long ago had held all the family spellbound as he lay idly on a couch, locked in verbal duel with Sir Jeremy, while the family's long *Seder* nights drew to a close. It was over a quarter of a century ago that John had disappeared into the South American jungle. John was utterly unreal for me, and indeed Myer always said he thought my Uncle John was dead. But somehow Myer always lingered on the word 'thought.' Linger or not, I could never imagine John and I could tread the same earth. So John became for me a legend, a whispered, guilty story half-told and half-concealed, a story told to entertain and warn and, of course, my childhood idol.

Because of excessive weight, exertion led to much sweating. Thirst always plagued me. One day I conceived a thirst during the midday school break. As I was too shy to go and knock at the doors of the nearby houses, I decided to walk to my Uncle Myer's to get a glass of water. It was about a mile. Thirstily I passed the terraced houses of Cowper Street, where in my mind's eye were rows of taps, forbidden to me by my timidity. I crossed Chapeltown Road and set off down Mexborough Avenue. On the way I peered over all the low garden walls in Mexborough Avenue, and plucked and fidgeted with the sooty privet leaves, and trailed my fingers over the rough black coping-stones with the rows of concrete-filled belly buttons where railings had once stood. But then, two or three gardens before Number 29, in the shade of the wall, an amazing plant. And for some reason, from the moment of seeing that plant, it was as though a steel pen started to engrave in my memory.

It was only a few inches high, with small flowers on a sort of arching spray, like the tightly curled-back tail of a very bouncy terrier. But what amazed me was the colour of the flowers. Bursting out of delicate soap-bubble buds, and grey with gentle down, flowers like little crinkly, paper-thin trumpets of pale powder blue and purest coral rose grew side by side on the same stem. I looked again, and it was true, two different colours, pastel-soft, on the same stem.

The front door of Number 29 was, as always, slightly ajar. Silently I opened it just a fraction further, and silently walked down the narrow passage into the living room. The only person in the house was my old grandfather Maurice. Like Myer and Harry, his hearing was very poor, and by this time he was nearly blind. Maurice was in the little kitchen-scullery, one step down from the end of the living room. Taking infinite pains not to make a sound, I slipped behind the old man, and down to the kitchen sink. A cup stood by. I filled it from the cold tap, and hurriedly gulped the clear water. It was delicious. And then, still unnoticed, or so I imagined, I now slipped once again behind the sightless old man. Even had I felt able to explain my presence to him when I entered the house, I now felt it impossible to explain my present position. I had to get out undetected. My heart was thumping.

Only then I noticed with fascination that Maurice had cut himself three slices of black bread, had taken a large scrape of butter on a knife, and was buttering the bread in what struck me as a very odd way, the butter on the knife acting as a sort of reservoir from which he was deftly spreading just the right amount of butter on to each slice. Behind him was the meat safe, behind whose metal grille stood an opened tin of condensed milk, with a spoon next to it, and the jar of treacle the old man so loved.

I slipped out of the kitchen, and out of the house. At once the nib ceased to write, and I remember no more. But in the years to come, I often wondered about the plant with two-coloured flowers, and for quite some time sought it. It was to be nearly 50 years before I found it again, and learned its name. If only I had spoken to the old man, how much he could have told me! Did he really see me? Maybe he did. All his life he had been so used to a house full of his children that probably now, at the end, one more would not have seemed strange.

I think I never spoke with my grandfather. The gap had been too great. I had been too young to cross it. By the time I was old enough, it was too late. But it was quite a different story with my Uncle Sam, the tenth of the Raisman children. Sam was every schoolboy's ideal of an uncle. He was the only Raisman who enjoyed football. He was a big, extroverted man, on whom the congenital Raisman inadequacy at growing hair had bestowed a high, shining forehead. His teeth flashed, his open face was smiling, and his open hand never left me without a welcome florin.

The untouchable photo of Sir Jeremy

Eggs and Peas in the Land of Chimneys

The Crash had occurred nearly ten years before I was born. It had irrevocably ruined the family business, leaving it with massive, unpayable debts. The disgrace was so great that no more business could be carried on in the family name in Leeds. Ralph changed his name and left Leeds. Sam also changed his name, and even in distant Burnley Jack changed his name. That name which was to have been so glorious had become too shameful to mention. In Leeds it was retained only by Ada and Maurice, John's wife, Myer and Harry, and in faraway India by Jeremy.

Sidney, Number 11, the youngest of the family, like Sam, Number 10, did not see why he should waste his time on education. He got up late in the morning, and often remained wandering round 29 Mexborough Avenue all day in a tattered thick woollen dressing gown, tied at the waist with a braided sash. There was always around Sidney an air of seediness and cynicism. His hair was lank and sparse, his complexion pale, his jowls hung loosely, and the down-set at the corners of his lower lips revealed a set of large, well spaced teeth, which betrayed a lifetime of cigarette smoking, and which seemed to say they belonged to a man who had seen the baseness of life, a man who was confident, a man of poise, wise to this world, and weary of it.

After some time mooning around Mexborough Avenue, awaiting the splendid fortune Fate had reserved for him, Sidney took jobs in various towns where high self-esteem and a confident patter could be rewarded. Finally, through postings in the Midlands he gravitated to Birmingham, where Raisman Number 9, his older brother Ralph was now established as a solicitor, and was going out with a local girl of a well-to-do family. Sidney was welcomed with open arms into the business. Sidney was also welcomed with open arms by the younger sister of Ralph's fiancée. So the two brothers celebrated a double wedding with the two sisters, and lived happily ever after. Sidney became the solicitor's clerk, and Ralph could devote himself to full-time bridge playing and preparing for the anticipated retirement that awaited him among the palm trees of Bournemouth just as soon as he could stash away enough loot to cover the high stakes without which the locals could not enjoy the game.

Jeremy continued to send a regular sum to keep his parents. Apart from

245

that, the tailoring, which was only to have been the temporary support while the business got underway, now became the sole source of support. Myer, Sam and my father, the only brothers left in Leeds, combined in an attempt to make ends meet. Their workroom was the attic of our house in Harehills. But by this time, Burton's and the other big tailoring factories with their retail shops had taken over virtually all the market and all the manufacturing. To find what few customers might be left over, the remaining master tailors had to spend days travelling by bus far out into the mining villages of South Yorkshire. This forlorn business was known as CMT - cut, make, and trim. Turning their backs for ever on the road to the prosperous north, the family now looked south of the river. For the family it was a riches to rags story.

The attic provided an irregular L-shaped workroom with a low sloping ceiling so it was only possible to stand upright at the cutting table in the middle of the room. It was airless, too hot in summer and too cold in winter. To keep his fingers active, Myer used to go down for a shovel-full of live coals from the downstairs fireplace on the ground floor and carry it flaming and smoking up two flights of winding stairs to the tiny attic fireplace. From time to time as the cold made his fingers too stiff to manipulate the cloth, he would get up from his machine with an impatient grunt of disgust and crouch over this minuscule fire, warming his hands in a kind of rinsing action right over the top of the burning embers.

The workroom was filled with tobacco smoke curling round the low-hanging light bulbs and in the intervals between the incredible din of the sewing machine, you could hear the clack of my father's tailor's shears on the polished surface of the cutting table. Dust was thick in all the corners and encrusted the flex of the hanging light bulbs like hoar frost round the dead stalks of mountain grasses in a blizzard. Apart from its shiny work surface under the needle, Myer's machine stood deep in the clips (cloth pieces) that he periodically gathered into a large sack that could be sold for a few coppers to be reprocessed to make shoddy.

Myer, so kind and playful at other times, never liked to see children in the workroom. He became at once uncomfortable. 'Don't play with the shuttle,' he'd command. 'It's not a toy. Don't play with the oilcan. You'll mark the cloth. Don't touch the drive belt. You'll get your hand caught in the buckle.' For Myer, these sordid workrooms were a source of shame and disgrace, the outward sign of the failure of his cherished

Family Plan.

About this time Jeremy wrote to Harry to say that he was finding himself
in some financial difficulties. He said he was sending Myer a lump sum
of £1 000 with the hope that Myer could set himself up in business and if
it went well, Myer might one day be able to manage without his help.
Until Myer said he could manage, however, Jeremy would also go on
sending the remittances.

   Myer had never seen such a sum of money. He was deeply anxious
about what to do with it, how not to dissipate the completely unasked-for
fortune Jeremy had sent him, and how to set up a business which would
relieve Jeremy of the burden of having to go on sending remittances. The
first thing Harry advised Myer to do was set up a bank account to put the
money in. That done, they considered how to proceed. Eventually, the
brothers decided they would buy a tailoring shop. Looking around,
Leeds prices were too high, and after some searching the brothers decided
on a tailoring shop at 9 Front Street in Pontefract, which was, after all,
where many of their customers were, and there was a bus stop outside
where the bus from Leeds stopped, and a shared entrance with a
newsagent-tobacconist-sweet shop where they could get four ounces of
the triangular chocolate Vienna slices on their way in to work. Across the
road was a liquorice allsort factory that made the flat chewy Pontefract
cakes, stamped like coins with the maker's monogram, and resembling
cow pads left by a miniature jet-black cow.

So up went the sign:

HARRY RAISMAN, BESPOKE TAILOR

over a shop door that led to a long narrow room with a counter, behind
which Harry stood with his tape-measure round his neck, a sharpened
fragment of triangular marking chalk at hand, and a mouthful of pins for
the try-ons. Myer even gingerly invested in some 'outfitting' stock,
which consisted of a cardboard box of flat, peaked caps of the type
favoured by the miners. Above the shop was a narrow, dusty workroom,
where Harry used to cut out the cloth, and stitch the jackets, a cross-
stitching machine for padding the lapels, and a sewing machine for Myer
to sew the trousers. Myer found one of the stock of caps useful to cover

his bald head, and Harry had a film advert made for showing at the local cinema. He never let me see it, since he still felt shame at giving in to using such a device of capitalism. 'All advertising is lies,' he said.

'Even your advert?' I asked. 'Do you tell lies?'

'Yes, even mine.'

'But what lies do you tell?'

'I say these are the best suits,' he said with some disgust. 'They're not the best suits. Just suits.'

'What is the advert like?' I asked.

'It shows a man in a barrel coming into the shop naked and walking out again in a new suit.'

Leeds trams were confined to the city and its suburbs. To get to his shop in Pontefract, Harry's journey beyond the city began at the bus station below Kirkgate Market. While he was still in the city, the architecture was Victorian and romantic. The civic dignity expressed itself in monuments like John Barran's Moorish fantasy. Churches were copies of famous German or Italian buildings, mills had bell towers from Renaissance Tuscany. The bus then passed the Marshall family's extraordinary stone factory. It stood in Marshall Street and was called Temple Flax Mills because it was a copy of an ancient Egyptian temple. The architect, Ignatius Bonomi from Durham had got the idea in 1838 from his brother Joseph Bonomi, one of the amateur Egyptologists who followed Napoleon's expedition to Egypt. At the front of the factory, massive sandstone pillars with papyrus and lotus flower capitals support a cornice carrying the winged sun disc, emblem of the hawk-headed god Horus. The temple, designed for the blazing hot Egyptian desert, was modified for the Leeds climate. The factory's flat roof, suitable for a country where it never rains, started to grow grass, and when it was first built sheep were put out to graze on it. The interior of the factory, denied the glaring Egyptian sunlight for which its original was designed, was illuminated by 66 semicircular glass domes erected over gothic arches raised on cast iron pillars which were hollow so as to act as concealed internal drain pipes to prevent the roof flooding.

Once the bus had left Leeds and climbed John o' Gaunt's Hill, the hillsides were clothed with acres of rhubarb. Towards Pontefract these were replaced by the juicy liquorice crop, from which were made the local delicacy called Pomfret cakes. The bus wound round slag heaps and open-cast mines, bumped over great dips in the road, where the surface had subsided over ground weakened by the ant-like tunnelling of subterranean coal galleries, and chugged along the main street of Featherstone lined by the miners sitting on the kerbside passing the time of day. Lines of chimneys crowded the wayside, peered in during the day and lit up the night. The chimneys emitted a chemical symphony. Over some, a delicate puff of white vapour hung frozen on the air. From others, voluminous black smoke belched as if the Vatican conclave had failed to elect a new pope. One steamed all the way up as if scalded, another burned with a fierce red flame as if its lower end poked into the fires of Hell. Yet another fed a smoky-yellow candle flame, hardly visible in the day, but flickering uneven bright and shadow on the slightest night wind.

Even with his eyes shut Harry could tell where he was by the changing smells wafting into the bus. From the tallest tubes at Stourton an orange thread of nitrogen pentoxide wound like a scarf, permeating great stretches of the defenceless valley with a smell like a desert battlefield littered with putrefying corpses. When the bus stopped by the crossroads at Cutsyke, sulphuretted hydrogen, invisible, made the whole area reek of bad eggs and the passengers were impatient indeed if the bus had to wait long for the queues to get on or off and uttered loud noises of relief when it finally nosed out into the open road again. Most corrosive of all, beside the iron foundries at Crown Point Bridge, were the acrid fumes of sulphur dioxide. And when Harry finally regained the summit of John o' Gaunt's Hill on his return to Leeds at twilight, he looked down to where the immense cooling towers of Skelton Grange wreathed in steam seemed to dwarf the entire valley of the River Aire.

One day a smart young lady came into the shop. 'I would like a black barathea costume for a special occasion.' By way of answer Harry cleared his throat and came round to the front of the counter with a tape-measure.

'Put your arm out,' he said, holding her arm crooked at the elbow, at a slight upward angle to the horizontal and deftly stretched the tape from here to there and back to here again around the furthest points of her anatomy taking care that his fingers hovered just a fraction of an inch above making direct contact. As it was a skirt he was spared the usual tailor's embarrassment of how to make the inside leg measurement. Harry handed the customer a book of patterns. 'I'll bring the try-on round to you later this week.'

And later that week, with the basted suitings over his arm, and the lining held with pins, Harry followed her instructions and took the Kippax bus to Cas (Castleford). Cynthia and her husband were charmed by this strange, quiet man from the big city with his peculiar, quiet way of speech unadorned with any swear words or bad language, his soft, educated accent and his heavy blue serge three piece suit. And as they brought in the tea and cake, Harry wandered vacantly round the little miner's parlour picking up trinkets and little boxes and lifting the lids and looking inside and opening drawers and Cynthia and her husband pressed him to talk and talk on any topic he would and listened in fascination to his conversation and did all they could keep him there as long as they could.

'My father has a farm at Ackworth Moor Top,' Cynthia said. 'I told him about you. He'd love to have a suit made.'

And so, a couple of days later Harry took the bus that went from Ponte to the South Elmsall pit at Hemsworth, and got off as instructed at the stop after the Quaker School, where Mr Sheldon was waiting for him. There was no road to the farm. With Harry in tow the farmer stomped off across the fields, crossed a stile and negotiated a half dried stream. Harry paused in horror. At the other end of the field a couple of horses were prancing. Plucking up all his courage, Harry scampered across the field and up a little rise to the farmhouse.

The farmhouse was stone-built with stone floors paved with large uneven flags worn and tilted by generations of farmers' boots. The never-closed door led through a small kitchen-scullery into a huge living room whose ancient furniture, soft, tattered, and sagging invitingly, crowded round a wide and high fireplace, while receding into the back corners the room was increasingly dimly lit, chillier, dustier and less frequently visited so it gradually turned more into a dumping or storage ground than part of a furnished room.

At the entrance to the living room Harry stopped, unable to control himself. Inside the fender, by the very grate of the fire, cats were sprawled out, comfortable and stinking in the heat. In fact a fragment of hot coal had just fallen out on one, and the smell of singed fur filled the room. With its thick coat the cat was unconcerned by this bit of accidental hairdressing but Mr Sheldon's wife recognised the problem at once. 'Tammy,' she commanded, 'Cats!'

A small black dog, which had up to now been disguising itself as a very ragged hearthrug, leapt up excitedly with its curls of hair flapping in all directions and barked shortly at the cats who, without a moment of hesitation, fled the room and Harry entered and it was long before he left again, having measured Mr Sheldon and sampled thick slices of white bread and thick slices of bacon from a pig that had hung smoking for several weeks half way up the Tudor chimney piece.

Harry was pressed over and over again to stay and when he did finally manage to extract himself Mrs Sheldon gave him a basket full of unshelled peas. 'Take as many as you can carry,' Mr Sheldon said. 'We're not allowed to sell them. This year the Government has paid us to plough them back into the fields.' And under the peas was a real treasure, half a dozen fresh eggs, which were then rationed and had to be concealed on the three changes of buses all the way back to Leeds.

The next day Harry took the bus from home down as far as the main bus station below Kirkgate Market. Before changing to the Pontefract bus he walked up Lady Lane to North Street and entered his usual cloth shop at the top of Trafalgar Street.

'Three and a half yards,' Harry said, handing the pattern to the cloth merchant. 'He's a big feller.' Often a suiting could be made from three and a quarter, or even three yards.

Cloth came in rolls of 60-70 yards, rolled in an oval round a board or in bolts, cuttled, concertina-wise. The cloth merchant pulled down a roll and threw it out on to the polished wooden counter. A brass strip, let into the side of the counter, measured out the 126 inches but as the cloth unrolled a small red thread appeared in the selvage.

'An acknowledged damage,' the merchant noted. The cloths, which were sold at the cheapest possible price to the journeymen tailors, were from rolls called seconds with more than four strings marking acknowledged weaving faults and rejected by the tailoring factories. The journeymen tailors used the services of highly skilled cutters to cut out the pattern so that the fault would not lie in a visible part of the garment, and allow the full fall of 43 inches for the trousers with two inches for the turn-ups.

There was a standard method of calculating the extra cloth to compensate for a damage and both Harry and the merchant at once agreed on one sixteenth. Neither used a calculator or a pencil and paper. Mental arithmetic was as essential for calculating the odds on race-horses as for tailoring. Harry fished in his trouser pocket, drew out a handful of coins from which he selected a large half crown and a crumpled ten shilling note which he smoothed slightly as he handed it over. Then, pocketing the florin change, he draped the suiting over his arm and walked along North Street and down Byron Street where he entered an open door beside the Pailishy Shul and walked unannounced upstairs into the cutter's workroom.

This was only the beginning of the travels of the suit. It was to do a lot of miles by bus and foot, draped over Harry's arm, accompanied by new cloth on its way out, or other half finished or fully finished suits on their way in and covered by an old raincoat or brown paper wrappings to protect them from the rain and snow in winter. After the cutter Harry called in at the trimming shop to buy the matching linings and buttons and replenish his store of thread, canvas and padding. All this was carried back to the workshop in Ponte. Harry stitched the jacket by hand and Myer the trousers by machine. 'Jets and flaps,' Harry said. If things were really busy, a feller hand, always female, was employed to insert the invisible stitches in the hems.

For the first try-on the customer might come to the shop, or more often, Harry would take it by bus from Ponte, to the customer's home, across the fields to Mr Sheldon and at this stage, with pins held between his teeth, Harry would tear out the basting stitches and often the armholes, marking up the new lines with chalk. And this process, so natural to Harry, seemed the very peak of luxury to the farmers and the miners, who had never dreamt of such personal attention ever being paid to them.

After the first try-on, the suit would return to Myer's workroom above the little shop in Front Street and be re-modelled and often a second try-on needed. And once the try-ons were satisfactory the suit would bus again to Leeds, back up Lady Lane on to North Street and be taken to a buttonhole hand to sew the buttonholes either by hand, always a female job, or later by machine. The tailor himself sewed the buttons on, keeping the thread lifted between his fingers from the cloth on a sort of stalk with the suit held high on his knees so he could more conveniently raise it to his mouth to bite off the thread between each button. Buttoning was carried on at enormous speed and without conscious application. Harry could identify a tailor simply by the pattern of button threads, diagonally in a cross or going round the outside in a square or whatever other individual pattern chance and tedium had built into that man's routine.

And finally the suit would be taken to the presser's to be steam pressed under the Hoffman presses. And here great skill was needed. If the iron was too hot, or too dry, or the suit was pressed for too long, the surface of the cloth became shiny. This damage was irreparable and the whole suit would be a write-off.

Harry was to make several suits and costumes for the Sheldons. His long relationship with them only ended when Harry declared that he could no longer fend off the increasingly insistent advances of Mrs Sheldon. Assisted enthusiastically by her young daughter, the farmer's wife did all she could to make him miss the last bus back to Ponte. Harry considered Mrs Sheldon extremely attractive, undiminished by the fact that she was severely hunchbacked after a fall from an apple tree but did not wish to risk the legendary anger of her well-built husband. Mr Sheldon, Harry said, was reputed to have lost his temper with a horse that had once pinned him against the wall in the stable, to have picked up a huge log that many a lesser man, and certainly Harry, could not have wielded and given the wayward horse a massive clout on the extremely sensitive hairless end of its nose, which is to the horse as his heel was to Achilles and, as everyone knows, is the most sensitive part of a horse's otherwise impregnable anatomy.

Gradually Harry learned the geography of South Yorkshire and its local dialect. The miners of Normanton and Featherstone and their families were delighted with these visits from the big city. Throughout a large part of the South Yorkshire coalfield Harry became known as a great savant and was asked his advice on all manner of family problems, and during these travels, Harry learned about the famous places of South Yorkshire. The crooked spire of Chesterfield's Parish Church was one of the famous sights of the railway journey to London. One day, it was said, they had been celebrating a wedding in the church and the bride was discovered to be a virgin. The spire was so surprised it leaned over to have a closer look and it has been leaning ever since. But should the event ever happen again the spire will think it commonplace and straighten up.

One evening while he was waiting at the bus stop Harry's attention was attracted by some tailoring detail of the uniform of a young policeman standing next to him in the queue.

'The policeman became very annoyed,' said Harry.

'After some time he said roughly, "What are you staring at?" Probably he had said something before that I hadn't heard.

'"Oh, I'm sorry," I said. "I was just wondering how that was made."

'The policeman's attitude suddenly changed. "I'm terribly sorry," he said, "I didn't recognise you. You're Mr Raisman, the tailor." And he said it so respectfully.'

Travelling back one evening from Pontefract Harry noticed a scruffy dog running out to the bus stop. A few days later on the same journey he saw it again at the same spot. His fellow passenger noticed Harry's interest. 'He comes every day to meet his master,' the passenger said. 'His master died at work two weeks ago and the dog is still waiting for him.'

In the South Yorkshire coalfield the onset of the cold autumn weather was the time when the smoke of the huge factories and the innumerable little coal fires in every home produced dense, poisonous fogs. On such evenings Harry had a hard time getting back from Pontefract to Leeds. Nothing could be seen as the bus reached the brow of John o' Gaunt's Hill. Only in the imagination did the city below, vaporous as a kettle of boiling sulphur, grind and hum along its arterial river banks. Buses took wrong turnings and got stranded in narrow cul-de-sacs and when Harry's bus finally crept through the swirling mists over Crown Point Bridge and safely reached the bus station the passengers were welcomed by the cheery yellow glow and familiar clanging sounds of the Leeds tramcars. Only tramcars on their iron tracks could keep moving and even then the conductor, carrying a torch, had to walk ahead along the tracks followed by one of these vast vehicles looming through the fog with its single central headlamp shining like a great yellow eye. 'Daddy travelled,' said

Myer, 'to 'Ull, 'Ell and 'Alifax.'

In the end, the travelling became too time-consuming and so Sam, with no skills of his own, acted as a kind of errand-boy, going out to buy the cloth, picking up the trimmings and taking the suits to the buttonhole hand's and the presser's. Harry even taught Sam to do the try-ons. Now Harry and Myer spent almost their entire time in the workroom. Despite all their efforts it was a doomed venture. The tailoring factories were rapidly evolving an automated method of production called the 'box-coat system.' They could make a suit for less than Harry paid for the materials. Myer's failing sight made it more and more difficult for him to continue. Finally one day Myer collapsed while working. Without a word, Harry went out and took a job as a tailor in one of the huge mass-production factories in Burley Road. Myer's last business venture was over. The only thing Myer brought back from the tailoring shop in Front Street was the old cloth cap he had taken from the outfitting stock. The rest was left unsold.

Since the death of Queen Victoria Myer had practised the habit of drawing the already polluted Leeds air through daily packets of Woodbines or of Player's Navy Cut Senior Service. Often he had been warned to stop, and tried, but failed. 'It's my only pleasure,' he said huffily. And now, increasingly he was paying the price. Deep in his lungs the macrophages were loaded with coal. The delicate pink tissue with which he was born was turning hard and black. It was a common enough ailment in Leeds and all of the South Yorkshire coalfield, the human price of the industrial revolution. No medical miracle had been found to give an old man new lungs. Even a single verse of the Lily of Laguna ended in Myer gasping and clutching the back of a chair to support a terrible bout of deep racking cough. The long, slow suffocation of Myer had begun.

When Myer was well enough to travel, Harry went with him by train to the equally smoky city of Birmingham to see Ralph and Sidney, who now shared a prosperous solicitor's business opposite a town hall that was only slightly less grandiose and no less black than that of Leeds itself. Ralph and Sidney had married two sisters. Out in the salubrious suburbs, where the clean western air blew in from the Welsh mountains, the bow windows of their fine houses a jaunty stroll apart looked out on to wide leafy streets and their two girls each played together and indeed looked, with their shared gene pools, like two pairs of twins, kissed by Fortune, and took holidays in Madeira and the south of France.

'Can you help Myer?' Harry said. 'He can't work any more. I've managed to get a job at Black and Luper's tailoring factory. As long as I have a home he will live with me. Celia and I will look after him. But I haven't any pocket-money to give him.'

It would have been uncharitable to ask their older brothers to return to Leeds the same day. Even if the railway timetables had permitted, the double train journey, Leeds to Birmingham and back again to Leeds in one day, would have been too exhausting for Myer. So, after seeing their older brothers to Ralph's home, the two solicitor brothers went back to the office to consider this request. Bending all their keenly honed legal skills to this professional conference, they went over many weighty legal matters, dusty tomes were taken down from the office shelves, many precedents and regulations were reviewed and a number of highly imaginative schemes evaluated.

At home Ralph's wife was delighted to treat her guests to smoked salmon on open slices of thin white bread. This expensive delicacy, so far beyond their means, was, she remarked in her shrill new respectable voice, so much superior to the cheap tinned salmon they were used to share out carefully and season with vinegar between thick slices of black bread.

Sidney

'It was the first time I had tasted smoked salmon,' Harry said. 'It was ghastly - slimy and horrible. They can keep it. I had to ask for a glass of water to take the taste away.'

In the morning, Harry and Myer prepared to go for the return train to Leeds.

'Sidney has to go straight to the office this morning,' Ralph said, apologetically over breakfast. 'We are short staffed at the moment. We discussed things yesterday. Legally, it's very complicated, you know. We could make a contribution, but we need to be able to claim tax relief. For that we need to register Myer as an elderly and incapable dependent without means.'

'Don't bother,' Harry said. 'We'll manage.'

On the way out Ralph sheepishly handed Myer a full packet of 20 Woodbines.

A Look in Myer's Box

The Crash had irrevocably broken up the family. Of the once numerous, noisy brood, few remained in their last home in Mexborough Avenue. Gradually, its liveliness and hope had been replaced by silence. Louis was in Canada. From the time he left Leeds the family never heard of him again in his lifetime. John, the brilliant scholar, the gay conversationalist after whom all the ladies' heads turned, was last heard of as a vagabond in South America. John, whose business was to have brought them all to the promised land of prosperity, had sent no word for so long that even his mother assumed he was dead.

Myer had given everything for the Plan. When it failed he was alone. He felt he was too old to marry. The children he had loved were the now dispersed family. He was never to marry or have any of his own. By now he was nearly blind. It was too late for him to take on any further training. In any case he felt he had nothing to work for. His hopes had been for others. He had wanted nothing for himself. Now he ceased to work, and almost ceased to live. He had no possessions, ate little and wore just one suit of clothes, summer and winter. The quality of Leeds suits was so high that nothing he could have done in the remainder of his time would have worn it out anyway. He was negligent of his personal appearance. He never unfastened his waistcoat. 'It covers,' he said 'a multitude of sins.' Myer's life now consisted of playing bridge in the nearby card club in Savile Mount, with his father as a partner. Fixed partners were not allowed in the club, but they made an exception for these two.

Fanny had married and gone to live in Sunderland, a town whose Jewish community had originally all come together from the little Lithuanian *shtetl* of Krettingen about 35 miles north of Yurberick, when a single disastrous market-day fire had destroyed their wooden houses in the late 1880's. In *Der Hame* they had been closely intermarried with the Yuberickers, and spoke the same dialect. Now, the continuation of this tradition linked their descendants in Sunderland and Leeds. During the Second World War Sunderland was the target of heavy German bombing, aimed at the Wearside shipyards. Fanny had one son Lenny and a little girl Joyce. To avoid the nightly air-raids, Fanny sent Joyce to stay with her grandparents in Leeds. Myer was delighted. He always loved the family children and he would dandle the little girl on his knee, and sing:

> *The wind, the wind, the wind blows high,*
> *The rain comes pattering down the sky.*
> *She is handsome, she is pretty,*
> *She is the girl from the golden city,*

and Joyce's tight black curls would bob and her dark eyes sparkle and she would shriek with excitement.

Myer's mother had noticed the pleasure he took in his younger brothers and sisters and now, as time passed, in their children. 'You must get married,' she said, grieving that such a man should be childless. Myer didn't answer and she, as everyone, knew that he had decided to look after her and even her will couldn't prevail against his.

Myer never lost his fascination with cards. 'It's a remarkable thing,' he would say, 'however often you deal you never get the same hand twice. It's a property of the structure of cards. It's remarkable.' Myer sat for hours happily playing *klabbiyash* with his mother as she grew older and weaker, her body scarred by a lifetime of childbirth and housework. Little Joyce, scampering about the house, watched as her grandma took longer and longer to walk the length of the long living room in Mexborough Avenue. But Myer told her the story of the two lovers trapped on the deep blue willow pattern plates as they fled, sleeves flapping, over the delicate nine-turn bridge and were at last transformed into two loving birds. Myer tried to answer all her questions and teach her all about this and that as they wandered round Potternewton Park on their walk to Harry's house in Harehills where Myer's dinner was waiting, stewed and roasted to the succulent richness he loved in the black-painted, cast-iron oven set into the kitchen fireplace.

Early each morning Joyce noticed how her grandpa Maurice got up long before the rest of the Mexborough household, to go to the market and buy fresh fruit and the freshest fish and, when he could get it, perch. On his way back he would stop at the bakers and pick up fresh bagels. And when he got back, the little girl would nestle her slender figure, topped with its mass of curly hair, silently close up by his side at the kitchen stove and watch his every movement as he stood, stirring the pan of freshly-ground coffee, whose aroma Joyce would never forget, carefully concentrating so as not to miss the exact moment to remove the pan, fill his pint mug and sit down to his breakfast of a raw onion and pieces of bagel with equal dollops of sweet jam. Then she would trot back after him to the kitchen to see how he held his great gold pocket watch open in one hand and meticulously timed the stewing of the plums or the gooseberries or strawberries for making into jam or conserves.

My mother Celia used to get on very well with Harry's father Maurice.

'The old man,' she told me, 'loved to come round and hold the baby and see all my latest gadgets. He was a very good cook and he loved modern things.

'Whenever he came he said, "Come on, show me what new things you've got now. What other new gadgets have you got?"

'"How wonderful," he'd say. "I wish I could have them."

'His wife was just the opposite. She hated any new things. So did Myer and Harry. When I got an immersion heater - they were very new then - Maurice was fascinated. "What's that red light on the wall?" he asked. "Tell me how it works."'

During his school holidays Fanny's son Lenny came down to stay at 29 Mexborough Avenue with his grandparents and his Uncle Myer. 'Let's reconnoitre,' Myer would say to Lenny, referring to the reccy planes circling overhead, checking that Yorkshire was not being invaded by the Luftwaffe. This was Myer's invitation for his little nephew to set out with him on long walks. Lenny's eyes would open in wonder at each new thing they saw on their way up and out of the city of Leeds and Myer would encourage him by saying, 'You ain't seen nothin' bo.' And so the old man and his nephew, deep in conversation, examining carefully each new sight, would wend their way ten miles over the Chevin and down into Wharfedale and the ancient market town of Otley with its narrow market place hemmed in by blackened sandstone houses and here, for a special treat, they would share a chocolate bar and Myer would take a coffee.

'What grandma liked most,' Lenny said, 'was when Myer took her on train excursions to the seaside, to Bridlington, or Flamborough, or our house in Sunderland. She loved going out in boats. She loved the sea. When I went to a café with her, she always insisted I behave properly. "Don't put pieces of bread in your soup," she said. "That's something you only do at home."

'But in the end she was so deaf,' Lenny said, 'it was difficult to communicate with her. But her eyes were always bright and shining, and her face was lively and intelligent. All her life she never lost her curly black hair and her clear, girlish complexion.'

Ada used to go to play solo with the Wolfe family every evening except Fridays and Saturdays in summer. Sometimes she would say to my mother, 'Come with me. I can't hear what they say,' and Celia would go with her and repeat *four spades* or *two no trumps,* and all the other bidding loudly into Ada's good ear. Mrs Wolfe had come from the town of Shkud, close to the Baltic port of Memel. The people of Shkud always carried a sort of aura deriving from the town name and whenever his wife made a mistake at cards the husband would say, 'Well, what do you expect from a player from Shkud?'

Ada had a large grey cat. On her daily round of the grocer's, the butcher's and the baker's, it followed her like a dog. If Ada slipped out while the cat was asleep it would rouse itself and go round to all the shops in order until it found her. The shopkeepers would say to her, 'Mrs Raisman, your cat's come for you.' Myer had immense respect for 'mother's cat.' Unlike his brother Harry, Myer liked cats and disdained dogs. 'Dogs are too cringing and servile,' he would say.

Ada's cat always went with her to her nightly games of solo. Maybe I can just remember, when I was five, seeing her sitting by the kitchen fire with the cat on her lap and her hand on the brass rail of an old-fashioned metal fireguard. Or maybe it was only a photograph. It was the only cat my father could ever bring himself to speak about. 'When mother was ill in bed,' he said, 'they kept the cat in the kitchen. Mother was in bed under sedation for ten days. The cat made every effort possible to get into the bedroom. Mother passed away at night and when Myer came down in the morning he found the cat dead under her chair.'

After his mother's death Myer started going to synagogue regularly, several times a week. He would never explain this change in his behaviour beyond saying, 'I did it out of respect for mother.' He was very touchy if questioned on this subject and would say, 'Don't ask me about it.' On several occasions when I wanted him to stay and play with me he said, 'If I don't go just once, that's it! I can never go again.' The reason for this was not clear to me and I would give in and even sometimes go with him, although I always regretted not arriving early enough to hear the poignant melody of the opening hymn *How beautiful are thy dwellings...*

In synagogue Myer knew all the intricacies of the service, when the cantor was speeding up and when he was slowing down. Myer explained in whispered tones about the holiest things, the Scrolls and, above all, the space in the Sacred Ark behind them. This space, which need only be a theoretical space, was the equivalent of the Holy of Holies in the long-destroyed Temple in Jerusalem. In it was the invisible Divine Presence. Myer used to tell me when to stand and when to sit and that you must not go in or out while the ark doors are open. There was only one point in the service where Myer always became very serious, got up and

Myer and his little nephew

rapidly chanted a short passage which seemed to be quite repetitive and had strange long vowels, including one word that sounded just like Myer. Before doing this he told me sternly that at this point I must under no circumstances stand up or speak. I noticed only a few people stood up and did this. The others remained seated. This was the prayer said for a dead parent.

Myer also pointed out the passage sung three times by the congregation in the closing hymn *Lord of the Universe*, which went *He will bring the dead to life in the abundance of his lovingkindness*, the passage which formed the topic of Mahler's Second Symphony.

Myer's father sometimes went with him to synagogue but none of the rest of the family did. My own father always expressed a keen horror of religion. 'It makes people vicious,' he would say and positively refused to be coaxed into a synagogue. If pressed only a little Harry would explain his anti-religious views with such vehemence that my mother would become alarmed and say, 'Sha! Sha! Harry, don't be silly, don't

262

talk like that,' and afterwards she would turn aside and, rolling her eyes mysteriously, mutter, 'Never mind, I'll pray to make it better.' My mother's view of God was judged on a personal basis but she gave Him a long time span. 'God has been good to us,' she would say, looking back over her entire lifetime.

It turned out that Myer continued his regular synagogue-going for some time and then one Day of Atonement, failing to resist the temptation to stay in bed, he missed the one fateful attendance he had so fearfully foreseen. Just as he had predicted, he never went again and would never be persuaded to go either.

For a short time after their mother's death, Sarah looked after her father and Myer. 'They'd stay at the club from two till six in the afternoon,' she said. 'Then they'd walk back up Chapeltown Road. I could hear them in the street arguing about the bridge, "He knows he can't make the contract, and he bids like that..."'

It was the final irony. After struggling all his life against the effects of his father's card-playing Myer now sat down to spend his last years playing bridge with him. 'Every day,' said Sarah, 'Myer had three ounces of pickled meat from Smuckler's. It cost ninepence. Come eight o'clock I'd put on the chips. Half-past eight he'd be eating. The same every day. And two slices of black bread and jam. Myer would never eat fresh bread. He said it upset his stomach. Nine o'clock they'd be back in the club.'

Sarah soon got married and left home. Now Maurice was getting very old and his sight was deteriorating. After the cards were dealt he would pass each card one after another, three inches in front of his good eye. Then he could remember them and play. When someone played a card and was about to scoop up the trick, he'd say in exasperation, 'What is it? Show me the card. I didn't see what you'd played.' Then, 'Oh yes, all right, the queen. Carry on.'

In the end he went into the Herzl-Moser hospital on Francis Street for a cataract operation. It was a disaster. When they took off the bandages, he was blind. 'It was the only time I've seen father cry,' Sam said. Maurice became seriously ill and now Myer on his own couldn't manage to look after him. For his last week Maurice was taken up to Fanny's home in Sunderland.

Harry rushed up to see him. Maurice was lying in bed. 'I could see a great lump in his side,' Harry said. 'It was the cancer growing.'

Myer noticed that he was continually repeating one phrase 'Quickly, quickly...'

'He's wandering,' Myer said to Harry.

'No I aren't,' said Maurice sharply and continued 'Quickly, quickly...'

'He didn't seem distressed,' Harry said. 'All his life father was never without a song on his lips, always singing, or whistling. He was always cheerful, the old feller, bless him.' Maybe he was already urging on his horse in the first race in the next world.

Maurice had reserved a plot of land where he was to be buried next to his wife Ada in Gildersome, nearly a hundred miles away from Sunderland. Sam was too impatient to go along with all the delays in the arrangements for a hearse so he put his father in the back of his van and drove him back to Leeds. 'I didn't drive straight back to Leeds with him,' said Sam. 'I took him a roundabout route, past all the racecourse towns, past Thirsk and Catterick. So he could have a last trip to the racecourses.'

This last act of respect for his father may not have been the only reason for my Uncle Sam's detour and maybe the police would have been difficult to convince if they had had occasion to look into the back of the van parked outside Thirsk or Catterick racecourses.

Louis died in Canada, so poor that his wife had to beg the family for a little money to put up a tombstone. Louis had never stopped gambling. When Myer, the second son, heard of Louis' death he said 'We're going in order.' And now, at last, Myer lived alone in Mexborough Avenue, the sole occupant of a house which had once been so full of people.

One of the grand-daughters of Moshy the Wine Merchant happened to be living a couple of doors away. It was that Nina who, as a little girl, had circulated so irreverently round the four-poster bed in which Moshy and Chayie die Shvartsy had been dying. She was now a comfortable, maternal sort of woman, with a great respect for Myer and his brothers. She took it upon herself to look after Myer's needs. It seemed as though Life was at last offering Myer the chance of marriage, a family, and a home of his own.

'Why didn't you ever get married?' I asked him.

He replied with a little Yiddish song:

If a man has a little wifey
Then he's got trouble;
If a man has a little wifey
She's an atonement.

'But don't say it in front of your mother,' he added cautiously.

Actually, my mother was quite addicted to this tune, which was a Russian folk song well-known to her own father, and she crooned it repeatedly and contentedly to me, and in the years to come to any other young children she could find, as a lullaby. However, she used only the words, 'Ayly lully,' and I never found out whether she knew Myer's version or not.

Myer once showed me the huge bed in which he slept. It had formerly held many young Raisman brothers. The vast spring mattress sagged in the middle, stretched over the years by the weight of the generations of young boys who had slept in it and played on it. Now when Myer slipped alone between the white sheets he found that, wherever in the bed he tried to sleep, he always rolled into the deep central well.

What it felt like he described to me by singing:

Oft in the stilly night, ere slumber's chain has bound me,
Fond memory brings the light of other days around me,
The smiles, the tears of boyhood's years,
The words of love then spoken,
The eyes that shone now dimmed and gone,
The cheerful hearts now broken.

When I remember all the friends so linked together,
I've seen around me fall, like leaves in wintry weather,
I feel like one who treads alone some banquet hall deserted,
Whose lights are fled, whose garlands dead,
And all but he departed.

But Myer never complained about his own life to anyone. 'Laugh,' he said, 'and the world laughs with you. Cry, and you cry alone.' And if I persisted, he would put me off by singing a snatch of a happy Al Jolson song, and winking or nodding significantly at me:

When there are grey skies,
I don't mind the grey skies,
You'll make them blue, Sonny Boy!

Myer walked everywhere, disdaining even the ha'penny rides in the Leeds tramcars. Once, on the anniversary of the stone-setting, Sam drove him out to Gildersome to visit their parents' grave. An old lady, seeing them together, took Sam aside.

'Who's that old gentleman?' she whispered.

'That's my brother,' said Sam. 'Why?'

'Every day, summer and winter I've noticed him walking here,' she replied. 'He goes over to that grave and stands over it and says, "Mother, why did you leave me?"'

Myer had had no childhood. He always was father and mother to the others. And only when he was, he thought, completely alone and unobserved, did he allow himself the luxury of grief. And however much he played the fool when he was with me, I could never understand why I couldn't get him to play the fool when any of my friends were there. In their presence he was gruff, dignified and aloof.

In the end Myer left Mexborough Avenue and came to live with my father. The last of the ten Raisman residences had served its term.

Meanwhile, my father, who had always hated tailoring, had tailored on regardless. There was nothing else he could have done. Once, in conversation with a business man, Harry had pointed out a curious architectural feature on the roof of a building. 'Well,' said the man, 'What's that worth to me?' and he looked pityingly at a person who was prepared to waste his mental energies looking at architectural oddities so obviously devoid of any money-making potential for the beholder.

My father, for his part, was not complimentary. 'He waddles along like a pregnant penguin,' he said.

'Your father,' Myer told me, 'could never have got on in business. He hasn't got it in him. You have to be ruthless. When you make a bit of money you've got to put it back into the business, not spend it on your family.' And Myer looked almost accusingly at me.

In our house Myer's life pattern was very peaceful. Every evening he went to the bridge club but most of the day he spent dozing in front of the fire in the room we called the blue room. By now the wooden mantelpiece clock was covered, except for the face, by a folded, tea-stained tablecloth on which stood a bird cage whose door was kept fastened open and whose tame occupant, Peter, had already tried several times unsuccessfully to land on the appealingly smooth surface of the sleeping Myer's bald head. These abortive landings usually ended explosively, with Myer waking up and waving his arms wildly, while shouting 'Geroff,' as the alarmed budgie attempted, in a flutter of feathers and claws, to convert its botched landing into an emergency take-off. I later discovered from a photograph of Churchill in bed that he had come to a much more cooperative arrangement with his budgie for landing rights on his bald head.

Anyway, both Myer and Peter gradually adapted to the new situation. Through these unfriendly gestures Peter discovered an unexpectedly aggressive aspect of creatures it had previously seen only as benign, while Myer took to sleeping with his cloth cap on his head, a practice which he retained to the end of his life, long after Peter had fluttered off to a bluer heaven than the blue room.

Celia did not adapt so readily and was never happy about Myer coming to live with us, even though he brought the old piano which Fanny had so loved in Carr Road. For my special education Myer went to the music shop in the Grand Arcade and bought sheet music of the old Victorian music hall songs. I soon learned to tap them out to everyone's delight and when the piano strains of *My Grandfather's Clock* were interrupted by the Westminster chimes from the wooden mantelpiece pyramid, Myer would cock his head to one side appreciatively.

My mother's favourite song was *After the Ball*, in which the jealous lover mistook his fiancee's affection for a man who he did not know was her brother, broke off his engagement and remained solitary for life. My mother never failed to be deeply affected by this tragic story, recognising it even after the first three notes. After its performance I couldn't help noticing that she was always a little gentler to Myer than was her custom.

When Myer left the family's last house in Mexborough Avenue he brought all his personal possessions with him. They didn't need a removals van, just a suitcase. Apart from his few battered clothes they all fitted into an old metal cigarette box. The box was beautifully designed, painted orange with a hinged lid. It was sparingly decorated with a marginal motif of a gold band enclosed in fine black lines and the name Wills's Gold Flake pleasingly worked in red and gold. I cannot remember ever seeing Myer open the box and yet it somehow came to identify itself with him in my mind and once, when he was ill in hospital, I peeped in.

The contents were trivial. There was an old photograph of his parents, his father standing, round-faced, round, bald head, small circular wire-framed spectacles, little button-nose and a small, bristly, pure white moustache. Ada sat on his right. She was unmistakably the carrier of the square Raisman face, large square nose, deep-set eyes, the eyebrows forming a beautiful smooth curve,

Ada and Maurice

and a high square forehead emphasized by the simple swept-back hair.

With this picture, was a sepia-tinted photograph on an unposted postcard. It was a young man in army uniform. He had exactly the same face as Ada, he held his head at exactly the same angle, slightly tilted forward and he had the same large widely-spaced front teeth. He stood in a totally unsoldierly stance, as if one leg stood to attention, the other at ease. Under his right arm was tucked a swagger stick. His uniform was most un-military, his sagging belt loosely held by an S-shaped buckle. His lumpy battledress hung in wrinkles. On the sleeve was sewn the red cross of the Royal Army Medical Corps.

The box contained three newspaper cuttings. Two of them described incidents in the highly distinguished imperial career of my Uncle Sir Jeremy. The third and oldest was a battered, faded, yellow piece of newspaper. It had been torn very carefully from the page and neatly folded into eight equal segments, only about one inch across. I opened it out gingerly. It contained an announcement, 'Sixty-four Exhibitions of the value of one pound ten shillings per annum, and tenable at the Central Higher Grade School were awarded as follows...' In the list was Louis' name, under Leylands School. It was the first academic achievement of the family. On the back was a despatch from the Ashanti War of 1891.

Perhaps because Myer's possessions were so few they held great significance for me. His three-piece-suit included a waistcoat with three rows of pockets. In them Myer carried on one side a gold watch, on the other the gold cigarette case Jeremy had given him in 1915.

The pocket watch was polished smooth with no ornamentation. It opened by means of a sprung hinge, carefully concealed and smoothed into the edge at one side, and released by pressing a spherical button milled in segments like a little gold orange and mounted on the winding handle at the middle of the other side. Apart from its sensuous feel the watch had a pure white, enamelled face and elegant, slender, Victorian-style hands. The hours were inscribed in delicate black Roman numerals. The large black and white watch face served Myer well as he became blinder. To see the time he would hold it up just a few inches from his own face. When he was in bed he couldn't see the distant clock. So he kept this watch in his shoe, placed just under the bed, close to his hand.

Town

Climb up on my knee, Sonny Boy!
You are only three, Sonny Boy.
You've no way of knowing,
I've no way of showing
What you mean to me, Sonny Boy.

Al Jolson

Once Myer came to live with us my education became shared in an unspoken pact between Myer and my father. My father took me out into the country, Myer into the town. Uncle Myer showed me transport. He lifted my tricycle down to the canal towpath and taught me the strange word 'barge.' Crossing Crown Point Bridge we stood beside a curious brick column looking rather like a wide chimney. A hundred feet in the air, a tall railing of elaborately decorated Victorian ironwork encircles the top of this structure, like a monstrous royal crown. This is the shot tower, from the top of which molten lead was dripped into the water below to make lead shot.

The canal towpath

Shot Tower   *Railway cut through a pub*

In our wanderings through the city Myer, his hand guiding my trike, took me down the turning off Vicar Lane by the curious elliptic building of the Corn Exchange and down the narrow lane by Kirkgate market to the embankment where the railway line was carried high overhead right through the middle of a pub. Next to this Myer showed me the cholera graveyard. When the railway line was built in 1845 it had cut through the churchyard of Leeds Parish Church where the victims of the cholera epidemic of 1842 had been buried. So the tombstones were replaced, like the scales of a snake, on the winding sides of the embankment and, so as not to disturb the peace of the untimely dead, the London and Northeastern Railway Company agreed to lay the lines on rubber sleepers and to forbid the train guards to use whistles as they passed this stretch of the line.

Myer also took me by electric tramcar to City Square. 'The Black Prince,' he said, and the bridle arm pointed our way to the station. For penny platform tickets we entered the dome of an enchanted world. Footsteps echoed on the platform under the high, arched glass roof. The hall reverberated to a loudspeaker *York - Darlington - Sheffield - Chesterfield.* I had no way of picturing these railway places whose names Myer repeated to me in an imitation of the strange sing-song voice of the announcer. Trains could rush past, 'An express,' said Myer. They could clatter by with forty wagons, 'A goods train.' They could have the engine at the front, at the back, in the middle. They could have two

271

The cholera graveyard

engines. They could come into the station going one way, and in a moment reappear going in the opposite direction. 'Shunting,' Myer said. They had a whole language devoted to them, 'the sleepers,' said Myer, 'the buffers.'

I stood holding Myer's hand beside an immense railway engine. The huge front wheels were linked by gleaming pistons. 'The fireman,' said Myer, 'the tender.' Myer thrilled me with these grand-sounding railway words, 'guard's van, sheds, junction.' Myer imitated the noises of the incoming trains, *Sh - sh - sh*, and maybe the driver was amused to see a little boy holding an old man's hand. The skin was shiny, the fingers tobacco-yellow, the nails ridged and curved, strangely horny from years of scrabbling out thread ends from the cloth beneath the steel foot of the sewing machine.

The driver set a lever as long as himself and the engine burst out smoke and steam. Myer raised his free hand in mock horror to his ears, half-raised the hand that still held mine and shuddered his head. 'Oooh!' he said and, as the noise got too loud for any sound of his to be heard, made as if to run away. But his hand always held mine, his face always turned towards me smiling and when in the end the train was ready, the heavy, leather-hinged doors slammed and the guard walked down and blew his whistle and waved his green flag. At first the body of the train seemed to shudder and then slid past, more and more smoothly until it finally delivered itself from under the glass roof and we looked out on an ever-increasing vista of criss-crossing tracks behind it as it sped towards York, or maybe Darlington or Chesterfield, while the smoke billowed slowly up against the sooty panes of the glass roof, filling every corner of the high station.

Myer remained silent for a long time, not spoiling the dramatic exit of the train. At last I felt a little tug, and a soft voice, 'Well, Geoff, is that enough?' and he stomped off, snorting rhythmically.

It was Myer who first took me on a train, to visit my Aunty Fanny in Sunderland, and there to meet my cousins Lenny and Joyce. It was a new experience sleeping in a strange bed and I followed Myer everywhere through the house. 'Look,' said Fanny to her children, 'he even goes with him to the bathroom,' while I trotted off upstairs to stand at Myer's elbow while he shaved.

Myer had a crooked smile. Years before, when he was only 16, he had gone to a music hall evening at the Queen's Theatre in Hunslet, south of the river. It was a stormy January night and on his way home he had battled through a blizzard which blew on one side of his face. When he woke the next morning this side of his face was paralysed. Despite all attempts at electric shock treatment Myer's facial palsy never completely recovered.

Myer had a great sense of humour. He took pride in always answering a question with a question. Even 'What time is it?' could be answered by 'What time should it be?'

A small man, he watched me growing without comment until one day he noticed my now immense shoes beside his small ones. 'Battleships!' he exploded indignantly.

But the pompous were his favourite targets, people with 'side.' As the Leylanders left the slums they began to take on the airs and graces appropriate to their new wealth. 'You would think he had never wiped his bum on a piece o' newspaper,' said Myer.

One day we visited a rich family who were renowned for being very careful with money. I had warned him how they counted the sugar lumps. We took tea, politely, in expensive, fine china. Our hostess delicately picked up the

The Black Prince

273

silver sugar tongs, an implement Myer regarded as an absurdity, and asked Myer, 'How many lumps?' Myer's head bowed humbly.

'Two,' he said in an offhand, modest sort of way, raising his eyebrows almost imperceptibly in my direction and after receiving these much noticed sugar lumps he sat back with all the delicacy of a coy debutante in an eighteenth century salon, only to find himself without a tea spoon. Myer turned to me, leaned his chin affectionately on my shoulder, in a perfect imitation of Tenniel's famous picture of the Duchess in Alice in Wonderland and asked affably, 'May I spoon with you?'

At first I was completely confused. I had never heard such politeness from Myer. Did he want me to join him in cadging some money? Was it a kind of dance based on the mating behaviour of some aquatic bird? Only his eyes, silently pointing to my spoon and then to his spoonless saucer finally explained his meaning.

But Myer was always very strict with me if I said anything harsh about a person. 'Let him enjoy himself. Live and let live.' Or, if in what I said he detected a note of envy, he would say sternly, 'Render unto Caesar, that which is Caesar's. Don't look at what he has. If you want it: Go thou and do likewise.'

'People in glass houses...' and Myer would wait provocatively, nodding me to finish the last line.

'What goes up,' Myer said, 'must come down.'

'What do you mean?' I asked.

Myer simply repeated, with added emphasis, 'Everything that goes up must come down.'

Myer was one of the musical members of the family. He never said anything if it could possibly be sung instead:

Oh! A tanner!
Two tanners make a bob
Three make one and six
And four two bob

When he took me to hear the Mikado at the Albert Hall, however passively I might sit, Myer reverberated every nuance of the opera to me by rhythmic breathing and nudges and knee-tapping and stifled snorts and silent singing, until in the end it was impossible to resist. And as we came out, 'Wonderful how Peter Peers leapt and danced about, and a wonderful voice!'

Myer punctuated his conversation with a special kind of communication, which I can only call his 'sounds.' One day I asked him why he didn't like liver. 'I did eat it once,' he said. 'Oh yes, I did eat it. Just once. When I was nine or ten. Mother made it.' He paused, and thought how to put it. 'It made me very ill. Very. I don't know why. Perhaps it was off. I've never eaten it since. Yes, very ill. B-p-fwerrrh!'

But this sound can hardly be represented on paper by any combination of letters. It began in the way of a normal word, but on reaching its climax Myer began a slight shudder which introduced a deep, soft vocal rumble, as if drums were being used to underline a passage of music. This shudder began in the throat and rose to the mouth. By this stage the lips were somewhat puffed out by the -errr- part of the sound, and his jowls picked up the shudder and amplified it by wobbling slightly from side to side while the throat now produced a low growling rumble as a bass accompaniment. And as Myer uttered this sound the hearer felt as if carried away on a magic carpet. He gained an extraordinarily clear picture of a man who had just suffered the intense agonies of delayed poisoning but had miraculously survived (although many a lesser man would have succumbed) and when he recollected it years later, still had the sensation of looking back into the fiery jaws of Hell.

Myer never rode in our Leeds electric tramcars or in buses. He walked everywhere. He knew the city backwards. I used to complain. A four mile tram ride cost only a ha'penny. 'Waste not, want not,' Myer said. And he would walk all day, with me riding my 'trike,' the knuckles of his familiar old tobacco-stained fingers guiding the handlebars. With a tilt of his head he would point to the newspaper sellers dressed in layers of grubby waistcoats and raincoats. They wore woollen gloves with the finger ends cut off for ease of handling the papers. 'Poor old woman,' Myer said to me, with exaggerated expression. But he meant it, and sang:

There are many sad and weary
In this pleasant world of ours,
Crying every night so dreary:
Won't you buy my pretty flowers?

Once, on the way down Chapeltown Road, I waited while Myer ducked into a small tobacconist's shop. 'Would you like to share my Mars bar?' he asked, and took a small, chromium plated penknife out of his pocket. It was a beautiful, silvery knife, with a neatly engraved decoration, and a little moon shaped dimple to put your thumb nail in to open it. Myer cut the Mars bar into thin slices, using the paper wrapper as a plate.

'I found this penknife in the street,' he said.

'Did you really find it?' I asked, 'Really?'

'Yes, I found it in Chapeltown Road, at the top of Mexborough Avenue.'

We ate the Mars bar walking along together.

Myer was adept at all kinds of games. He could look through a pack of cards and say which one was missing. There was a game of patience, which was played only to see how many of the cards could be sorted out into four clean runs of the suits. Myer not only taught me this but he would often sit for hours playing it on his own. 'How much would you have to pay to break even?' he asked. 'If you paid the bank an "in" of ten shillings would you come out winning or losing?' I suppose a mathematician could work it out. If all cards come out, you got 52 shillings, and were 42 shillings up. If none came out, you lost your ten to the bank. Strangely, however many times I have played this game since, ten always seemed to be the right number to break even.

Myer taught me chess. At first he gave away the queen, then a rook, and finally a smaller piece, like a bishop or knight. At this handicap he could still beat me. So he played blind.

'Pawn to king 4.'

'Pawn to king 4.'

'Knight to queen bishop 3.'

'Which knight?'

'There's only one knight that can move to queen bishop 3.'

Even then it was hard for me. Then, once, his concentration must have wavered and I pounced on a piece. Myer laughed, 'Oh, I'd forgotten that was there.'

One day Myer took off his glasses, put his head back so it faced the light bulb in the ceiling and passed the four spread fingers of his right hand back and forwards in front of his eyes a couple of times, then put his left hand over one eye and passed the fingers in front of the uncovered eye. Then he repeated the action on the other side.

'What are you doing?' I asked.

'Ehhh!' he said, in disgust, 'that one's blind altogether.'

Myer had a deep, rich, singing voice. Puffing away at his cigarette, he would sing Brahms' lullabies with the expansive warmth of a bachelor with a love of the family children. To me as a child the plump Myer in his stained, shiny-backed waistcoat, with its untidy hanging straps was the incarnation of the jolly, rounded Mr Pickwick I had seen in Phiz's famous illustrations of Dickens. This was not surprising as he spent so much time reading Dickens aloud to me. I was very proud of Myer's interest in me. Myer was the head of our family. No one failed to be deferential in his presence. But he made every effort to inculcate the fact that my father was to be the most respected man in my life.

Myer loved to be called 'Unky.' Unky was a word I played with endlessly. There were tunky, runky, and sunky, hunky, stunky and frunky, and there was all the difference in the world between the benign bunky and the gruff grunky.

Myer never gave instructions or said what he thought directly. Instead, if he thought I was wasting time, he would quote a proverb, such as 'Satan will find evil yet for idle hands to do.' But Myer himself never made judgements about what other people did and never told me to do anything, or not to do anything. If he disapproved of something I said or did he would grunt 'Ah-ha' in a soft, questioning voice and put his chin down, lowering his eyes and peering at me over the top of his glasses. If I persisted he would tilt his head still further down, and maybe repeat 'Ah-ha?' even more questioningly. And then, when I got it right, he would relax and say broadly, 'Now you're talking!' Most of all Myer disapproved of any sign of envy. He always responded badly to questions such as 'Are you a better singer then he is?'

'Comparisons,' Myer would say, 'are ojous.'

We were a very undemonstrative household. Anniversaries went unrecognised, birthdays (except for mine, of course) were unmentioned and unknown, apart from Myer's. Uncle Myer, was uncertain what his birthday was. Apparently there had been a delay or confusion between his birth and its registration. So, like the queen, Myer had two birthdays, an official one, and the day he came into the world.

For most of my youth at home I shared a bed with Myer. By night the uncertainties of daylight life became rounded into a cosy world. The warmth of the bed was a luxury in the unheated bedrooms of our northern city. Indeed the bed was a geographical entity. It had equatorial regions, it had polar regions and it had temperate zones. And a hot water bottle. After we switched the light out I loved Myer to sing his versions of the old music hall songs in broken English:

Von veek I tought I'd like a shvim in die vater
I hadn't had von since a yerr ago.
And for it I did not vant to pay von quvarter
So to a brook I vent vere it vas low.
I took off my clothes - very quvick
And by an apple tree I laid dem.
Den into die vater I vent - very quvick.
A lady came and sat right down beside dem
And she stayed dere from nine-a-clock till six.

In die shade of die old apple tree,
Vere die vater came op to my knee
I had to bend down
Vile dat lady vas aroun'
So dat my face she only could see.
And de bees dey vas stinging my nose - out die vater
And der fishes vas biting my toes - in die vater
But I stayed dere all day
Till dat lady vent avay
In die shade of die old apple tree.

In bed I listened with fascination to Myer's rendering in Hebrew of the Jewish religious liturgy. My favourite was a single clarion call, sung just once on each Sabbath by the synagogue cantor at the most dramatic moment in the morning service.

The heart of the Sabbath service is the weekly recitation of a passage from the Five Books of Moses. The cantor stands in the centre of the hall at a reading desk on a raised platform. The reading desk of our synagogue suggested a boat; it was ascended by a short flight of steps on its west side and its gunwales were formed on each side by marble balustrades. The cantor stood at the reading desk, like a forward bridge in the prow. Before him, the doors of the Ark were draped with rich velvet curtains, lettered in gold thread, and above them the eternal light flickered in a ruby-red glass vase suspended from the ceiling by three silver chains.

When the Ark was to be opened the congregation stood and the cantor, flanked by two assistants, all wearing long blue and white tasselled prayer shawls, left the reading desk and walked up the steps to the sacred Ark. The curtains were drawn to the sides and the Ark doors opened to reveal the glittering Scrolls. This was a moment of deep silence and anxiety.

As the Ark doors were opened, the cantor had to turn and face the congregation. The assistants removed the Scroll from the Ark, taking immense care not to knock its tall, bell-laden spool caps against the Ark doors and laid it lovingly in the arms of the cantor who, embracing it and resting it over his shoulder, would carry it, tinkling, down the steps, back along the aisle and up to the reading desk, where he laid it on the velvet cover to be opened.

During its passage along the aisle the people in the front row of the congregation would lean forward, gather up the knotted fringes of their prayer shawls between thumb and two fingers and touch the cloth against the bejewelled red velvet Scroll cover, or, even better its silver breastplate encrusted with the twelve semi-precious stones representing the Twelve Tribes of Israel. Then, stepping back as the Scroll went by, they kissed the shawl fringes reverently. Myer, reaching forward from our place in the second row, liked to carry out this custom but he always did it with an irreverent little snort, and a mischievous twinkle in his eyes as he glanced back towards me.

Myer explained to me that, should any harm or violence be done to the Scroll, should it ever happen, God forbid, that the Scroll be dropped in its difficult passage from the open Ark to the shoulders of the waiting cantor, then, it was believed, a boundless calamity would befall. And it was no easy task to transfer the Scroll. The cantor must stand facing west with his back to the open Ark where stood the Scroll with its breastplate also facing west. Only with the concentrated help of the two assistants working behind his back could the precious Scroll be safely consigned to the left shoulder of the waiting cantor.

Thus it was that at this moment the synagogue fell apprehensively silent and when the cantor finally possessed the Scroll, rested it on his left breast over the heart, steadying it with his right arm and took two paces forward to the top of the short flight of stairs going down the platform before the Ark, he pierced this silence by a triumphal call: *Hear, O Israel, the Lord our God, the Lord is One!*

It was this precise moment that Myer recreated for me over and over again at my insistence during the dark hours.

In the morning, Myer used to wake me up with ragtime:

Come on 'n hear! Come on 'n hear! Alexander's ragtime band.

Then, after breakfast, Myer used to walk me the first part of the way to school, seeing me off on the corner where the fissured cast-iron base of the rickety gas lamp and the cracks of the pavement grew rayless mayweed whose golden globules stained my fingers yellow, with a sweetish odour.

Myer involved himself with every part of my schooling. He had unending patience. He used to laugh at the way my father read a book. 'Daddy's so impatient. Look! As soon as he's read the first chapter, he turns to the end.'

When I started biology my father was very excited He saw the first step to medicine and the lost career that he had always secretly regretted. 'I'll learn with you,' my father said, but when I came back with the first lesson, the shape of leaves, he lost heart. Starting with linear, lanceolate, ovate, obovate, cordate, shaped like a heart, obcordate, peltate and mucronate, and the outlines getting steadily fatter, was too far and winding a road.

Not so Myer. Everything I needed to learn, he studied. If I marvelled at how he was ready to take in anything, he would say, 'Under the sun, there's nothing new.' And so Myer learned calculus or French, Latin, physical chemistry, nuclear physics, anything, as long as I needed to learn it, nothing was too abstruse or too irrelevant, since all was part of Myer's dream, and floated gently in his mind as in an immense, placid ocean.

If I was impatient with my homework he would say, "Rome was not built in a day," or else, "Great oaks from little acorns grow." And be careful, "There's many a slip 'twixt cup and lip." In the morning, before leaving me, he would test me on those facts I had got wrong the evening before, and say, "If at first you don't succeed, try, try again," and I later thought how many times he must have said these things to himself over half a century at the treadle.

Sometimes when I managed to fix some piece of information in my head, he used to quote:

And still they gazed, and still the wonder grew,
That one small head could carry all he knew.

Before school in Cowper Street we had an assembly, with songs like Blake's 'Jerusalem,' and Old Testament hymns. The classes sat in neat rows, cross-legged on the floor, one class slightly separated from the next. Over us the high-ceilinged school hall echoed with the pure sound of massed boy's voices, while beneath the wooden boards of the school floor exuded a special odour distilled from generations of sweaty, stockinged boys' feet, an essence transformed by long maturing in the wood into an almost resinous fragrance, by no means unpleasing. But while this aroma regaled my nostrils, my ears were charmed by a plaintive hymn:

Hushed was the evening hymn,
The temple courts were dark;
The lamp was burning dim
Before the sacred ark.

I saw the little red light flickering high above the ark doors, beneath the marble plaque with the Ten Commandments:

Oh! give me Samuel's ear,
The open ear, O Lord
Alive and quick to hear
Each whisper of Thy word.

And the image of the flickering red light, the old deaf High Priest and the little boy Samuel, listening in the dark, became fused with Myer singing to me in bed.

Country

Here, where the world is quiet;
Here, where all trouble seems
Dead winds' and spent waves' riot
In doubtful dreams of dreams.

Swinburne

Compared with the comforting warmth of Myer, my father was a reserved, inscrutable figure, always away to work before I got up, always home late in the evening. He talked about the moon and stars. We used to go to the glass-fronted bookcase in the front room and he read to me about the Argonauts' search for the golden fleece, of the magic name of Colchis, of the bull-monster, the Minotaur and the silken thread that was the clue to the labyrinth and of Perseus and the mirror which he used to outwit the gorgon Medusa who had living snakes for hair and whose single glance turned the onlooker to stone.

My father had gained his education from his life-long passion for doing crossword puzzles in the newspapers. Over the years this strange curriculum put him in command of a peculiar accumulation of facts. His deafness came between him and the outside world and when the occasional word percolated through a chink in this wall of silence he rolled it around inside, contemplated it for a long time unmodified by any further contact with the outside. When it finally reappeared it often had acquired a strange colour.

There was a radio programme called *Gardeners' Question Time*. It seems unlikely my father could have heard it but he must have read about it in the Radio Times, and used to entertain me with the sort of exchanges he imagined:

'Question: What shall I do? When I turn on the tap, water comes out.

'Answer: Go jump in the river.'

My father did not feel that the truth could be obtained by the crude method of asking questions but only after a long period of silent inner thinking. Two of his pet hates were the words 'secret' and 'difficult.' If he read in the newspapers 'This is the text of a secret communiqué,' he would snort with indignation and if I tried to disagree he would say dismissively, 'That's ridiculous. If it's secret you can't know it,' and 'There are no such things as secret weapons. You can't send power on a ray.'

And no one ever pressed him further, since there was always about him something that showed he had access to a hidden knowledge, something of the aura of a mystic or holy man, that said 'Don't touch me.'

Throughout his life my father never touched a drop of alcohol, however dilute. 'Even the smell of it makes me dizzy,' he would say, and raise his hand, palm open towards me and move it from side to side and say *Pffwerh*.

My father could always see unexpected relationships between things, or people, or events, relationships that no one else had ever seemed to see before but which, once stated, were surprising by their obviousness. Many people repeat things twice but my father, who always seemed uncertain whether others could hear him, usually said them three times, adding slight elaborations each time round. But conversations with my father had to be brief. You didn't get another chance once he had switched off.

People admiring the way he would come out with all kinds of abstruse bits of information for a crossword clue often asked, 'How did you know the answer to such a difficult question?'

'There are no such things,' he would say, 'as difficult questions and easy questions. All questions are the same. You either know the answer or you don't. All questions are easy if you know the answer. That's all there is to it.'

My father loved to solve difficult mathematical problems in his head. But he used a system of his own. Algebra was a complete mystery to him. He rarely used paper, and then only to put down unintelligible columns of figures which he lined up in special ways that clearly contributed to his solution of the problem. My father was fascinated by conjurers and magicians. 'I know it's not magic,' he said, reassuringly. 'It's just a trick,' but somehow his voice always left the matter just a tiny bit open. He himself had a vast store of superstitions he would never admit to. As for the past, no one should ever express pleasure or satisfaction at any achievement. And if he felt the conversation was in danger of leading to this he would try to prevent it by putting his finger to his lips and saying, 'Sha! Sha!' Any suggestion that something good might happen in the future was even more dangerous, and at this he got quite agitated and said, 'Touch wood,' or, 'May no Evil Eye see!'

When he made a suit and finally got to the last try-on, and was satisfied, and ready to hand it over, he would put a penny in the pocket and say, 'Wear it healthily.' If I asked what it meant, he shook his head as if an explanation would weaken the effectiveness of the blessing.

'That's so you should always have money,' my mother explained.

My father believed that only women should have umbrellas. Men had hats. Boys never; only caps. And it was dangerous to bring an open umbrella into a house. On rainy days he always watched carefully to be sure that my mother never came into the house with an umbrella still open. And naturally this dislike of umbrellas can only have been strengthened by his memory of the geriatric, ill-assorted teeth of the dying Chamberlain, squeezed into a craven smile as he returned from Munich, having grasped the nettle danger, waving a scrap of paper and carrying the ridiculous rolled up umbrella, ready at once to protect from Nature's unpredictable squalls the scant, wind-blown locks of the man who had just betrayed Czechoslovakia.

My father spent hours on jigsaw puzzles, tapping triumphantly with his finger tips as he inserted the final element that assembled a stormy sky, a galleon in full sail or an English country cottage nestling in a summer garden full of hollyhocks and Canterbury bells. And all the while, as he fumbled with fragments of cloud or leaves, solving the problems of the fractured jigsaw world, he crooned contentedly to himself. He would begin with a snatch of a song that related to the work in hand. His usual start was, 'Turn it round the other way-ee,' but from here the train of imaginary sound would detach itself from the visual world of the jigsaw puzzle and wander off quite independently through a stream of other half-recognisable musical fragments related to each other by all manner of tenuous links.

'Generally speaking,' my father explained to me, 'a star arises two minutes before the sun. For six months of the year Venus arises before the sun, that is, it's a morning star, and for six months it arises after, that is it's an evening star. And a part of the year it can't be seen because it's behind the sun, it catches up with it. The ancients thought there were two different stars. When they saw it in the evening they called it Hesperus, and when they saw it in the morning they called it Lucifer. It's the only star that's bright enough to be seen in daylight. The later astronomers worked it out. Of course they were mathematicians. If ever you notice the brightest blue-white star in the night, it's Sirius, the Dog Star. According to the Ancient Greeks Sirius was Orion's dog. There's a constellation nearby that is regarded by some as the most beautiful in the sky. It's called Orion, the Hunter. You can see it in the southern sky in summer. Orion takes three months to rise and three months to set. In the hunter's belt there's a very beautiful nebula. It's green. You can only see it with a telescope. But you can't mistake Sirius if you see it. It's a brilliant blue-white star. It outshines every other star in the sky.'

I'm pretty sure my father had never looked through a telescope and I don't think he would have managed to decipher how to use a pair of binoculars. But for some time after talking about the stars he would sit silent, occasionally pursing his lips or shaking his head in mute admiration, as he turned over in his mind the beauty of the imagined constellations. In fact, the conventional representation of things presented my father with problems. He was completely unable to understand how a map worked. The ideas of scale, direction and orientation simply confused him. After turning it round a few times in his hand, as though it was a compass, and reading the familiar place names in total bewilderment, he would push it quite forcibly into my hand and say, 'Here, take it away! This map's no use. I know how to get there. I'll tell you which way to go.' If pressed to explain the route on paper he would draw an uncertain wavy line, like a piece of string with Peruvian quipu knots in it, by which he tried to illustrate how to get from one place to another.

For all our wanderings over our extensive county I never knew him forget where anything was that he had been to, nor where anything happened. He could recall exactly how many yards up a lane he had turned left or right at such and such a gate, whether the ground was smooth or rough, wet or dry, uphill or down, on which stump he had leaned his bike in 1910, where Charlie Blass had leaned his, on which bench he sat to eat his sandwiches and what was in them. He seemed to have an internal picture of every part of his beloved Yorkshire. I think I could have made his way blindfold to the field in the Plain of York where the ruins of the thousand year old Cowthorpe Oak stand beside the battlefield of Marston Moor. 'It wasn't like this,' he used to say, 'when I used to cycle out here. It wasn't like this. There wasn't this wide road, and all this traffic. This was a narrow, winding country lane. It was all open country, green fields. Now it's all built up.' And he shrugged in disgust.

I looked around and the houses on either side of the road and their blackened sandstone garden walls were clearly Victorian. From their style there could be no doubt that they had been built before he was born and even from the layout of the flagstones of the pavements it was obvious that the road could not have been narrower in his youth than it was now. It seemed to me that he could never have cycled along the winding lanes between the green fields on which he spoke so confidently and so clearly saw. I know better now.

One day we found ourselves in York Minster. It was one of my father's favourite places. He looked around outside at the flying buttresses, and inside up at the high Gothic arches of the ceiling vault, the Rose West Window, the Three Sisters. We stood at the foot of one of the massive stone columns of the nave. 'You know,' my father said, 'I never cease to wonder. How did they know how to make this? Who thought of it? How did they know how to do it?'

On the way home we paused by the open, wind-blown road at Wetherby. Over scraggy, low hawthorn hedges, the bare ploughed fields invited no footsteps and offered no warmth. The flatness of the earth mirrored the sky and my father stood motionless, intently scanning the low, white, featureless sky. There was no sign of the position of the sun. After a long silence, he said, 'They are skylarks. They fly straight up so high they are out of sight and then, up there, they sing.' He dropped his eyes to my face questioningly. But the sound he heard was beyond my ears.

My father found machinery inscrutable. Simple tools such as hammers and screwdrivers he always managed to break, bend, or otherwise render useless in some grotesquely inappropriate job. He gardened with a penknife. My father disliked even the simplest machinery. He never learned to open things. A metal jam jar top clipped on and vacuum-sealed was a major problem. To help the innocent user these tops were inscribed, 'Pierce with a pin to open.' I could aways recognize the ones he had opened. Like Caesar's body the metal was hopelessly rent by as many as a dozen fierce jabs of a large table knife.

My father did not reveal his emotions. 'I don't like a man who wears his heart on his sleeve,' he said. If I rushed home proudly from school with some achievement my father said nothing.

'He doesn't show it,' said my mother, consolingly. 'He's really pleased. I can tell,' she added, somewhat mysteriously. Much later I was told, by more than one lady, that my father had a shy, mischievous smile. But I could never remember having seen it myself.

My father found the animal kingdom a little dangerous. Horses, sheep, pigs and cows were to be avoided. Swans and geese were threatening. But his major bête noire was the simple domestic cat. The word 'cat' or even the description of the animal made him shudder. He could never enter a room with a cat and left immediately if one appeared. It took him several minutes to recover his composure. Mere mention of a cat would interrupt his meals and he would become angry. If he encountered a cat in the street he would cross the road, but in a narrow street he would turn back and go another way, or even abandon his journey altogether. Only in one rare moment did I manage to persuade him to speak of his loathing for cats. And that was just to tell me that it was something about the softness, the appearance that suggested the animal would be soft and pliable to the touch, that made him so horrified, as if it had no bones. Indeed one day a dog brushed against his leg beneath the table and he, thinking it was a cat, screamed out loud. Monkeys are terrified by snakes, and elephants by mice and I suppose it was similar.

'It's a well-known condition,' my father said dismissively. 'Lots of people are known to have been like that. I read that Napoleon was like that. One day one of his officers came into the room and saw him standing on a table threatening a cat with his sword. He was terrified.'

Cartoon drawings of animals contained hidden information for my father. One particular advertisement for ice cream never failed to fascinate him. A large friendly-looking bear pranced along to the centre of the stage and then reared up on all fours, at which moment the artist froze it in a heraldic posture like a sort of bear rampant. However often he saw it my father would follow its motions with delight, miming its actions and uttering an exclamation of satisfaction as it adopted its final dramatic pose. In the weekly comics he was acquainted with all the sayings of Desperate Dan and Corky the Cat. But he saw in the cartoons things I could not see. In these drawings each artist had his own particular style. There were some over which my father always puzzled.

'Why don't you like them?' I sometimes asked.

'I can't make them out,' he said distastefully. 'I can't understand the drawings. I can't see what they represent.' He never explained further. I looked at them and couldn't see any difference from the others of which he did approve.

Once or twice I woke him whimpering in a dream. 'I am glad you woke me,' he said. 'I was having a nightmare. I have it often. Strange creatures are sitting on a wall looking at me. They have all kinds of monstrous forms, humans with the heads of cows, that kind of thing.'

Hilton Road was wide and cobbled and gas-tar, oozing up between the cobblestones, melted and gleamed temptingly when the summer sun was hot. It smelt of ancient collieries, it could be worked like plasticine and was immediately destructive to any clothing it touched. The back street was much narrower and overshadowed by a huge Baptist Church on the other side. In fact it was so narrow that when Uncle Myer, trying to see whether he could still ride a bike, fell off, he tumbled right across the street and into the hedge of variegated laurel that grew in a sunken row beside the church.

Our house at Number 34 Hilton Road was one of a long terrace of identical red brick houses with low, blackened sandstone front walls spotted with dollops of long hardened cement where the council men had filled the holes left when the original ornamental railings had been taken down. The houses numbered from the top of the street. Without the house numbers it would be difficult for a stranger to work out where he was. There were only subtle differences. Three houses down, on our side, the spinster sisters, the Misses Duce, long retired infant school teachers, had a row of curiously shaped limestone rocks cemented along the top of their front wall. But the one who made most attempt to stand out was Mrs Pearson, our higher neighbour at Number 32.

Mrs Pearson was a large woman, with a large round face, flowered frocks, and a dresser of never-used china in the front room. My mother attempted, fruitlessly, to teach Pitman's shorthand to her daughter, Ann. On one occasion my father measured Mrs Pearson up for a barathea costume. But for her part, never having worn anything but off-the-peg ready-mades, she could never understand his appreciation of hand stitching, the many try-ons needed for bespoke tailoring, the 'lay' of a sleeve, or the fine 'finish' of heavy cloth. And for his part my father abandoned any further attempts to teach her his sense of fine taste in clothing.

Mrs Pearson's house was immaculate to a degree that horrified my father and mother. They had almost a moral objection when she broke the uniformity of the long terrace by having her front room windows replaced by new diamond-shaped leaded lights in place of the peeling rectangular ones with which the houses had been equipped when they were first built. But when she went on to have a turret of ornamental ironwork surmounting the front window my father decided she was totally insane. Not so her wizened little husband, Mr Pearson, a retired station master from the railway. Coming back from Bolton Abbey one evening, my father had met him outside the Devonshire Arms, striding off up the green bank of the River Wharfe, walking stick in hand. 'He has a country cottage in Kettlewell,' my father said in admiration. 'It'll only be a simple stone hut. He uses it at the weekends.' And with that my father hurried me off to Bell Busk Station and the train back down home to smoky Leeds, while his imagination roved with Mr P high up the darkling valley of the River Wharfe.

My father disliked the city and its polluted river, devoid of plant or animal life forms. 'There was a man,' he said, 'who decided to commit suicide. So he decided to hang himself from Leeds Bridge. To make sure of it he drank a glass full of poison and to be doubly sure he took a revolver and shot himself. Unfortunately the shot missed his head and cut the rope so he fell into the river. Well, the taste of the water was so vile that as he swallowed it, it made him sick and he got rid of all the poison.'

Sometimes we would stop at a newsagent and he would buy me a packet of stamps, maybe the coloured triangular giraffes and snakes of Mozambique, the diamond-shaped wrestlers and yaks of Mongolia, or the strange cars and planes issued by the last Nationalist administration of mainland China. I learned that 4 stamps in a sixpenny packet cost a penny ha'penny each. And, scraping together all his spare cash, he even took me to a stamp shop in town and ordered the 1948 Silver Wedding set of the entire British Empire. I have no idea where or when he had got his knowledge about stamps. He explained to me that Victorian stamps and stamps of Bosnia and Hercegovina would become very valuable because Queen Victoria was dead, and Bosnia and Hercegovina didn't exist any more. He knew about perforation gauges and watermarks, and errors, and floating stamps off envelopes.

But town and shops soon bored him. When the summer days were long my father took me far, by long distance bus to Knaresborough. You had to wait for ages at the bus station in Lady Lane, behind Trafalgar Street where we got big soft, white precious tickets, costing a shilling and a penny, far different from the little coloured cards, with a different colour for each price, from a ha'penny to the maximum of sixpence, that were used on the city buses and trams. Or we cycled to Spofforth Castle, Plumpton Rocks, Follifoot, Pannal, or Spacey Houses, North Deighton and Little Ribston and my father repeated the names, half to himself, such as Micklethwaite.

'Mickle,' he said, 'means small, and muckle, big.'

My father loved biological speculation. 'It's a curious thing,' he said, 'I've noticed it often and wondered. If you see a field full of cows, they're all facing in the same direction. Cows know when it's going to rain. They all huddle together in the corner of a field. They have a sense that tells them that it's going to rain.

'There are seven salts that make up sea water,' he said. 'It's a great mystery why the sea-fish need salt water to survive. What I would do to investigate it is extract the salts one at a time to see which ones the fish need.'

He loved to take me out fishing to collect sticklebacks and minnows to bring home and keep in jamjars and buckets. We devised the most detailed and totally improbable methods of capture of these prized fish. The agile sticklebacks could be taken by a method similar to that used for centuries by the North African octopus fishers. You had to choose a swiftly flowing and sunny part of the beck. A jamjar was placed in the deepest part of the water, its mouth facing downstream. As the mud settled, the water within the jar became still, and the sun's rays, magnified by its convex sides, warmed it. Into this seductive haven the sticklebacks were attracted, and they hovered there, lazily fanning their fins. Coming back at the end of the afternoon, the jar could be carefully raised. During this operation, the fish, as though enchanted, seemed totally unable to find the way out of the jar, and it was possible, in this way, to take as many as a dozen splendid adult specimens furiously charging about within a single jar. And anyone who doubts this method needs no more than a jamjar, a stickleback stream and a sunny afternoon to try it out.

Another favourite method was to lie flat on our stomachs at the stream bank, head and shoulders projecting over the water edge. Then with a glass dessert dish, which we called a scoop, we hunted the wily fish. Many hours of concentration went into catching one tiny minnow. Pressed full length against the earth, breathing the fragrance of the fallen leaves, nose almost touching the water, carefully manipulating one's shadow so as not to alarm the fish, through deep concentration we entered into the mind of the fishes, observing how they darted in and out of the weeds trailing from the overhang of the stream bank. And what to the uninitiated might seem an ordinary little stream was for us a treasure house as full of miracles as Alph the sacred river of Xanadu. My father showed me how to spot the good places where fish could be observed, how to recognise the yellow cow-like female stickleback, fat with spawn, and the male, its sides brilliant with angry red mating colours, and the three spines on its back aggressively erect as it charged furiously against any foe, however much bigger than itself.

Beyond the stickleback stream, the path led by the house that had belonged to Oates. There was a memorial plaque that my father loved to read. 'Oates, the gallant Oates,' my father called him. During Scott's Antarctic Expedition he had crawled away from the camp and into the snow so as to leave food for the others to survive.

As far back as I could remember my father used to take me out every weekend into the woods. When something caught his eye he would poke in its direction with a twig or with his foot. 'What have we here?' he would say and at this signal I would pounce excitedly upon an oak apple, a curiously coloured autumn leaf, or an odd mushroom. In Meanwood, my father and I scrambled through the brambly undergrowth which buried the broken stone walls. We explored the abandoned water cisterns, and the disused quarry with its ruined workers' cottages. Wandering in the deep green shadow of Adel Woods my father would take me under the stone aqueduct called the Seven Arches. We used to imagine this was a Roman ruin. In fact it was the remains of an early Victorian scheme to introduce water-wheels, later abandoned in favour of steam-power. Transfixed with shafts of sunlight penetrating the dense tree cover, the rough stone arches seemed to grow out of a carpet of pink campion and bluebells. And no weather stopped our outings. One hot summer, just past Oates' house, a group of school boys had caught a crayfish. And in the Spring thaw after the icy winter of 1947, trudging in Wellington boots, we saw a wall of water, like a tidal wave, cascading off the thawing hillside.

Nearby, on Adel Moor, stood a large crag, very good for scrambling up, and beneath the moor emerged a clear stream of drinkable water which was led through a strange stone sculpture in the form of the head of a baby from whose mouth the cool water gushed. This was known to local people as the Slavering Babby. On a hot day you had to queue up politely behind other families with thirsty children. There was a laurel bush nearby, remains of a former Victorian garden and as clean cups, people plucked the shiny green leaves and folded them into little boats which could, at a pinch, hold a small mouthful of water if you were quick. From here the path by it led to a little valley of great interest to children. Here there were stone pigsties with real pigs and a little wooden tea-shop from which trays loaded with cakes and little tea services could be taken out to rough benches along the dry stone walls of the meadows running down to the beck.

In these outings we discovered the place in Adel where miller's-thumbs hid under stones, and the weedy goit at Golden Acre where the stone loach hung by its barbels. We knew the place and time when frogs spawned. We also knew a marsh where, between marsh marigolds, a thin film of stagnant water covered a soft, fine silt. Here we crouched on hummocks of grass, rolled up our sleeves to the armpits and pushed our arms full depth into the oozy mud. I was always surprised to find the depths were warm to the touch. They stored the heat from the sun. Feeling around gently among the roots, our finger tips could recognize the slithering movements of the long bodies of newts. With great care not to harm these delicate creatures we could raise them to the surface. To secure one of these fascinating animals made me happy for days and even the thought of it kept me awake at nights.

I never found out where my father had learned this trick. He seemed to have a special understanding of little creatures. 'You've no need to be afraid of spiders,' he told me. 'They're much more afraid of you.'

My mother, on the other hand, shared the general disgust of the Leylanders for any form of creeping or aquatic life. 'Worms!' she exclaimed in horror. 'Worms!'

My father was always curious about the animal life of the woods and streams, none more than the life of frogs, with their strange metamorphosis, and his memories of their miraculous appearance in the new shell craters in Flanders. For years he had puzzled over why there were frogs in Golden Acre but not in the lake formed by the Gipton Beck in Gledhow Valley Woods close to our home in Harehills. Why had frogs or tadpoles not descended the course of the Beck through Adel and Meanwood to the confluence of the becks at Sheepscar and then worked their way up the Gipton Beck? Was the water of the Gipton Beck unsuitable for frogs? The frogless marshy lake in Gledhow seemed very similar to that of Golden Acre where you could hardly walk without stepping on frogs.

Finally he decided on an experiment. One icily cold March day, filling several buckets with frog spawn in Golden Acre, my father and I started the day-long trek by three changes of buses to Gledhow and dumped the spawn in what seemed the most similar part of the lake there. For several years we watched the Gledhow Lake but saw no trace of frogs.

However far from town, my father did not look like a countryman. His only suit was a dark blue three piece heavy diagonal serge, summer or winter, white flannel long johns and a white flannel vest. Cold was man's enemy. There was never a day too hot, or a spot too remote for a white shirt, with the loose, flowing sleeves kept from falling around his wrists by shiny chrome concertinas. And only rarely, cycling up a long gruelling hillside, would he take off his waistcoat with its shiny silk facings (that he called a vest, and children were not allowed to have) and loosen his tie.

'Don't tell Mammy I drank so much orange juice,' he said, slipping off the metal trouser clips that kept his turn-ups out of the bicycle chain, and relaxing in his elastic braces that on or off never left his trousers and his tie that loose or tight never was unknotted. We sat together on a wooden bench outside the little outdoor roadside café at the top of the hill. 'She'll think I've got diabetes.'

The hairs on the back of my father's neck knew all kinds of unusual dangers. Among the few ragged black farms that still survived between the collieries and open-cast mines of South Yorkshire, thistles and the burrs of hardheads tore at his turn-ups as he fled across a field at Ackworth Moor Top in the failing evening light and his black lace up shoes with their slippery leather soles slithered on the muddy banks of a ditch he was putting as quickly as he could between us and the dangers of a couple of distant horses. 'Horses can be very vicious creatures,' he said with relief as we slowed down to a walk for the last few yards to the safe haven of the Sheldon's Hill Top Farm.

'Don't go near the water. Two inches of water is enough to drown.'

I protested, 'There's more in a teacup.'

'Don't joke. It's perfectly true. You can laugh about it. A child can drown in two inches of water face down.'

'But why,' I asked myself silently, 'did the child continue to lie for the fatal moments face down separated from life-giving air by only two inches? Why not simply move his tender mouth a couple of inches, let alone get up?'

But my father knew about a power of enchantment that bound down the hapless suckling to its grisly fate. It was the same as when, in some country lane, we crossed a railway line, whose parallel tracks ran far to either side, converging in a geometrical illusion, that disappeared in the distant perspective of the empty horizon of the plain of York as if into the vast emptinesses of Patagonian pampas. 'Never walk on the tracks,' my father warned. 'A train can come. The distance is deceptive. You get hypnotised by the oncoming train. In a moment it's on you and it's too late.'

Moors which were majestic in the day became places of terror as the dark clouds lowered over the quaking mosses of Fountains' Fell and the daylight waned.

'This fine drizzle. You can't see it, it's like a mist, you can feel it on your face. It's called Scotch mist. Come on, let's be getting back. It's getting late.'

'But it's only 3 o'clock,' I complained.

'It can snow,' he said testily, trying to cover the panic in his voice. 'Easily. Then we'll be stuck up here all night.'

'What, in May?'

'Certainly in May. It can snow in June.'

And as he resolutely turned his handlebars, and mine, downwards, back to the safety of Leeds, I looked sadly as the others carefree and light, around us, some even seemed foolhardy enough to be setting out upwards, and the hill farmers and their dogs loitered around indifferent to the impending catastrophe that he saw could so soon engulf them.

'When there is a snow fall the farms in the Yorkshire Dales can be cut off for weeks. They are well stocked up for this. They know all about the weather. A few years ago when we had that heavy snowfall in March (1948) the farmers on Ilkley Moor asked for volunteers to come up and help them find their lambs buried in the snow, and dig them out.'

In any case it was a good thing not to get back too late, or Myer would tell my father off. 'School in the morning!' he would explode. 'How can you … ?' And my father would simply remain silent and look sheepish.

'Children grow when they are asleep,' he explained later.

Once in a green valley beside the ruins of an abbey church gleaming by shallow stepping stones the River Wharfe wandered, my father chose a small flat stone with care and for the only time I saw him suddenly, this strange, dreamy untouchable man, as a boy too. He was showing me how to play ducks and drakes. But neither I nor he never matched again his first low throw till we tired of trying, on a summer afternoon to match that first glorious, carefree throw that before sinking out of sight, skimmed as if in magic seven times on the crystal ripples.

A little upstream lay Barden Towers and the great estates of the bold bad Percys, wild and robber Dukes of Northumberland, marauding down the lawless feudal centuries through the northern valleys from their ancient seat, the marble halls of Alnwick Castle. Here the river ran through a wood, where it seemed to dwindle to a mere trickle of slow water, or so it appeared, the Strid. On either side footsore people wandered among the cool woods far from any bridges that could cross the river and the tiny silver star flowers of Circaea, the enchanter's nightshade glittered in the shadow. The Strid was a mere tempting, easy stride across to the other side from one rounded slippery rock to another, maybe even less than the stride of a tall man, saving an hour of weary walk.

'Look,' my father said, 'it's deceptive. Underneath the river has carved out an enormous rounded channel in the limestone. Under the surface the water is churning and boiling, thirty feet deep and wide. When a person falls in they are sucked down in there and held under the surface and the river does not give up their body for weeks. A couple fell in on their honeymoon and they were not found again for two weeks.'

'But,' I said, mischievously, 'it's dry now. The stones are not slippery.'

'Oh, no, no, no, no, NO,' my father replied, in the sternest, magisterial tone he could make, ending in a short haughty and dismissive laugh. 'Come on.'

'I'm going to jump it,' I teased, and made a step as if in that direction.

'Don't be silly,' he said in alarm, his voice rising in pitch. 'Don't joke about it.'

Years later I was surprised to read in the paper that a young honeymoon couple had been drowned at a famous beauty spot in the Yorkshire Dales, called the Strid. Their bodies appeared weeks later and miles down the river.

In these country outings, my father was taking me to the places where, when he was a boy, Myer and Jeremy had taken him. Harry had been denied the opportunity to see the world. So he made up for it by his love of Yorkshire. And for him the wild scenery of the Yorkshire Dales held all he could wish, as in some of his favourite lines from Wordsworth:

Oft have I heard of Lucy Gray
and when I crossed the wild
Methought I saw at break of day
that solitary child.

But just once our most ambitious cycling trip took us far beyond anything Harry had done with Myer, far to the north, across the dusty wind-blown Plain of York, past the marble halls of Alnwick and right over the Cheviots to Scotland. In Edinburgh's high stone streets we lost the way. A distant ridge was home to Corstorphine Zoo where we found a noble eagle standing aloof. Its claws grasped a blasted naked branch and its neck was slightly bent forward, its shoulders hunched as if peering into the distance. Its eyes were fixed regally on the misty blue Borders to the south and it ignored the unseemly throng gawping through the bars of its enclosure. 'Its sight is very keen,' my father said, noting in admiration that nothing we could do, no hand-clappings that would startle whole flocks of dismal pigeons, no arm-wavings, no bar-rattlings, no sounds nor antics moved the great bird for one moment to relax its visionary gaze and take even one hooded eyeblink of notice of the morons gesticulating idiotically at its armoured feet. 'It can see things invisible to the human eye.' My father chuckled, 'It's probably eyeing a sheep on the distant hillside, thinking of its dinner.'

Then we got completely lost. Our goal was to cross the Forth to see the castle at Dunfermline. I looked despairingly at the map, while my father watched me with unconcealed disdain. 'Well?' he asked after a while, looking in mock enquiry from my face down to the useless bit of paper in my hand.

'We need to go through a place called Barnton,' I said.

The back streets of Edinburgh were not equipped for foreigners. Natives old and young, men women and children milled unconcernedly everywhere, knowing clearly where they were going, unaided by maps. 'We'll ask someone,' my father said.

A burly Scot was approaching, with his shoulders hunched. 'Barnton,' my father said to him.

The native stopped and looked in amazement at a fat boy sweating in the August sunshine, and a tailor in silk-backed waistcoat and slightly frayed braces.

'Barnton,' my father repeated.

The native was good-natured, powerful, but good-natured. Visibly his mind pondered the situation. Meanwhile my father absent-mindedly took a gold pocket watch out of his waistcoat pocket, consulted it, snapped it shut and returned it to its place. To the native the tone of his adversary's speech resembled that of a question. The strange pair before him did not have a war-like aspect, more the hangdog demeanour of lost wanderers. He glanced at the chromium plated armbands, like concertinas holding up the baggy sleeves of my father's shirt. It seemed unlikely that this was a knight in armour challenging his honour. 'Barnton,' the travelling tailor said for a third time, and the southern word sounded much like the bah-ing of the sheep on yonder hillside - Bahh-nton.

The gillie's jaws worked silently for a while, no doubt mouthing various possibilities silently to himself and then, as if a light had been switched on, 'Barrrr nton!' he uttered fiercely, 'Barrrr nton!' Kilted raiders, sporrans swaying even now descended on the soft southern lowlands. 'Barrrr nton!' A war cry propelled through a matted, curly lifelong growth of facial forest, in which the sprigs of purple heather glinting danced. So loud was his utterance, so fierce and clear that even my father heard it. Recognition flowed between gillie and tailor, no less warm than when Stanley met Livingstone in the depths of Africa.

'Yes, Barrrr nton,' my father replied, trying his best to imitate this wonderful new sound he had just heard.

A long burst of speech followed, fluent and expressive, punctuated by commas, full stops, semi-colons, question marks and exclamation marks. Several sounds were hyphenated. But the words interspersed between these marks were completely lost to us. Many strong vowel sounds occurred, some resembling the French 'u,' others the Russian 'yerri,' and great rolling 'rrr's' poured out like mountain streams in Spring. Eventually the native put one hairy hand on my father's rather travel-grubby shirted shoulder and pointed. His other hand constructed a city in the air. Towers, and battlements, turrets, thoroughfares and back streets streaked the sky and then he walked on with the somewhat rolling gait of a sailor who had just landed from a stormy sea. His destination was not far, an unassuming pub door about twenty yards down the terraced street behind us. We had caught him in the nick.

But my father stood like a man transfixed. 'Barrrr nton,' he said, and repeated this in wonder, looking almost affectionately towards the pub door (a place he would never enter) and then, with deep feeling, 'Donald Macpherrrson, M'Gregor, McPhee.' And soon, elatedly following the sky map, we reached the gleaming grey waters of the Forth. But my father remained a man released from a prison of silence. Scales had fallen from his eyes, words flowed out of him. 'There are hills beyond Pentland and seas beyond Forth.' He made more than one reference to McGillycuddy's Reeks, and he implored, 'Ye Highlands and ye Lowlands, O, where hae ye been?' But most of all 'Barrrr nton.' My father rolled the word around and polished it like a newly discovered jewel and for many years it reappeared, at happy moments, often in his speech.

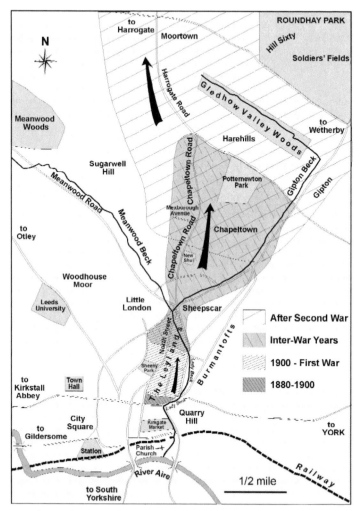

The Leylanders travelled north at about thirty years per mile

The Bridge Game

For Leeds the words 'north' and 'wealth' have the same significance and Chapeltown Road was the arrow pointing in that direction. In the eighteenth century the busy cloth market of Briggate was the beginning of the modern city's prosperity and in the next century the mansions and parks of the wealthy industrialists crowned the hills on the northern edge of the city.

The Leylanders' migration was determinedly northwards. Starting at the Templar Street Fortress just before 1880 the Leylanders travelled north at about thirty years per mile. In the first thirty years they reached Carr Road at the level of Sheepscar. In the next they reached Mexborough Avenue at the level of Chapeltown Road. But the Raisman family were never to reach the northern heights, nor cross the ridge to where the ruins of Harewood Castle frown over Wharfedale and the road runs on, fifteen miles from Leeds to Harrogate where Montague Burton and the other plutocrats of the Leylands lived.

At each stage of their migration the Leylanders established the twin institutions necessary for their spiritual well-being, the synagogue and the gambling club. At the earliest stage the Greenhorns' Synagogue stood in Merrion Street behind Saint John's Churchyard at the top of Briggate and across the road was the Lonsdale Club, both founded by the egregious Maishy Goodman. Moshy Raisman, the Wine Merchant, had been a president of the Greenhorns' Synagogue. His nephew, my grandfather, was a president of the Lonsdale Club. A mile north and thirty years later the synagogue was in Wintoun Street at the level of Sheepscar and a club, mysteriously called 'The Institute' was across the road. Its popular secretary, Velfky Priceman, was famous for his verses:

What my son does
At night
I wonder.
He is an ox
*He plays the box.**
            (chemin-de-fer)*

'About that time,' said my father, 'I was made secretary of the bridge section of the club. Father was very well regarded. In fact they had set up a competition called the Pa Raisman Trophy.

301

'Well, I was speaking to a meeting, going over the future programme of matches when father got up and said, "Isn't it time you were in bed?"

'"Yes, I'll be going in a minute," I said.

'As a matter of fact I think it was the first time in my life he had taken any notice of me. He'd noticed I was the only one of his sons who didn't gamble. When I lived at home, before I was married, I used to be going to bed just as the others were setting out on their night forays. That, combined with the difficulty in communicating with me about gambling, owing to my deafness, he probably thought that I was mentally defective.'

Thirty years later the Greenhorns' Synagogue had been reconstructed in the form of a mosque a mile further north up Chapeltown Road and here once again, across the road, was the 'Institute' where now Myer, Harry and Sam played cards. And the advance guard of the Leyland wealthy had already begun to invade the hilltops far to the north, faithfully carrying with them the temples of their twin deities, the god Jehovah and his female counterpart, Tyche, goddess of Chance. Which temples finally stood triumphantly side by side in the suburb of Moortown on the coveted northern heights, where the Leylanders could worship and gamble in splendour.

But in the end people became dissatisfied with even this small separation of their worshipping places. In bad weather the gamblers found it inconvenient to have to put their coats on and cross the road to pray. So a club was built right on the synagogue premises, attached directly to the synagogue itself. Both institutions found this very satisfactory. Now, when as often happened, there were not the required ten men for some little remembrance service the beadle came out of the synagogue to ask for someone to make up a quorum. 'Wait a minute,' one of the card players would say, 'Don't start without me. I'll just finish this hand.' So the service waited to start until he had finished his hand.

Cards were played very fast and no one ever minded the short wait. 'A working man has to gamble,' one of the old tailors told me. 'It's the only way he can make any money.'

'I heard that twenty percent of the people in prison are there because of gambling,' I said.

'So that means that four-fifths of the people in prison are there because they didn't gamble,' he replied without hesitating.

Actually, none of the Raismans was immune from gambling, even Myer.

'We had a system,' he said. 'You backed second and third favourites. It was scientific. There was a slight advantage. Over time you could win. But that was all changed when they introduced the tote. After that there was no advantage.'

From the card room of the Institute a door led to a darkened room, where huge shaded lights hung low over the brilliantly lit green baize tables. The hushed voices, the wisps of tobacco smoke appearing for a moment as they traversed the light and the peculiar clack of the cues on the balls made this forbidden room fascinating to me as a boy. I only got in once and then my embarrassed Uncle Sam hastily led me out.

Because of his fear of my gambling I never thought there would come a day when I could persuade my father to let me learn how to play cards. But in the end the Goddess of Chance worked in my favour. We were on a trip to Knaresborough and visiting the Dripping Well where Jeremy and Harry had been so many years ago on the day when the fatal decision about his education was forced on Harry. At the entrance was a slot machine. I put in a penny and pulled the handle. The wheel stopped at white, the jackpot. Twenty pence clattered out (one and eight). It was the first time I had ever bet. Within a few minutes I had lost all the twenty pence and all the extra pennies in my pocket. My father considered I had been immunized and from then on he began to show signs of relenting his prohibition on the subject of bridge.

Uncle Myer, sensing a change in my father's attitude, set about teaching me how to play bridge. There were certain strict rules. I was never to play in a club, never with strangers, never for money. And most important I had to endure my father continually reminding me 'never to play cards for money.' I felt like a traveller who planned to visit an area of endemic disease and who was being repeatedly vaccinated. And so, chastened but excited, one winter evening Myer, Sam and my father sat down to play bridge with me. There were no fixed partnerships. One rubber was played with each combination of partners. Myer was the teacher. His bridge playing was almost magical. He seemed to have a complete awareness of the position of all the cards and of all the possible ways of playing. Bridge appealed to something deep in his nature. It combined chance with intelligence.

A fire burnt in the grate. The card tables occupied the middle of the room. Myer was in the warmest spot, his back to the fire. Outside the window, unseen, a blackened stem, its last leaves curled and dry, its thorns encrusted with the smoke of Leeds, raised a solitary rose hip, no bigger than a pea, tap-tapped against the window, behind the curtains, in the dark, softly, heard only by me.

Tap, tap-tap.

Like his father, Myer's sight was bad and he had acquired his father's habit of passing each card in front of his good eye and memorising them. If I threw down a card quickly and immediately scooped up the trick in triumph, Myer would stop me severely and say, 'Wait a minute. What is it? Show me the card.'

The first hand was dealt, and an uninteresting two spades bid and made. The second hand was dealt and bid and desultory conversation started.

'I used to spend a lot of time playing billiards,' said Sam.

Sam was almost the baby of the family, Number Ten. Before the Crash he had been the junior helper in the family business. After John's flight Sam was at a loose end. For years he went out with a girl called Evelyn. People used to talk about how beautiful Evelyn was, but hardly anyone in the family had ever seen her. Then one day he came back and announced, 'Don't ever mention Evelyn to me again!'

His mother had never stopped grieving over John, and worrying about him. 'How can John look after himself?' she used to ask. When it became clear that Sam had really broken with Evelyn, Ada took her opportunity. 'You're at a loose end,' she said, 'Go and find John and be with him. Look after him.'

'It was 1936,' said Sam. 'John had been away over five years. I could see how hard things were here. When I heard that John had finally crossed Brazil and Uruguay and was in Argentina I decided to go out to him. Maybe I could make my fortune in Buenos Aires.'

'How can a person make a bid like that?' Myer snorted in indignation at my father, interrupting Sam's story. 'How can a person learn (Myer nodded his head towards me, the pupil) if you bid like that?' Whether it was teaching bridge or telling stories or acting an imaginary part Myer always put all of himself into anything he did. If bridge was to be taught, it was to be taught properly. About Myer there was such consistency that, like the symphonies of Mahler, every part, however small, of what Myer did was Myer.

My father was a good card player but very impatient and erratic. Myer was forever reproaching him with the bad example he set me by his impatience. My father would apologize meekly but not mend his ways.

Tap, tap-tap.

'Sorry,' said my father, pulling down the tops of a couple of cards in Myer's hand so as to verify the position of the ace of spades. 'Go on then, enjoy yourself. You can say *kaddish* (the prayer for the dead) for this contract.'

'That's not the point,' said Myer huffily. 'We're trying to teach, aren't we?' Myer had a curious habit of snorting rhythmically as he thought about a bid or played a card. It seemed to soothe his indignation.

It was stormy outside but the heavy velvet curtains covered the windows from ceiling to floor. The curtains were the colour of old gold, and old, a lot older than me, slightly dusty and not a little ragged, but they were quite thick enough to shut out the cold of a Leeds winter. Meanwhile I pressed Sam to continue with the story, and Sam went on, obediently and with enthusiasm. 'John had a remarkable knowledge of languages. He learned Portuguese on the boat crossing from France to Brazil. He could bet fluently in five languages. I remember my first Spanish lesson when I arrived in B.A. We were sitting having tea in a café. John pointed across the street, "*Si yo dijiera* - If I were to say - *que aquella mujer* - that that girl - *al otro lado de la calle* - on the other side of the street - *es muy hermosa* - is very pretty, - *estaría usted* - would you be - *de acuerdo conmigo?* - in agreement with me?"

'Quite a mouthful for your first sentence in a foreign language, Eh?'

'Children, children,' said my father (who wasn't listening to Sam) 'be quiet in school.' Long after Yiddish had been abandoned for all other purposes it was still used while playing cards. My father was excited because he had just picked up a big hand. 'Are you listening? Two clubs!' My father sat back dramatically, fished his handkerchief out of his pocket and blew his nose.

The shape of my father's nose exemplified the interaction of nature and nurture. Nature would probably have given him the square nose of his other brothers but nurture intervened in the form of his fall and the repeated nasal surgery thereafter. A doctor had once told him, 'Your nose is so modified by surgery that I can't tell what it originally looked like.'

The bidding went round and Sam continued, 'I soon learned to speak Spanish. In the end I spoke it better than John. John was so lazy he never bothered to acquire a good accent. His accent was always terrible.' There was a pause in the game. In the moment of silence I heard the gasping of the wind outside. Myer and my father were too deaf to hear such a soft sound. Sam, if he did, made no sign. The general consensus was that it was time for tea. I disagreed, impatient to pick up that good hand that I had been denied all the evening but I was overruled 3 to 1. My mother went out to prepare tea and biscuits. I tried to get Sam to continue the story of Uncle John but somehow the thread seemed to have slipped.

Meanwhile, for his part, my father sat abstractedly, ignoring all this faint conversation, and waiting for his tea to come. I noticed he was drumming his fingers rhythmically on the table and chanting contentedly to himself. I moved closer and looked enquiringly up into his face. My father at once politely stopped drumming and then, obliging my curiosity, without a word started again at the beginning for me. Tonsured monks, rope sashed in brown robes, sprang from the card table, chanting and swaying orgiastically to his fingers:

Back and sides go bare, go bare,
Both hand and foot grow cold,
But belly,
God send thee good ale enough,
Whether it be new or old.

The mediaeval procession swept by in unholy venality, its undulations obedient to his finger beats, its plainsong disappearing slowly into the distance. The drumming stopped, the tea came in, and we were once more between rubbers in a bridge game in which I was doing decidedly badly and the strange, dry wind I had never felt before was curling.

My mother had brought a tray full of refreshment.

'Would you like a slice of melon?' she asked Myer.

Myer eyed the crescent-shaped delicacy dubiously, not wishing to offend. 'I don't like to get my ears wet.'

Sam got up and went out of the room for a moment. 'Is Uncle Sam a good card player?' I asked Myer.

'They're all good card players,' Myer replied. 'But he gambled all the time, just like John.'

'Let this be a lesson to you, Geoff,' said my father. 'Never play cards for money.' He waggled his finger at me and I pretended not to notice.

'I took Sam to the ship,' said Myer, lowering his voice and glancing at the door to make sure Sam was still out of earshot. 'Sam would never bother with a university education. Oh No! Not him! Everyone else could make money so why shouldn't he? That's how he thought. Well, of course after John had gone Sam hadn't anything. So we gave him money. From the tailoring factory. No good. Gamble, gamble, gamble.

'So I said, "Well go on out to John. I'll pay the fare."

'So I went to the boat to see him off. I didn't dare give him the money. He'd have gambled it straight away. Anyway I got to the boat,' Myer spoke even more softly, eyeing the door nervously, 'No Sam. Waited, waited, still no Sam. In the end he arrived, with a girl. So I gave him the ticket and that's how he got to the Argentine. And now he's back here in England we still have to help him. Daddy still makes up suits for him for nothing.'

'And you?' I asked. 'Do you make them for nothing?'

'Ehh, me,' Myer said dismissively, as if I had mentioned something absolutely worthless, and he stopped talking.

We waited for Sam to come back. Myer pushed his chair slightly away from the fire and I idly poked the coals. 'Too hot!' Myer said, as the sparks flew up and in a dying moment seemed to whirl in a dusty wind passing a thousand miles across dry grass, stiff under an endless sky.

Sam came back shortly and play recommenced.

My father was getting bored. It was too much of a strain for him to try to follow the conversation so he started reciting poetry to himself:

Sir Rolf the Rover tore his hair,
And beat his breast in wild despair...

'Harry,' said Myer 'stop burbling. It's your bid.'

Sam went on with his story. 'Billiards is a passion in Argentina and all Latin America. John and I used to play the tables. People used to bet on my playing. Well, some people put bets on for John. I used to have a secret signal that told him whether I would win or lose. Of course I wasn't always right. But we made a good screw out of it. It wasn't any good. Whatever we made John gambled away on horses. Sometimes he won too. Sometimes he made a lot of money. A lot. I used to say, "John, buy yourself a suit of clothes. Buy yourself a new suit. You've plenty of money." It was no good talking to him. But as soon as he had nothing, as soon as he was skint, he'd come home and lie on the bed, as happy as anything reading, reading. I decided to come back.'

'Well?' asked my father, interrupting. 'It's your bid.'

Sam bid and the play continued.

'I always get these hands,' I cried in disgust. 'Where are all the aces?'

'Ask me a nuddy,' said my father, unsympathetically. 'I haven't got them.'

'Stop weeping and wailing,' said Myer. 'I'm notorious for picking up bad hands. Anyway, all the best contracts go one off.' I played out in bad grace, carelessly throwing out an ace, then a king, 'beating the air.'

Myer set his cards down on the table. 'Aces and kings,' he said severely, 'should not be used to kill deuces and trays.'

'Well you've got them all, anyway,' I said, nearly in tears.

'I'll show you,' said Myer with a smile and proceeded to make all the rest of the tricks with his low cards, throwing his aces and kings away without using them.

It was a major feat. The rest of us looked on amazed.

'*And things, quoth he of Houndsditch, have come to a pretty pass,*' said my father.

'Well, we won't score that one,' said Myer gently, not wanting to hurt my feelings.

'If you think Myer's good at cards,' said my father, 'You should have seen father play.' I still couldn't help looking crestfallen. 'Let that be a less...' my father began.

I couldn't take it. 'I ought to play for money,' I snapped. 'It's obvious. I'd back the opposition.'

'Game and rubbish,' said Myer. 'Let's change partners,' and he pushed his chair back from the table and looked down at his knees. 'Legs,' he said, 'Do your stuff!' and with an effort he stood up, stiffly, took off his cap, laid it on the chair and walked twice round the chair in an anticlockwise direction. 'It changes your luck,' he said.

My father dealt, and snapped his fingers. 'Ahh! A card short. Misdeal.' He scooped up the cards and started re-shuffling the pack.

'He can't even deal,' whispered Myer. 'That happened last night at the club with Malkin the baker. I said, "Why don't you stick to baking bread?"'

My father did not hear this, but continued half to himself:

And the little dog swore,
By Odin and Thor,
And the canine Valhalla,
He'd stand it no more.

'Well,' Myer said louder, so my father could hear it. 'Have you finished messing about?'

My father looked glumly at his poor hand. '*Here we suffer grief and pain*,' he intoned religiously and knocked his cards on the table to indicate no bid.

Tap.

''E thinks we're playing dominoes,' chuckled Myer.

'*Now who be ye, would cross Loch Gyle, this dark and stormy water?*' my father recited, now relaxing back in his chair and once again shutting out the extraneous noise.

The auction ended. My father led out the king of clubs. We watched in suspense. It lived and my father followed at once with the ace, exclaiming, 'Oh, Ye of little faith!'

'Roman leads,' Myer said.

I looked enquiringly.

'Leading from the lower of touching honours,' Myer explained.

'What happened when you decided to come back?' I asked Sam.

'Well,' said Sam, 'at that time Myer wrote from England that mother had been knocked down. She was completely deaf and one day she was crossing Chapeltown Road to go to play solo. She couldn't hear the traffic and a car knocked her down. She had recovered but she was very ill. I decided to come back. There was no way to raise a fare to England. John couldn't keep a penny. I once asked him where all the money went. "*Où sont les neiges d'antan?* (Where are the snows of yester year?)" he replied. Then the Second World War came. I joined the British Army and they sent me back to Europe. That's how I got back. I could speak Italian. There's a large Italian-speaking population in Buenos Aires. I'd learned it there. So I was sent to join the Intelligence Corps of the Eighth Army under Wavell. They had just conquered the Italian colonies in East Africa and they needed Italian speakers. I was sent to Eritrea. We were called the Middle East Forces.

'Well, the Italians had been very popular in their African colonies. They'd made great progress in irrigation and agriculture. The people were grateful. Everywhere there were posters: *Viva Il Duce!* - Long Live Mussolini! It was the job of my unit to seek out fifth columnists and disguised Italian officers.' Sam smiled broadly.

'At last,' I thought to myself, 'a Raisman who was a hero.'

Sam dashed my hopes. 'The people of Eritrea are very beautiful. They have small, delicate features, perfectly formed. My commanding officer told me that the most likely place to find the fifth columnists was in the brothels. So in every town the British Army occupied we first had to investigate the brothels.

'Jeremy was delighted to find he had a brother in the army. He wrote and told me that he could get me a commission. He knew the Commander-in-Chief, Wavell. I said, "No, thank you."

'I didn't want to be a dead hero. I suppose,' Sam went on bitterly, reflecting something Harry must have told him years before, 'it would suit Jeremy's position in India to say he had a kid brother who was a dead war hero.'

'Your anathema!' said Myer, interrupting at such a precise moment that I guessed he must have been listening. I had the impression he didn't like a turn in the conversation that was critical of Jeremy.

'What?' I said, surprised.

Myer swept one of his few locks of white hair out of his eyes and repeated, 'Your anathema: two no trumps.' He was referring to the fact that I thought that this high conventional opening bid was very dangerous. 'Two no trumps,' he said again. He was my partner.

I tried to concentrate on the game. In the distance, curls of dust flew in the meaningless wind, alone, all alone. 'Are you getting tired?' Myer asked. I blushed and went on to bid. We ended in five clubs. Myer was dummy. He sat looking at me as I played. 'Partner having none?' he asked when I trumped a diamond lead from my father.

'*Je n'en ai pas,*' said my father, putting the words into my mouth. A queen was played. '*From Blessed Virgins and Holy Martyrs, Good Lord protect us!*' said my father, conceding the trick. '*Stap me vitals!*'

I was getting confused.

'Time,' said Myer. 'It's late.'

'*The witching hour, when churchyards yawn and graves give up their dead,*' said my father.

I wanted to hear the end of Sam's story.

'*Uncle me no uncle,*' said Myer, laughing. 'Enough's enough, and too much is plenty.' Myer shifted his chair to one side, and I looked at him enquiringly. 'I'm getting a singe,' he chuckled, nodding his head in the direction of the red glowing coals in the fireplace behind him.

'Another deal?' I asked and the game continued grudgingly, at my insistence.

'We captured lots of Italian officers,' said Sam. 'Just like your father

Sam (front row, third from left) with Italian prisoners

in the First War I was their jailer. Every weekend my driver and I would go back to the stores, turn in our rifles and indent for shotguns. Then we would go off into the bush with our Italian prisoners. We went for long weekends and shot lots of game. Wonderful game. Some of our prisoners had been professional cooks in Italy before the war. They made wonderful dishes. Mind you, the British orderly didn't like our commanding officer. He used to put cockroaches in the middle of his sandwiches. But the Italians - marvellous cooks! I've never tasted such delicious venison.'

Sam had come to the end of his story. We started to add up the points for the last rubber. I had lost heavily in all three rubbers.

'Let that be a lesson to you,' said my father as he left the room.

The Liniera

*And Cain said unto the LORD: Behold thou hast
driven me this day from the face of the earth; and
from thy face shall I be hid; and I shall be a fugitive
and a vagabond in the earth. And the LORD set a
mark upon Cain, lest any finding him should kill him.*

Genesis 4, 13-15

What pangs of remorse, if any, John might have felt on the boat to Rio he
did not impart to Sam. Sam's tale of Buenos Aires had left a shadowy
pause of the five years the fugitive John had spent, a Scholar Gypsy,
alone. John was on his way south, across the vast land mass of Brazil,
'riding the rails.' 'You just waited around,' said Sam, 'and the local
police got fed up with you and put you on the next train.' I seemed to
glimpse the lone gambler with his battered cigarette and his equally
battered trilby hat waiting on the dusty wooden platform boards of a
deserted country station, the open goods wagons and the shiny steel
railway lines disappearing into the unending flatness of the scrubby,
sunbaked pampas:

Good morning Mister Railroad man.
What time do your trains roll by?
At nine sixteen and two forty four,
And twenty five minutes till five.

Standing on a platform,
Smoking a cheap cigar,
Waiting for an old freight-train
That carries an empty car.

Well, I pulled my hat down over my eyes,
And I walked across the track,
And I caught me the end of an old freight-train,
And I never did come back.

John was what was called a *liniera*, a hobo riding the rails. Around him
came a small group of fellow *linieras*. They couldn't even begin to
fathom the mind of their mysterious comrade, this man who had a first-
class honours degree in Latin and Greek, whose learning had surprised

even his teachers at university. To them he might as well have been a man from another planet. They scraped a precarious existence. Anyway, John's needs were small. He survived by his wits. Later he gave way to his natural laziness and survived by his fellow tramps' wits. They began to complain. 'Here we are begging, and you do nothing.'

John bore it till it was clear he could no longer. Then he said, 'All right, I'll show you how to beg,' and strode ahead of his disgruntled companions and went into the next little town, where he made at once for the office of the notary. What happened therein he never told anyone. He emerged with five pesos, not a large sum to anyone but a beggar, but to them, a fortune. His comrades were amazed and never again asked him to beg. He became their honoured guest. He was obviously a man of importance.

In a small town in the south of Brazil the police held him for questioning. They asked his opinions about England and her parliament. John answered readily and with some pride for the institutions of the country he had been forced to flee. They threw him in jail. 'My prison,' John said later, 'was a hole in the ground with no light. The sun beat down on the roof. It was terrifically hot inside. I was held there for ten days in the same pit with murderers and homosexuals. I had to sell my clothes to get money to buy food.' John's replies had included the word 'socialised.' It was all the interrogators had understood and they concluded that he must be a communist agitator. After ten days they decided to save themselves the trouble of burying him and they released him while he could still walk. A scarecrow, John continued south.

He had reached the Brazilian province of Parana and wanted to enter Paraguay. With or without papers, it was not easy to cross the torrid Latin American frontiers. At this point the two countries were separated by a river. John found a ferryman. What would the man take? The ferryman searched greedily through John's few belongings. There was only one thing of value left. It was an overcoat, made in the warm, heavy wool of the Hebrides, Harris tweed. In Leeds it was a very valuable object. The cloth was the best, thick, soft and warm. And the cut was equally good. This was the overcoat made by Barney Bailey, the legendary master tailor of Leeds. But what use was it to a peasant ferryman in a tropical jungle? No matter, the ferryman would accept nothing else and John entered Paraguay.

The next frontier led to Uruguay and also crossed a river. John had no more overcoats left. A single track railway bridge spanned the deep gorge. John walked over this bridge. Had a train come he would have had to hang from beneath it, over the chasm. 'This,' said Sam, 'was a man whose mother said he couldn't cut himself a slice of bread.'

The wandering John continued his way south. He now had to cross yet another frontier river, into Argentina. The road here passed over a wide bridge with a town on each side. John stopped in the town on the Uruguayan side and considered the problem. In the morning he walked across the bridge to the armed frontier guards on the Argentine side. They stopped him. 'I have heard,' said John, 'that the bread in that shop is far better than on our Uruguayan side.' Covering him with their guns, they let him go to the shop. John bought a roll, sauntered back to them, wished them 'Buenos días' and returned across the bridge to Uruguay. Each morning he repeated this performance. The guards were flattered, and so was the baker. John had charm. Then one day when their vigilance was relaxed, he simply didn't come back.

Wandering, John reached the great Argentinian port of Rosario. It had a Jewish community and John hastily gave the slip to his little band of now Argentinian layabouts and sought Jewish hospitality. It started off lavish enough but soon they grew tired of him. So they gave him work ,to paint the synagogue. John, the impractical idler, did not relish the task. So he found his little vagrant band and set them to work. The respectable Jews of Rosario were horrified at this shameless act of sub-contracting by a beggar and John was soon on his way again. But his journey was nearly over. He had reached Buenos Aires, the capital of Argentina.

The port of Rosario

In Buenos Aires John was to stay for the rest of his South American exile. He lived by horse-racing and by teaching English and Latin at private schools. From here he finally wrote back home and five years after he had left England he was joined by his younger brother Sam. Here John acquired quite a coterie, who loved to listen to him speak. One university professor would come every day to listen to him. The professor was happy to hear John's opinions on any subject at all. He wrote all the sayings down in copious notes and edited them under the title *Ideas Claras y Lucidas*.

Sam stayed with John for six years. Then, when Britain went to war with Germany, he took the opportunity to sign up and get a free passage back home and so, finally, John was left alone:

Now we come to discover that the moments of agony
Are likewise permanent
With such permanence as time has.
We appreciate this better
In the agony of others than in our own.

For our past is covered by the currents of action,
But the torment of others remains an experience
Unqualified, unworn by subsequent attrition.
People change, and smile: but the agony abides.

T.S. Eliot, from the Dry Salvages

The End of the Raj

In 1943 the tide of the war was turning. Germany was being driven out of Africa and Russia. The Allies were contemplating invasion of Italy, and America's entry into the war had stopped the Japanese advance towards India. Everywhere people were beginning to realise that an Allied victory was going to be the outcome and the various Allied Governments were starting to consider how the world was going to look after the war was over.

502 Linlithgow to Amery   ***Delhi, 20 Feb 43***
Raisman's tenure as Finance Member does not expire until April 1944, my own considered view is that the portfolio ought to continue to be held by the reappointment of Raisman who has done very well in it.

I mentioned that he had sounded me as to a possible Governorship.

157 Amery to Linlithgow   ***London, 1 Oct 43***
I am grateful to you for letting me have your considered views about Raisman. It looks as though there will be a difficult decision to be made in relation to his replacement as Finance Member before very long.

In June 1943 Linlithgow came to the end of his term as the longest serving Viceroy of India. In his place, Wavell was promoted to Field Marshal, raised to the peerage as Viscount Wavell of Cyrenaica and of Winchester, and appointed Viceroy of India, a post he held until India was on the verge of independence in 1947.

Linlithgow was tall and thin, Wavell was short and broad. Wavell had an amazing memory for other men's poetry but was himself very difficult to communicate with and for one who had the misfortune to sit at the side of his blind eye communication was virtually impossible.

The War Cabinet instructed the new Viceroy to bring India completely under martial rule. This gave Wavell every opportunity to wear his uniform and decorate his broad chest with his medals.

244 Wavell to Amery   ***Peshawar, 28 Nov 43***
The best course seems to be to give Raisman limited extension. He knows the problem intimately, and his extension would

excite less criticism than a new appointment from home, for which I imagine suitable first-class men would be difficult to find.

In London, the India Office duly noted Wavell's opinion:

246 Note by Monteath   London, 2 Dec 43
Sir Jeremy Raisman is giving signs of fatigue - so much so that it would only be fair to him that he should have a spell of leave, at any rate after he has got his next budget through. If no suitable European can be found an extension of Sir Jeremy's term would seem to be the safest course.

261 Wavell to Amery   Delhi, 10 Dec 43
Raisman is not afraid of taking decisions and has a clear mind. I would sooner extend him than take an outsider.

289 Amery Memo   London, 30 Dec 43
The normal term of office of Sir Jeremy Raisman, the present Finance Member of the Viceroy's Executive Council, comes to an end in April, and it is very desirable that a very early decision should be reached as to the appointment of a successor. Sir Jeremy Raisman himself agrees with the Viceroy that if the change is to be made it is as well made now as later on.

298 Wavell to Amery   Delhi, 5-6 Jan 44
Raisman, as I told you in a private telegram the other day, is pressing for a very early decision because he is sending his elder boy to school in England this spring, and if he is to go himself it would naturally suit him best for the whole family to move together. I do not think you need worry further about his future. My impression is that he would stay on as Finance Member if asked to do so, but would not be sorry to go. I doubt if he expects the offer of a Governorship, and he is not fitted by temperament or experience to be a Governor.

304 Amery to Wavell   London, 6 and 7 Jan 44
I have received a telegram from Winston urging retention of Raisman. Failing success in our search the War Cabinet will probably recommend extension of Raisman.

305 War Cabinet Minute   London, 8 Jan 44
Wavell is of the opinion that it is no longer necessary that the

Finance Member should be an expert. What is required is rather a Finance Member, capable of weighing the advice of his experts, and having come to his conclusion, of convincing his colleagues.

360 Wavell to Amery   Delhi, 8 Feb 44

It may interest the Cabinet to know that Raisman's presentation of budget proposals to Council was admirable and that he dealt most skilfully with strong opposition by some members.

369 Amery to Wavell   London, 10 Feb 44

I believe Monteath has shown you Winston's enthusiastic commendation on Raisman's handling of his budget proposals in Council. It seems to me that we had much better make up our minds to do as Winston suggested and prolong Raisman for a year.

381 Wavell to Amery   Delhi, 15 Feb 44

I am interested in your views about the Finance Membership. Raisman is now very restless and says that while he is quite prepared to accept retirement or an extension for a definite period, he is not willing to stay on as a stop-gap until His Majesty's Government finds it convenient to replace him. He says, quite reasonably, that at 52 with a young family he cannot afford to do nothing, and that he does not want to be kept hanging about. I hope you may be able to let me have a decision very shortly.

390 Minutes Amery & Churchill, India Office
London, 18 Feb 44

The Cabinet asked whether we could recommend an extension for Raisman. The Chancellor and I have agreed to recommend an extension of one year. Raisman has produced a good budget with strong anti-inflationary measures and Wavell speaks in increasingly high terms of him and of his handling of Indian colleagues.
L.S. Amery
Yes Raisman
Winston S Churchill

399 Amery to Wavell   London, 24-25 Feb 44

You will be relieved, as indeed will poor Raisman himself, at knowing he is to be prolonged for a year. I imagine when he gets through his budget it might be quite a good thing for him to come home and discuss the sterling balance situation with the Cabinet's Indian Finance Committee. Incidentally that might give him a little leave as well.

401 Wavell to Amery   *Delhi, 25 Feb & 7 Mar 44*
I am glad it has finally been decided to offer Raisman an extension. He is not, I think, very pleased at his extension, but he has accepted it with a fairly good grace.

He would like to go to London about mid-May to mid-July. I am telegraphing to you agreeing that he may go home on duty for a couple of months this summer.

But the main purpose of the May 1944 meeting in London was for Jeremy to coordinate with Keynes the positions of the Indian and British delegations at the Bretton Woods Conference to set up the International Monetary Fund. From London Jeremy wrote back to his family in India. 'I am appreciating this leave - after all, only the second break I've had since the war began. I was invited to a dinner at Claridges. All the top people were there - Amery, Monteath, the economist, Keynes, Montagu Norman, the Governor of the Bank of England. We had a three course dinner with superb wines and delicious cigars afterwards. I was invited to make a speech on the finances of India. Afterwards they congratulated me.'

38   Amery to Wavell   *London, 3 Oct 44*
I imagine that sheer high finance is not so important now as it once was. I promised Raisman faithfully that I would try to secure an early decision. He certainly is not anxious to stay on and I gather his wife wants to come home too. Also I imagine his prospects in the City would be much better if he came home next year than if he let another year pass.

165 Wavell to Amery   *Delhi, 27 Dec 44*
I am glad you spoke to Cabinet about Raisman's future, about which Raisman is still anxious. My present idea is that Raisman should lead India's delegation to the Bretton Woods Conference, being made an additional Member of Council if necessary. Raisman knows more about sterling balances and their history than anyone else, and I understand that his non-official colleagues would put up a good case for India.

320

Jeremy's days in the service of the British Empire were coming to an end. He was to be spared the last two years of the crumbling of the Raj. By now the future of the British Empire itself was looking increasingly shaky and His Majesty's Government in London was finding that it was fast losing control of events in India.

302 India Office Minute   London, 7 Mar 45

I think it is perhaps mildly relevant to this problem that I have to listen, during my visit to India, to attacks made upon the manner in which the India Office does its business. The main point of attack has been that we seem to assume that if we give instructions to the Government of India, that is the end of the matter, and that those instructions can be carried out as easily as they would have been thirty years ago. The attackers (Coates and Raisman) pointed out that they are in a minority of two to eleven in the Council and that neither they, nor in the last resort the Viceroy, are really able to carry out instructions to which their colleagues are not prepared to agree.

383 Colville (for Viceroy) to Amery   Delhi, 10 Apr 45

Raisman leaving this week.

'During the war,' John Michael said, 'my father produced five budgets and was able to mobilise the finances of India to support the tremendous war effort that they had to sustain. In the end India was producing more steel than Britain. And warships.

'He was in close touch with Tata. Tata came to stay with us in Peterhof. They were having discussions. He and I played table tennis together. There was a ping pong table in the back of our hall. He was a good table tennis player, JRD Tata. Nobody talked about his first name. Everyone knew him as JRD. They would have been discussing credits for setting up the factories, probably for expanding the factories, discussing how to maintain and expand his steel production which the government was very interested in indeed. My father could have provided loan finance either from the Reserve Bank of India or directly from government funds. He could do that if that was going to be contributing directly to the war effort.

'The other great problem my father had at the time was raising taxes in such a way as not to be too oppressive but nevertheless to raise the money that was needed to pay for the huge growth in military hardware. That

Tata enterprise has stood India in good stead. Their biggest industry. Probably still is. Certainly was then. My father was a strong and very important supporter of that enterprise.

'The table tennis game? JRD was brilliant. I was 13 or 14 at the time. I thought I was quite good. We had a good game but he won. He was slim and good looking. He wasn't old. He might have been only in his 30s or early 40s. So it wasn't too humiliating for me. The summer of 1942 or 3, I suppose.'

After Jeremy left India, the end of the Raj was not long in coming. Two weeks later, Clement Attlee led the Labour Party out of the wartime coalition government. Two months later the elections resoundingly voted Churchill out of office. Leo Amery retired from the India Office. During the war his son had been executed as a traitor. The new Labour Prime Minister dismissed Wavell on 31 Jan 1947 with 4 weeks notice. Wavell reminded Attlee that it had always been the custom for the Viceroy of India to be given 6 months' notice. Nonetheless, he accepted Attlee's offer of an earldom and spent the three remaining years of his life ennobled, with the ermine of the 1st Earl, Viscount Wavell of Cyrenaica and of Winchester, and a tiara for the Countess.

Jeremy, on the other hand, refused Attlee's offer of the Governor-Generalship of Kenya. 'I didn't want to become a Labour peer,' he said. So he was spared any responsibility for dealing with the Kenya insurrection, in which the Mau Mau terrorists assassinated Wavell's son, bringing to an early end the line of the new Earldom.

At midnight on 15th August 1947 the British Raj in India ended in a bloodbath and the bitter break-up of the state. Offered an honour for his part in ending the Raj the retiring Chief of the Indian Army, Sir Claude Auchinleck replied he would take nothing for what had been 'the most painful and distasteful episode of my career.'

'When we were in India,' John Michael said, 'tiger shooting was a great sport and the viceroys, like the Moguls before them, used to do it on a massive scale. They'd go and shoot 30 or 40 tigers. They reduced the tiger population.

'My father shot a tiger, oh yes - in the days when it was politically correct to do so. And I was with him at the time. I was on the next elephant. He and my mother were on one elephant and I was on the elephant behind. It was in the United Provinces, near Lucknow. One of the Nawabs invited mother and father to go on this. It was in his state - the Nawab of Chhatari, a small state I suppose, he had. The Nawab of Chhatari (Sir Muhammad Ahmed Said Khan, KCSI, KCIE, GBE was a Lieutenant Colonel in the Indian Army, and President of the Executive Council of the Nizam of Hyderabad, 1941-7) was a great friend of the family. In fact he gave me my first 2-2 rifle for my 12th birthday. He was often at our house in Delhi.

'I remember very well when we arrived. I was 11. It was 1940. The villagers of the nearby village came to tell us that a villager had been attacked. So there was a man-eating tiger on the rampage. So the women and children were left behind and the men went out that afternoon looking for this tiger but they didn't succeed in putting him up, so the next morning we all went out and whether the tiger we shot was the man-eater or not I don't know. I don't think history relates that.

'And I went along on this shoot, which was very exciting, on the *shikar* (hunt). We stayed in a bungalow. We were up in a *machan* for a time. This is where you sit up in a tree hide, and they have a *kiyor* - a goat tied to a tree. Then we went out on elephants. We had beaters and they were

Hunting tiger

hard to find, the tigers. Normally you only saw them if they came on to *nullahs*, on to river beds, *nullah* is a river bed, usually dried up. And that's where he saw this one and he had Mama on his elephant as well. The mahout was a chap who was an experienced tiger hunter and he pointed it out to my father and said, "There you are. There's your shot."

'It was a forest and I was on the elephant just behind him. It was quite a long way away. It was a hundred yards and he managed to get him with his first shot. The elephant keeps still enough. The elephant is an ideal base from which to go tiger hunting because (a) no tiger will ever attack an elephant, and (b) you're high enough to see over all the long grass and so on. The Indian elephant is smaller than the African elephant but they're much more efficient and more highly trained. And the African elephant can't really be used for anything.

'I saw it all. I saw him taking aim and I saw the tiger before it was shot and then of course he had to put another couple of bullets into its head before one dared to go up to it. He could shoot. Being short sighted didn't necessarily mean that the couldn't take aim. It was a 375 magnum, a powerful and accurate rifle, not telescopic sights, but ordinary sights. It was a very good shot he had actually. You could call it a lucky shot because he didn't practice shooting much although he had done some training when he was younger. He probably hunted *sambar* in Bihar, a kind of stag. Possibly bear but I don't suppose so. I don't think father'd been on a tiger shoot before. He might have been, but certainly he'd never shot a tiger before. He was very chuffed over that. The Nawab was very bucked. He was thrilled. He was delighted that his guest had got a tiger. I suppose when we came back we had a sort of party to celebrate it. Everyone was very excited. I think we went on to visit the Governor of the United Provinces in Lucknow straight after that. So it may have been a combination of an official and a friendly visit. It wasn't an official visit to Chhatari.

'It was a magnificent tiger. We had the skin hanging up in Peterhof for a couple of years. It was hanging up with the head below and the whole hide above just above the landing. But the Indians took the whiskers because they believed that they would give you sexual potency. So they pulled them out. A sort of aphrodisiac. I think they ate them. I think they sort of crunched them up. So one by one the whiskers started disappearing. There were still a few left when we left and brought the tiger back to England.

'The Nawab of Chhatari was a splendid looking fellow with a marvellous moustache and lots of curly black hair. He was wearing jodhpurs.

'Now, let me think. What happened to him? I read something about him. Chhatari. Where would it have been? They all lost their power and everything. Yes they all lost their power. Here we are, in Wavell's Diary:

Chhatari: Renounces his titles... page 338

'They felt they'd been let down. Yes. Well they had. Here we are:

The Nawab of Chhatari came to see me (that was in '46) about the position of the loyalists who'd always helped the British. Were we really going so soon and leaving them at the mercy of Congress, who'd always been anti-British. And now we'd got at odds with the Muslim League too, and what were our friends to do. Did I advise them to surrender their titles as they were being pressed to do by Jinnah? Couldn't we stop another ten years or so anyway? The Labour government were surely going much too fast in handing over India.

These interviews of which I had already had a number, and shall doubtless have many more, are rather trying and very painful. August 1946. Some of them I don't have a great deal of sympathy for, but some like the Nawab are really genuine and a great gentleman. And I'm sorry for them.

'A great gentleman. That's what my father thought about him. And again on page 338:

I was sad to see a letter from the Nawab of Chhatari, renouncing his titles. I'm sure he didn't really wish to. Any more than His Highness of Bhopal really wishes to abdicate and become a private Muslim Leaguer.

'These people didn't do at all well. They were just displaced. They did go to Pakistan. They just lost their position and so on, their titles and their lands and became ordinary private citizens. They had been great supporters of the British. That's why he invited people like my father to go and visit him.

'They wouldn't have imagined at that time what was going to happen. Absolutely not a partition. But it was only five years away, only five years. Yes. That way of life was about to disappear for ever, everything, my father, the Government of India, Wavell, Chhatari. It's going to be as though it had never been there. The forest, even the tigers. Yes, even the tigers.

'They all felt very let down, those people . It was all on the verge of collapse and yet not many saw it. Well certainly not with the immediacy with which it happened. As poor old Chhatari himself said, "Can't you stay another ten years?" Even Nehru and Gandhi were overtaken by the momentum of events, however much they'd stirred them up. Wavell had sent London a plan for leaving India in stages and advised that we need to state clearly that India is to be given independence and to announce a timetable. The Labour Government didn't even reply to Wavell. They didn't want to listen to what Wavell was saying. Attlee had lost confidence in Wavell and didn't want to be tied down.

'Attlee had all sorts of economic and social problems at home and India was a dimension he could do without. It sounded intractable. And it was getting more and more difficult to handle, and so on. So I mean it was all understandable. But with a firm enough policy... But once the statement had been made that they were leaving in '47 then all the pent-up forces began to explode. If the statement had been made were going in December '48 they'd have been held in check for that much longer. But it would nevertheless have been felt that it was in the pretty near future.

'But it was Mountbatten who said, "Let's do it in August 1947." All Mountbatten did was to accelerate and lost control. Actually he went out with a brief from Attlee to do it in '48 but Mountbatten thought he'd score brownie points by bringing it forward by a year. Instead of which he just caused the death of millions of people. It was a complete scuttle. My father was very lucky to be out of it and he was desperately sorry about what happened. And pretty critical. We didn't have to leave India when we did. Not that we could have perpetuated the empire. Oh, no! He never thought that. But we could have taken at least another year and done it in a much better way. We could have dealt with it better. We got out of it with indecent haste. It was a tragic end.'

Hyderabad, in the centre of India, was a rich Moslem ruled state whose 61-year old Nizam, Osman Ali, was a direct descendant of the first Nizam appointed by the Mogul Emperor Aurangzeb in 1713. The Nizams had been consistent allies of the British Raj supporting them in their war against Tippoo Sahib and remaining loyal during the mutiny of 1857. In 1947 Chhatari, who had now lost his own state, negotiated a standstill agreement of one year on behalf of the Nizam's Council with the newly independent Indian government in Delhi. Meanwhile the Nizam was in discussion with the new Moslem state of Pakistan. But Pakistan was a thousand miles away. Hyderabad was completely surrounded deep in Congress India. On September 13th 1948 Indian troops attacked. The Nizam appealed to the newly formed United Nations and to his fellow monarch King George VI, whose father had designated Hyderabad as a faithful ally. But Osman Ali was on his own. Over four days, Hyderabad's irregular troops resisted fiercely, suffering murderous losses before the Indian army entered the 13 gates of the ancient stone wall surrounding the capital. The City of the Four Minarets, proverbial for its splendour and its riches, now formed part of India's Central Provinces. Thus fell the last Mogul state, its glories entered into history. It had outlived the British Raj by a year.

Tiger Country

Raisman's farewell Budget was Churchillian in its comprehensiveness and interest. In his handling here and abroad of the country's finances, Sir Jeremy Raisman has proved himself a courageous and faithful servant of India.

The Times of India, March 2nd, 1945

'For my last five years in India,' Jeremy told Harry, ' I had to prepare the budget. It had to be absolutely secret. With one word of what I knew a man could become a millionaire overnight. The authority of an official depends upon him being completely above any hint of scandal. Many men in my position did not live up to that.'

Now he was back in London.

'The government pension was so small,' Lady Raisman said, 'we could hardly afford the rent of our London flat. We had no savings. On my first birthday back in England Jeremy looked in his wallet and saw a five pound note. He gave it to me and said, "Get yourself a present. Get what you would like. I can't give you any more. That's all we've got left." So I had to buy my own birthday present.'

As far as Jeremy was concerned India was over. He advised his son, 'Don't go into the service of governments. You'll get no thanks for it.'

But India was not over with him and in some ways, belatedly, he did. The British Government wanted to get the maximum benefit from his experience of running the finances of India. As Chairman of the British Indian delegation to the Bretton Woods Conference, which set up the International Monetary Fund, Jeremy was the British government's most experienced finance expert on India. In the cool winter weather of 1948 he was asked if he would return to India and three years later to Pakistan to advise on setting up the arrangements for the Reserve Banks of India and Pakistan.

On his return trip in 1948 Jeremy took the opportunity to go back and visit the Legislative Assembly. India was now independent and so he was sitting in the Strangers' Gallery when he received a message from the Speaker asking him to join him in his room after the debate. And there he found assembled many of his former political opponents from the

Congress Party, who welcomed him most warmly and said how pleased they were to see that he had returned to the scene of so many of his former battles. These were the leading politicians in the Congress Party who had voted against every one of his five budgets because they were in the opposition. By definition the opposition never supports the government. They had decided to be in opposition. The Congress Party had always voted against all his budgets on principle.

Jeremy had been anxious to get back to England while he was still young enough, and while he had his contacts in the banking world and the City, prominent people like the Governor of the Bank of England. Jeremy wanted to use the contacts he had already started to build up, and extend them. The contact which was to mean most for him was the introduction to the Chairman of Lloyds Bank. Jeremy was invited to join the Board and in this way he started what he always liked to call his second career. He was 53 when he was invited to become a Director of Lloyds Bank. Then he became Vice-Chairman and finally, Deputy Chairman. He had an office at the Bank's Head Office, in Lombard Street where he worked four days a week.

And then he had a number of other things that he did. He became Chairman of the Public Works Loans Board. He was on boards of the Alliance Assurance Company, BAT and Glaxo, where he became Deputy Chairman. Glaxo had been founded by two old ladies in New Zealand to sell powdered milk for babies. In 1946-7 it went into the newly discovered antibiotics just as they were coming through.

The family had been living in Kensington for some time and now they felt they wanted to live in the country. They took some time hunting around until they hit on Fieldhead. Jeremy didn't use the train much, as he had cars with chauffeurs who picked him up. But Guildford wasn't too far away and had a good train service to London so he could easily meet people who were coming to visit, many of them old Indian friends who made a point of visiting him whenever they came to London. It was far out enough not to be in the commuter belt, which he didn't want to be in, and it was pleasant country.

Now, secure in his bank career, Jeremy had accomplished the childhood dream he had dreamt when he paused with my father by the Dyneley Arms at the top of Poole Bank more than fifty years before. And on his daily drive to and from the Bank, Jeremy and his drivers, especially his favourite, John Greenway, gradually explored the various possibilities of the steep, winding green lanes behind whose towering hedges and impenetrable laurels were glimpses of many an elegant mansion and no doubt took many a wrong turning on that maze of tiny roads, unsign-posted, for those who lived there had no call to reveal the plan of their private paradise to strangers, coming down from Cobham, cutting the corner towards Shamley Green and then coming across Farley Heath. Finally, having worked out the most scenic and exciting way, Jeremy would say to his driver, 'Let's take the Tiger Route today.' And from that time all the Lloyds Bank drivers called it the Tiger Route.

Meanwhile the British Government was struggling with the questions of dissolving the rest of the British Empire and many a problem that had been met in India reappeared in Africa. Three times more the British Government called on Jeremy's help. In 1952 he was asked to lead a commission to advise on setting up the tax constitution of the new Federation of Rhodesia and Nyasaland, in 1958 the Federation of Nigeria, and in 1961 Kenya, Uganda and Tanganyika:

From The Times
Nairobi, August 21, 1961

Sir Jeremy Raisman, Deputy Chairman of Lloyds Bank, returns to East Africa tomorrow and the second half of the Raisman Commission begins forthwith. The original talks began with wide differences of opinion and with both Tanganyika and Uganda claiming large sums from Kenya. Meanwhile the three Finance Ministers have held their half-yearly meeting in Nairobi, and, according to Sir Jeremy, the unusual sight of the captains of rival teams sucking their orange slices together at halftime is a sign that the Raisman inquiry has gone well. In many respects, Sir Jeremy suggests, the quarrels are like those of three brothers growing up in the same house and feeling circumscribed by the others' close presence. Sir Jeremy feels he has the job of the father who teaches his sons the lesson of unity.

After coming back from Nairobi, Jeremy wrote plaintively to his brother Harry. 'They expect me to help them settle the financial claims of an

330

empire in dissolution.'

Fanny had spent all her married life in Sunderland. Her husband, Maurice, was a door-to-door salesman, selling anything that he could carry by bus or by train or on foot round the villages of the Geordie miners, for whose families an income of £5 a week would have been untold riches. Maurice was a popular figure, a wizened little man with a deeply wrinkled face, a merry chuckle that would dissolve into a terrible smoker's cough and an ever cheery hello for anyone else he met tumbling about on Life's uneven cobblestones, and always ready to give credit and keep a tally through lean times, and there were many of them during the Jarrow Hunger March and the hard thirties in all the little mining villages of the Geordie country. And through Fanny and Maurice's efforts and frugality, both their children had been able to go to university, and the little cut glass dish on their kitchen table had never lacked a portion of pickled herring, where the wind blew in the scent of the sea from the sands of Roker Beach. And now finally, when the children had grown up, qualified, married and moved to London,

Fanny

Fanny and her Maurice gave up their house in Sunderland and followed their children south to spend their last few years with them.

In her younger days, Fanny had had a fine singing voice but was put off performing in public because she was embarrassed about her size. Thus discouraged, Fanny had long ago given up any attempt at elegance and dressed with the comfortable abandon of a Lithuanian fishwife. Soon after arriving in the capital, arms akimbo Fanny Dreebin, scattering aside the soft southerners, strode down Streatham High Street, where she found herself outside a branch of Lloyds Bank. On the spur of the moment Fanny decided to call on the famous older brother she hadn't seen since their days in the Leylands. So, unaware or indifferent to the fact that Lloyds would have hundreds of branches all over the country, she stepped in and asked to see her brother.

It was some time before the branch manager could make any sense of this large lady with a hardly comprehensible but strident Geordie accent, and a tightly fitting knitted woollen bonnet who had never used a bank in her life, and seemed to be accusing him of hiding her long lost brother somewhere at the back of his office. But finally a message was telexed to the Lloyds Head Office in Lombard Street. 'Sir Jeremy Raisman's sister is in Streatham and wants to see him.'

Jeremy was not in the country at the time and when the message reached him he took some days to decide how to respond. Finally, he decided that only Myer could handle this delicate matter. 'Tell her,' Jeremy wrote sternly to Myer, 'that I am glad she is well, and I would be happy to see her. But I have duties at the bank, and I can't mix them with unannounced family reunions.'

Myer, furious with Fanny, dutifully relayed this to her, adding a number of further admonitions and embellishments of his own. But Fanny didn't trouble to respond to Myer's letter. By that time she had long since forgotten the whim that had taken her into the bank. She had her own life to live, it had not been an easy one, and she took only a passive interest in Jeremy or in any of the others who, by accident of birth had shared her childhood home in the Leylands. She made no further response to Jeremy's offer for them to meet. It was all too long ago. Life's paths, over half a century, had graven too differently on them. As in Darwin's Origin of Species the individuals had diverged to the point where they could not come together again. The gulf was unbridgeable. And so it was the Livery Street babes of 1892 and 1895 were not to meet again. But events were to show that there was life yet in Myer and Jeremy's extraordinary Family Plan.

At this time I left Leeds to go to university and for the first time since I could remember, I slept alone. My father was very worried about how I would manage the expenses at Oxford.

Leeds
21st Oct 1957

Dear Geoffrey,

I am entirely satisfied with your accounts. I was prepared for the initial outlay, most of which will not recur. It's the avoidable expenses that matter, and if you will look after these all will be well. You have not sent any laundry home as you said you would. Is it that the packing is too much of a nuisance? Laundry is a great expense for you and I think we ought to work out some system for dealing with it. How do you find the other expenses of living? Can you keep them within bounds?

I'm pleased to read about the work you are doing and happy to feel that at last you are getting down to serious business. Work is what I'm chiefly concerned about. I knew when I first launched you on this course that it would be no joy-ride financially for me. Also it means sacrifices on your part. I should like to see you on your way to the very top. It matters not what course you would have taken, the same conditions would have applied.

Men who succeed enormously do so because they are fired with ambition and allow nothing to deflect them from their purpose. You must be prepared to work hard and sacrifice some years of time. You have the ability and you now have the opportunity. An intelligent man can only be happy doing intelligent work. Fix your eyes on the summit, and no matter how hard the way you will achieve it and find the reward has been well worth the struggle.

Be determined to get away from this horrible poverty which has oppressed me all my life. Poverty robs you of all the pleasures of life. You have not yet experienced the horribly depressing effect of financial insecurity. Profit by my experience and develop a determination to avoid it no matter what temptations you may meet. Intellectually you are miles ahead of your contemporaries. Use your brains to seize whatever Oxford has to offer and you will in due course reap a material reward as well as personal satisfaction.

I am looking forward to seeing you at the end of term. I'm hoping that your stay at Oxford will have had a beneficial effect on your outlook on life, to the extent that you will have developed a heightened sense of responsibility, and have become more capable of handling your affairs and life's problems generally. It is not enough to have an intellectual capacity for scholarship. One should be able to apply one's intelligence to all matters affecting life. Matters for which there is no specific school or university, but which have to be learned by experience, and which a man is expected to cope with according to his natural ability. Oxford is claimed to produce and develop this capacity for responsibility and leadership. Who knows one day you might even be able to help me with my problems, and take a little of the weight off my shoulders when I'm a little older and a little more tired than I am now.

Unky and I have decided that we shall find the money to keep you at Oxford. We know you will not incur avoidable liabilities. It remains with you to make the most of your chances. No matter how much I write I can never put down on paper all my feelings for you and my hopes for your future. Remember always, Geoffrey, that I am your very best friend, and that no one will ever consider you in the same light as your affec

Daddy

And now, in this new place, of all the family, I found I was the only one who had entered a social plane accessible to Sir Jeremy and after all I belonged, like him, to that minority of the family who still shared the same name. Sir Jeremy had been made Senior Honorary Fellow of his old college, Pembroke, and on the occasion of attending one of the annual college gaudies he took the opportunity of his trip to Oxford to call on me.

I was astonished as a huge black limousine drew up outside my house. My famous uncle walked in.

'Will the chauffeur come?' I asked.

'Oh no, he stays in the car,' Sir Jeremy replied.

'Does he need anything?' I asked.

'Oh no, he's a very good man. I've always had him. He has a flat over the garage.'

Trying to hide my curiosity, I looked at the chauffeur, and he smiled genially back at me, as if at a child in his care, as if beckoning me to a vacant throne which was, through my uncle, my rightful place in fairyland.

John Greenway dozed over the steering wheel, with his peaked chauffeur's cap shading his eyes and the car radio softly playing, while the Deputy Chairman of Lloyds Bank visited his nephew.

'Can people get past?' I asked embarrassed, indicating the shiny black Daimler in our narrow street.

'The police are always very kind,' said Sir Jeremy. 'They make allowances for cars like this.'

As Sir Jeremy came in I reached out to take his hat, but I was too slow, and to my horror he had already glanced around the bare, narrow hall and placed it on top of the wardrobe, a place I knew to be thick with dust.

During his visit Sir Jeremy asked me in detail about my course, my progress, and my objectives. It was all stern and friendly. Together we tried to see what Life could offer this young, first-year medical student. I felt a strong hand behind me, supporting, guiding. It was as if, in the unspoken running of the family plan, I had passed from Myer's care to Jeremy's. Shyly, at the end of this I mentioned that Myer had taught me how to play bridge. 'If I can't win at a game,' Sir Jeremy said, 'I won't play.'

I asked him what bidding conventions he used. 'Bidding at bridge is just a sophisticated form of cheating,' he said. 'There are two types of people,' Sir Jeremy told me as he left. 'One type worries about what others think about him. The other type lets others worry what he thinks about them.'

He was on the way to a formal college dinner when he said this.

'I always worry about how I look,' I said innocently, admiring my great uncle. 'I panic at the thought I have forgotten to shave.'

Sir Jeremy's hand flew instantly to his chin and as he left he took his hat from the top of the wardrobe. I felt a sinking feeling. What would such a great man do when he found his hat was dirty? Sir Jeremy lightly brushed his cobwebby hat with no more attention that one might whisk a speck of dust from a sheet of paper, showing not the slightest sign of distaste or disapproval.

A few weeks later I got a letter from Myer, bursting with pride:

My dear Geoff,

I have had a letter from Jeremy advising me of his coming visit to Leeds on May 18th for his honorary LL.D. He is coming by train. The University is arranging a car to pick him up and take him direct to the College for lunch, at which the Chancellor, the Princess Royal, will propose a toast to the ten Honorands. Jeremy is booked to make the first speech in response. They then go on to the Town Hall to don their robes and receive their degrees, 3.0 to 4.30 p.m. After this they go to the Lord Mayor's tea-party at the Civic Hall. These arrangements will keep him occupied till about 6 p.m. Then we shall probably have him for a few hours to ourselves. He has booked a sleeper for the return journey. This does not leave until 2.36 a.m, but he can go in to sleep at 11 p.m, which he intends to do.

He writes, "I have deliberately cut my visit to the inside of a day, as I want if possible to dodge the press hounds who may try to work up a headline story about the Leylands boy made good."

Incidentally, he mentions his visit to Oxford. He says he was extremely interested in your work and plans.

Did you read the report that he had turned down the Chairmanship of Lloyds from which Sir Oliver Franks was retiring. Some job to refuse!

My love to you,

Unky

But later, when I asked Myer if he had gone to the ceremony, or seen Jeremy, he became evasive and rather gloomy and muttered about something being difficult and problems and I did not need to be told in words of one syllable that the two brothers had not met during Jeremy's honourable one day visit to his home city.

Life is nothing if not unpredictable. Alas for my father's dreams of splendour for me! He had not taken into account the endocrine development of the adolescent male. I was not able to give him total satisfaction, although I have to say he did go on a bit.

Leeds
Nov 14th, 1957

Dear Geoff,

I have just read a letter of yours dated Tuesday, which I can only describe as extraordinary. Your utter indifference or ignorance (the effect is the same) of my circumstances and your own leaves me shocked and disgusted. I would point out to you that when you left Leeds I gave you almost my entire capital. The little I had left has been entirely eaten up by your further demands while at Oxford.

To ask me to help you with money for your marriage is utterly preposterous. I haven't any. Further, I would draw your attention to the fact that I am in my 60's. I am a manual labourer and have arrived at an age when physical disabilities strike suddenly and without warning. Also my job is not secure. Employers look askance at men of my age, and once my famous speed of output begins to decline I shall find myself on the scrap heap. I have no provision for the future, and I daren't think of the probabilities of the next 5 or 6 years. This is the exact financial position. I made arrangements with Jeremy to help you through. These arrangements will dissolve on your marriage, and I, I repeat, have no money.

I should be scared to let Jeremy know of this. Not that he would oppose your choice or your eventual marriage, but he would consider that you are letting us all down when in view of your age you could well afford to wait a few years. I'll try to help you as much as I can, but it will not be much. I cannot promise that Jeremy's contribution will continue. It may, but I cannot be sure.

It passes my comprehension that you should be so incapable of self-control, so regardless of the necessity to plan your future instead of rushing about like a bull in a china shop. Are you of such a weak character that you cannot look before you leap? Can't you see that all the circumstances are massed against you. And are you so unable to see clearly the way ahead? If you two are so determined on marriage, do something yourselves about it. Let V go to work and you try to earn some money during the vacations, and so make it possible to do what you wish. Quarrelling with your family and V's won't get you anywhere.

Your affec

Daddy

P.S. Your attitude and behaviour on this matter surprises me so much that I can hardly believe a person of your intelligence can be so short-sighted. I would draw your attention to what I can only describe as a rake's progress since you met V. Consider the closing stages of your school life, your headlong trip to the continent, and now the threat to our family unity. A cloud of gloom and depression envelops me. I do not write this letter in anger, but I am very, very sad. I am not opposed to your marriage at a suitable time, but I disapprove of what I consider to be a reckless premature action.

Getting married was always a hazardous occupation in our family. I did not feel able to repeat my father's biblical-style engagement of seven years and even that had not been long enough for Myer. There followed a long period of coolness and I lived under a cloud, lifting a little at times but only finally dispelled when, despite all gloomy predictions, I completed my degree. But in the meantime Fate was preparing something so unlooked for and so insoluble as to totally eclipse any remnants of my father's righteous indignation about my reckless behaviour.

The Fairy Tale Hero

'John,' said I, 'you seem to have taken an erroneous view of life and its duties. Pushed on by ambition, you are dreaming rather of what it might be glorious to attempt than what it would be possible for you to accomplish. Believe me, it is not necessary to a man's respectability that he should commit a murder.

Many a man has passed through life most respectably without attempting any species of homicide - good, bad, or indifferent. We cannot all be brilliant in this life. And it is in your interest to be contented rather with a humble station well filled than to shock everybody with failures, the more conspicuous by contrast with the ostentation of their promises.'

De Quincey: Essay on Murder as One of the Fine Arts

That expected day came when my father didn't go to work. He went up to Butterworth's, the little newsagent-cum-stationer's shop and post office at the top of the street, and a few steps on the other side of Harehills Lane. He came back with a little buff coloured book with the Royal coat of arms in one corner. 'My pension book,' he said. 'Sixty five.' He shook his head, sadly. 'It doesn't feel as though I've had all that time.' But then he looked at what he had in his hand and his face brightened up. 'Ten pounds a week! That's more than I've ever earned in my life!.'

My father never felt the need for any social actions. He didn't even go to the funeral of his cycling companion Charlie Blass. I went for him. One day we were visiting Leslie Alberts, who had stood next to my father singing and joking away the so many tedious years at the shiny workbenches at Burton's. 'How will you get back?' Leslie asked my father.

'He looks after me now,' he replied, jerking his head in my direction. It was one of those defining moments in life, the wheel was being passed into my hands.

When Sam had recalled his memories of John at my childhood Passover

Seders it was more than ten years since anyone in the family had had any news of him. Even letters telling John of the death of his parents had aroused no reply from Argentina. Now, for 25 years no one had heard anything of John. John was missing, presumed dead.

Although John's flight and the Crash had occurred so long ago it never ceased to be painful for the brothers to recollect and shameful for its survivors. I found it hard to get facts. 'Why didn't John make money out of his solicitor's business?' I asked Myer.

'You needed money, influence, contacts,' Myer replied. From the dignified, self-conscious way in which he said 'influence' and 'contacts,' I could see that he himself hadn't any idea what they might entail. Myer was getting reluctant to continue this conversation.

'Constant dripping wears away a stone ,' he said, warningly.

I changed tack, 'So you mean to say that Uncle John's failure wasn't anything to do with his gambling?' I had reached the edge of what even I, his favourite nephew, could say to Myer.

'We-elll ...,' Myer said. It was one of his sounds. A prize one. It only lasted about five seconds but it had a world of meaning. It began brusquely, as if to say, 'How dare you ...?' But almost at once it turned into a high, wheedling falsetto, 'Now you have put me on the spot, Geoff...' From here it descended into a long, straight passage, indicating reflection. There was even, like kettledrums in an orchestra, a hint of a throat rumble. Finally it ended up expanding the initial, defiant and indignant tone, 'No, we haven't anything to be ashamed of, he tried to make a go of it. The conditions were against him.'

During the Christmas of my first year as a student, Myer came to stay. I had bought and resuscitated a wreck of an old AJS 650cc twin motorcycle, with upswept exhaust pipes. It was a former racing machine, and still kept enough of its former glory to do the ton. We planned to go into town, about two miles.

'Could you manage on the back of the motor bike?' I asked Myer, who by this time was too unsteady even to ride a bicycle on his own.

'I think so,' Myer said. 'I'll try.'

I installed him very carefully on to the pillion, and checked that he was stable.

'Are you comfortable?'

'Yes.'

'Sure?'

'Sure.'

'Hold on to me.'

Myer obeyed, and we were off.

But of course, on the way down the long straight stretch of Marston Road, I couldn't resist one little burst of speed. To my surprise, Myer showed absolutely no signs of nervousness. As we reached our destination I held the bike very steady as he eased his arthritic legs off the machine and on to the ground. I marvelled that he seemed absolutely calm and relaxed, and I couldn't help asking him: 'How was it?'

'Fine,' he replied simply.

'You weren't afraid?'

'Afraid?' Myer repeated. 'No. Whither thou goest,' Myer paused, grasping at how to express the thought in his mind, and then, 'If you go, I want to go with you.'

In that wet mid-winter, I had my first vacation job, my first and only experience of the real world of labour that Myer and Harry knew so well. I found the ten days extremely tedious and was not happy, one evening when the slush of melting snow was piled high in the streets, to find my rubber overshoes had been stolen by a fellow worker. Returning home with delight and relief when it was over I tore open my very first wage packet. To my horror a vast sum had been deducted at source for National Health Insurance. Out of my first week's wages nearly two pounds had been deducted from a total of eight. Worse still, out of my second, part week, the same sum had been deducted from a total of only four pounds. I spent a long time complaining in various

Myer

colourful ways to anyone who would listen. Myer, the old socialist who had spent so much of his working life fighting for state welfare, remained silent. In the end I had worked myself into a frenzy of righteous indignation. 'I never even use the hospitals,' I shouted.

Myer was finally stung to speech. 'No,' he said sardonically 'They're for the old 'uns like me.' I was chastened, but it turned out that Myer himself was soon to have his own charitable instincts tested to the full. Shortly after this I got a long distance call from my mother. Long distance calls were expensive. Obviously something unusual had occurred. My mother's voice was full of excitement. 'Who do you think has come?' I guessed in a flash. It could only be my childhood hero. Neither my father nor Uncle Myer had wanted me to be told. They feared my career might be compromised even by contact. Gambling was to them a fearful disease. Anglo-Indians are said to be peculiarly liable to leprosy and to contract it in circumstances where others remain unaffected. I was a Raisman.

I couldn't have been more excited. I hadn't really expected John was alive, let alone that I would ever meet him. My imagination couldn't tackle the question of what such a man would be like. What would it be like to meet a person reputed to be as brilliant as John? How did a man live with having so wantonly destroyed the lifetime hopes and struggles of Myer and my father? The brilliance and the guilt I anticipated, but what I had never foreseen, and what surprised me most when I met him, was the irrepressible childishness.

John was summoned before the family conclave. Astonished brothers and sisters converged for a two-day meeting at Sarah's home in Leicester. I was to be admitted for the second day's events. Apart from their parents, who had passed away, Louis, who was in Canada, Fanny, Sir Jeremy and Jack, all the rest of John's generation of Raismans attended the spectacle.

Sarah was a short lady with large features and a manner resembling the Duchess in Alice in Wonderland. Sarah had studied history at Leeds University, where she was aided by her phenomenal memory for dates. She knew every birthday, marriage day, and death day in the family, and could effortlessly recall every day when I or anyone else had visited her.

The family's passion for numbers had been vital for the gambling of my grandfather and his sons, it had helped my father calculate the reduction in cost of cloth with faults, and in Sarah it took the form of dates. And Sarah was also famous in the family as a tireless talker. Even Myer acknowledged her prowess in this direction.

'Your Aunty Sarah,' Harry said, 'could talk the hind leg off a donkey. You need a surgical operation to get away from her.'

Sarah

Sarah had been the last of the brood to leave Leeds, having taken care of Myer and her father almost till the time Myer left Mexborough Avenue. After years of longing for a child, Sarah had married late, to a much younger man. To conceal the difference, she had adapted her speech to sound like that of a baby and would always call monks monkeys and never used an adult name for someone when Tibberly, or Stinky, or Chubbs, or Tunky, or some other baby name could be discovered. When Sarah married, she had first moved to Mickleover in Derby, where she called her house Midmay to commemorate the time of the greatest event in her life, the birth of her only son. Shortly after they had moved to the house in Leicester where we were now sitting.

The family sat John in the corner of the small, packed parlour and he recounted his experiences in Argentina. His wondering siblings sat around, dumbfounded. Myer, the acknowledged head of the family, sat in another corner, speechless with indignation. He resembled an offended matriarch who had just had an exceptionally naughty boy brought home from school.

But as the proceedings wore on Myer was unable to contain his feelings in silence. He occasionally said, 'Good God!' or used Yiddish expletives, of which there was quite a range available. They all began with the word, 'Oy,' followed by a bewildering variety of possible calamities such as, 'A fire! Woe! Woe is me! A curse! A curse that shouldn't or didn't happen to me! A cholera! A blessing be upon us to protect us from what I have just heard! Pains of childbirth!' and so forth. The proceedings were long and so Myer used many of these, selected to suit the particular moment. But most of all he used a sound at which he was so adept that he really made it his own. It was his groan.

Actually this sound combined groan and sigh and a lot more beside. Myer's groan was deep and rich and he used it in an unending series of variations. Its purpose was to give the hearer a glimpse into Myer's soul. For groans were never frivolous. Although the emotions conveyed by a groan were always on the sad side they varied from sharp, pungent sorrow to deep, ingrained woe. Groans could be short or long drawn-out, simple or complex but once started a groan must continue to its end. Occasionally one fell to a low intensity and the hearers, mistakenly assuming it to be over, continued their conversation. At such times the final part of the groan would be heard softly in the background proceeding a little indignantly to complete its burden of woe. There was even a special groan which ended in a tremulous repetitive vocal shudder, signifying that the train of thought led Myer to something so hideous to recollect that even he did not dare expose either himself or his hearers to the final awful sound which that particular groan would attain if he let it proceed to its natural conclusion.

On the occasion of John's return I think Myer ran through his entire repertoire and indeed for some time after the historic meeting in Leicester, as he turned over in his mind what he had heard there, Myer still spontaneously uttered the occasional forlorn or indignant groan.

I knew John the moment I entered the room. An emaciated old man dressed in a very dilapidated old suit, broken glasses, unfastened shoelaces, a stinking old briar pipe half-detached at the joint. But above it was a noble but unmistakably Raisman head with a stern expression, with the large Raisman nose and a back-and-sides fringe of unkempt white hair. The only special features were his big ears. I think my father introduced me but his words seemed miles away. I was in heaven. My childhood idol, my legend, had been resurrected. I neither greeted John, nor he me. It seemed unnecessary. Strangely, both of us addressed my father, thanking him for the courtesy of the introduction. Neither John nor I felt we needed it.

There were no chairs left in the small parlour so I sat at John's feet. John's conversation was wild. Gradually I became aware of my shocked uncles and aunts. Naturally they, who were now prosperous and respectable, whose very names were changed, dreaded the scandal that the return of this ghastly spectre threatened. Moreover he was destitute and conspicuously in need. They might be expected to spend money on him. Why on earth hadn't he died? Their deliberations were to the point. What was the least expensive way they could get him to go back quickly and quietly to Argentina so he could complete the act of disappearance he had so sadly bungled at the first attempt?

John, for his part, said he had had to decide whether he was destined to be a fairy tale hero or a tragic hero. Since he had not died, he must be the first and not the second. He was quite apologetic about it and assured the family he had had every intention of relieving them of his presence by disappearing into the wilds of Brazil but since the staple food of the region, manioca, was so ghastly he had not been able to do it.

344

As I sat at John's feet in Leicester I slowly became aware of the contempt of John's now respectable brothers and sisters. 'John's language is not very refined,' a shocked aunt told me warningly. And of course at that I listened even more intently, but found that John's conversation poured out in a confused babble which was very hard to understand at all. For some time I wondered if he was actually insane, and every one was just being polite about it.

Myer, who was not one of the respectable ones, dozed off from time to time, waking occasionally to utter an, 'Oh, Woe!' or a groan, and then falling asleep again. Actually John was very nervous. He later told me he felt like King John at Runnymede, confronted by his armed barons requiring him to sign Magna Carta.

Myer sat among his smartly dressed brothers. His jacket was unfastened, revealing his old, repeatedly stained waistcoat, a mass of buttons, pockets and creases. But regardless of their relative incomes, all the family still looked on him as the head. Whoever spoke never failed to have Myer in view. The slightest gesture of disapproval or the shade of a frown from Myer was enough to silence instantly even the most eloquent speaker in full flight. This was not to be a time for recriminations. Myer had lost everything in the Crash and if he could forgive, they all could. It was not for the juniors to indulge in expressions of disapproval of John in Myer's presence.

They started to discuss whether John would be arrested. 'He is quite safe,' said Sidney, the youngest. It was not clear whether Sidney regretted this or welcomed it. Sidney's manner was opulent. He was the youngest and richest of the brothers and the most indignant at being asked to contribute money to the cause of sending John back to Argentina. Sidney began to lecture on the legal aspects of John's position, 'The Statute of Limitations...'

Ralph, Sidney's senior, interrupted him by a cough. Ralph was Sidney's boss in the legal office. Sidney was silenced at once and turned his attention to his teacup. Ralph was almost the image of Sam. Bald, shiny head, cheerful open face, never at a loss for a joke. He didn't even bother to continue the legal discussion.

John had not shown too much concern about his own possible arrest. In fact he was waiting for a pause in the conversation to start his own line of argument. 'This question of whether a man is arrested or not,' said

John, discussing his own fate in a completely detached way, 'is an apparent paradox. Now, for example, in the Roman games what is meant by the sign thumbs up?' John addressed this to his sister Sarah.

Sarah seemed appalled at this frivolous diversion and spluttered, 'To save...'

John seemed delighted. 'Of course,' he said. 'That's what everyone thinks.'

'Now, for example, if in the Roman games the emperor gave the sign thumbs up, everyone assumes that means the gladiator was to be spared. But Juvenal has a poem in which thumbs down means to save. Now here we have two contrary opinions. Obviously if the artist depicted on a fresco that thumbs up means to save he must have known that it was so. And the people like Juvenal that wrote in the poems that thumbs down means to save, must also be right. Whenever you meet contradictions in history you've got to use your imagination and try to solve them. In matters of custom it is possible for two customs to prevail. After all the Roman Empire was big. One of them may have prevailed in the West and the other in the East. One of them may have prevailed for two hundred years, and the other for another two hundred years. If two statements although they are opposed are both stated then both must be right. There's no question of choosing between them. That's my way of solving contradictions in history.'

John sat back triumphantly, as if he had scored a great debating point against fierce opposition.

Myer had turned to me, 'I went with him to see Jack in Lancashire. On the way back we had to change buses at Halifax. John was talking all the time.'

'What did he talk about?' I asked.

'I talk about?' asked Myer, mishearing me.

'What else did he talk about?' I repeated, emphasising the 'he'.

'Now you're talking,' said Myer, and paused. No one else in the room appeared to be listening to my conversation with Myer.

'Did he stop talking?' I asked Myer, eager to see what he thought of John.

'He didn't stop talking at all,' said Myer emphatically. 'He turned to me and he said, "I hope I'm not boring you," he says. "Still I've amused you. I've made you laugh," he says, "Icould have made you cry as well, if I wanted."'

Myer paused again.

'So what did you say to that?' I said, trying to keep Myer's account going.

'I said, "Don't make me cry," said Myer and he chuckled throatily. 'You know he's... he's talking, talking, talking...' Myer was getting exasperated as he thought about it. 'Here am I - I'm looking up the programme...' Myer spluttered with indignation '... I'm looking up the bus timetables. Here I am at Halifax Station - I'm looking up the bus timetables and he's talking away... talking away. I can't concentrate on what I'm doing. He's not bothered about getting home. O, no! He's talking, talking, talking.'

Myer paused, at a loss for words to express his frustration at John's impracticality. 'I told him to shut up.'

At this I glanced up towards John and noticed that he was listening appreciatively. He was clearly delighted to have elicited this reaction from Myer and now he sat quietly just outside Myer's line of vision and without interrupting.

'What was he talking about?' I asked, trying to prolong Myer's reliving the incident.

'What was he talking about?' Myer echoed my question indignantly. 'Anything under the sun. He talks about all sorts of things.'

'For instance?'

'I'll tell you,' Myer began and stopped to think, 'I'll tell you the truth, Geoff, it went in one ear and out of the other.'

'Were you not taking any notice?' I asked, provocatively, keeping Myer on the verge of exasperation.

'No,' said Myer, 'I wasn't taking any notice. Blathering ... blathering away he was. A lot I couldn't hear as well.'

'Did you not understand it?' I asked.

'Well ...' said Myer, prolonging the sound, 'he talks about all sorts of philosophy - of - why - of why he's a gambler.' Myer was becoming inarticulate with indignation. 'He explained why he's a gambler! He starts talking a lot of bleddy rubbish about why he's a gambler! What do I know from why he's a gambler,' Myer exploded, dropping into broken Yiddish-English and laughing despite himself, as he thought of how ridiculous it was. 'I didn't take any notice of him,' Myer went on. 'Just a lot of nonsense - trying to explain why he's a gambler - a lot of bleddy rubbish.'

By now, several independent conversations had sprung up all over the room. The meeting was clearly getting nowhere. Sidney was exchanging compliments with his sister Sarah, who secretly envied his plutocractic poise.

Myer began again, as if he was alone and speaking to himself: 'I didn't know whether to tell Jeremy.'

Silence fell in the room. Religious Jews may not utter the name of God. The family's high priest had come close to it. I kept my eyes cast down, aware that I was the only one who had been admitted to Jeremy's presence. 'But I did,' continued Myer. 'I phoned him.

''E said, "John should go and live somewhere like Spain where the income tax is low."'

Myer now turned directly on John and even John paled. 'Do you think you could manage to live in Spain?' Myer asked testily.

'Of course,' John said, trying to regain his poise. 'My dear fellow,' John began, turning away from Myer, and speaking as if to an imaginary hearer, 'live in Spain? Why, I lived for two weeks without food in a pit with murderers and homosexuals in Brazil! Why shouldn't I be able to live in Spain?' John turned back to Myer, who had asked the question, but to whom John had not dared to address such a disrespectful answer.

I could see Myer was seething with indignation. To blunt the blow I quickly asked John, 'Where? Where were you in a pit?'

'In Santa Maria de la Campaña,' John replied, delighted at an escape.

It had only partly deflected Myer.

'He thinks he's an Argentinian,' Myer snorted, explosively. 'He doesn't think he's English at all. He talks as though he's an Argentinian.'

No one wanted to see Myer upset. Sarah rushed a cup of tea to John, interposing herself between him and Myer. Sarah leaned across John with the milk jug.

'Oooh, this is a good idea!' said John in mock surprise, as if it had never occurred to him to add milk to tea. 'One could put some milk into it.'

Sarah added two huge spoonfuls of sugar. John waited, and Sarah added more sugar. After the sixth spoonful, when John still didn't seem satisfied, she said, 'Well taste it. See if it's sweet enough.'

John stirred the semi-solid mass. The spoon grated on the bottom of the cupful of sugar. He took it out, sipped the syrupy mass and said, apologetically, 'The English sugar isn't as strong as the Argentinian sugar.'

Fortunately Myer had subsided by now and wasn't paying attention. 'In Argentina the Indians in the country drink tea with a metal straw that they call a *bombilla*. The tea's called *maté* and they drink it out of a sort of gourd.'

'What is it like?' I asked.

'Ghastly,' John replied.

John drank his tea without further comment. Several conversations were going on in different parts of the room. Myer was fast asleep and snoring loudly, my father was singing quietly to himself, and no one was taking any notice of John, who seemed to feel challenged by not being the centre of attention. He turned to me, 'Have you been following the Profumo scandal?'

'Yes,' I mumbled.

John continued, 'In his book, *The Skin*, Malaparte takes the view that homosexuality is a way of expressing disapproval of society. And in this matter, the Brazilians are very much like the English. In South America the Brazilians have got a reputation for backwardness. In fact, as worshippers of the posterior they are considered to be the most backward of people. And of course, in Europe the English have the same reputation. Homosexuality is known by the French as *le vice anglais*.'

John paused and turned to my younger cousin, David, 'What's the German for gay?' John asked, and without waiting for an answer, 'Must be *fröhlich*.

'You know, ever since we were at university, both Jeremy and I have tried to understand the source of the imperial power of Britain. We both noticed a connection with the classical world of Greece and Rome. But in my opinion, it was the homosexuality of the classical world which was the root of its strength. For example, it is said of the Greek master that he had to be always firmly behind his pupil. In classical antiquity such tendencies were regarded as...' and here John turned to me, enquiringly.

Not knowing the answer to this, I remained silent.

'In classical antiquity,' John went on, answering his own question, with mock severity, 'such tendencies were regarded as sacred. It was only later that the puritanical Judaeo-Christian ethic introduced heterosexuality as a virtue. For the Greeks and Romans, homosexuality was a source of power. For example, in the Battle of Leuctra, the first defeat on land of the Spartans, the armies on both sides were homosexuals. In fact Gibbon is of the view that it was the overthrow of the Roman Empire by heterosexual barbarians that started the decline of the classical civilisation. And so, in the same way, the British Empire was also ruled by an elite administrative class, who were trained in public schools where homosexuality and flogging were a route to the acquisition of wisdom. And according to this view the fall of the British Empire can be regarded as due to a decline in flagellation of the posterior, the seat of administrative wisdom. In other words, as men seek to become more and more untouched, there is less and less flagellation of the posterior. And if we want to return to our former greatness men must sacrifice their posteriors for the good of the British Empire.'

At this point John paused for breath and looked around the room. No one responded and he continued. 'I have illustrated this by a poem on the Profumo affair.'

'Can you remember it?' I asked.

'I call it A Posteriori,' John said. 'You know what an *a priori* argument is? Well this is an *a posteriori* argument. It begins:

> *England, the Queen of the Waves,*
> *You beat your free, not your slaves!*

'Not bad, Eh?' John asked, turning to me for approval.

'Go on,' I said.

'Well,' John said, 'it goes like this:

> *When we go to kingdom come*
> *From the palace or the slum*
> *For whom shall they beat the drums*
> *For the smacked or the unsmacked...'*

John turned again to me questioningly.

'Bums?' I ventured.

'Very good,' John said, picking up a sweet biscuit but not eating it and he went on:

> *Cephalocentric clods*
> *Have become the people's gods*

And so the man in the street
Bears rule with his untouched seat.

'Cephalocentric clods refers to the election of Harold Wilson after the defeat of the Tories following the Profumo affair. But naturally, I take the opposite view. What Profumo did was a patriotic action. To delay the decline and fall of the British Empire, he had to sacrifice his posterior, and so I wrote:

They spread your sway far and wide
The men of the smacked backside
But now that your long day wanes
Their bums go in search of canes.'

John started to eat. It was the first time I had seen it. With his left hand he broke up a sweet biscuit, covering the table with crumbs. He then started to convey the morsels to his mouth with a spoon. 'I always like mis-shapen food,' John said, 'like broken biscuits that you could get for a penny a bag, or the finger breads that mother used to make. I used to like the ones whose shape came out wrong, any kind of defective food.'

'I'll get you an egg if you're hungry,' said Sarah, and went into the kitchen.

'How much money would the family need to raise to get you set up in Spain?' Myer asked.

This met with no response from anyone. Indeed, sporadic conversations on a variety of topics started again all over the room. Sarah reappeared with a fried egg. John fixed her severely with his right eye. His face was stern, like a schoolmaster who had just triumphantly asserted an important point against a strong but now defeated opponent. 'For the goose?' asked John, not releasing her from his strict, imperious gaze.

Sarah was puzzled. John never asked for things directly. He was very coy about his personal desires. Then, understanding, she came back with a choice of two sauce bottles. John took one of the bottles and started to pour its contents all over his egg. Sarah was about to remove the other. 'No, that's all right,' John said, taking it from her and deluging his plate with the second sauce as well. The fried egg glistened with masses of red and brown sauce. John picked up a spoon in his left hand.

'Your glasses need cleaning,' said Sarah to John. It was an

understatement. One of the spectacle lenses was cracked as well.

John looked up with mock severity, 'I take a Platonic view of society. I am a follower of Plato. Gardening is to be done by gardeners, and I leave the cleaning of my glasses to the maid.'

Sidney looked despairingly at Sarah. John, the unrepentant pauper, was once again mocking the wealthy he had cheated and now expected to support him.

Myer turned to me, 'His wife won't have anything to do with him. Won't even see him.'

'What do you expect?' asked Sidney. Myer turned his head and silenced the youngest once again.

Meanwhile, in response to the mention of his wife, John had started a long lecture on Plato. In the curious repetitive rhythmic speech so characteristic of him, John described three stages of Platonic love. 'According to Plato, first of all you need the body of a woman, and the woman needs the body of a man to get the conception of beauty. So that's your first stage. In the second stage you get the conception of beauty, like in mathematics, but still need the body. In the third stage you get the conception of beauty but don't need any body. That's why I left my wife. As Plato said, " Any fool can amuse himself with the body of a woman beside him to make love." That's the lowest stage. I reached the highest stage where I can get the conception of love and beauty without a woman. So why do I need my wife? So I left her in England for 33 years. That's the reason I had to leave my wife in England for 33 years to practise Platonism. I am the purest form of Platonist. A Platonist has to go from one woman to another so he can get the abstract idea. With one woman alone you can never get the abstract idea of beauty. It's only by comparing one woman with another. You have to go from one woman to another to get the ideal of pure beauty and love.'

At this moment Sam arrived. He had already seen John in Leeds and he now strode breezily into the house, as usual without knocking. His face beamed and he flashed his expansive mischievous smile at all his brothers. He was clearly at ease with John.

'Well, what do you know?' Sam said.

'Did you get me my new false teeth from Lenny?' John asked. They were soon chatting freely. Waiting my chance, I intervened where I could, pressing Sam to repeat John's exploits, the ones Sam had told me about year after year, here in front of John. Sam obliged with a tale or two. I watched John closely. He sat delighted, nodding approval, flattered to hear himself the subject of such attention.

'You were a legend to me,' I said to John.

'Well, and now?' John asked eagerly.

'Still a legend, better than a legend,' I replied. 'Much, much more, a living legend.'

Several of the younger generation became interested. John's nephews and nieces began to cluster round him. John eyed the younger generation. The teenage nieces looked very innocent. John's face took on a mask of extreme school-masterish severity. He rarely smiled, but his eyes flashed and twinkled with mischief. He began, 'When I was in Argentina, Peron became dictator. His wife was Evita.'

Sidney, clearly detecting mischief in John's tone, had started to hover behind his innocent daughters.

'Actually, Evita was nothing compared with Theodora,' said John, apparently changing the subject.

'Who?' I asked, provocatively.

'The empress Theodora was the wife of Justinian, the Byzantine emperor,' John replied. 'She was a remarkable woman.'

Sidney relaxed a little. It sounded like history, an improving subject for young ladies' minds.

John continued, 'Theodora was a courtesan. Her speciality was to lie down naked in public with her legs apart and cover her body with corn seeds. Then geese were allowed to come and eat the seed. Apparently the changing expressions on her face as the geese pecked up the seeds delighted her onlookers.' John cackled to himself. 'Pretty terrific, Eh?' he said to Sam.

Without attempting the useless task of stopping John's conversation, Sidney, Sarah and Ralph all descended on their horrified youngsters and on various pretexts started to shoo them, like a gaggle of geese, into the kitchen.

Sam sat back. It was years since he had been treated to such a performance. John turned to Sam, 'Do you remember all the stories about Evita? How she used to go to the girls' schools to pick schoolgirls for Peron?' Sam nodded enthusiastically.

John turned to me, 'One day at dinner Evita was sitting with her legs apart. She noticed the Archbishop of Buenos Aires gazing between her thighs. "What does your Excellency see?" she asked. "The gates of heaven?"

'"No," the archbishop replied. *"The Casa del Pueblo."*

'The *Casa del Pueblo* means the *House of the People*. It was the name of the socialist club in Buenos Aires.

'I have known over a hundred women,' said John. But I later decided that John's female exploits were probably all verbal. Despite the fact that my father was convinced John had remarried (probably several times, he said) John seemed ignorant of women. 'I was giving an English lesson to a married lady one day, when she hopped on to my knee.' John didn't continue this story, but changed course, 'There was a lady who went on a journey. A friend sent her husband a telegram which read *Negocio* - it means business in Spanish. But he read it backwards, *oi cogen* - today they are making love.'

John paused to see what impression he had produced. Then he went on, aimlessly 'I won a lot of money at the casino at Mara Plata. On the way home a man with a gun stopped me. I threw my hat in his face and escaped. So I decided there's no point in staying in a country where you can't keep your winnings. So I used the money to buy a ticket back to England. That's why I came back.'

John now turned his attention to Sarah's young son: 'Have you heard of Casanova?'

The boy murmured a confused reply of 'Yes.'

'Not many people know the difference between Casanova and Don Juan. Both were famous lovers but Don Juan only loved very beautiful, high-placed ladies. Casanova, who was a librarian, loved anyone from a duchess to a washerwoman. It didn't matter to him.'

It was clear who John admired most. John's impudence had silenced the bourgeois elements. Sam, Ralph and I clustered round him, laughing. Ralph and Sam sat back and started to relax and enjoy their older brother. Together, Ralph and Sam looked and behaved more like twins than brothers, with their high, shining foreheads, their moustaches, their open friendly smiles, and above all their happy, devil-may-care conversation. A stranger leaving the room at the end of a joke or funny story by one of them would have difficulty knowing, when he returned, that the next story was being told by the other. And now John's charm had asserted itself. The years had peeled away. John was destitute, a beggar, begging from those he had wronged, probably a man on a police wanted list. But for us, he represented eternal childhood.

Myer snored quietly in his corner and the meeting was turning into a reunion.

John picked up a biscuit and held it appreciatively between finger and thumb.

'Do you remember the finger breads mother used to make for breakfast?' he asked, his voice dropping respectfully to a purring croak. 'Wonderful!'

He turned to Sam, who nodded, smiling broadly.

'Milk breads, weren't they?' John continued. 'Or what did she call them? Oooh, so many different types ...'

The mundane biscuit, still held aloft unbitten, like a communion wafer, became transformed into a delicate and delicious morsel. John started to nibble its periphery, scattering a shower of crumbs over his waistcoat.

'My mother was a remarkable woman,' he said turning to me and continuing his low honeyed purr of admiration. 'Her concept of the philosophy of time was amazing. She used to say, "It doesn't matter how old you are. Time's all the same." In this philosophy she resembled the ancient Greek philosopher...'

'What can he do?' said Ralph to Myer, laying his hand gently on the wrist of the slumbering head of the family, and waking him with the question.

Myer gave a slight grunt and went back to sleep.

John, waiting until it was clear that Myer was not going to speak, turned accusingly to Ralph and asked 'Do you wear a bowler hat to the office?'

'Yes,' replied Ralph, not taken aback by the suggestion that he took on airs. 'But so did you in your office.'

John mumbled for a moment. 'I suppose I did,' he admitted.

Then he caught sight of one of the young family females again. 'When Link came over to Buenos Aires he asked me to take him to the Palace of Pleasures,' John began. 'There were over three hundred girls ...'

Myer woke up at this point. 'Good God!' he spluttered, and fell asleep again.

In the small parlour, my father had carefully selected a position in a corner of the room where he could sit with his right ear as close as possible to the wall, making it impossible for any speaker to creep round to his deaf right side. Those who knew Harry always approached and sat on his left side, making sure that their lips were completely visible when they spoke. If ever I forgot, my father would remind me with scant ceremony, 'Take your hand away from your mouth when you speak!' or 'Speak to my good ear!' Harry's deafness, however, was not a complete disadvantage. For his eyes, anxiously following every attitude of the unheard speakers, detected much that their words would gladly have concealed.

Unable to hear most of John's mumbled conversation, Harry had tired of the long meeting and his mind had, as usual, wandered along in its own parallel channels. From time to time he hummed, or pursed his lips and frowned at some passing thought. Now he suddenly remembered something. 'Stand up a minute,' he ordered John, and John, without pausing in his talking, shuffled obediently to his feet.

'Put your arm out,' my father said. John held his skinny arms out horizontally, giving an excellent imitation of a scarecrow. My father took a tape-measure from his waistcoat pocket and measured the distance from the middle of John's back to his cuff. Then he took a folded envelope from his other pocket and consulted it.

'Why did you do that?' I asked.

John, meanwhile, was continuing the story of how his guest in Buenos Aires refused the girls who offered him *La Bicicleta* or the *Tableau Vivant*.

'I forgot whether I had taken that measurement,' said my father. 'We are making John a suit. Look at him, he's dressed in rags. And so emaciated.' It was true. John looked like a couple of planks of wood nailed together with an old suit flapping on it. Suddenly I realized what a frail old man stood before me. His speech had been that of an adolescent schoolboy. His eyes twinkled but his body was a wreck. A third of a century of wandering on the South American pampas had wasted it. 'Sit down, John,' said my father, and the word John had a tenderness I had never heard before.

John sat obediently but never stopped talking. I felt very proud of my father.

'Where I stayed in Rosario,' John was saying, 'there was a statue of the

Virgin Mary outside my house, very keen on the Virgin Mary those people. In the end they had to put railings round it to prevent the drunks from molesting her on their way home at night.'

My father heard none of this.

'Your cousin Len (Fanny's son) is making him a new set of teeth,' my father said to me. 'Lenny's a good dentist.' I realized John's teeth didn't fit. He couldn't eat solid food.

Meanwhile John's conversation had changed course. 'The urine from the public urinals was collected by the fullers and used in their dry-cleaning establishments to clean togas.'

'Urine? Togas?' What had I missed? John was happy to repeat it all. He was justifying the action of the Roman Emperor Vespasian in levying a tax of one obol on public lavatories in Rome.

'Vespasian's argument,' John said, 'was a legal one. That urine was property and that the fullers should therefore pay tax on it. Vespasian's son Titus objected that it was beneath the dignity of a Roman Emperor to collect a trifling tax on urine. In reply Vespasian held up an obol, the smallest coin, and said, "*Pecunia non olet* - Money doesn't smell."'

'And that is why,' concluded John, 'public urinals are to this day called *vespasiano* in Spain and Italy and *vespasienne* in France.'

John was looking straight at Sarah. Obviously we had not understood something. John's expression became stern, and he continued, 'You are at Cambridge?' he said to one nephew. 'Yes,' was the meek reply. 'Have you heard of the famous economist Keynes? He was famous for his work on international liquidity.'

During all this John was still looking unblinkingly at his sister Sarah. At last she understood. 'The lavatory is at the top of the stairs on the right,' Sarah said.

'Oh,' said John, feigning surprise, as if he had not enquired. 'Really? Splendid.' And off he went. He paused at the door. 'When the Argentinian dictator Peron was alarmed at some setback, one of his close advisers said, "No tenga miedo mi general. Aún Napoleon tenía su Waterclo. (Do not fear, my general. Even Napoleon had his watercloset)."' John shambled off upstairs.

Sarah turned to me, 'He never talked like that before. Not about women.'

'He is mad,' said her husband. It seemed a good formula to save face.

No one could be responsible for what a mad person said even if he was a relation.

'Well he always ate in bed,' said Sarah, 'and that's a sure sign of madness. Don't you eat in bed?' she asked me. I demurred. 'Oh, but Unky told me that you always do,' Sarah insisted.

What could I say? It was common knowledge that I shared a bed with Myer.

John came back, talking as he entered the room. 'You have studied history?' he asked me. 'Splendid. Do you know which king died in a loo?'

The meeting was breaking up. Sidney appeared with his daughters again to take leave. John took a parting shot at them.

'Who were the four homosexual kings of England?' asked John.

Myer was fast asleep again, and after all, I thought, what were these many different chattering voices but part of Myer's dream?

In fact, while the main performance had been going on so indecisively, the spectators in the parlour were provided with tea and a biscuit, a modest entertainment since the usual ostentatious junketing which marked our normal family reunions at weddings and the like was obviously not appropriate to the return of a renegade after a third of a century of absence. There was no social advantage to be gained out of spending money on John. The frequent journeys to the kitchen to replenish the teapot were the scenario for a complete subplot to be enacted therein. This was an altogether more business-like affair. It was conducted by a largely female cast. The older females, of John's generation, took this opportunity to disclaim all knowledge of John's present disgusting talk. They were embarrassed and felt the need to excuse themselves to their offspring. They did not want their children to imagine that their now respectable bourgeois parents had ever been exposed to such earthy talk. 'He was never like that before,' repeated the uncomfortable parents, shaking their heads disapprovingly. 'Never talked like that about women.'

But this subplot had a much more important, but unspoken purpose. These ladies were trying out each other's strength, trying to decide just how little each of them would be able to contribute to the expense of trying to get rid of John. In the end the bourgeois siblings all went away, nursing their sense of outrage. Myer, Sam and my father, the Leeds contingent, were left to take care of John. Myer's sewing machine rattled again, my father's tailor's shears clacked on the cutting table, and John for the first time in a third of a century was clad again in a hand-made suit of Leeds cloth.

'I had to decide,' said John, 'whether I was a tragic hero or a fairy tale hero. I decided I was a fairy tale hero.'

But the sonnet written to his daughter from his exile in Argentina shows quite another side:

These meagre gleanings from the barren years
A long-missed father sends. Daughterless tears
Watered the furrows that a stubborn field
Refused a richer harvest for its yield.
The past here to your filial gaze revealed
Is tenebrous but in its gloom concealed
There lies pure gold, the memory of the morn
When you, resplendent to these shores were borne.
Three months from out each year Ceres forewent
Two months alone by you with me were spent
In a whole year. To the Goddess of Corn
Returned her maiden. From that vanished dawn
Rests but your image. Back to me is sent
No living likeness for my heart's content.

Getting Rid of John

On the way back from the meeting in Leicester I took my father and Myer to see a famous beauty spot. A baroque palace floated on an ornamental lake. Great avenues of trees formed a guard of honour for a noble duke. The two brothers strode out along the carriageway, Myer, with his bald head and stumpy gait, looking the image of Winston Churchill, for whom the palace was an ancestral home, but a comparison which would have greatly offended Myer's socialist temper. My father sniffed the air. 'What an odour of sanctity!' he said.

I began to enthuse on the history of this elegant place. My father listened, unimpressed. 'The history of England,' he said and paused, 'the history of any country, is nothing more than an account of the bitter, continuous struggle of the common people against their rulers, the kings and queens, the dukes, barons, earls...'

He paused again, ruminating bitterly. 'As for that ruffian Edward VIII, it was said of him that he retired from being First Admiral of the British Fleet to take up the post of second mate on an American destroyer. Kings and queens, they're nothing more than a bloodthirsty gang of thieves and murderers, with a thin veneer of civilisation. Usually not even that.'

Myer smiled furtively at me, as if to say, 'He does go on.'

'What do you think, Unky?' I asked.

'Live and let live,' Myer replied.

'Let's be going,' said my father. We had only walked hurriedly around.

'What's the hurry?' asked Myer, lingering over the view of the lake with its Italianate bridge. 'I don't expect I'll see it again.'

Despite great complainings, the family conference in the kitchen at Leicester had raised just enough money to send John back to Argentina. But their fear of scandal was not over. Getting rid of John did not turn out as easy as they had hoped. Within a year he was hankering to come back to England.

All the years after Sam had left Argentina in 1941, John had never written a word to his parents. They had gone to their graves convinced he had died before them. Now he started to bombard the family with letters.

La Lucila, Argentina, April 8 / 65

Dear Geoffrey,

I was delighted to hear from you, and I am looking forward as impatiently as you are to our meeting as soon as possible, and the spirit of adventure that animates you finds a ready response in me.

As far as my staying in England is concerned, it was certainly not my original intention to do so, though after the enthusiastic reception I received from certain members of the family (including yourself as not the least of them) I felt inclined to alter my plans. But in the end I decided that we were all of us much too near the events to appraise them properly, and that my return to the Argentine for a short while would provide the necessary breathing space. My idea at the moment is to pay a hurried visit to England. Perhaps in view of the fears expressed by some of the family, I shall adopt a disguise when I walk abroad.

As no letter can be complete without some reference to him who doth bestride the family like a Colossus - my dear brother Jeremy - I should like to state that I am quite satisfied at not having seen him, and my desire to see him was really in contradiction to a principle expressed by De Quincey in his essay on Murder Considered as one of the Fine Arts. This lays down that a person who is a public figure is not a proper subject to be murdered. A public figure has no real existence. Jeremy is too much of a public figure to have any real existence.

I am submitting myself to medical examination. Of course in these cases I believe the subjective element is much greater than the objective. Each doctor sees what he wants to see. The doctor is making a discovery of the X-ray findings, and I am having to deliver a sample of my tax-free urine, which I smuggled into the country past the Customs without declaring its value for inspection. Other modern equivalents of the tortures employed in the Spanish Inquisition, such as blood examination, are being applied. I will let you know the findings in due course. If adverse, my departure from the country will be hastened.

Freud was of the opinion that successful Swiss bankers collect postage stamps and retain their excrement. In order to rescue my financial affairs from chaos and confusion, and get back to England, I shall have to indulge in a continuous course of constipation and avoid all recourse to laxatives and supposi- tories. So it is immaterial to me whether toilet paper is single, as it was before I left England in 1931, and as it still is in the Argentine, or double as in England now. It may even be tripled or quadruplicated by later scientific discoveries. Though I have been compelled to hand over my urine to the doctors' henchmen - or rather henchwomen - I shall resolutely retain my excrement.

Yours affectionately,

John

P.S. In view of J's crowning infamy in having become a director of Glaxo, I am quite content at not having seen him. The danger that threatens both of us is that he might visit me if I settle in England.

To raise the money for this anticipated return, John first decided to tackle his admirer, Sam:

Lisbon, Jan 14th 1966

Dear Sam,

I have just received a letter from Geoffrey in which he tells me that you and Myer were strongly opposed to my coming. If I had gathered from your last letter that your opposition was so extreme, I should certainly never have left the Argentine. I was rather surprised at not receiving a letter from you, as you had promised to send me a further fifty pounds. Had you done so,

I should have paid the return fare, taking advantage of the 10% discount and the difference in the two money rates in the Argentine.

Although I was doubtful when I wrote you, I had already made up my mind to do so. I should like to recapitulate the circumstances in order that we may see clearly what seems a confused situation. When you promised to help me with a monthly remittance, it was never my idea to subject you to a permanent burden. I looked upon it and still do as a temporary loan to tide me over a difficult period until I could become self-supporting.

If this action of mine has caused you and Myer any worries, I deeply regret it. It was undertaken with the idea of making things easier for you. It is often very difficult to know what decision to make. If I have acted irresponsibly in your opinion, you will forgive me, realising that it is part of my struggle for existence and not a wild adventure. Will write you further from Spain and Love to you and your family, Myer, Harry and Celia.

John

This elicited an anguished letter from my father:

Leeds, Tuesday, 18th Jan

Dear Geoff,

You will see from the enclosure what an utterly irresponsible creature John is. He has been told in the plainest terms that money is not to be had. The 'wealthier' will not help and the poorer cannot. In spite of all that was written to him, he has involved himself in an expenditure of what is to us a very large sum of money, which from his letter he expects us to find. Sam, Myer and myself are too disgusted and dismayed to know what to do about him. He always was an intractable problem and always will be. He appears to think that you and Fanny encourage him in his peregrinations and if this is so, I should wish you to disillusion him if you can.

Affec, Daddy

P.S. 'Gambler' is the saddest and most tragic word I know. Neglecting any natural gifts he may possess, and heedless of any opportunities his mature talent may offer, he casts his all at the mercy of blind chance, and spends his life glued to the poverty line, stumbling through a desert of alternating fears and hopes, chasing a mirage. Whilst those who knew him best watch with despair the early promise wither and the hopes and ambitions for him dashed to the ground.

But the wandering John was inescapable. Now I found that my own hero worship of John was getting me involved. And John was doing his very best to keep it so.

La Lucila, Argentina, Feb 9th 1966

Dear Geoffrey,

It was with great pleasure that I received your letters which confirm, what I had noticed from the first, in the historic meeting at Leicester that we take the same attitude towards life, and hence our futures are destined to be inextricably interlinked. If you chance to read any of my poetry, remember what Horace says, 'Painters and poets have always enjoyed the same licence to venture on anything.'

I must apologize for having kept you so long without an answer to your letters, but I have been waiting for the news from the family, since the non-receipt of same may seriously affect my plans for the future. As an Epicurean god who sits above the thunder in undying ease I can give way neither to rage nor depression. My equanimity cannot be disturbed by the fact that my brothers, who see things as through a glass darkly, fail to burn incense on my altar...

As far as my own position is concerned, the family have dealt me what, if I were not a Fairy Tale Hero, would have been a knock-out blow. In spite of their promise, they have sent me no money since the first week in December, and have not even let me know what is happening, to enable me to take steps to protect myself in the struggle for existence. As a consequence, having practically no lessons for the summer, I am compelled to use prestige instead of money.

Spengler, in his 'Decline of the West,' says that our Western Civilisation invented contrapuntal music and credit democracy. You take the democracy with your ordinary people, and I take the credit with my prestige.

It is pleasing to note that the thesis that 'life copies literature' is justified in my case. You remember that in the fairy tales, the hero who is the third son is just about to live happily ever afterwards when the two wicked brothers put a spoke in the wheel and attempt to destroy him. Myer and Jeremy are the two elder brothers and I am the third son. It is rather ironic to think of poor Myer as a wicked brother.

In spite of all difficulties, it is my intention to return to Europe this summer. Toynbee in his Study of History makes play of the fact that the great man or great nation has a long period of withdrawal until it returns to play its part in the full light of history. The withdrawal in my case has lasted 33 years. It is time for the return.

The lack of funds may cause a delay of a month or so. I like your confidence in my ability to overcome difficulties, and to get through life without being worried by material consider-ations. In the present crisis, the adventurer and the soldier of fortune has to abandon the ivory tower of the philosopher and become a man of action. I shall let you know later development.

Your affectionate Uncle John

Reading this letter, I felt that I had to admit my father was right, John was indeed an intractable case. Any lingering doubts about John's innocence were over. I began to see him as a captive struggling desperately to awake from someone else's, Myer's, dream.

My passivity was soon rewarded by another letter:

Dear Geoffrey,

Not having heard from you, I have a feeling that my last letter may have produced an unfavourable impression on you, and that certain expressions I used therein might have been misinterpreted. It was my impression that it would not meet with a favourable reception on the part of your father or your Uncle Myer.

It might seem that what I said about my brothers was base treachery on my part, especially in view of their very generous treatment of me. I believe Myer to be the noblest, most self-sacrificing and disinterested person in the world. And at every moment in the family history, in the most difficult circumstances, he has always responded to any call made on him. He took an enormous amount of trouble looking after me, and, at the last moment, gave an astonishing display of his nobility and generosity when he saw me off. Your father is equally disinterested as far as he himself is concerned, and also gave every manifestation of his brotherly love. But both of them wish for you what they do not desire for themselves, the fame and fortune which they consider the adequate reward of your genius. In this respect, they are not at all interested in research or scholarship, except as it is represented by the outward success of which Jeremy is an outstanding example.

I have the same deep attachment to the family which I know you to have, and would never harbour any sentiments that were hostile to its unity. You might think that the description in my last letter was infelicitous, but as I have the most complete confidence in you, I felt quite certain that there could be no doubt in your mind as to my meaning. If your silence means that you have finally discovered that your idol has feet of clay, I am not at all surprised, conscious as I am of my many imperfections. In that case I release you from any promises you have made to me. But if you are still of the same mind, I shall return to Europe by Easter.

There is more I could write but I await your response before treating of subjects more worthy of the frivolous Muse. You will notice that I have changed my digs, owing to a pecuniary difficulty with the hotel-keeper. Fighting with landlords is a favourite amusement of mine in the slack season.

It may be that, owing to my having been away for so long, I have lost touch with things, and have completely misunderstood the situation with reference to you. You will as a consequence, have to be guided by your own inner light without taking into account what I think.

With love to you and the family,

Your affectionate Uncle John

And despite all the family could do John came back to England, once again penniless. Once again they packed him off to Argentina. And once again he came back. His shambling gait did not seem able to sustain such wanderings. His bald head with its fringe of white hair, and his sticking out ears made him look more and more like Gandhi, a bent, emaciated figure with a crab-like shuffle, as if thick layers of dhoti cloth were wrapped between his skinny thighs. His fingernails were filthy and broken; he had never learned to use a knife. His glasses were always half-opaque. But behind them twinkled the most youthful and mischievous eyes. His eyes never grew old.

Now there was not enough money to send him back again. So the family, always worried that he might be arrested, arranged for him to go to Genoa. But John seemed to have acquired a sense of being Spanish.

'*El que tiene alquilado el culo no puede sentarse quando quiere*,' he said. (He who has a hired-out arse cannot sit down when he pleases.)

So, like Columbus, John went from Genoa to Spain. But John had no wish to go back to the New World. 'Do you think,' he taunted his outraged family 'the price of fallen women is higher in Spain or in Portugal?'

John's to-ings and fro-ings had lasted the entire period of my university course. At last I passed my final examinations and obtained a college prize. This began to soften the family's anger at my marriage, and all four brothers all expressed themselves in their own particular ways:

Leeds

Dear Geoff,

We have received your always welcome letter. I am very pleased to learn that your interest in academics is back to its old standard. I too hope that once you are settled down you will find happiness and contentment in your work and domesticity. You must never think that any of us here think of you with anything but affection and kindness and always have your interest at heart. We are always prepared to help you and if at times we have differed from you as to a proposed line of action, we have always been animated with a desire to further your best interest. However, the differences are now past and gone and I sincerely hope that the future will bring you success.

The telephone rang at about 10 this a.m, with the message that the Bridge Upholstery had been broken into and petty cash to the tune of £70 or £80 in Mammy's charge had been taken. M. has been in a state of great excitement. Obviously this was superior to T.V. It had actually happened in real life. M. was taken down by car to the C.I.D, watched fingerprints being taken, volunteered a lot of information, useful and useless, and generally had a wonderful experience. She has not yet simmered down, and having gone through the entire rogue's gallery from Dick Turpin through Charles Peace down to the present day, has delivered herself of the most extraordinary opinions. I am quite thankful she is at Coles' at the moment. Let them suffer.

I should apologise for my scanty letter writing, but I really have been very busy with my own work and helping Sam in his new venture.

Yours affec

Daddy.

P.S. I have been considering why the night sky is dark despite the existence of millions of great suns all emitting light in all directions. Dare I put forward a suggestion - viz. light when subjected to gravitation gives up some of its inherent qualities to every source of attraction, with the result that only a very attenuated beam eventually reaches the earth. This suggestion may be treated with contumely. I don't mind, but having thought of it, I had no one else to burden with it but you.

I have been considering why the night sky is dark

My academic success also brought a forgiving letter from Sir Jeremy:

Flat 5, 16 St James's Street
London S.W.1
Whitehall 4751

Dear Geoffrey,

I send you my belated but very sincere congratulations in securing the Theodore Williams Scholarship in Anatomy. I am very happy to know that besides the financial advantage it has completely rehabilitated you with the Pembroke College authorities. This has its pleasant effects for me, for on the last occasion when I dined at the High Table I was not a little embarrassed by the circumstances attending the forfeiture of your college scholarship, which your tutor thought I might have been able to influence. However, that is all past history, and I am grateful to you for the magnificent achievement which has eased my position.

I send you my best wishes for a continuance of your successful career. Also a cheque for £25 as a belated wedding present - and an olive branch!

Yours
Jerry

P.S.

Don't quote to me Sam Johnson's letter to Lord Chesterfield, "Is not a patron, my Lord, one who looks with unconcern on a man struggling for life in the water, and when he has reached dry land, encumbers him with help?" The circumstances are different.

This welcome letter helped soothe my guilty conscience and I wrote of it to John. John now replied with a very different appraisal of Sir Jeremy:

Avenida Principe de Asturias, 11
Barcelona

Dear Geoffrey,

I was delighted to receive your letter and to learn about Jeremy's letter.

369

It does not surprise me that you have found him so likeable. It corresponds to the picture of his true self which I have always had. Before I came to Leicester and telephoned him I was telling him what a great admiration I had for him and still have.

The question of the Decline of our Western Civilization links itself with Jeremy's comments on modern youth and communism. Whilst I admire Jeremy very much, I don't quite see that the argument against them not being constructive necessarily condemns them. They are prisoners trying to free themselves from the bonds of tradition, the heritage of our complex civilization.

I read through the modern Greek grammar you sent and did all the exercises in a couple of days. Apart from a few simplifications, it is not much different from Ancient Greek. The difficulty is the change in pronunciation from what we learned for Attic Greek. I am sure that if I went to Greece, I should be speaking the language quite fluently in less than a week.

With love to you and the family,

John

I also phoned Myer at once, and read Jeremy's letter over the phone to him. His response was rather different from John's:

Leeds

Dear Geoff,

Many many thanks for your phone message last night. I deeply appreciate your desire to please me. You rightly recognised that I would be profoundly pleased with Jeremy's letter. Having been instrumental in soliciting his interest on your behalf, I had been very unhappy that your marriage should have caused estrangement between you. As for the letter itself, I think it is splendid. He has apologised most handsomely. Apart from his fulsome praise of your achievement, I hope it will soon be possible for him to visit you in your new home. And now I just wish to repeat how overjoyed I am at this turn of events. Jeremy's letter will perhaps help you to understand the constancy of my devotion to the kid brother of my earlier years.

You will recall how ill I was when you were last here. I have not improved since. Without going into details, I have not been out since mid-December. I have been warned that it is dangerous for me to go out in wintry weather.

I was pleased to hear that you are still having your Sunday bridge parties. It brings back many hours I had with you all.

I am having some eye trouble, so please excuse my closing now.

Love
Unky

Two Spades

And Moses went up from the plains of Moab unto the mountain of Nebo. And the Lord showed him all the land unto the utmost sea. And the Lord said unto him: This is the land which I sware I will give it to thy seed. Now I have caused thee to see it with thine own eyes, but thou shalt not go thither.

Deuteronomy 34

I was only just back from a year in America. All the while Myer's illness had not got better. I got a call from my father, 'Unky wants to talk to you. I'll pass him the phone.'

'Wait!' I commanded. 'First tell me how he's been?'

'Not so good. Here he is. He'll tell you himself. Speak clearly. He's having trouble with his hearing aid.'

'OK.'

I waited. There was a lot of shuffling in the background.

Then, 'Geoff?' Myer's familiar, soft, crackling voice.

'Yes,' I replied loudly.

I heard finger nails scrabbling frantically at a hearing-aid pressed to the phone. The hearing-aid whined higher and higher, rising to an almost painfully loud screech, then falling soft again and extinguished, like the heterodyne whistle as a lone wireless operator stranded on a jungled Pacific island turned the wavelength dial of his radio, desperately searching the airwaves for a human contact.

'Unky!' I shouted.

No answer, some more shuffling, then again, agonisingly, 'Geoff?'

I jumped to my feet, pulling the phone up to the maximum stretch of its cable, and 'Yes,' I shouted at the top of my voice, holding the phone in front of my mouth like a microphone to get the maximum loudness and the minimum distortion, then rapidly placing the receiver to my ear.

At the other end I heard muttering, aside, 'It's no bleddy good,' Myer was saying to my father, 'I can't hear.'

I waited. Then, into the phone, Myer spoke again. He was relaxed now, resigned and comforting. He'd worked out what he wanted to say and his rich, Brahmsian voice spread over me like a warm rug.

372

'Geoff, I can't hear you but I know you can hear me. It's all over with me. We're waiting for the ambulance to take me to hospital. I just want to tell you: I've had my life. Now you have yours. Do well. Enjoy it. And be happy.'

'Unky, Unky,' I shouted, 'I'm coming up to Leeds.'

There was no reply, only a shuffling at the other end, some muttering which I could not catch, and then a click as the phone was put down. I could not accept this was the end of the banquet. I drove up to Leeds.

He was lying in bed with the white winter sunlight streaming over the back of the Town Hall and through the tall grimy windows of the ward. 'We'll soon get you out of here,' I said.

'Me,' Myer smiled wryly, and he changed to the broad Yorkshire accent that he liked to use in moments of intense irony. 'The only place I'm going is t' boneyard.' He laughed. 'Kicking daisies.'

'I picked up an interesting hand at lunch-time yesterday,' I replied. Myer's eyes twinkled. 'It had 17 points and a strong AQ10 to 5 times spades, but not 8 quick playing tricks. The question was whether to bid an unadventurous one spade, or take a chance and go up aggressively for two spades.'

Myer nodded approvingly, to show he agreed with my call of two spades. I was pleased to have got the approval of the master and turned away, thinking the matter was at an end. But Myer stirred restlessly in the bed, as if something was still unsaid, looking up at me, raising his eyebrows questioningly.

My father, used to not hearing anything himself, clearly understood what Myer wanted, and nudged me with his elbow, 'He wants to know what happened. Did you make it, the two spades contract?'

'Yes,' I said loudly to Myer. 'I made it.' Myer smiled and settled back.

Myer's smoke-ravaged lungs could barely supply the oxygen needed for his brain. Over the next two days his consciousness flickered as he passed in and out of a kind of delirium. I saw his mind in glimpses, as one sees the sun, momentarily revealed between the scudding clouds of a stormy day. But the shortness of Myer's future did not reduce his interest in the world.

In a clear moment he described to me in detail the odd visions of his over-clouded hours. No situation was too strange for him to apply his curious analytic intellect to it. Like Socrates after taking the hemlock,

Myer was giving his pupil a blow-by-blow account of the end.

Myer looked fondly at me and said, 'I dreamt you were in America... you were getting a prize or something, an honour... it was a great hall... there were columns on either side... statues...' And here Myer stopped with a final snort of self-mockery at how ridiculous it all was, his hopes and all for which he had striven over such a long, strange path and rested back on the pillow.

At the New Synagogue on Chapeltown Road, the beadle was the same Mr Segal who had been beadle in my younger days, when I had first gone with Myer to see the wondrous opening of the ark. Now Mr Segal too was very old and quite decrepit. With a holy razor he made the ceremonial cuts in the mourners' clothes, symbolising the rending of the garments. Originally they were made in the lapels of the jackets, but a less spiritual generation economised and had them made in their ties instead.

Myer's funeral crossed that Victorian arched bridge of delicately carved sandstone over which his grandfather Hoshy and his parents had crossed before. There was hardly any vestige of the narrow little streets from which the slum kids had once pelted Jewish funerals with stones. We passed unmolested and unnoticed, and took the hill road to Gildersome. We seemed to have arrived so quickly. In the burial chapel I stood by the coffin during the ceremony and was filled with an urge to pat its lid and laugh with Myer at the pomposity of the service. He had always enjoyed debunking ritual.

Myer's grave was in a plot reserved for him in the very oldest part of the cemetery. There couldn't be half a dozen spaces left and then it would be full. Giving him this place was a last honour from the community where he had spent his eighty years. The graves here were very old and decrepit, many of the soft sandstone memorials illegible. The scorched ground, cracked by the wind, grew withered rayless mayweed, its golden globules devoid of fragrance. The remains of a low brick wall separated the Yurberick graves from the Marienpolers' burial ground. Broken bits of ornamental ironwork lay rusting under the branches of a stunted oak. A straggly rhododendron and one solitary little rosebush, white with mildew, were all that man had planted, but scrub was spreading in from the surrounding ragged fields as tousled Yorkshire reclaimed its borrowed ground.

At the graveside the men formed a disconsolate little queue, to pick up the spade and throw a few clods of earth on the coffin. Each passed the spade to the next in line. As there was a gap after me, I laid the spade on the pile of newly turned earth. The rabbi stepped forward and reproved me sharply. 'Don't put it down with the blade facing out! Always put the blade in the earth!' I wondered if there was somewhere a book of rules, with clear, written instruction on the techniques to be followed when putting down spades at funerals. Maybe, at this raw moment, when the connection between this world and the next was open, the normally innocent, simple spade temporarily acquired magical destructive powers, and could have been pointed fatally at an enemy. I decided that the rabbi would definitely have bid one spade and not two.

The Knight of Number Eleven

In Spain, John had taken lodgings in a decrepit, roomy old apartment in Barcelona. He enjoyed the light and the heat of the city. Its noise didn't bother him and the outward-looking, liberal Catalonian people were to his taste.

Barcelona is a city set out on a regular rectangular plan, with streets crossing at right angles. Across this plan, diagonally from corner to corner, the wide central avenue cuts a straight course at an angle to all the other streets. After the Franco forces had finally captured Barcelona, at the end of the Civil War, they had named this central avenue the *Avenida Generalíssimo Franco*. The citizens, who hated Franco, never used this name. They simply called it *El Diagonal*.

On Barcelona Station John was fascinated by a group of hippies. He noticed that they were required to observe strict social rules, such as wearing long hair and dirty clothes, and smoking marijuana. They spoke a special jargon, had their own music, and despised the older, wealthier generation, who they called 'the system'. Apparently these particular hippies accepted John because of his tramp-like appearance. They thought of him as a man of their world.

'Do you know where I can get b*****m in Barcelona?' one of them asked him.

'No,' said John.

'I'd never heard the word before,' John told me later. 'It sounded like some kind of fruit conserve.'

John's lodging was Number 11 in the *Avenida Principe de Asturias*, the Avenue of the Prince of Asturias. John liked this name. He would refer to himself as *El Caballero de las Once*, the *Knight of Number Eleven*, after the style of Don Quixote. His landlady, Aurora, was an old lady who came from a once distinguished Catalonian family, now fallen on hard times. Aurora's husband, a retired civil servant, was old and bed-ridden and Aurora took John and another lodger to help pay the rent. From Aurora John began to learn about Catalonia. 'She was a very intelligent woman,' he said. 'She was always asking my advice about crosswords.'

John seemed to find Aurora glamorous. It was nothing about her person. She was plump, matronly, rather short-sighted, and not a little decayed. What attracted him was her name. Aurora was the ancient Greek goddess of the Dawn. 'When Tithonus was a young man,' John said, 'he was so good looking that the goddess Aurora fell in love with him. She was so enchanted she offered to fulfil any request he made. Tithonus asked for immortality and the goddess granted it. However, although he didn't die, he grew older and older, because he had forgotten to ask for youth. In the end he prayed for death. Tennyson describes it in his poem, *Tithonus*:

> *The woods decay, the woods decay and fall,*
> *The vapours weep their burthen to the ground,*
> *Man comes and tills the field and lies beneath,*
> *And after many a summer dies the swan.*
> *Me only cruel immortality*
> *Consumes: I wither slowly in thine arms,*
> *Here at the quiet limit of the world,*
> *A white-haired shadow roaming like a dream*
> *The ever-silent spaces of the East,*
> *Far-folded mists, and gleaming halls of morn.'*

John's fellow lodger was a bald-headed old man who used to pester John for translations of Shakespeare. In return he entertained John with his strange habits. Every morning at breakfast he would take five slices of bread, lay them out on the table before him in a fixed pattern and solemnly eat them in a set order. This never varied.

'What did you eat in Spain?' I asked John.

'Spanish omelette, fruits, I went to the market,' John replied.

'Which fruits?'

'Peaches, strawberries,' John mentioned the most unlikely diet. 'In Catalonia they eat strawberries with vinegar,' he went on.

I couldn't imagine John, with his sweet tooth could like that.

'With vinegar?' I asked, surprised.

'There was a lunatic asylum,' John said, 'where they decided to take the inmates out to learn farming. The idea was to soothe them. One inmate was watching the farmer spreading manure on his strawberry patch.

'"What are you doing?" asked the lunatic.

'"Putting manure on the strawberries," replied the farmer.

'"Well," said the lunatic, surprised, but with humility, "I always put cream on my strawberries, but then, I'm mad."'

377

Avenida Principe de Asturias 11

Dear Geoffrey,

You would like to hear about my progress. You make me think I am fleeing from a world on the point of destruction. And indeed, escaping from our declining W.C. I have found salvation in the strangest of places - in a girls' school. Incidentally, I don't know whether your idea of me is influenced by your knowledge of Freudian theories. All myths of returning heroes, according to them, really express a desire to return to the womb. Thus as a returning hero, it is rational for me to have this desire, feeling as I do the agony of separation from the womb by the cutting of the umbilical cord.

In your letter you ask me to write about my mother, but in view of the fact that such a study might err on the side of MGM-ism (Hollywood sentimentality), I prefer to defer it and substitute a study of Jeremy. Actually, I can understand what appears to you as Jeremy's aloofness. The family was too close for him.

To return to my teaching, I am working 9 hours a week and earning a little more than five pounds a week, which is sufficient to keep me in comfort. I teach on Tuesday and Thursday evenings in Barcelona, and on Friday mornings I travel to the girls' school, which is situated in a seaside mountain resort in the province of Gerona, about 80 miles from Barcelona, in the direction of France.

I am the only male in the establishment, and I receive every attention from the headmistress and the staff. The taking off of my weight, you see, was evidently the preparation designed by the Fates to enable me to be sufficiently debonair to be a Squire of Dames. I now weigh more or less what I did sixty years ago, when I was a student, and am in the best of health. I have dropped about a quarter of my weight and I am in excellent condition for teaching. I have never been so brilliant. My pupils are filled with an unbounded enthusiasm. The headmistress and vice-principal and the teachers all attend all my classes. The headmistress congratulated me after I gave my first lesson. They all admire me greatly and consider that I am unique as a teacher of English, and indeed I am. My Dear Fellow, there is not a teacher of English in the state of Spain

378

can hold a candle to me! I can teach in one year what the average teacher cannot teach in three years.

John

The girls' school was a convent which belonged to a strict teaching order of nuns, the Order of Clarissa. The only man who had ever been in there was a holy priest. The Fairy Tale Hero was accepted at once. The grave Mother Superior cherished him. He taught Latin and English. 'Strange,' he said 'for a Leylands Jew to be teaching Latin to Spanish Catholic nuns.'

When he had first been appointed to teach at the convent John had rather coyly asked the nuns if he should teach the girls modern English. 'Certainly,' they told him.

'Splendid,' he replied. So he began with what the schoolgirls wanted to know, how to say, 'I love you,' and, 'Give me a kiss.' The Mother Superior didn't object but had a nun sit in the class with him to keep order while he taught. The girls' English developed rapidly.

'Wordsworth,' said John, 'expressed a view that the new-born child comes from a heavenly home, where its immortal soul knew purity. As children grow up, they forget this knowledge. Wordsworth says "Shades of the prison house begin to close upon the growing boy." Now, if this view of Wordsworth is correct, it's perfectly obvious that education has no value whatever, quite the contrary:

Our birth is but a sleep and a forgetting,
But trailing clouds of glory do we come,
The Child is Father of the man.

'In other words, we come already bearing these divine ideas, and lose them as we grow up. Mind you, Plato takes a different view from Wordsworth. Plato accepts education. Plato says that when you come into the world you forget what you knew in your heavenly home, and therefore education is a species of remembrance, what he called *anamnesia* - unforgetting.'

Part of John's theory of education was that he never disciplined his pupils. So he saw no reason why the children shouldn't eat their sandwiches in class if they wanted to and he left discipline to others to maintain or not as they pleased. As a lawyer, John believed that the purpose of law is to reform the criminal not to punish him.

The Mother Superior was concerned about John's physical pleasures. She found out his needs and likes, made him tea, and had him accommodated in the convent. For her he brought back from England a whistling kettle, a teapot, a rubber hot water bottle for the cold Pyrenean nights, and all his favourite sauces, Daddy's, HP, but above all his beloved Lea and Perrin's Worcestershire Sauce. In this way he dutifully assisted the Mother Superior in her desire to make him comfortable. In the convent he was able to study the officially discouraged Catalonian language around which all the local anti-Franco sentiment centred. Living languages attracted him. He marvelled at the delicate way the pious Mother Superior, when irritated did not say *Drat*! but *Me cag' en diez*. (I shit on ten: *diez* is a euphemism for *Dios*, God).

The religious sentiment of the Catalonians finds an outlet in the pilgrimage to the mountain grotto of the Virgin of Montserrat. John visited this shrine, and sent back a poem about the toilets:

Montserrat

Virgin of Montserrat
I with my Panama hat
Totemic vestigial gear
Thy grottic presence revere.

How shall our W.C.*
Not an A One but a B
By some miraculous sign
Arrest its early decline.

Only a virginal power
In our most critical hour
From this their bodily grave
Our damned souls can save.

(*W.C., Western Civilisation; 'A One,' first-class)

But for all his bravado John was running from one place to another. He had to take a long train journey from the convent to a college in Barcelona, where he also taught several days a week. The Mother Superior worried about him. One day he left the convent a little late. It was essential for him to get to Barcelona in time for his evening class. 'I'll pray to the Virgin Mary for you,' said the anxious Mother Superior.

380

John shambled off but missed his train despite the Mother Superior's prayers. He caught the next one and arrived late in Barcelona Station. Now, instead of having time to walk to his college, as he usually did, he had to catch a taxi. On his small income it was a major financial blow.

As he got out the taxi driver quoted the fare. John gave him what both John and the driver thought was a thousand peseta note. The driver gave John his change. Only later John noticed that both he and the taxi driver had been mistaken. The note John had given was of a hundred pesetas, smaller in fact than what he had been given in change. John had arrived at his college in time and had actually made a profit on the journey. 'When I told the Mother Superior,' John said, 'she smiled and said, "The Virgin Mary works in mysterious ways." '

John taught at the convent for a few years but in the end, despite the prayers of the Mother Superior, his health became too poor. He was taken to hospital in Barcelona, where the medical bills soon exhausted his small funds. The Virgin Mary, who had been so helpful with the taxi fare, did not seem inclined to make any more miraculous economic interventions on his behalf, so he flew back to England where he was to pass his last short time.

A little before he left Barcelona his landlady's husband had died. Her needs were now fewer and she dispensed with her second lodger but kept John. In the end she proposed marriage to him. John, 80 years old, was deeply flattered. Barcelona is a rich city by the sea. Rising steeply out of the town on the seaward side is a tall hill which the citizens call the *Tibidabo*. The reason for this odd name is to be found in a chapel on the summit. From here a splendid panorama of the city spreads out. Within the chapel, in the wall facing the town below, is a stained glass window with a biblical scene from the temptation of Christ. Christ is seen in the desert, cast down and naked. Overshadowing his half-prostrate body is a magnificent Satan, in rich flowing robes. Satan's arm is extended flamboyantly, his open hand pointing to a picture set in the stained glass panels. The picture shows the rich city of Barcelona which lies on the other side of the window. Satan is offering the city to Christ, with the condition set out below the picture. It is in Latin, from the Vulgate:

Haec omnia tibi dabo
    (All these things I will give to you)
Si caedens adoraveris me

(If, falling, you will worship me)

Christ's answer is not recorded on the window:

Post me Satan!
(Get thee behind me, Satan)

John refused Aurora's offer. He could have spent the end of his life in ease, in Barcelona, *El Caballero de las Once*, enjoying her Spanish omelettes. Who can tell why he returned to England? Maybe he felt the strange pull of the dark northern city where he was born.

When he returned to England he came to live in London with Fanny's son Lenny and his wife Dena. In return for their hospitality, John talked incessantly. Night after night all the experiences and thoughts of his life poured out. John's habits changed. He started to became an ascetic and take his tea without sugar. 'In view of the fact,' he explained, 'that I have put on weight, and have grown so disgustingly fat that most people think I look thinner, the whole thing seems ridiculous. I must prepare to diminish, like the Jain sages for whom the greatest virtue of old age was to starve yourself slowly to extinction.'

John's walk was indescribable. It had the characteristics of prancing and shuffling at the same time. What should I say? A mincing shamble? It attracted favourable attention from females of all ages. Once, when he was walking down the street with me, he dropped his disgustingly tobacco-stained, creased handkerchief. A lady passer-by flew at it, and handed it back with the strange, reverential mixture of maternalism and lust that he seemed to evoke.

John became a pilgrimage for the young ladies he had taught English in Spain. They sought him out, brought him offerings of goodwill and blessings from the Mother Superior, spent their meagre au-pair wages to buy him presents, wrote him letters, and sat admiringly at his feet. And, looking straight into their eyes he acknowledged them by a quotation from the Rubaiyat:

Ah moon of my delight that knows no wane,
The moon of heaven is rising once again.
How often rising, on this same spot,
Shall look for me in vain.

To a young admirer who once wrote to him and mentioned proudly that she had managed, by dieting, to lose some weight, John wrote back, 'I note that you have lost some weight. I hope that when I see you next, there will be enough of your body left for me to embrace.'

John wore a jaunty, dirty, old red-brown hat. Its rakish angle always gave him a mischievous, racy air. He was very vain. I showed him a photograph of himself as a First World War officer, seated beside my father. John looked on his own open face and big ears. 'What does that photograph of me tell you?' he asked. It was not meant for me to answer.

That's my Roman Emperor look

'What innocence!' he went on. 'Did you know that the artist Kramer wanted to use me as a model for a portrait of Christ?'

I photographed him, staring straight at the camera, knuckles clenched, pipe fiercely gripped in his jaws. His trilby sat at the same rakish angle as long ago. 'That's my Roman Emperor look,' he said.

Then I showed him a photograph of his brother Jeremy. 'Oh!' John exclaimed. 'This is the great Jeremy! You can see there a thinker, the family genius, you can see the genius there can't you? The genius, the sophisticated one. Look at that. You see there a man who has examined the smile of the Mona Lisa. Now gaze upon this portrait of me. As Hamlet says:

> *Look here, upon this picture, and on this.*
> *Now, gaze upon Hamlet's father and Hamlet's uncle.*

'Obviously I was destined to fall a victim to the more sophisticated. Whereas look at my brother Jeremy. He's a man will always master the world. I, on the contrary, am too innocent, too impractical. I'm the one that will only arrive at truth by a long road of suffering, the Via Dolorosa. But after I have the agony and the suffering I will arrive at the truth. I will always wear my heart on my sleeve. All my history is written in that photograph.' John paused, looked at the picture of himself as an open-faced teenager, and then went on, 'Gaze upon it, and you know everything that's going to happen to me. Obviously I will be so optimistic that I will believe that it's only necessary for me to enter into a casino to abstract thousands from it. I could never possibly believe that money could ever be taken from me. You see, I'm so innocent that I believed that anybody in the world would open their hands to pour fortune into my lap. That's my innocence.'

Dena was fascinated by John and impressed by the trail of young female pilgrims crossing the snowy Pyrenees and the fair fields of France and daring the dark fogs of London to find their way through the maze of suburban Streatham streets to seek out the saintly relic staying in her house. She admired the pair of yellow silk pyjamas a 17-year old brought reverentially to John and listened, spell-bound to every word John had to say. 'I'm normally a very late person anyway,' she said, 'but after John came I got so little sleep. I was always very tired at work because I had to get up in the morning. John, of course, stayed in bed till afternoon.'

Finally Dena arranged for John to live nearby in an old-age home run by a Nigerian girl and her husband. He soon became their favourite and they would look after him patiently. He was very grateful and did what he could in return. 'What did you do?' I asked.

'I taught her how to bet,' John replied.

'Was your teaching successful?' I asked.

'Well,' he said, 'she learned all the simple bets but the more complicated ones she left to me.'

I later asked her about it. 'I hear my uncle has taught you how to back horses?'

'Oh, yes,' she said, 'I've lost a lot of money.'

As John had written in his poem:

The Goddess of Chance
Now held her luckless worshipper in thrall.
To her he duly his orisons made
No travesty of his prayer will it be
To put his Domina Nostra into words:

Our lady which in heaven dost abide
Grant me to earn each night my nightly bread
From games of cards in clubs and in casinos

Mingling therewith the daily manna too
From horses fleet of foot and greyhounds swift
And lead me not into temptation
Of wending home to close my eyes in sleep
'Ere the sun rises bringing hateful light
To those that shun the indignity of toil.
O Goddess, powerful and glorious!

And if ever I mischievously recited the odd line, or even phrase of John's poem, my father recognised its origin at once. 'Oh,' he would say, trying not to smile, 'is that more of your Uncle John's rubbish?'

Harry wagging his finger at John in 1976

Two and a Half Centuries

In a narrow road where there was not room to pass
My carriage met the carriage of a young man.
And while his axle was touching my axle
In the narrow road I asked him where he lived.
'The place where I live is easy enough to find,
Easy to find and difficult to forget.

The gates of my house are built of yellow gold,
The hall of my house is paved with white jade,
On the hall table flagons of wine are set,
I have summoned to serve me dancers of Han-tan.
In the midst of the courtyard grows a cassia tree,
And candles on its branches flaring away in the night.

Meeting in the Road, transl. Arthur Waley

My uncle Sir Jeremy's letters always occupied two sides of a small sheet of writing paper under a neatly centred, embossed letterhead in royal blue announcing Fieldhead, Shamley Green. They had between 13 and 15 evenly spaced lines of writing on the front and never more than that on the back. There were about 6 words on a line. They were never cluttered or crowded. The words strode evenly across the page, and there was a military angle to the capital letters, like soldiers saluting on parade.

The messages were brief, precise and could admit no error:

Sat. Aug. 12

FIELDHEAD
SHAMLEY GREEN
NR. GUILDFORD, SURREY
BRAMLEY 3128

Dear Geoffrey,
We shall be here on Saturday

Sat Aug 12
Dear Geoffrey,

We shall be here on Saturday next and shall be delighted to see
you here. If you could arrive by about 1 p.m. (or a little
earlier) we would like you to have lunch with us. The drive

from London will take from 1 and a half to 2 hours depending on the traffic. The best thing will be to come down the Portsmouth Road (A3) to the point, about a mile south of Ripley, where (opposite the large Fisher's Garage) a road to the left takes off for W. Clandon and Newlands Cross. If you could arrive at that point about 12.0 noon (having left London about 10.45 a.m.) I would meet you on that side road in a beige Rover saloon FPL 737 and pilot you to Shamley Green and Fieldhead via Newlands Corner.

Will you drop me a line (to 16 St. James St.) to say if you can come in time for lunch and if the above time plan is possible for you. If it is not I can send alternative instructions for the journey.

Yours
Jerry

P.S. In your reply you may call me Jerry

You can imagine I did not dare to leave London a moment late. But to my horror my old Morris Minor did break down on the way. The starter motor jammed. I finally got it going again by a smart and anguished blow with the starter handle but not before a major panic punctuated by a breathless call from a public phone box to Sir Jeremy.

The beige Rover was waiting in the country lane, precisely as described. On arrival I explained my black fingers and car problem. Sir Jeremy was very understanding. 'Did you ever have such a problem with your car?' I asked.

'Oh yes.'

'With a Rover?' I asked incredulously.

'I can't remember which car,' Sir Jeremy replied.

I was the only member of the family who had ever been there. Before us the Sussex Downs rose, misty blue on the horizon. Behind us the square Tudor windows of the dining room revealed hints of white linen, mahogany and silver. Blue and green of Aubrieta speckled the crazy paving. A lawn sloped down past manicured banks of heather swelling in the southern sun. 'I call it the Warden of the East,' said Sir Jeremy, pointing to the stately green-gold column of a huge conifer.

We stepped under a string of creosoted rags and entered the rose garden. 'Lot of trouble with the deer eating the buds,' he said.

The drive was a tunnel of glossy green laurel, the house encrusted with firethorn. 'Pyracantha,' Sir Jeremy told me, 'Greek for firethorn. Some cottage,' he went on, after a pause and I recalled what Myer had told me was Jeremy's favourite song:

Take a tender little cot,
Quite a miniature affair,
Hung about with trellis'd vine...

When Myer had died I had finally taken possession of his Gold Flake tinful of papers and his other things. Now I had come to give the cigarette case to Sir Jeremy. I didn't know its history then, but it had seemed to me the only object sufficiently grand to give such an important person as a memento. Sir Jeremy accepted it with thanks, gravely, rather like the dodo accepting the box of comfits from Alice, but showing no sign he had ever seen it before.

'I would like to have seen Myer,' he said, 'but there was nowhere suitable for us to meet.' We were standing by his pond. The fragrance of Osmanthus filled the air.

'They're called Notonecta,' I said, pointing to the water boatmen, and feeling proud of my knowledge.

'It means swimming on the back,' said Sir Jeremy, 'Greek.'

We wandered on through the garden. A mound of heather rose on the slope beside us. 'Last year,' Sir Jeremy said, 'I was walking through the former Imperial Palace, the Schönbrunn, in Vienna. I was at an international conference and I was taking some exercise between sessions. An American stopped me and said "What are you doing here?" He was a complete stranger to me. I said, "I'm sorry, you have mistaken me. Who did you think I was?" "Oh, I'm sorry," he said. "Now I can see I made a mistake. But from a distance you are the absolute double of a close friend of mine. His name is Valentin Raisman."

'It seems his friend had lived in Moscow and had recently emigrated to New York.'

We were now deep in the garden well out of earshot of the house. We walked in silence for a while. Without any explanation, Sir Jeremy gave voice to a thought that had been on his mind. 'Swifter than eagles, and stronger than lions,' he said, quoting the four Hebrew words from David's lament over Saul and Jonathan. I had never heard him speak

Hebrew before and I never heard him do it again.

'Wonderful,' he went on, huskily, 'the depth of meaning in such a short phrase.' We continued round the garden in silence.

Back in the house Sir Jeremy told me about each of his grandchildren, noting carefully their interests and laying down the way that each of their inclinations could be developed usefully, markers that would help in the formation of their future careers.

Sir Jeremy poured me a fine glass of sherry and stood it firmly on an odd little coaster made of silver-gilt wires plaited in the form of a small wicker-work mat. 'Would you like a chocolate?' Sir Jeremy asked. 'These are very superior sort of chocolates.'

The seemingly endless list of granddaughters' names tripped off his lips, each one affording him a momentary, lingering satisfaction, names of Greek goddesses and water nymphs, names for graceful, slender cotton frocks on Oxford college lawns or in languid punts or English summer gardens. And while listening to these floral details, of considerably more interest to him than to me, my gaze wandered over the high, glass-fronted book case behind his head. Its highly polished door frames supported a criss-cross of equally highly polished slender frames carrying the diamond shaped glass panels. Behind them, the rows of well-bound books had a well-used, but not worn look, their gold embossed letters only just legible at this distance. I caught sight of one title *The Founders of India*.

I did not like to peer too closely or to press my great uncle on details of his past, especially at a time when he was so intent on telling me about the future. However, during the brief intervals I could steal from paying attention to Sir Jeremy's speech I managed to read a few more titles. They referred to the lives of great and famous men, men of achievement, financiers, statesmen, stern imperialists. My eyes roved shyly over the room. On the sideboard were large, precious objects, skilfully worked in Indian brass, silver and ivory. Rounded or bulbous forms seemed to predominate, but each with a twist of imagination or an ingenuity of ornament that made it exciting to the eye. Sir Jeremy had mentioned some of these objects before. 'This was a gift from so-and-so,' or 'This was given to me on my retirement from this or that board.' He also made it clear that the object referred to was a one-off production of a famous artist or craftsman.

On a low coffee-table a new book was still in its shiny dust jacket. It was a copy of Anthony Sampson's *Anatomy of Britain*, a collection of sketches of the top people in politics and industry, the sort of power-nexus running the country.

Sir Jeremy followed my eyes. 'I know most of them, personally,' he said.

'There is a picture of me in my paraphernalia,' he said, pointing to a small, framed photograph on a little writing-table. 'That one's the Star of India, that one's the Cross of the Indian Empire, and that's the Order of Michael and George. Each has three levels. The lowest is a simple Knight Bachelor. These are the highest levels. Indian princes always wanted to be given them. There's a medal with each order. You keep them. The rest, the chains and so on, you give back.' Jeremy pointed in the photograph to a little medallion around his neck. It was a sort of rose confection. 'I call that one the order of the squashed tomato. I've got them upstairs in the bureau. I'll go and get them to show you.'

He went off upstairs, and returned with three beautifully polished wooden boxes, in which the medals lay on rich velvet linings. 'Take that one,' he said. 'Keep it for a while.' It was gold, with pink and white enamelling. I must have looked astonished, because he repeated, 'Keep it for a while.' I think he saw it as a good luck charm for my career.

Sir Jeremy never lost his fine physique. During the week he lived in a flat in fashionable St James' Street, and would stride across St James' Park in the morning before his chauffeur drove up for him in the great black bank limousine.

The park was a refreshing oasis of green in the middle of the city. Its serenity was accentuated by the succession of limousines glimpsed behind discreet rows of trees, sedately gliding along Piccadilly and The Mall, and around the elegant portico of Apsley House at Hyde Park Corner. In spring, necklaces of green spiky bobbles dangled amid the small new leaves of the plane trees, and the horse-chestnuts were loaded with stubby conker candles. To each side, the ceremonial park entrances were guarded by cast iron sphinxes with curiously feminine haunches, squatting like lions on heavily rusticated limestone columns.

As Sir Jeremy crossed the park his spirit was lifted by the fine house fronts flashing through the gaps in the trees, reminding him of

Palmerston and Wellington and great statesmen. The spirit of Macaulay, he had read sixty years before in the bedroom over the gambling den in Trafalgar Street, seemed to preside over this elegant scene.

Sir Jeremy's walk was not unnoticed. One morning a neatly dressed lady handed him an envelope. 'You don't know me,' she said, turning to go. 'I have watched you every morning.'

The envelope was faintly pencilled, 'Verses from an unknown lady.' It contained two typewritten sheets, pinned together:

I see him approaching, my heart quickens its beat,
Deign he to notice me or will he look at his feet?
Is he a surgeon, a banker or spy?
Is it intrigue I see in his eye?

Whatever he is, he seems so discreet,
Always alert, so trim and so neat,
Not too fat, nor yet too thin,
Old-world charm he brings with him.

Is it for exercise he crosses the Park
Or to find his secretary there on her mark?
Muddling through letters, his papers and things,
Does she bring his coffee as soon as he rings?

Well, if winter comes I expect he will cruise.
Leaving this Island is so little to lose.
Maybe he'll come back when Spring's in the air,
And if he does I hope I'm still there.

Next morning Sir Jeremy handed the lady a note, smiled and paused before striding away to his car.

Your verses touch me, and your smile
A heart revealing, free of guile.
How sweet for one of seventy-five
To learn romance is still alive.

Can Nature trick us in these ways
In the dark winter of our days?
Alas, we see the beckoning hand
But cannot reach the promised land.

Affections mortgaged to a wife
And business duties fill my life

And many a grandchild at my knee
Ensures that time is never free.

Let mystery remain unsolved,
Nor hearts too deeply be involved.
And so, like ships that pass at night,
Just beam - as now - a friendly light.

A couple of years later my father was staying with me in London. He always got up early in the morning, shaved, and was always dressed in a white shirt. He was not used to receiving daily newspapers and always considered them to be complete distortions of the truth. When he stayed with me he seized the paper the moment it came through the door. After finishing the crossword, however, he could not refrain from reading the news, although always with the deepest scepticism, and then he spent some hours turning over the day's new events in his mind, so that over my breakfast some hours later the talk inevitably turned to politics.

My father's views had an unchangeable quality. The hero of the news was always the Soviet Union, a country which, in his lifetime, had destroyed Tsarism and Hitler and which might as well have been on the moon as far as his direct experience was concerned. For my part, as usual, I attacked the loss of freedom in the two great communist super-powers and their satellites. 'No use believing what you read in the newspapers,' my father used to say. 'Much of it's pure fabrication, or else the original meaning is completely lost in the translation.'

With each round of this oft-repeated argument, I had over the years become more and more venomous, goaded in proportion to the unshake-ability of my father's view. This time, however, my eloquence had a startling effect. I had rarely been able to see clearly what my father thought about things. But on this occasion I noticed a sudden darkness about his eyes and forehead and an unmistakable sense of defeat. Too late the inhumanity of my attacks was clear to me. All his life he had fought for the socialist principles of justice and humanity, looking to the Soviet Union as the standard bearer of civilisation. It was not I who had been betrayed, it was he and all those who had struggled along with him. If now he chose to refrain from saying what was so bitterly obvious to all, what right had I to force the words out of him?

It was during this visit that an opportunity arose for Sir Jeremy to come up for a meeting in the City. Since it happened that John was also in London at the same time, I decided to try to bring Sir Jeremy and Uncle John together. But, even wearing the mantle of Myer, I always remembered the fate of Fanny's attempt to visit Jeremy in his office. Such a plan was stretching my new-found family authority to its utmost. I felt it was a mischievous thing for me to do, and I didn't dare warn Sir Jeremy that I had also invited John.

I met Sir Jeremy off the train and took him to my home. On the brief car journey he told me: 'Last week, I was introduced to Professor Sir Wilfrid Le Gros Clark at the Athenaeum. He asked me if I was related to you.' Sir Jeremy laughed. 'That's the first time anyone has asked me if I am related to someone they know. Up to now it has always been the other way round.'

'When I first started work,' I said, 'Le Gros Clark asked me where the name Raisman came from. I said I thought it was a form of Redman or Roseman.'

'I think it may mean "an archer," Sir Jeremy said, rather uncertainly. I suppose it would have been a comforting thought for him that we had come from sturdy yeoman stock, the sort of men of old who would have given loyal service to a feudal lord during some patriotic English campaign at Crécy or at Agincourt. And so much better than my view of its origin as a 'cheap jack' or the Russian equivalent of a door-to-door brush salesman. Later, however, I discovered that certain Maronite Christian community headmen were indeed called Raisman, and referred to by Arabic writers on the Crusades as archers. So maybe Sir Jeremy did have a point.

Now, nervously, as we got close to home I screwed up enough courage to tell Sir Jeremy that his brother John would be there. I concentrated on the driving, since my courage was not enough to look him in the face as I told him. He took the news with little comment and to my relief, as he stepped into the house, greeted John in a completely relaxed way. The three brothers, who had shared the same bed in Sheepscar Place, now sat together on the couch talking. This was the first time they had all been together for over sixty years.

'I see you have gone bald,' said Jeremy, looking at John's shiny head.

'You too,' said John.

'Oh yes, I've been bald for years,' said Jeremy.

393

'*Calvo sed non calvinisto* (bald but not a puritan),' said John laughing.
'Very good,' said Jeremy, laughing too.

Civilities over, they at once resumed the arguments of the past as though those years had been so many minutes. I saw before my eyes the very scene Sam had described to me at our Passover evenings. John sprawled lazily on his seat and fiddled with his pipe. Jeremy sat upright, righteously arguing, and my father, the kid brother, listened. They were now all over eighty. 'So now you're a social parasite,' said Jeremy, referring disapprovingly to John's pension from the state. It was what was called a Supplementary Benefit, little more than a pittance. It had just been enough to keep John from starving.

'I'm entitled to it,' said John, more ruffled than I had ever seen him. 'I'm a British subject.'

Jeremy nodded very slightly, as if to say 'A man with your opportunities...' There followed a long pause, and Jeremy continued 'The people of this country are paying themselves too much. They are not producing enough, to justify the wages they give themselves. Socialists,' said Jeremy contemptuously. 'Anyone who isn't a socialist before he is twenty hasn't any heart. If he is still a socialist after thirty he hasn't any head.' So saying, Jeremy turned to Harry and his voice at once lost its accusing tone. 'We're on different sides now, Harry,' he said gently but firmly.

My father looked on, the obedient younger brother, his head held forward stiffly, trying hard to catch John's mumbled speech. No kind word passed between them and yet there was no mistaking their closeness. They were all three sitting on the long couch. Jeremy had sat down first, in the middle, as befitted his rank. John had sat on Jeremy's right. Harry had no choice but to sit on Jeremy's left, with his bad ear towards them both. Now Harry sat well forward, put his right hand on Jeremy's wrist, to hold his attention and turned his head far round so as to bring his good left ear into play.

'Did you do the Times crossword this morning?' Harry asked Jeremy.

'Yes,' said Jeremy. He paused. 'And you?'

'Oh, I did it all. I always do,' said Harry. 'I do *Ximenes* as well.'

'Me too,' said Jeremy. 'I couldn't get "It's not for ever," - five letters,' said Jeremy.

'Amber,' said Harry. '*Forever Amber*'s the name of a book. I think it's

394

about a prostitute. The clue refers to traffic lights. They don't stay amber for ever.'

Jeremy paused, and thought. 'They've a special language of their own. *Weekend*, for example means *k*.'

'And *butter*,' said Harry, 'means a ram or a goat. *Flower* means a river.'

Jeremy nodded.

'What else didn't you get in this morning's Times?' Harry asked.

'*Gild the other bath first* in seven and seven,' Jeremy said.

Harry replied without a pause. '*Turkish delight* - an anagram of *gild* and *the*.'

Jeremy shook his head and was silent for a while. Then he said bitterly 'With a mind like yours, it's a terrible shame you never had an education. What a career you could have had! A mind like yours - wasted.'

All three were silent. The air hung heavy over John.

'The only thing I regret now,' said Harry 'is that I can't ride a bicycle any more. Going off into the Dales was the greatest pleasure in my life.

'The last time I went out, a few years ago, I cycled as far as the roundabout at Wetherby, you remember it, on the Great North Road.' Jeremy nodded. 'A lorry came by and confused me and I fell off. The lorry stopped and the driver came over quite disgusted and looked at me and said, "What! drunk at this time of day?" '

Harry sat back again, taking his good ear out of action. It was a sign that he had no more to say. The subject was closed.

There was a lull in the conversation. Sir Jeremy sat silently. John shambled to his feet and wandered round the room aimlessly, muttering 'Splendid!' or 'Remarkable!' a few times.

After a pause Sir Jeremy began on a new, impersonal topic. 'Last month,' he said, 'the bank had its annual lunch. Mountbatten was the guest of honour. He sat next to me and I was surprised at what he told me.

'"You know," he told me "In my opinion you were responsible for the death of Gandhi."'

'"How do you work that out?" I asked him.

'"Well," he said, "it's what Nehru told me."'

At this point Sir Jeremy turned to Harry. 'After independence and the partition of the territory, there was a financial crisis. The Reserve Bank of India was holding all the gold and currency reserves. The new Reserve Bank of Pakistan appealed to the British Government to intercede for them. I was asked to go out and advise. I refused, but in the end they insisted, and I agreed to go out, but only on the condition that I would give advice, but I would not enter into any discussion. I would give my opinion and that was that.

'Well, I advised that the gold reserves should be shared out between the two national banks. It was only fair. Both countries had paid taxes. They were entitled to it. Without reserves, the national banks couldn't function. It was only common justice.

'Well, what Mountbatten told me was that after I had left, Nehru, the new Prime Minister refused. "What!" he said "Give them the money! They'll only use it to buy arms to murder our people with."

'So there was an appeal to Gandhi. Gandhi's influence was tremendous. People worshipped him like a god. Well, Gandhi at once backed my decision. He agreed it was only natural justice, and with that, of course, it was agreed to transfer the gold and currency reserves. They included the sterling balances I had fought so hard for at the War Cabinet that time when I visited you during the war.

'In fact,' Sir Jeremy said, 'I had gone to see Nehru on the morning of Gandhi's assassination and Nehru said to me, "You know the old man's being very difficult and causing me a lot of worry because there's a lot of opposition building up to him."

'That very afternoon, Gandhi went out as usual, to pray in public, and the rest of the story you know. One of his fanatical followers just walked right up to him with a revolver and shot him dead at point blank range.

'Of course I told Mountbatten that I didn't agree I was responsible.'

Sir Jeremy sat back.

John, fumbling with his pipe, remained totally silent.

'Let's have tea,' said Harry, playing the host. 'A couple of nights ago,' he said, 'I dreamt about father. He advised me on a horse in the Lincolnshire Handicap. The peculiar thing was that the horse was only a four-year-old. It had been born long after he had died.'

'Remarkable,' John said, absent-mindedly.

'Did you back it?' I asked.

'No,' Harry replied, and paused.

'And?' I asked.

'It came nowhere. Just like all his other bets,' Harry answered.

Again there was a pause in the conversation. I looked towards Sir Jeremy's last official photograph, bedecked with insignia. 'That photograph was at the coronation,' Jeremy said. 'I had a wonderful seat in Westminster Abbey. It was the only time I wore the GCIE and the KSI together. I forgot the gold elephant chain and left it in the taxi on the way home. The gold chains are kept in the bank vaults. They are very valuable. You don't keep them, you know. I was terribly upset but then, half an hour later, the door bell rang and there was the taxi driver with the chain.

'They belong to the Order. They have to be returned for the next holder. But not all the orders,' he went on sadly. 'Some of them are extinct now the Empire is over. There will be no more holders.'

'Remarkable,' John said, noisily breaking a biscuit, showering crumbs all over his saucer.

Jeremy paused again. 'I call them my toys. My grandchildren love to play with them.'

At the mention of children John and Jeremy both softened. 'You know,' said John, 'I have four grandchildren. One of them noticed the kettle boiling. He was just beginning to speak and he came rushing in and said, "Grandpa, grandpa, the water's kettling." So much more logical than saying, "the kettle's boiling."' Jeremy smiled broadly. Love of the family children was something they all shared.

We looked again at the photograph of Jeremy in his regalia. 'Actually, you can't wear all the insignia of all the different knighthoods together,' said Jeremy. 'When you go to get them you are given strict instructions how to kneel, "Not to go into a huddle with the monarch," you're told. "It's very undesirable."'

'Remarkable,' John said again, in an even more sarcastic tone. Jeremy ignored this. 'My name's on a plaque in St Paul's Cathedral,' he said. 'I can never remember exactly where.'

'This tea's very good,' said John, absent-mindedly. My father obediently poured John another cup.

It seemed all too soon that the meeting was over, and the three brothers were going out of the front door. On the way I diverted Sir Jeremy into the room where I had hung Kramer's browning little sketch of him. I had hardly managed to smooth out the creases from where it had lain folded in a drawer. The tea stain clearly spread out from one corner. For a moment Sir Jeremy's eyes glinted. 'Where did you get that?' he asked, and his voice had a keen edge that made me afraid he was going to ask me to return it.

I felt that since both he and Myer had so carelessly discarded it, taking no more care than Jeremy had of the historic telegram about Italy's entry into the war, that it, their past, was now by right more my possession than theirs. I was not about to relinquish now, when, so late in the day, Sir Jeremy might change his mind. 'Oh,' I mumbled, 'Myer brought it from Mexborough Avenue.' Sir Jeremy offered no further comment.

Like John, Jacob Kramer had remained a complete, impractical wastrel. His talent too could never be harnessed. For years he had been a familiar sight in Leeds pubs, holding forth on his theory of art, a wild-eyed figure with a huge hook nose and dense mountains of tightly wavy hair. To relieve his chronic shortage of money he would run up a rough sketch, take it to someone and obtain an advance on a portrait. He hardly ever finished one. After the completion of the final vast wooden panels of the Day of Atonement procession, his productive life had come to an end.

In the hall outside the open door John and my father were getting their coats on. 'He should have been an academic,' Jeremy said, inclining his head towards John, and still thinking of where and why the family plan had failed. 'He would have been very successful as professor in a university.' Sir Jeremy left the room.

Meanwhile, John had got as far as shuffling mincingly down the front steps, his shoelaces unfastened as usual. My father followed, his arms outstretched to steady his weak balance, placing his feet gingerly so as to transmit the least possible shock to his arthritic hips. Sir Jeremy strode ahead regally. He was martial in his bearing, a body of iron, driven by an indomitable will. He was nearly ninety. He had never retired. On taking up one job in his latter years he had written to Myer: 'The harness holds up the tired horse.' A friend who had known him years ago had described him to me as 'that indestructible uncle of yours.' Now he reached the front gate well ahead of his two younger brothers, paused, turned his head and frowned as he saw me trying to help both John and my father down the steps.

'I am not impressed by the condition of my juniors!' said Jeremy.

On the drive back to the station, Jeremy was trying to be friendly to John:

I remember, Heraclitus,
How often you and I
Had tired the sun with talking
And had sent him down the sky.

John nodded appreciatively. 'Not a bad memory, ' said John. 'Of course the poem's much shorter and more elegant in Greek.' He paused, mockingly, then recited it. It was his revenge for the comment at the gate.

Jeremy, who knew the Greek as well as John merely said, 'You always had a magnificent mind.'

At Waterloo station the three brothers streamed out across the platform, hats in hand, looking so similar with their large square noses and high bald foreheads, in all two and a half centuries of them.

The Round Ocean

He walked in glory on the hills;
We dalesmen envied from afar
The heights and rose-lit pinnacles
Which placed him nigh the evening star.
William Canton, Heights and Depths

Of all the gaping brood of naked chicks whose nest Myer had feathered and Myer's treadled miles had led to rich and comfortable lives, Ralph and Sidney had jointly contributed a packet of 20 cigarettes. It was only Myer's ancient co-conspirator Jeremy, who had ever given anything in return.

All his life Sir Jeremy had never failed to send an annual allowance, first to Myer for his parents, then to Myer for himself, and finally to Harry, 'for looking after Myer,' he said. When Sir Jeremy became ill, he wrote to Harry, 'This year I am sending you a double amount. If I am still here next year I will go on sending you the annual allowance as usual.' It was the seventieth instalment. He was still working at the Family Plan hatched that Friday night when he was only eight.

In 1967 when he reached 75, Sir Jeremy had served on the Board of Lloyd's Bank for 22 years. He had been offered but turned down the Chairmanship. His second career was complete. 'It would not be right that a man of 75 should remain on the Board of an important public company,' he said, and despite great reluctance, the Board accepted his resignation.

Years passed and now Time was beckoning my great uncle to his last appointment. I got a phone call from Sir Jeremy.

'Get me a prayerbook,' he told me. 'A Jewish one in English.'

'In English?' I asked amazed. Sir Jeremy would have had no difficulty with Hebrew.

'Yes, the Reform Jewish prayerbook is in English,' he said.

I questioned him no further, and got a copy for him.

'I am a confirmed agnostic,' he said.

I didn't say it struck me as a contradiction in terms. Agnostics are uncertain. But if I had said so, maybe he would have quoted Socrates, *the only thing we can know is that we do not know.*

'I want there to be some Hebrew words, I mean some words of the Hebrew service, some words...' and his voice trailed off.

I told my father of Sir Jeremy's elaborate preparations for his funeral. 'Perhaps he'd like a mausoleum,' said my father.

We were both so amused I plucked up courage to phone back and ask Sir Jeremy, 'Would you like a mausoleum?'

He paused a long time. 'They're very expensive. Some of my acquaintances have them but they're very expensive.' Then he too laughed.

'I'll come over and we can talk about it,' I said.

This time I had not taken with me the detailed military instructions for the traverse of the Tiger Routes. But I tried to follow them from memory. And sure enough, in snatches, here on the way to Peaslake, and Albury, the dog-leg across the road to Dorking and Leatherhead, the turn led into the familiar, short village stretch of low, old houses, with Shere Church on the left; I recognised it. Here I was right, but there I missed the way, and wound along roads much narrower, much greener and more winding than I had remembered, when the early golden Spring was over, and crooked wooden signposts pointed the way to ancient settlements, still dozing in the warm cradle of lost time, dreaming of the glory days and derring-do of empire, of tropical suns, and the smell of leather tackle on steaming horses, pith helmets and white ostrich plumes. And sure enough here was Shamley Green again and the familiar last turn into Fieldhead.

We discussed the route I had taken, my uncle trying to work out where I had been. The names fascinated him. 'Wonersh,' he said. 'There's Winnersh and there's Wonersh.'

I walked with him once again in his magnificent garden. Snowballs hung on the snowball tree. He leaned on a stick, furious at his disability, refusing all help. At the side of the warm, south-facing garden slope there was a tidy row of raspberries, now heavy with glistening berries and carefully restrained in wire netting. 'We'll have some of those berries for our tea,' Sir Jeremy said to me, with the tone of a regimental commander looking down over the enemy troops before a skirmish. Then, skirting the battlefield determinedly, he wielded his stick, showing no sign of pain. But, suddenly a stab came to me from long ago when I had gone blackberry picking with my father in Gledhow Valley Woods. 'What you need,' my father told me, 'is a good stick.' I said nothing to my uncle, realising that I was drinking again from a long ago spring.

But after a few passes at the forbidden fruit it became quite clear that Sir Jeremy found it altogether too painful to bend down to get under the wire. 'Those berries are beyond reach,' he said, with firm regret. I too regretted the succulent berries, but there was no question of anyone else helping him.

'Did you know John wrote a poem?' I asked Sir Jeremy. 'I ought to say he "composed" it, because he never wrote it down. I got him to recite it to me from memory, and then I tried to write it out. It took me a long time to work out all the classical allusions and quotations. I'm still not sure I've got all of it right.' I handed Sir Jeremy my transcription of *Non Est Inventus*.

Sir Jeremy read the dedication and then went through all 20 odd pages of the poem and my notes. He read slowly, steadily, without pausing or going back and in complete silence. No change of expression gave any clue as to his feelings. During the reading I tried not to move. When he got to the end he handed it back to me still without a word. Maybe his lips were a little more tightly compressed.

'Err... ?' I said.
'The dedication is a sonnet. It has to scan. You've got the line ends in the wrong place,' Sir Jeremy said, and the conversation was over.

'I've taken to listening to music on the Third Programme,' he said. 'I enjoy the modern music on the Third Programme. It's very interesting - not at all difficult if you concentrate.'

On my way out, he insisted on guiding me back down the tunnel-like drive of laurel and standing in the middle of the little country lane to indicate when the traffic would allow me to turn out. Once out, he told me there was to be no hesitating, no time for further farewell. 'Drive off at once,' Sir Jeremy ordered firmly.

In the driving mirror I caught my final view of the broad shoulders and pure white hair but the road was so winding that the image was gone in a flash.

His last day was the first he had ever failed to get out of bed, go downstairs and make his own breakfast. The iron constitution had weathered 86 years. His mind and his memory would have been good for another ninety. 'He believed that the mind was very important,' his wife told me. 'He used to say to me "As long as the mind is all right ..." He believed in the power of the mind.

'He did the Times crossword every morning. He couldn't see. I had to read out the clues to him and tell him what words were across and what letters. He did it all, every day till the last day. The paper came in at 9 in the morning and he did it all except one word. He just couldn't get the last word. In the end he got it. It was a word I had never heard of. He had to spell it out for me. It was at 11 o'clock. As soon as he got it he closed his eyes and drifted off into sleep. It was the last word he ever said.'

In the end he was cremated. No words from the Hebrew service were included but he had carefully selected a number of passages to be read. They included Wordsworth's mystical Pantheistic lines:

> *And I have felt*
> *A presence that disturbs me with the joy*
> *Of elevated thoughts; a sense sublime*
> *Of something far more deeply interfused,*
> *Whose dwelling is the light of setting suns,*
> *And the round ocean and the living air,*
> *And the blue sky, and in the mind of man.*

Afterwards I showed Uncle John the service. 'Jeremy must have gone soft in the head,' he said. And then, unable to conceal the edge of malice in his voice, he went on, 'What did you say the name of his house was? Fieldhead? I must remember that for my next poem.'

Both had studied Rome. But they saw different Romes and took different messages from them. As John had said, 'the Roman Empire was big. At one time one custom could have prevailed, at another time another.' For Jeremy, Rome was the upright, marble-white nobility of the Roman Republic, for John it was the colourful debauches of its later emperors.

I went up to Leeds to break the news to my father. In clear weather I took him out on his much-enjoyed drive into the Dales. Somewhere in Upper Wharfedale, after our usual hours of comfortable silence, I asked, 'Well?' The question could have meant, 'How do you feel?' or, 'Do you like the view?'

My father took it as, 'How do you think the car is doing?'

'In the old days,' he replied, 'it was a real test of a motor car, whether it could get up hills like these.' We drove again in silence for some time before he continued, 'It's not the same feeling as cycling, the struggle up the hills and the elation of coasting down them again.'

'No,' I answered sadly. That pleasure I could not bring him back.

'I can respect a man who believes in God,' my father went on. 'What I can't respect is all the rigmarole of religion, all the ballyhoo.'

'Oh, really,' I answered. 'I have the opposite view.'

Sir Jeremy's obituary in The Times was encrusted with Imperial letters like GCMG and GCSI. His entry moved from *Who's Who* to *Who Was Who*.

'I disagree with your picture of my father in India,' his son said.

'You knew your father,' I replied. 'Let's try to get it right. Tell me what was your father's special contribution. Explain to me about the sterling balances and the War Cabinet.'

'It was the most important single act that he did,' John Michael replied. 'And he did it on behalf of India. And that is now referred to today by people as being one of the most remarkably unselfish acts of a Britisher in India on behalf of India.'

'So where,' I asked 'did these principles come from? Where did your father get them from? From Macaulay? From Rome?'

'In some degree, yes. Nobility. And courage. What was in the interests of his country. An ethic which hardly exists today. It was a Roman virtue. Honour, and behaving according to high standards.'

John Michael paused.

Taking advantage of the pause, I said, 'My father loved to repeat the story of how Horatio kept the Bridge:

For the ashes of his fathers and temples of his gods.'

'My father liked that too.' John Michael replied. 'And I did:

Lars Porsena of Clusium, by the nine gods he swore
That the great house of Tarquin should suffer wrong no more.

'Honour. And I was brought up with that. And that was Macaulay again, *The Lays of Ancient Rome*. It was Macaulay who wrote it.

'When I went to stay with my father at Carignano,' John Michael said, 'it had a library with marvellous books, mainly novels, romantic novels which I used to read as a boy with great enthusiasm. And when we went back there many years later, those same books were there on the bookshelves. The place is closed now, hardly used. Every now and again somebody goes up there. But the same books are still there. I remember them.

'Peterhof was burnt down in 1980. I remember how distressed my mother was.

'It's not right to say my father was an imperialist. He was a servant of empire. But he was lucky to leave India when he did and avoid the final terrible debacle.'

There was a silence. We both thought back over it all, that long life journey, all the things he had seen and done and the man behind it all and we wondered silently together, each in his own way, how to bring to life a life that was gone. And then John Michael said, 'John Greenway, my father's favourite Bank driver told me, "I always remember the Tiger Route I used to drive your father. He loved that, the little back roads, the winding hills, the wild country."'

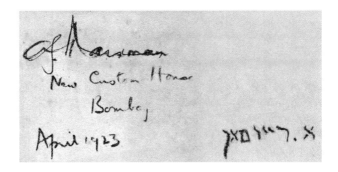

Horse Races in Heaven

Harry never lost his love of reading, and his love of poetry. On his granddaughter's birthday he sent her a book of Edward Lear's Nonsense Verse. In the flyleaf he wrote:

Edward Lear in his prime
Wrote this work to pass the time.
You may read within this book
Rhymes he made by hook or crook,
And reading may remember too
Grandpa who made this rhyme for you.

Recently he had got hold of a book on Ancient Egypt and it fascinated him. The amazing variety of animal- and bird-headed gods must have awakened memories of old nightmares for him.

'Now I understand why they came to monotheism,' he said. 'There must have been too many different gods for people to remember them all. Just like the innumerable saints of the Roman Catholic Church.' But soon his investigations came to a point of special horror. 'Ancient Egypt,' he told me 'was divided into 14 provinces. Each one worshipped its own animal. All kinds of things. One worshipped crocodiles. And there was even one that worshipped cats. It was called Bubastis. They used to mummify the cats, and collected enormous numbers of them in a huge cemetery they called the Necropolis. If anything could make me have an even poorer opinion of religion than I do, that would be it!

'Primitive religions worship the sun and the moon. The ark is always to the east of a synagogue. And at certain points in the service the congregation stands up and faces east. That's a relic of sun worship. There's always a full moon on the first night of Passover. The first Sunday after the first full moon of Spring is Easter Sunday. Obviously these are relics of moon worship. The fact that the Jewish day always starts in the evening is evidence that there was moon worship. And what else is the crescent flag of the Mohammedans except a relic of moon worship? The moon has a cycle of 19 years. The golden number is the number of the moon's years. It's called the Metonic cycle because a feller called Meton discovered it. The golden numbers are used to calculate the time of Easter. Somewhere I've got the different golden numbers that explain the Jewish leap years.

'The Christian calendar is not used by the Moslems or the Jews because the Jewish calendar dates from the supposed creation of the earth. Year 1 is the year when the earth was created. Julius Caesar had the calendar adjusted and it was quite accurate until Pope Gregory, and he altered it again. There are different ways of reckoning. The Sothic cycle is a cycle of 1460 years. It's the old Egyptian calendar. Their year was 365 days, so they were a quarter of a day wrong. If you multiply 364 by 4 you get 1460, and then they were straight again. When Sirius the Dog Star rises in sunlight that's the start of the Egyptian year.'

As he got older my father's eating habits changed. My father loved fish and ate it for breakfast, dinner and tea. He made no secret of his liking and even not at meal times would enlarge on the delights of fish and most of all on 'Herring, the King of Fish!'

All their married life my mother had dutifully prepared chopped herring, skinned and boned and diced with egg and various ingredients, soaked in white vinegar according to the Leylanders' ancestral *Litvak* method. At every meal a dish of this Baltic delicacy would be placed on the table. He used it as one might use a dish of butter and pressed it enthusiastically on anyone eating with him. 'Don't you want to use some of this?' he would ask. 'It's very good. Herring! The king of fish!'

Then, suddenly, one day he said to my mother: 'Don't make any more chopped herring! I don't want it! Don't make it! If you do I won't eat

407

it!' His tone was so decisive she didn't feel there was any possible question.

I was fascinated. 'The other night,' he explained, 'I had a vision. A large fish appeared and said, "Do you speak French?"

'"I'm sorry," I said, "I don't."

'"Italian, then?" asked the huge fish.

'"No," I said, "I'm afraid not."

'The fish went through many languages. In the end I said, "I essay a little English."

'"Well," said the fish, "I don't want you to think I'm aggressive, but I've got some unpleasant news for you. I'm the king of the fish, and I take a dim view of you eating my subjects, chopping them up and mixing them with apples and oranges and vinegar. I don't like to have to say this, but if you don't stop, I'll see that next time you eat herring a bone will get stuck in your throat and choke you."' Harry never ate chopped herring again.

Maybe as a result of his Egyptological studies, my father's views on cats began to change. 'One day,' he told me, 'I happened to go into a room in someone's house. I didn't notice it, but a cat was there. And at first the cat also didn't notice me. When we caught sight of each other, the cat looked at me with such an expression of terror - Uffppw! - such indescribable terror, and bolted from the room. Another time I saw something very few people ever see. A ring of cats. They were females surrounding a single male which was attending to them. It's a very unusual thing to see. Later on I was told that it was a very dangerous thing, and I was lucky not to have been seriously hurt.'

My father had acquired a few of the books that Myer brought with him when he came from Mexborough Avenue. One of his favourites was the Everyman edition of Macaulay's Essays. One day I took it down from the shelf and idly turning the pages. I discovered the neat pencil line which recorded Sir Jeremy's pleasurable discovery of the sturdy Elizabethan yeomen so many years before. I passed it to my father. To my surprise my father completely ignored the pencil line and scrabbled at the page with his finger nails. 'This,' he said 'is how Jeremy studied.'

I looked completely bewildered.

Pleased with the success of his little joke, my father mischievously retrieved something from the book and rolled it between his finger tips.

I wondered if it was going to be a fossilised bedbug. Then he opened out his hand to show me. It was a piece of candle grease, fallen from a candle in the brothers' bedroom over the gambling house in Trafalgar Street, perhaps as Jeremy closed the book in a fit of impatience at the waves of Yiddish swearing that swept up, like the monkish chant in the *Carmina Burana*, from the gambling bacchanal below. 'You know,' my father said after a long silence. 'Jeremy never lost the memory of having been a slum dweller.' This was obviously something he had been turning over in his mind for some time.

'Why do you say that?' I asked.

'Well,' he replied. 'You remember the last time we saw him, he was describing his house, and he said, "A retired admiral lives next door." And he said it with such pride, "An admiral!" Did a man like Jeremy, with a career like Jeremy's, need to be impressed by the fact that an admiral lived next door? Only a person with the outlook of a slum dweller would take pride in the fact that an admiral lived next door.

'But still, he never looked down on the Leylands. He used to say "Dirt is only matter out of place." He had an orderly view of life.'

Later, when I met a close family friend of Jeremy's from his India days, I came to see this in another light. She was describing the glittering scenes at the palatial official residence, the tea parties, the engagements, the relaxing and informal moments of the famous men of power and influence, the government dignitaries and financiers who passed through. I listened, eager to try to understand, to try to find what to ask to gain understanding. 'Do you think he enjoyed it?' I asked her.

'No,' she said, obviously surprised at such a question and she paused to think. 'No, I don't think he enjoyed it at all. He gave me the impression he'd much rather be at home with his family. That's how he seemed to me.'

The family were leaving few mementoes. After Sir Jeremy's death I visited his widow. She handed me *Verses from an Unknown Lady* and Sir Jeremy's reply. I made admiring noises. 'That's nothing,' she said. 'He wrote verses for me every day when we first went to India.'

'Is there anything you would like?' she asked. I shook my head. Then, on the doorstep, I remembered the cigarette case.

'There is one thing...' I said.

'Wait a minute,' she said and without waiting for me to tell her what it was she disappeared into the house. 'He left this for you.' Something in her manner suggested an almost superstitious fear of the little object, some link with that part of her husband's life which she had never been allowed to see.

Jack had a tragic life. His first wife was what Myer called a religious maniac. She erected crucifixes all over the house, especially in the kitchen and over the marriage bed and refused to allow any member of the family to see her husband. They had two daughters. All three died young, and Jack was left on his own, living in a run-down terrace house in the poorest quarter of the town, surrounded by the crockery and cutlery, unused and unwashed, collecting the dust of the increasing years that had passed since they had been the symbols of his late wife's attempt to rise to the bourgeoisie.

The relationship between Jack and my father was something inscrutable. It was, of course, not Jack's fault that in Myer's Plan he and John had been chosen for an education, no more than it was Harry's fault that he had not. And until one moment I never had any impression that Harry felt that Jack owed him anything. But, searching for any scraps of information that might light up the past, I took the chance to drive my father past Howarth and over the winding Pennine lanes to Lancashire, where Jack lived in Burnley.

To my amazement, Jack greeted us with blank hostility. 'Oh, you,' he growled, at Harry. 'You did me a dirty trick.'

I was shocked. My father said nothing. He seemed completely taken aback, at a loss for how to respond. But I could not help noticing a guilty expression on his face. Jack said nothing more and a terrible silence fell on the room. No one moved. The tension between these two old men was almost intolerable. As a self-appointed disciple of Myer I was deeply pained by any sign of hostility within the family.

Jack was already very frail, his hands trembling with Parkinson's disease. I stood over him in his deep and ragged armchair and called upon the spirit of my Uncle Myer, 'What would Myer say to this?' I asked with all the faltering sternness I could muster.

Jack turned on me and the white stubble on his face, unshaven for some days, bristled with rage. Despite his frailty he seemed about to launch his stocky frame out of the chair and lunge at me as in the old, glorious days in Templar Street when he was brought home from a brawl on a shutter.

'Myer,' Jack spluttered, with inarticulate rage, 'Myer...' he paused for breath, and his eyes rolled. 'Myer... Myer was a saint!'

During all this, my father said nothing. I waited. Jack subsided into his chair, his energy all spent but never allowing his eyes to leave those of his brother Harry, nor abating one whit the heat of their anger.

'Well,' Jack said, finally making the effort to stand up and offering his hand to Harry, 'Let's forget it! Let's shake hands.'

They shook hands, like strangers, a strangely tragic sight for two old men who had shared a bed.

'But you'll be sorry,' Jack said, 'I don't forgive you!' and we left the house. It had all taken but a few minutes.

I did not dare to ask my father what he had done, especially as I suspected he had somehow taken money from Jack. On reflection I realised I had never bothered to ask myself where my father had lighted on the windfall he had given me to buy the car we were driving in.

We drove away from Burnley in silent dejection. The last thing I had wanted to uncover was discord, discord far too late in life for Time to heal, to find my father might have carried out a base deed or to see him, like Noah, humiliated. I had lifted up one stone too many.

After half an hour, my father said 'He was always like that. When I was young he scratched my face with a nail,' and with a gesture he indicated his cheek, like a little boy running to his mother to complain.

'What had you done?'

'Nothing.'

But I was not so sure any more.

Jack committed suicide shortly after. We heard he thought he had cancer and had decided not to bother allowing it to go through its natural course. Whether his diagnosis was right I very much doubt. Harry was cut completely out of his will and thus a crucial link in Myer's plan had failed. Jack was buried in the *Englisher* Cemetery at Gildersome. His house was converted into a mosque.

A couple of years later I visited Myer's grave. I picked up a small white marble chip from his plot. I wrote 'Unky' in pencil on the stone, put it in a paper clip box on my desk, and forgot its existence. Only a little while passed, and now John was taken ill. I got a phone call from my cousin

Lenny at about 5 o'clock in the afternoon. I went out to eat, and returned to my desk at about 8 o'clock to finish some letters. At the end of a letter and without lifting my eyes from the blotter, I reached blindly into the box for a paper clip. The white marble chip leapt out.

'Don't be impatient, Unky,' I said. 'I'm going to see him.'

I found John in bed, too weak to move. When he was first admitted to Nuffield Ward in Crystal Palace he had been able to phone in his bets every day. Now, he didn't have enough strength to hold the phone. He was attended from time to time by chaplains and assistant-chaplains. They were delighted at a patient who would argue with them about the authenticity of the gospels, especially one who had such an outstanding classical knowledge at his fingertips.

While I was there a young assistant-chaplain in plain clothes turned up and introduced himself. John said he already knew who he was.

'How?' asked the young man.

'I can always tell a man who is near to God,' said John.

'You know,' John said to me after the young man had left 'as religions get weaker, they come together. Its what happened in Greece and Rome. They worshipped all known gods and goddesses. It was called syncretism. That is what will happen here with modern religions. As they both get weaker, they will come together.'

'Gambling,' John said 'is like the Hindu Trimurti. There are three gods, Brahma, the God of Creation, Vishnu, the Preserver, and Shiva, the God of Destruction. When you win, you are created, and when you lose you endure destruction.'

> *Like to the august king on Bosworth field*
> *He would have given his kingdom for a horse,*
> *A greyhound chasing an electric hare*
> *Was in his eyes a sight fit for the Gods.*

> *Now some there be that win, and some that lose;*
> *He had the lack of perspicacity*
> *Always to be found upon the losing side.*

The assistant-chaplain was God-sent. John lingered, very weak, for some days, and each morning the apprentice man of God obligingly phoned the bookmaker with John's Yankees, Heinz-bets, and accumulators. John's bets from the hospital prospered. Maybe at last, Tyche felt remorse.

During these days of enforced idleness John passed the time by developing his theory of the cause and origins of the Trojan War. 'Before the war,' John explained 'the Greeks and the Trojans used to meet at the racecourse at Sandy Pylos. Menelaus is described as *He of the Loud Shout*, from which we can know that he was the bookmaker. Well, on one occasion, the Greek king bet his wife Helen as the stake, and lost. After the Trojans had gone back to Troy, it was discovered that in fact they had been doping the horses. Homer describes them as *Horse-Tamers*, which obviously means *Horse-Dopers*. So the Greeks went to war to get Helen back. During the long siege, the Greeks passed the time gambling, and it was here that Palamedes invented dice. The Greeks were so pleased that they dedicated a set of dice at the temple of Tyche in Argos. At her shrines, Tyche, the Goddess of Fortune is represented with a horn of plenty over one arm and a rudder in her hand, to signify she controls the destiny of men. In other statues she is seen holding the wheel of fortune, or standing upon a razor's edge to show that she is kind one moment and unkind the next.

'After a long time outside the walls of Troy, Ulysses, The Wily One, thought up a plan to entrap the Trojans. The Greeks made a wooden horse and pushed it up to the city gates, taunting the Trojans, "Dope that if you can!"

'The Trojans could not resist such a challenge and so they admitted into the walls the horse that caused the city's final overthrow.

'You know,' John said. 'I'm celebrating my golden separation.'

The hospital staff, anxious to be helpful to John, offered to call his wife. He didn't say no. John's wife refused to answer the call. After fifty years separation, she didn't want to start again. 'After I get out of here,' John said with a weak smile, 'I'm going to get together with my wife again.'

I phoned my father. 'John's very ill,' I said.

'Is he very ill?' my father asked.

'Very.'

'I hope,' said my father, 'there are horse-races in heaven. I'll come.'

Himself in poor health, he made the long journey down to London, and thrust a crossword clue at John, '*A stern and just judge*, in twelve letters?'

John barely reflected. 'Rhadamanthus,' he mumbled toothlessly. My father, not hearing, repeated the question several times. John repeated the same answer, each time only slightly louder. My father finally sat back, contented.

It had always been the fashion in Leeds for men of a certain age to wear hats. For many years the fashion was a medium-brimmed black hat, the crown indented to a particular depth, and worn at a precisely casual angle. But finally the fashion changed. Narrow, sloping-brimmed hats in checked brown or grey were in. My father's tastes in hats had not kept up, and when my mother bought him a new hat, he had accepted in silence, but later secretly tore out the little multicoloured feather tucked in the narrow band.

I helped him down the hospital steps. He was regretting his age. 'I bought this hat to celebrate the arrival of Julius Caesar,' he said. 'I think it was in 44 BC.'

'I thought it had a feather,' I asked. 'Where's it gone?'

'Oh,' he said 'it grew into a bird and flew away.

'You know, a few weeks ago I was down in the market. You know people say we look alike, the brothers. Well, I was passing the stall that Sam used to have before he died. And that's six years ago. The man at the next stall stopped me by putting his hand on my arm. For the way he did it I knew he had spoken to me, but I hadn't heard it. He repeated, "Hello! I haven't seen you for a long time. Where've you been?"'

'So?' I asked.

'I told him, "I'm Harry."'

The next day I mentioned this story to John.

'Oh,' John said. 'Do you think your father looks so young?'

'He looks twenty years younger than his age,' I replied. 'Don't you think so?'

John ignored this comment. 'How do I look?' he asked eagerly.

'You look not a day over sixty,' I replied.

John was well over eighty. He swelled with pride. Then, after a pause for reflection, 'Do you really mean it?' he asked anxiously.

'Yes.'

'Thank you very much,' he replied, and lay back, clearly gratified. 'When I get out of here I'm going to get together with my wife again. We'll find somewhere to live.'

My daughter Ruth, one of his many grand-nieces, came wearing a badge which read, 'Don't blame me. I didn't vote Tory.' John was delighted. He had never lost his fascination with children.

'You know,' he said to the bright-eyed youngster, 'we have something in common. You were born in Nuffield Ward in Oxford, and now I'm in Nuffield Ward in Crystal Palace. When you were born you cried so much that I could easily tell you would have an outstanding career as a professional mourner.'

He never mentioned dying. It was a tiny tug on the fine line, the line invisible to outsiders, invisible to even the closest of non-blood relatives, that joined the Raismans. Here was a very old Raisman addressing a very young one. But he knew she would understand. For the last word he had lost all breath, and not even his usual mumble emerged.

As she left he groped for a retort, 'This was the noblest non-Tory of them all.'

'I will see you tomorrow,' I said, putting my hand on his fleshless shoulder.

I lip-read the familiar reply, 'Splendid!'

As we left my daughter said to me, 'What a pity I didn't know him earlier.'

Every afternoon for those last few days in hospital John watched the horse-racing on television. One day I had the mistaken impression that the set was working even though it was not plugged in. John was amused. 'Must be a numinous intervention,' he said, using the unusual word 'numinous' instead of 'divine,' and waiting till he thought the young assistant-chaplain was out of earshot. He didn't want to hurt the feelings of his new-found friend by profane sentiments.

John gambled steadfastly. He knew he would not live to collect any winnings. John did not gamble for gain. His last hours were very restless. Long after he had ceased to communicate he seemed to be grappling with some internal questions. It was impossible to guess what they were. A phone call came later, in the night. Tyche had finished her sport with John. I found on his bedside table a crumpled envelope with the names of horses and races in his shaky script. The nuns who laid out the body returned his meagre belongings. These included several betting slips that they had found between the bedclothes. He had been steadfast till the end.

Few people have heard of Tyche, the Goddess of Chance. John would have been pleased if he could have known that shortly after his death, excavations at the ancient Hebrew city of Beth Shean, capital of the Ten Cities, scorching below sea level in the Jordan Valley, revealed the 2000-year old temple of its patron goddess, Tyche, the Temptress. There, glowing in a mosaic, a pearl-festooned trilby hat on her head, she holds in her arms the cornucopia, horn of plenty, overflowing with the untold riches promised, glittering, always just out of reach of her faithful, ever-hopeful devotees.

Tyche... glowing in a mosaic

Non est inventus. There's your gamester's end.
The votary of fortune here's no more.
The bookies shout the odds. The croupiers call
Lay your bets Messieurs, Faites vos jeux.
The wheel has made its final spin,
Les jeux sont faits, Rien ne va plus.

No more will he on his way homeward to a wifeless bed
After an all night vigil at the tables
Tarry for breakfast at the roadside bar
Watching with wistful eyes the weary waiter
Set out the buttered rolls and coffee.

Uncle John

416

The One is Not

There was now no space left at the Hilltop Cemetery. Myer had had
almost the last place and now the burial ground had closed. The
Gildersome kids hunted rabbits about its deserted tombstones. The Leeds
Jewish Workers' Burial Society had for years collected weekly penny
dues so that its members could have tombstones. Mr Schiffer, the consci-
entious president, was at his wits' end. Finally, after much anxious
negotiating, he stood up triumphantly at the meeting and announced:
'We've got another four acres so, thank God, we can bury 500 more
people.'

'They've built a new synagogue up Shadwell Lane,' my father told me.
'It's all swank and polish. It doesn't even look like a synagogue.
Ordinary people, old-age pensioners, can't afford to join it. It looks like
a Chinese pagoda. There should be a more solemn air about a synagogue.
If they were going to build a synagogue they should build one like the
one in Chapeltown Road, a copy of Solomon's temple. This one looks
like a night club.' It didn't appease my father that the architect had
salvaged from the former Francis Street Synagogue an old sandstone
sculpture of the Lion of Virtue biting the Serpent of Evil.

The remnant of the family did not want John brought back to Leeds. So
he never completed the last leg of his longed-for return. His body must
rest in a foreign cemetery in London. The task of arranging his
tombstone fell to me. It was to be as simple and as cheap as possible,
merely to mark the site, in case any of us who chose to go and mourn him
might weep over the wrong mound of earth. There was to be no upright
headstone, just an inclined slab covering the plot.

Despite these restrictions I couldn't resist trying to insert some flavour of the debonair gambler into the inscription. Nothing seemed better than *Non Est Inventus* (He is not to be found), the title of the irreverent poem in which John's deserted wife tells the story of his fall and flight. But it was not to be so easy. For one thing, *Non Est Inventus* is Latin, and the religious body that controlled the cemetery had strict rules of propriety. The bereaved should be respected and not subjected to flippancy, however learned. The authorities did not look favourably on any inscriptions apart from the expressive 'Sadly Missed,' 'Deeply Mourned,' 'Asleep,' 'Ever in Our Hearts,' and so on. They were very happy to have very long inscriptions (charged at an extra sum for every letter) with ever so many names of heartbroken relatives. But apart from such lists the rules were quite clear. Any words had to be in Hebrew and from the Holy Scriptures. I could find no Hebrew word for *luftman* or gambler.

In the end I found the solution in Genesis Chapter 42 Paragraph 13. Joseph's brethren had abandoned him in the pit. They assumed him dead. Later, when Joseph was in a position of authority in Egypt, the brothers came to him for help in a famine. They didn't recognise him but he recognised them. So he amused himself by playing a little game of deception with them. He accused them of being spies. They tried to clear themselves:

> *And they said to him: My lord, thy servants are twelve brethren, the sons of one man in the land of Canaan; and behold, the youngest is this day with our father, 'Ve-haekhod eynenu* (And the one is not).

The *one* they referred to was their brother Joseph, who stood before them, enjoying their confusion. By saying, 'the one is not,' they didn't quite say outright he was dead. It was evasive, embarrassed but a perfect translation of John's idea of the missing gambler in *Non Est Inventus*. When I mentioned their holy origin the two words *Ve-haekhod eynenu* were approved without any further question by the cemetery authorities.

I described my plan to my father. 'What do you think John would say?' I asked.

'I think he'll pop up out of his grave to read it,' Harry replied.

'And?'

'He'd be amused.'

'Do you think so?'

'Yes.'

418

And so, cut into the middle of the cheap stone that lies over John, the lead-filled Hebrew letters declare to the eternal heavens the childish impudence of that magnificent mind.

The summer of 1980 had a hot sunny August. Even the afternoon before, I had had to water the lawn. Then, in the night, the thunderstorms began. By morning the roads to the capital were flooded. Of even the few who were left of the once numerous family some couldn't get through. I went to pick my father up at the bus stop from Leeds. As I drove round, looking for somewhere to stop, I saw him. It was an ordinary, middle-class street, with ordinary people, doing daily things, kids coming from school, housewives shopping and a trickle of cars. He was sitting quietly on a bench, by the bus stop. He wore a grey suit, an overcoat, and a grey trilby. His face was gentle and lost in thought. His lips were pursed in a half-pulled expression, meant for some unseen companion who, in his mind, he addressed, in the situation he was thinking about, that said he did not hear the street sounds around him. He looked awkward, shy, trusting as a child and as defenceless as a fallen leaf upon the forest floor.

By the time we got to the consecration the rain had stopped and the clouds had risen to a sullen black ceiling. It was humid and hot. 'Are there ten men?' asked the minister. 'Not yet. I expect more,' I said, embarrassedly, looking hopefully in the direction of the road along which the mourning brothers should any moment appear. 'Don't worry. We'll wait,' he said, gently.

Meanwhile I enlisted the services of a gravedigger who was standing by. To make one of a minyan (quorum), the only requirements were to be male, over thirteen years old and prepared to stand up wearing a hat. Finally we scraped ten together.

'I hope you don't mind it being such a simple stone,' I said to my Uncle Ralph. 'We couldn't raise any more money.'

'That's quite all right, 'Ralph said.

'When I think of what John did to me,' said Sarah's husband, my Uncle Wilf, 'I think what I gave was a lot.'

I didn't answer.

'Of course,' Wilf went on 'you don't know what John did to me. I never told you.'

As we went into the burial chapel, my father noticed an old man with a long white religious beard. 'Who's that?' he hissed to me. 'Rip van

Winkle? Listen, when they start calling people up tell them not to bother with me. I can't read the stuff.'

The minister did everything he could to make the consecration personal. He even read the inscription to the mourners. 'Why does it say *Ve-haekhod eynenu*?' he asked me in a whisper.

'The one is not,' I whispered back. 'From the story of Joseph.'

The minister was pleased to have this personal detail to add to his speech. He might have been a little more concerned had he known the reason for those two Hebrew words on John's stone. But maybe not. Times change.

'Actually it's the title of John's poem,' I said quietly to Ralph.

'Sounds just like one of John's abstruse comments,' Ralph replied smiling.

My father picked his way unsteadily across the clay clods still glistening from the downpour. 'I'm pleased with the stone,' he said. 'It's more than John deserved.'

Uncle Ralph helped his older brother Harry reverently into the car. Despite his ever-increasing unsteadiness my father remained steadfast in his prohibition of walking sticks. To use a walking stick now would have been a surrender.

As Harry got into the car he turned to Ralph. 'A slight attack of *anno domini*,' said Harry, at once both irritated at the stiffness of his joints and pleased at his younger brother's concern.

We drove off, John's grandchildren in the back.

'I dislike the traditional burial ceremony,' said Harry. 'The falling of the earth on the coffin. To me that's the final separation. When John came back to England,' my father went on 'he said he would commit suicide if we didn't help him. We should have let him do it.'

I could see John's grandson's eager face shining in the driving mirror. 'Why does your father hate my grandfather?' he asked curiously.

Fortunately my father's deafness prevented him hearing the question.

'Don't you know the story?' I asked, pitching my voice at a level my father couldn't hear.

'I thought I did,' said the grandson, tentatively.

'What did you hear?' I asked.

'That my grandfather was a scapegoat for the family.'

'It's a long story,' I said.

420

The Biting Frost

Ten years passed. The story seemed to be over. There seemed nothing to add. Any remaining curiosity must remain unsatisfied. The past had at last fallen silent. I got a letter from my father:

Leeds, 3rd May, 1986

Dear Geoffrey,

'An honest man,' wrote Burns, 'is the noblest work of God.' But consider honest or dishonest he suffers the vagaries of metabolism, the organic malfunctions, and the so often painful task of stepping from this world into the next. Noblest is not the adjective I would choose. And sometimes as I lay awake through the silent watches of the night, I recall the hopes that are now no more than faded memories, and I think:

Backward, turn backward, O Time in your flight

Make me a child again just for one night.

I am slightly bewildered by Araucaria's efforts at a crossword puzzle. Why they are described as crossword puzzle is beyond me unless they're intended to make people cross. To solve requires knowledge esoteric, eclectic and extremely erudite, which is quite beyond me.

You mention Jeremy. His first reaction to my writing dates back to my school days. I wrote him a letter during his first year abroad. I still have a faint recollection of the soft soap he worked into a foaming lather in his reply.

He was never comfortable debating with me, he being right and I left. He agreed with Shaw and Wells, who maintained that the right to vote should depend on proved intellectual standard. Politically they were both useless creatures whose vanity and conceit were swollen by the money and adulation poured on them. Their ideas would have resulted in an oligarchy, government by a small group, in this case a couple of intellectual snobs. They spent a large part of their time in futile controversy about the work of Pavlov, Wells supporting and Shaw deriding. Shaw thought nothing of P's work, and in the discussion more or less called Wells a damn fool.

421

It was not given to me to visit faraway places, and so I take what may be called a vicarious pleasure in the wanderings of your restless feet. Our activities are restricted to those whose passions and ambitions are but a lingering memory. But as your progenitor I can claim a little responsibility for the work you have done. It does lighten the depressing nostalgia of old age to feel that I have been of some use after all.

As far as I am concerned you need not grieve about your English. You realised the hopes I once entertained and the ambitions I once dreamed. I would not have you different. And as for your own literary ability remember the invention of the wheel was more use to humanity than all the artistic charm of the Renaissance.

You ask about my letters. Many years ago, as a soldier in France, I wrote a letter to Sarah, then a scholar at secondary school. I remember some of it:

The moon shines uncomplainingly,
Out of a cloudless sky,
And all the world writes letters,
And I wonder, 'Why can't I?'

At my efforts lyrical
You look down from a high pinnacle
Of modern school critical,
Hyperaesthetical,
Towering thought.

Alas, the fluency has departed, and I find it very difficult to write. Even the physical effort has become a strain. I dislike stressing this deterioration, but it's useless flogging a sterile imagination and perhaps next time I write I may do better.

Affec
Daddy

It was a cold winter day when I drove up to Leeds. The afternoon was short and gloomy. Grey flurries of rain or sleet swept the motorway. The bloom was almost over in the blackthorn hedges of north London, the dying white blossom turning a nondescript brown as the leaf buds began to open. But as I approached Leeds, the clouds broke, revealing a washed, whitish-blue sky, and an unusually clear winter sun. In the severer weather of the north, the blackthorn blossoms grew new, still white as snow, with the promise of a second spring.

In the last moments of daylight I opened the back door and walked through the kitchen into the living room. The room was full of strange brilliance. After the raw cold of the outside air the gas-fire gave a soft, orange-glowing warmth. But the strange light was not from the gas, nor from the electricity, nor from the multi-coloured glass trinkets with which my mother loved to adorn the mantelpiece, sideboards and window ledges. Rather it came from my father's head.

My soft footsteps on the carpet were not enough to alert my father. He was sitting at the far end of the room, as close as possible to the west-facing window, so as to catch the last rays of the setting winter sun. He was almost bent double over a thick garment spread over his knee. His face looked down, wrapt in a concentration so great that he whistled slightly in his teeth as he drew in the breath. With machine-like regularity his fingers fed the heavy cloth between needle and thimble. My father's once tight black, wavy hair had become pure white, and from it the low winter afternoon sun streaming at an angle through the glass, was reflected with the silvery radiance that had struck me when I first entered the room. Falling from his luminous hair across his inclined face and on to the needlework, the shaft of pure white light was soft and warm. I paused, reluctant to break the spell of this silent vision, and then walked quietly into his field of vision. It seemed improper any longer to spy on his solitude. I felt like Alexander standing before Diogenes.

My father looked up mildly, 'Oh, hello Geoff.'

I didn't speak but looked enquiringly at his hands. 'I'm making a costume for Mammy. She's for ever complaining things don't fit her. So I made this.'

I looked again. It was nearly twenty years since I had seen him sew. 'Did you make that?' I asked. He cleared his throat in reply. 'All of it?' I persisted.

'Yes, I can do any part of tailoring,' he said with pride.

'What, even the machining parts?'

'Every part,' he said with pleasure. 'I made this whole thing by hand. Of course you need time.'

He paused. 'It helps to pass the time.' As he moved his head, the gleaming, silvery hair sent points of light splintering through the room.

He paused again. 'But these are no use now.'

I looked puzzled.

'These are no good any more,' my father repeated, indicating his stubby, calloused finger tips. 'They don't obey you?' I asked with a smile.

'What was it John said to that Greek don?' my father asked sardonically. '"You must hasten your decrepitude."'

Over the last few years deafness, dizziness, failing sight, and great weakness of his legs had one by one curtailed his favourite activities. He had lost the fight first to cycle, then to drive and finally even to walk. 'I am virtually house-bound now,' he said, 'especially in winter.'

For a few years now, if I offered to take him to visit some close friend who had shown effusive admiration and warmth, he would say 'I don't care to go. They'll be all over me. They make such a fuss of me. Just because I've survived. No, I don't want to go there. Let's go for a ride in the country.' Now he spent many hours in his chair, doing crosswords or reading. He had already worn out several copies of Chambers Dictionary. Gradually, in the hours of silent solitude, he was breaking down the barriers between the inner and outer worlds. Now when spoken to, he would often ignore some remark, apparently not even having heard it. But some time later he would repeat it, more or less intact, to the speaker, as if it had only just occurred to him.

'One of the disabilities of old age is a defective memory,' he said. 'I can't do the crosswords at the rate I used to do them. At one time I did them without hesitation. 'But I still manage in the end. I do them completely, much to my own surprise. I get very annoyed with myself. Sometimes a word escapes me. I have to consult the dictionary to be sure I have done it correctly. I spend most of my time in this chair. I read. I was just reading about this feller, Dante.' He nodded at the book on the chair arm. 'He fell in love with a girl called Beatrice. It seems he decided that she was the Virgin Mary.

'Sometimes Mammy gets very impatient with me. She talks and talks. I can hear she's talking, that is, I know she's talking, but I can't hear what it is she's saying.' My mother listened to this impassively. 'She gets very het up when I don't reply,' my father went on. 'She can't stop talking. She's like the Brook:

I chatter, chatter as I go

To join the brimming river,
For men may come, and men may go
But I go on for ever.

'If there was no one for her to talk to she'd open the door and talk to the rooftops and the chimney pots and the sky and the stars.'

There was a long pause. 'You know,' my father said, 'she's got a defective memory now. She'll ask me, "Do you remember that woman? I met her in the hairdresser's today... you know, that woman..." And she gets quite annoyed when I say I don't know who she is talking about.'

At this point I glanced curiously at my mother, and she felt the need to say something. 'Isn't he awful?' she said, admiringly. Her respect for Harry had, over the years, never diminished.

Although he had now been for some time the oldest surviving member of the family he had, unlike me, never taken on the mantle of Myer. His younger brothers and sister, now themselves all retired, had never been able to accept this shy, reserved visionary as head of the family. His strange fancies, especially in France, had left him branded by them as a hopeless dreamer and eccentric, a position he showed absolutely no desire to contradict.

'The other day,' my father said, 'I was dozing in the chair, as I often do. I woke up and I saw two brown, fur-covered animals, one following the other, pass under my knees. It was only a fleeting image. I couldn't recognise them as any animal I had ever heard of. I believe they are inherited memories from a time before I was born. Long before. On another occasion a large animal ran past. It was a kind of large, multicoloured thing, I'm hanged if I know what it was, some kind of prehistoric monster. But not frightening or unpleasant.

'And sometimes when I'm in bed I wake up and I feel a touch on my shoulder and I look up and mother is looking at me. It lasts only a fleeting moment. The first time it happened I spoke to her and said "What do you want? What's the matter?" She never answers and is gone at once. Now I don't bother. I know it's just an image.'

'Your father,' Sidney once told me, 'got shell-shocked in the First World War and never recovered.' I too didn't trouble to contradict.

In fact the family story seemed over, the family itself a thing of the past. On the mantelpiece the clock still tremulously struck the quarters, but with such hesitancy that I wondered if it would get through all the hours. Idly I opened the little wooden door at the back and watched the mechanism of the old hammers falling wearily on the brass chimes. Only a wisp of fluff and the faint white trace of a bird dropping remained of its chequered history as a flower vase and a birdcage.

'You know,' said my father, intercepting my train of thought, 'I never knew what happened to Myer's old cap, the one he always used to wear when he dozed in front of the fire.'

My father now tired of the conversation, slid forwards in his armchair and reached out to pick up the tattered Chamber's Dictionary, its back broken from being repeatedly opened out and doubled back on itself. Settling back with The Guardian on his knee, he set about the crossword. After a short while he suddenly looked up. '*Philoprogenitive*,' he snorted with a mixture of satisfaction and disgust. 'That's the answer, *philoprogenitive*. It means having a lot of children. A good description of my father.

'In those days, it was a religious duty to have as many children as possible.'

'But your father wasn't religious.'

'Not in the least. He had them so there would be someone to keep him while he gambled.'

'Is that why you only had one?' I asked.

'I'd have liked to have more.'

'How many?'

'Four or five.'

'So why didn't you?' I asked, disappointedly.

'We would have done if we could have afforded it,' my father said sadly. 'Mammy always wanted more children.'

Meanwhile my mother had made tea. She still baked practically every day. 'I wake up early, and I can't bear to lie in bed any more,' she said. 'So I do some baking.'

So there was always at least one tin full of ginger cake and two or three large metal dishes with apple pies and tins of ginger biscuits and for the umpteenth time I plagued my father with questions about the past and with absolutely no sign of impatience he replied, with total accuracy, simply, with no temptation to elaborate, to questions put him so many times before, always attentive enough to weed out the planned falsehoods I had so carefully woven into my interrogation to test him.

I was beginning to feel that the book was ready, that its many strange tales really did reflect what had occurred and I was scraping the bottom of the barrel. By chance the dog brushed against my father's knee. Without thinking, he put his hand down to fondle its furry ears. 'Was Trotsky like that?' I asked, ever hopeful of even the smallest scraps of additional information.

'Trotsky was mother's dog really. When she wasn't having any more children she got a dog. She used to look after it and feed it. It was devoted to her. Meanwhile Trotsky's modern successor had placed herself as close as possible to the fire and was concentrating on the difficult task of trying to scratch a particularly tantalising but inaccessible spot behind her left ear. My father stopped talking and looked with amusement at the preoccupied dog. 'Sorting 'is livestock,' my father observed. ''Erraway,' he growled and gently pushed the wobbling dog with his slippered foot.

The precariously balanced dog at once collapsed, uttering a grunt of surprised indignation as she landed on the floor. Slowly picking herself up, with a great air of offended dignity she retreated to the far side of the hearth a few carefully estimated inches out of foot-range, whence she looked with mournful reproach at my father, who was by now unable to control his laughter at the dog's woe-begone expression. At this burst of laughter the dog looked even more reproachful and woe-begone and my father became even further convulsed with mirth.

This cycle of human laughter and canine reproach continued for some time until my father, gasping for breath, relented. 'Come on then,' he said, putting his hand down repentantly to console the ruffled dog, who trotted up forgivingly. 'Mother would never tolerate any cruelty to the dog,' Harry said. 'She used to say "A deaf mute".'

Now I saw my opening. 'What?' I asked loudly, 'What did she say exactly?'

'She said, "a dumb animal".'

It was as though a new, long-closed door to the past had opened. In vain now were my father's protestations that he had been deaf, that he couldn't hear. I forced my way in, mercilessly. 'This weather,' I jerked my head at the winter landscape beyond the window, 'how did you manage then?'

'We used to huddle round the coal fire, eleven of us.'

'Did your mother complain?'

'No, they never complained. Mother told us about the intense cold in Russia. She remembered it from her childhood. "The great frost," she called it.'

'The great frost?' I echoed.

'"The great frost," Mother used to say, "The biting frost."'

I realised that maybe with the clarity of his 94 years, a new door in his mind had indeed opened. But with the same excitement I felt, there was also a distinct feeling of sadness. For I realised my task had only just begun and that now I could never find time to complete it. Bitterly I reflected on my struggle to find time to write the book, ironically reflecting on how short a time ago I had been congratulating myself on its accuracy and its completeness. Now my own words had come back to me with a vengeance. Truth, the mocking, elusive truth indeed, like the Hindustani elephant, varied with the position of the observer.

But during all this dull conversation the dog, indifferent to these philosophical concerns, had been eyeing my father's slippers secretly, cocking her head to one side and the other and pricking up her ears with each closely observed movement of the coveted prey. The slippers were of soft wool with a turned out furry margin that she found absolutely irresistible, despite our continuous scolding. As the conversation went on the dog had dropped on to all fours and was inching forward with intense concentration directed towards the furry goal. Finally, the temptation became too much and at one bound she leapt upon the slipper, sank her teeth into its quivering woolly edge, drove her front paws into the ground and started to pull frantically.

'Ey! Gerraway! Clear Off!' my father spluttered, once again overcome with laughter as he ineffectively shook his slippered foot with the dog still attached. Sheepishly the dog gave one last self-indulgent gnaw of the fluffy slipper and retreated under a chair.

When I got up in the morning, I discovered my father was outside furiously attacking a hydrangea. He had decided he could no longer keep the plants under control. 'I'd like to get rid of them,' he said. 'Next time I buy a bungalow, I'll buy one without a garden.'

'He's worried that I won't be able to manage the garden,' my mother explained.

Looking around I saw he had already completely eradicated the wonderfully fragrant yellow rose bushes he had nurtured for 20 years. Grateful for any exercise before the confinement of the long motorway drive I took a spade and fork and attacked the last remaining shrubs, two miserable, frost-bitten hydrangeas and the neatly clipped flowering currant that I had salvaged from an old house years before and which my father had converted into a small globe, rather like a privet bush. And thus we waged allied war together on the wretched plants. In the earth I felt the tines of my fork against the edge of his spade. Even though he could hardly stand up he was directing his fury quite accurately and when the last roots gave that terrible shuddering sign that they were about to release their final hold on Mother Earth he uttered a grunt of satisfaction and went back into the house.

'You know,' my father said, 'I think I am going to reach a hundred.'

As I drove off I noticed he had taken up a seat at the opposite end of the room, before the east-facing window, the half-finished garment across his knee, crouching forward to catch the weak, pure rays of the morning winter sun. Flakes of silvery light flashed from his pure white hair and he whistled slightly in his teeth with the exertion of concentrating on the needle he held in his calloused fingers.

Epilogue

And so these men of Hindostan
Disputed loud and long,
Each in his own opinion
Exceeding stiff and strong,
Though each was partly in the right
And all were in the wrong.

Saxe

And with that we have traced all these four long lives and nearly all is said and the time comes when I must take you back to the place from which we set out on this long journey and set you down again on the streets of Leeds where we first met.

Any of the four brothers would have told a better tale than I. But none of them would tell it. For those who lived through its events it was too painful, or too shameful, or too humdrum or too all of these together to be worth recording. It seems for them it was anything else but never full of wonder as it was for me.

The frenzy of the industrial revolution is over now. Pennine wool is no longer carded in the valleys. The westering sun, unseen by the shirt-sleeved workers at the cutting tables within, heatedly in the tobacco smoke laden air discussing who would be the winner of the 2 o'clock at Doncaster or at York, has long ago gilded for the last time the turrets of the great clothing factories of Burton's, Hipps', Alexandre's, the Fifty Shilling Tailors, those once household names, now memories as faded as the vast, proud empire to which they had sent out clothes and only we linger here, our story nearly over.

The community to whom those factories fed the unleavened bread of Passover has passed. It is only the ghosts of the cloth-capped workers who throng now the narrow streets. South of the river bob-tailed venison deer graze grassy hillocks where once colliery slag heaps fumed. The horizon is no longer pierced by a hail of chimneys falling like the arrows of Agincourt on the French host. The sky is as innocent a powder blue as one whose face had never been blackened by the sin of smoke. Everywhere the debris of the ramshackle factories has been cleared away, the rolling rain of seasons has all but washed the soot off the remaining walls and trees and the silent Spring of an older, forgotten Yorkshire is re-

430

greening itself, coming up among the ruins, endlessly ready to refresh the spirits of those who will come next here.

But still, tantalisingly silent witness, the two-hundred-year-old sandstone mansion stands in Potternewton Park, just as it did before ever a greenhorn from Lithuania set foot in the Leylands. The grassy park slopes still clothe the dry valley between Chapeltown and Harehills. But the park railings and iron gates were taken away to make armaments for the Second World War and even the huge carved sandstone blocks of the gateposts are now gone. Beyond the gates the two flowering cherry trees still stand, just as they did when Myer scurried past them that late summer afternoon over half a century ago when he first heard of the Crash.

The cherry trees are no longer slender saplings girded in gleaming bands of copper bark. They no longer stand like temptresses, beckoning the passer-by to the soft spring grass, shaking the pollen of their delicate white blossom from one gorgeous flowering head to another as if in some mysterious botanical act of love. Now they are like stout washerwomen. On their bulging trunks innumerable woody knobs encrusted with buds, and little twigs, and leaves, and even the occasional flower obscure the once graceful outlines, splitting the copper bands into shreds and tattered ribbons.

More than fifty times have the chestnut trees scattered their early morning treasures to generation after generation of Potternewton kids, but now the Leylanders are gone, gone to the northern hills and far beyond and on the green-painted wooden benches under the cherry trees you will not find the old people sitting out the summer evenings, chattering in Yiddish. All round the park the same sooty, redbrick terraces still clothe the maternal hills but the young conker seekers are new immigrants to Leeds. Their story has hardly begun though I doubt these cherry trees will see it out. But perhaps we may still be in time, if we go on a summer evening, when the insects buzz, and sit very quietly on the still-warm bench seats, to hear the elderly cherry trees whispering to each other of old Mrs Bloom who had a very wrinkled face and sold bagels in that little shop, that little one, just across the street, just over there.

Daddy,
it all
seemed
so
real.

Ruth, aged 14

The Leeds Jewish Tailors' Strikes of 1885 and 1888, by Colin Holmes. Yorkshire Archaeological Journal, 45 (1973) 158-166

Yorkshire Post, Leeds Mercury, Leeds Times, Leeds Evening Express, and Leeds Daily News, 1885 and 1888

Homage to Tom Maguire, by E.P. Thompson, pp, 276-316 in Essays in Labour History, Eds. A. Briggs and J. Saville, Macmillan, 1960

Report of the Lancet Special Sanitary Commission on the Sweating System in Leeds. Lancet (1888) 3380, 1146-8 (June 9th), 1209-10 (June 16th)

The City of Leeds. The Housing of the Working Classes Act 1890. Quarry Hill Unhealthy Area, November 1900. Book of Reference. W.J.Jeeves, Town Clerk, Leeds. Jowett and Sowry, Printers

The Persecution of the Jews in Russia. Special Restrictive Laws. A report of the Guildhall Meeting on 10th December, 1890. Text of the Memorial to the Czar. Russo-Jewish Committee, Wertheimer, London, 1891

Leeds in the Great War, 1914-1918. A Book of Remembrance, 1923

The Destruction of the Jewish Community of Yurburg (1941) translated from the Yiddish by Regina Borenstein Naividel from Yahadut Lita vol. IV pp. 295-7

Leeds Jewish Representative Council. Leeds Tercentenary celebrations of the Resettlement of the Jews in the British Isles. 1956

The Leeds City Archives (Sheepscar)

The Yorkshire Archaeological Society

The Joseph Porton Library, Leeds

The Leeds Jewish Historical Society

The Talmud: Selections by H. Polano. Frederick Warne and Co., London, 1890

V.D. Lipman, Social History of the Jews in England, 1850-1950. Watts, 1954

Lloyd P. Gartner, The Jewish Immigrant in England, 1870-1914. George Allen and Unwin, London, 1960

British Parliamentary Papers (BPP) and other Crown Copyright:
Report by the Labour Correspondent of the Board of Trade on the sweating system in Leeds. (Accounts and Papers 1888, vol 22). BPP 1888 Vol LXXXVI, p. 561-567

Report from the select committee on emigration and immigration (foreigners): together with the proceedings of the committee, minutes of evidence, and appendix. BPP 1888 Vol XI, p. 419-784

Report from the select committee on emigration and immigration (foreigners) with the proceedings, minutes of evidence, and appendix. BPP 1889 Vol X, p. 265-403

Fourth Report from the select committee of the House of Lords on the sweating system; together with the proceedings of the committee, minutes of evidence, and appendix. BPP 1889 Vol. XIV, part 1, p. 1-633

Board of Trade. (Alien Immigration). Reports on the volume and effects of recent immigration from Eastern Europe into the United Kingdom. (Accounts and papers). BPP 1894 Vol LXVIII, p. 341-566

Mansergh, N, Lumby, EWR, and Moon, P, eds. India: The Transfer of Power 1942-1947. 12 vols. London: HMSO, 1970-1983

ALSO BY THE SAME AUTHOR
SOON TO BE AVAILABLE FROM HAREHILLS PRESS

GHOSTS

The author goes to Lithuania on the trail of his ancestors. He visits Yurberick, crosses the River Niemen and meets Sorele, the last Jewess in Shakee who, to his surprise, can show him the house of the horse dealers. By accident he discovers the escape route along the River Niemen.

But how to paint the pastel shades of Lithuania when my palette had only crimson and black? A land of bandits and thieves, and murderers, police with white armbands, and highwaymen, and woodlands and rivers, and a branch of the Snoras Bank in Grumbliai?

* * *

The silver eyebrows still betrayed they had been once jet black. Deep furrows of his caved in cheeks, and fallen upper lip tight shut a mouth that seemed to keep in words of what he once had seen, something beyond motion, gesture, tears or speech, or any sound a man can make. And yet, when all around him smiled, the corners of his mouth turned up a little too, and seemed to make his eyes weep even more, and looking straight at me I saw transfixed by what he saw, frozen forever in a time that killed his soul and bound it to a long and living death far crueller than all he had seen done to them.

www.harehillspress.com

MYER'S DREAM

The author continues his autobiography, describing his medical course in Oxford, his introduction to science, and the observations that led him to the search for the repair of spinal cord injury

* * *

So, preserved in these prints we see the skin turned back over the dead criminal's head, like a sort of gory, old woman's bandage, the skull cap neatly sawn off, and the soft substance of the brain carefully scooped away, layer by layer, to reveal the object of our story, the first human view of the hippocampus, the house of dreams.

But when I nearly four centuries later repeated with less elegance the prurient delvings of Arantio, and first saw this gleaming structure, and with trembling fingers, delicately turned it over and saw the knobbly under-surface of the convolution, puckered into ridges like a row of teeth, that gives its name to the dentate gyrus, my finger tips detected no premonitory thrill that would inform me that upon this object I was to spend the most part of my working life.

www.harehillspress.com

THAT WAS MY MOTHER

Conspicuous by her absence from The Undark Sky, the author tells the secret history of mother, Celia Raisman.

*   *   *

At the bus station, she often stopped to go into the market to buy the oranges or grapes or other fruit she would carry in her ragged shopping bag to my father and peel for him. And this sometimes caused trouble for, as the years passed, although Celia who had been born beside the market and was street-wise, and never in the jostling crowd of all the villains of Leeds who infested the narrow alleyways of Kirkgate Market where the fruit was cheapest got her purse snatched or her bag slit open, she started to become confused, and since the bus station was the central point for buses all over Leeds and its area, she sometimes got on the wrong bus.

But Leeds is a friendly city, and the poor who ride buses all talk to each other like long-lost friends, and so the strange ride was only another series of conversations on the occasions when Celia went north by first going south or east or west, floating light and unsinkable as a feather on the mass of humanity on which we all must learn to float, or sink.

www.harehillspress.com